Small and Medium-Sized Enterprises and the
Global Economy

# Small and Medium-Sized Enterprises and the Global Economy

*Edited by*

Gerald I. Susman

*The Pennsylvania State University, USA*

**Edward Elgar**
Cheltenham, UK • Northampton, MA, USA

Published by
Edward Elgar Publishing Limited
Glensanda House
Montpellier Parade
Cheltenham
Glos GL50 1UA
UK

Edward Elgar Publishing, Inc.
William Pratt House
9 Dewey Court
Northampton
Massachusetts 01060
USA

A catalogue record for this book
is available from the British Library

ISBN 978 1 84542 595 1

Printed and bound in Great Britain by MPG Books Ltd, Bodmin, Cornwall

# Contents

# Contributors

## ACADEMIC CONTRIBUTORS

**Arnaldo Camuffo**, Professor of Management, Department of Economics, University of Padua, Italy.

**Gino Cattani**, Assistant Professor of Strategy, Department of Management and Organizations, The Stern School of Business, New York University, New York, USA.

**Dave Crick**, Professor of Marketing and International Entrepreneurship, Business School, University of Central England, UK.

**Hamid Etemad**, Professor, Desautels Faculty of Management, McGill University, Montreal, Canada.

**Mark Freel**, Senior Lecturer, Innovation and Entrepreneurship, Management School, University of Edinburgh, Scotland, UK.

**Andrea Furlan**, Assistant Professor of Operations Management, Department of Economics, University of Padua, Italy.

**Roberto Grandinetti**, Professor of Marketing, Department of Economics, University of Padua, Italy.

**Terrence Guay**, Clinical Assistant Professor of International Business, Smeal College of Business, The Pennsylvania State University, USA.

**Marian V. Jones**, Senior Lecturer in International Business and Management, Department of Management, University of Glasgow, Scotland, UK.

**Allen Kaufman**, Professor of Business Administration, Whittemore School of Business and Economics, University of New Hampshire, USA.

**James H. Love**, Professor of Economics and International Business, Economics and Strategy Group, Aston Business School, Aston University, UK.

**Jane Wenzhen Lu**, Assistant Professor of Management, Lee Kong Chian School of Business, Singapore Management University, Singapore.

**Carleen Maitland**, Assistant Professor of Information Sciences and Technology, College of Information Sciences and Technology, The Pennsylvania State University, USA.

**David J. Maslach**, PhD student, Richard Ivey School of Business, University of Western Ontario, Canada.

**Rod B. McNaughton**, Professor and Eyton Chair in Entrepreneurship, Department of Management Sciences, University of Waterloo, Canada.

**Johannes M. Pennings**, Marie and Joseph Melone Professor of Management, Department of Management, The Wharton School, University of Pennsylvania, USA.

**Irene J. Petrick**, Director, Center for Enterprise Informatics and Integration, Assistant Professor of Information Sciences and Information Technology, College of Information Sciences and Technology, The Pennsylvania State University, USA.

**Stephen Roper**, Professor of Business Innovation, Economics and Strategy Group, Aston Business School, Aston University, UK.

**Philip Shapira**, Professor, School of Public Policy, Georgia Institute of Technology, USA.

**Martine Spence**, Associate Professor of Marketing, School of Management, University of Ottawa, Canada.

**Jenna P. Stites**, Research Assistant, Smeal College of Business, The Pennsylvania State University, USA.

**Gerald I. Susman**, Robert and Judith Klein Professor of Management, Associate Dean for Research, Director, Center for the Management of Technological and Organizational Change, Smeal College of Business, The Pennsylvania State University, USA.

**Paul M. Swamidass**, Professor of Operations Management, Director, Thomas Walter Center for Technology Management, Ginn College of Engineering, Auburn University, USA.

**Deniz Ucbasaran**, Associate Professor in Entrepreneurship, Nottingham University Business School, Jubilee Campus, UK.

**Venubabu Vulasa**, Technology Commercialization Intern, Thomas Walter Center for Technology Management, Auburn University, USA.

**Paul Westhead**, Professor of Enterprise, Warwick Business School, The University of Warwick, UK.

**Craig H. Wood**, Associate Professor of Operations Management, Whittemore School of Business and Economics, University of New Hampshire, USA.

**Mike Wright**, Professor of Financial Studies, Director of Centre for Management Buy-out Research, Nottingham University Business School, Jubilee Campus, UK.

**Zhijian Wu**, MSc, 2004, Business Policy, National University of Singapore, Singapore.

**Jan Youtie**, Principal Research Associate, Enterprise Innovation Institute, Adjunct Associate Professor, School of Public Policy, Georgia Institute of Technology, USA.

## EXECUTIVE CONTRIBUTORS

**Joan Andrews**, Vice President, Global Sales, X-Rite Incorporated.

**Savvas Chamberlain**, CEO and Chairman, DALSA Corporation.

**James Hoban**, Executive Vice President and Chief Financial Officer, Markel Corporation.

**Mark Kujawa**, Vice President of International Business Development, Diamond V Mills.

**Karen Lint**, Chief Operating Officer, Lake Shore Cryotronics, Inc.

**Vivienne Ojala**, President, Brock Solutions, Inc.

**Thomas O'Shaughnessy**, Vice President for Business Development, Revere Copper Products.

**Manuel Rosales**, Associate Administrator for International Trade, US Small Business Administration.

**Markos I. Tambakeras**, Chairman, Kennametal Inc.

# Preface

The theme of the Third Klein Symposium on the Management of Technology originated in research that my Penn State colleagues and I undertook for the National Institute of Standards and Technology (NIST). The Manufacturing Extension Partnership within NIST has responsibility for enhancing the productivity and effectiveness of small and medium-sized enterprises (SMEs) in the United States. These firms are defined by the US Department of Commerce as having 500 or fewer employees. A major premise underlying our research was that SMEs must become more innovative in order to compete effectively in the emerging global economy. Recent entrepreneurial start-ups already have this capability and can serve as role models for others, but many SMEs (97 per cent of all exporting firms in the US) are not innovative and face increasing competitive pressure from low-cost foreign producers. Operational efficiency is necessary but not sufficient to compete in such a world. Differentiated and less price-sensitive products are becoming increasingly important to competitive success.

When our research began in 2003, I was a relative newcomer to the study of SMEs and, more specifically, to aspects of internationalization, which include importing, exporting, foreign direct investment and strategic alliances to sell products abroad. An extensive international network of scholars has been writing in this field for years and has produced a significant body of literature. My colleagues and I faced a steep, but fascinating, learning curve. When exploring themes for the Third Klein Symposium, the idea of linking its theme to our continuing NIST work seemed quite natural and promised great synergy. It also implied hard work and the opportunity to work with a new community of scholars, and ideally to form some new lasting friendships.

Thirty-two academics were invited to write papers for the symposium that was held at Penn State on 12–14 October 2005. The invitations included a list of issues and questions to serve as catalysts for what these academics might like to address. As appropriate for a symposium that concerned the global economy, the academics included representatives from the United States, United Kingdom, Italy, Canada and Singapore. The first two days of the symposium were devoted to brief overviews of the papers, and to comments and critiques of them. Authors were expected to revise their papers accordingly. On the third day of the symposium, senior executives from the public and private sector were invited to present their experiences with internationalization or their views on the role of SMEs in the global economy. Their presentations were made to a large and more general audience. Four of the presenters were winners of US federal or state awards for exceptional export performance. Two Canadian firms were recognized as among the 'Top 100 Employers' and/or '50 Best Managed Companies' in Canada. The Dean's Office of the Smeal College of Business contributed financial support for this day of executive presentations.

My deep and enduring gratitude and affection go to Robert and Judith Klein, who endowed my professorship at Penn State. The symposium that bears their name would have been impossible without the financial support that their endowment provided. I am privileged and fortunate to consider them as dear friends as well as benefactors, a rare and wonderful combination that few faculty members with endowed positions enjoy. As was the case with this symposium and the two preceding ones in 1990 and 1997, Bob and Judy Klein were continually in my thoughts during the planning and hosting of these events, and in the preparation of this book.

I struggle to find words of praise that are expressive and profound enough for the many contributions that Barbara Kinne has made to this entire endeavour. She has taken the initiative from preliminary planning of the symposium to final delivery of the manuscript, undertaking many tasks before I thought of them or hesitated to ask her to do because I feared imposing on her good nature and personal time. My effectiveness as an academic and an administrator has increased considerably since she became my administrative assistant in 2004. I can now undertake many more initiatives and be in many more places because of her skill and dedication to excellence.

Finally, but very importantly, I thank my wife, Liz, with whom I share everything in my professional and personal life. We both knew that holding the symposium in the same year that I assumed new duties as Associate Dean for Research would test our endurance and patience. I do not think I could have borne the long hours of work if we could not share brief interludes of conversation and support. Being an academic herself, she understands the seduction and consequences of overcommitment. I hope that I am nearly as worthy of praise and appreciation from her when it is my turn to reciprocate, an occasion that will surely arise soon.

# 1. Introduction

## Gerald I. Susman

The continuing worldwide trend to eliminate trade barriers and expand global trade presents small and medium-sized enterprises (SMEs) in developed countries with an opportunity and a challenge. The opportunity is to enhance revenue by selling more products to end-users or intermediaries in more foreign markets. SMEs can do this with their own sales force or through contracted distributors or representatives. The challenge is at least twofold. First, SMEs often lack the human and financial resources to take advantage of this selling opportunity. They need help from domestic or foreign partners or from public sector organizations to leverage or supplement their modest resources. Second, SMEs find it increasingly difficult to compete on price at home and abroad against competitors that have lower resource costs than they do. Consequently SMEs in developed countries are turning increasingly to innovation as a source of competitive advantage in order to protect their home market and participate in expanding foreign markets. Innovation can lead to development of products and services that competitors cannot imitate and for which customers will pay a premium price.

This book addresses the resource supplement/leverage and innovation challenges that increased global trade represents by exploring how SMEs can become more competitive at home and in foreign markets as stand-alone firms or as members of supplier and customer networks. The book contains 17 chapters, 16 of which are organized into six parts. Each part focuses on dimensions and issues that relate to the above challenges. These dimensions and issues are presented below with a follow-up summary of the chapters within each part.

Part I of the book focuses on innovation as a competitive strategy and the source and location of ideas for enhancing innovation capability. Does distance matter in the ability of firms to learn from each other? If it does matter, how can collaborating firms compensate for distance, especially when the information they exchange is tacit or context-sensitive? Can firms learn on their own as readily as they can from their customers and suppliers? Also how much innovative capability must a firm develop internally in order to absorb knowledge effectively from others? What are the essential elements of an innovation strategy? What types of firms and industrial sectors are most likely to adapt an innovation strategy and pursue it successfully?

Part II focuses on network dynamics. Networks vary considerably in their degree of coherence and structure and even in the extent to which members are conscious of network membership. Networks can aspire to function as virtual organizations, in which case one or more firms exercise leadership and control over others. How often can SMEs exercise leadership and control in such networks if much larger firms are also members? Networks can also be a looser arrangement in which participants only share information and ideas, but undertake no coordinated action. Finally, networks can be links between clusters of firms that share limited information indirectly, but are unaware of firms in other clusters. Can learning how to form networks and alliances (with the right partners and governance) become a strategic asset for SMEs?

Part III focuses on the way SMEs can leverage technology for competitive advantage. The Internet, for example, permits SMEs to search for information and ideas and to reach suppliers and customers as readily as large firms can, and to act in concert in 'virtual' organizations with other firms with complementary resources. Computer-aided design (CAD) and associated knowledge codification may be a prerequisite for collaboration with customers and suppliers worldwide, for example, with exchange of data files. Collaboration on operational issues can build trust, which, in turn, can stimulate further and more comprehensive collaboration on strategic and value-based issues.

Part IV focuses on internationalization, a process that can stimulate innovation as well as be stimulated by it. Firms that compete on innovation may sell products with shorter lives, thereby encouraging firms to pursue scale economies through international sales before the onset of commoditization or obsolescence. Innovative products may also be sold in smaller, niche markets, thus prompting firms to seek international sales before quickly exhausting domestic sales. Innovative firms may also expand their search for ideas and partners worldwide. Whether or not a firm's products are innovative, internationalization is an entrepreneurial act that only some SME managers are willing to undertake. The chapters in this section explore why some SMEs internationalize, their pace of internationalization, their choice of markets to enter and their entry mode.

Part V focuses on the role of the public sector in helping SMEs to overcome resource deficiencies that limit their ability to innovate and internationalize. SMEs can benefit substantially from partnering with universities that receive federal research grants, thereby supplementing their often modest R&D resources. Federal and state agencies can help SMEs to internationalize by financing or guaranteeing loans for foreign ventures or by introducing SMEs to reliable customers or suppliers in foreign countries. As SMEs vary considerably in their interest and capability to internationalize, no single policy or set of activities is suitable for all firms.

Part VI of the book includes summaries of presentations by senior executives of seven companies that earned recognition and awards from government agencies or industry associations for their outstanding exporting performance. Also included are summaries of presentations by two distinguished executives from the private and public sector, respectively, who were invited to discuss the economic and political context in which SMEs operate, and to highlight some government initiatives that have been designed to help SMEs to compete effectively in international markets.

## PART I   INNOVATION AND COMPETITIVE ADVANTAGE

Mark Freel explored the issue of geographical scope and innovation. He hypothesized that firms that cooperate with customers, suppliers and competitors outside their region tend to produce more radical innovations than firms that interact primarily within their region. The latter tend to produce incremental innovations. Broadening a firm's geographical scope expands the diversity of its idea pool. If radical innovations required exchange of tacit knowledge, firms would be challenged to maintain face-to-face exchanges as geographical scope expanded. Freel suggests, however, that innovation relies at least as much on exchange of codified knowledge (science-based) as on tacit knowledge, and that technological, organizational and cultural 'proximity' between firms can substitute for spatial proximity. Also increased R&D expenditure and technical personnel enhance a firm's ability to recognize and interpret non-local knowledge. Physical proximity is necessary for building trust among cooperating competitors, but this is not the case among cooperating customers and suppliers.

Love and Roper explored the role of knowledge source (internal R&D, supply chain or non-supply chain) on innovation success (percentage of sales from new products introduced or updated in the last three years) and business performance (productivity and sales and employment growth). Process innovation was also measured. Data from Irish manufacturing plants show that innovation success is related to R&D (percentage of R&D employees/total employees) and number of supply-chain and non-supply-chain sources. These three sources tend to be complementary, but there is some degree of substitution between them. Innovation success is affected positively by organizational context (large batch, multi-plant member), skill level and capital investment. Innovation success in turn positively influences sales and employment growth, but negatively influences productivity, at least temporarily. Process innovation unambiguously improves both productivity and growth.

Youtie and Shapira explored the competitive strategies of SMEs in Georgia in the southeastern US with special interest in firms that compete on innovation. A small percentage of firms competed in this way and tended to be in science-based or electronics/electrical/transportation sectors. Innovation in these firms was general and evident in product, process, organization and marketing innovations. Firms that competed on innovation gave some priority to adapting to customer needs and offering value-added services, but gave least priority to low price. Innovation and low price were virtual polarities. Firms that compete on innovation seem to have a core competency that can manifest itself in multiple ways. They may develop this competency because they cannot compete on price or may consciously reject price as a strategic option in preference to innovation.

## PART II  NETWORK DYNAMICS

Petrick and Maitland view SMEs as potential members of networks that compete like virtual companies against similarly organized networks. Economies of speed may be more essential in such competition than economies of scale and scope. Original equipment manufactures (OEMs) usually lead these networks with varying degrees of influence over the design, production, distribution and sale of components and end-products. Their influence is greater in industry sectors where low cost dominates differentiation, and is shared with SMEs in sectors where the latter enhance differentiation through their intellectual property. Other factors related to the comparative size and value of exchanges between buyer and seller also determine influence. The critical challenges for network management are to synergize the complementary assets of network members, take coordinated action when and where appropriate, and increase and distribute rewards that are sufficient to maintain member loyalty. The authors suggest that networks can address these challenges by building social capital through the continuous exchange of knowledge, thereby enhancing the situational awareness that is essential to formulate and implement complementary member and network strategies.

Pennings and Cattani followed the chemical to digital transition in the imaging sector from 1975 to 2005. The authors tracked the patent count and forward citations for three large firms (Kodak, Fuji and Sony) and three smaller firms (Adobe, Indigo and Interactive). Patent count measures a firm's research productivity; forward citations measure the impact of a firm's patents on other sector firms (that cite its patents). Brokers are firms that link otherwise unconnected clusters of firms that often cite each other's patents, and have higher growth rates and profits than non-brokers. Pennings and Cattani show that the above six firms were brokers in chemical or digital technologies at different times, and that Kodak's broker role was related to patent counts and forward citations[1] in digital technology, but less so in chemical technology (patent count only). Adobe, Indigo and Interactive emerged early as brokers in digital technology but the latter lost this status quickly (to Indigo via acquisition).

## PART III   TECHNOLOGY AND ENHANCED CAPABILITIES

Etemad emphasizes the role of Internet-based technologies (IBTs) in SME growth and development, or more specifically, internationalization. He shows how fast-growing Canadian SMEs exploit IBTs very effectively as complementary resources. They use IBTs to leverage their initial resource base (for example, financial, entrepreneurial, knowledge) to make potential customers aware of their products or services or to reach out to potential customers. IBTs do not create competitive advantage by themselves, but, if appropriately configured and aligned with a creative business model, they can allow SMEs to compensate for their small size and inexperience. The richer the initial resource base, the more there is for IBTs to leverage. The environment that SMEs seek to enter also varies in richness (number and quality of customers, suppliers, competitors and so on, and their degree of connectedness). Again the richer this initial environment, the more there is for IBTs to leverage. For example, IBTs can help SMEs build on the initial connectedness in their environment to form extraregional networks or join existing ones, thereby creating in cyberspace many of the advantages that regional clusters enjoy. IBTs can facilitate a virtuous circle in which the resources of the firm (push) and those of the environment (pull) grow and reinforce each other.

Grandinetti, Furlan and Camuffo show that Italian district subcontractors vary considerably in their design and marketing capability. This variability results from the desire of some subcontractors to reduce their dependence on local customers and suppliers. They attracted non-local customers by shortening development time and lowering design cost via CAD. Their design capability was enhanced further by applying what they learned from these customers (for example, quality, safety and legal standards) to the design of other customers' products. A similar bidirectional dynamic exists for supplier management. More broadly knowledge codification enables such capability development by standardizing internal routines (software, blueprints, procedures and so on), and thereby facilitating communication with customers and suppliers. A major strategic shift (such as managerial succession, or financial crisis) or an important customer's mandate for ISO certification or compatible CAD system may initiate the codification process.

Wood and Kaufman offer insight on the ability of suppliers to collaborate with their customers and on the content of their collaboration. Suppliers' ability to collaborate depends on their technology sophistication and sensitivity to the value of forming knowledge and learning networks with their customers, suppliers and so on. This collaborative ability is related to the type of products and services that suppliers offer their customers (for example, commodity or proprietary product). Collaboration builds trust, which, in turn, can lead to greater sharing of operational risk (manufacturing, product development, marketing) and asset risk (equipment and personnel) and to addressing corporate social responsibility (CSR) issues. SMEs address CSR issues by recognizing strategic stakeholders, aligning CSR activities with strategy, and using an explicit system of accountability. They tend to communicate about operational issues with suppliers and customers, but communicate about CSR issues only with suppliers with whom trust is crucial and furthest advanced (collaboration on proprietary products). SMEs may face more pressure to address CSR issues from European suppliers and customers than from those in the US and Asia.

## PART IV    INTERNATIONALIZATION

Maslach and McNaughton tested the 'small domestic market' hypothesis with comparative data on US and Canadian SMEs. It is widely assumed that SMEs in countries with small domestic markets will internationalize sooner than those in countries with larger domestic markets. While this is generally true, especially for SMEs that produce high technology products, there may be exceptions. The authors' data show few differences between US and Canadian firms on number of countries entered, number of countries with subsidiaries, diversity of the countries entered and overall foreign to domestic sales. Although Canadian firms derive sales from more countries and are more reliant on foreign sales overall, US firms internationalize more quickly (corrected for years of operation). Some special factors may explain the US–Canadian comparison, including exchange rates (which help Canadian exports, but hinder foreign direct investment (FDI)) and pool of venture capitalists (fewer in Canada than in the US).

Lu and Wu explore the differential impact of product diversification and international diversification strategies on innovation in SMEs. They show that product diversification has little impact on innovation (R&D/sales), which is contrary to the negative impact shown for large firms. International diversification has a positive impact on innovation when measured by export intensity (exports/total sales), but not when measured by number of countries in which firms had FDI. Product diversification interacts positively with international diversification (both measures) to enhance innovation. Lu and Wu speculate that international diversification facilitates innovation by exposing firms to more countries and ideas, and that innovation completes a virtuous cycle by encouraging innovating firms to diversify internationally in order to achieve an adequate return on R&D that is invested in products with relatively short product lives.

Jones contends that stage theories of internationalization ignore the many internal and external conditions that SMEs face during their development and imply thereby that internationalization follows a fixed sequence of stages rather than a set of options from which SMEs can choose. A comprehensive review of the literature suggests, however, that internationalization is a more fluid and malleable process than stage theories imply. SMEs may not progress steadily to more advanced market entry modes (such as from exporting to FDI) and to more psychically distant countries. Instead their choices of market entry mode and country to enter depend on the firms' initial resources and capabilities, business model, technology, degree of market development, and proactive or reactive stance toward innovation. SMEs may internationalize early or late after inception, by importing or exporting, and involve their research, production or marketing functions. Their choices and the sequence in which they are made depend on the opportunities they confront. Internationalization may not be their primary objective, but is a derivative of the globalization of their suppliers, customers and alliance partners.

Crick and Spence conducted a qualitative, comparative study of the internationalization strategies of 24 UK and Canadian SMEs that sell high technology products (for example, software, electronics). Such firms (HTSMEs) often internationalize faster than those that sell low technology products because they have smaller domestic markets, shorter product lives and so on. The qualitative analysis of interviews led to the identification of four main themes. Canadian firms are generally more comfortable with differences in language and culture than UK firms. Senior executive international experience, social networks and company websites are critical resources that facilitate recognition and exploitation of opportunities. Choice of countries to enter is influenced by ease of entry, low transaction costs, non-price competition, customers' ability to pay and potential to build reputation that enhances access to other countries. Finally lifestyle preferences and family dynamics of senior managers influence their attitude toward risk and play a significant role in their strategic choices.

Susman and Stites review three major theories of internationalization that offer explanations of SME behaviour regarding pace, initial and subsequent market and entry mode choice. The three theories are stage, network and rationalist theory. Eight hypotheses were generated from these theories. They were tested with survey data that were collected from 19 firms that won federal or state awards for exemplary exporting performance. These 19 firms were part of an original sample of 21 firms that participated in a study in 2003–04. The results suggest that SMEs initially export to countries that are psychically close, use the same entry mode in foreign and domestic markets and use their initial entry mode in successive market entries. The authors used rationalist theory to test whether product, sales and service complexity and high intellectual property (IP) content and protection influence entry mode choice. The results suggest that firms use a direct sales force when customers require extensive training in use of the product, and use a contracted sales force when IP content is high. The latter seems more likely in countries with strong IP protection laws.

## PART V   ROLE OF THE PUBLIC SECTOR

Guay cautions that national statistics on trade and investment obscure regional and state differences in internationalization. The 'Sunbelt' states had the largest percentage increase in exports from 2001 to 2005; the Midwest and Northeast states had the highest export value because of their longer exporting experience. New York and New Jersey have the most SMEs per capita and the highest percentage of exporting SMEs. The Northeast and Mid-Atlantic states attracted the highest percentage of FDI from 1999 to 2003, but employment by non-bank foreign affiliates declined during this period. Most states offer firm-specific advice or training on exporting (such as paperwork, market research, finding foreign distributors). Few states offer state-sponsored financing programmes, but many help firms find public or private financing. Some states lead trade missions or have opened foreign offices (mostly in the EU and Asia). Finally states compete to attract FDI by offering tax or other incentives, but these tend to offset each other. A less focused, more general, but essential factor in attracting FDI to states is investment in education, worker training, infrastructure and R&D.

Swamidass and Vulasa believe that US competitiveness will depend increasingly on innovation, and that universities and small businesses can contribute significantly to innovation enhancement. The Bayh–Dole Act of 1980 played a major role in stimulating innovation by granting to universities and small businesses the patent rights from federally sponsored research. This encouraged the development of university-based innovation parks where research was commercialized. One respected study found that university research accounts for 10 per cent of new products and processes commercialized in seven industries. SMEs commercialize 60 per cent of university-based research and are likely to be within 100 miles of the university where the research was conducted. Few SMEs can conduct their own in-house research because of lack of resources and training. Universities can provide the training and complementary skills that SMEs need to commercialize research, and partner with them via Small Business Innovation Research (SBIR) grants to facilitate commercialization.

Westhead, Wright and Ucbasaran advise that government agencies that promote internationalization should tailor their programmes and policies to the needs of different types of SMEs. The SME population is quite diverse. It includes recent start-ups and mature businesses, 'micros' (one to nine employees) and 'macros' (ten to 49 employees) and firms that sell or use traditional and knowledge-based technologies. SMEs vary in their interest in internationalizing, responsiveness to entrepreneurial opportunity, proactive or reactive reasons for internationalizing, resource availability, attitudinal or resource barriers and preferred modes of entry. Also the link between internationalization and performance appears to vary by the sector in which firms are engaged and by the performance measure used. Consequently government agencies need to devote sufficient time to identifying differences between firms so that they can then provide appropriate resources when and where they will be most effective.

## PART VI  EXECUTIVE SUMMARIES

The summaries by senior executives from seven award-winning companies indicated that they started to internationalize at different stages in their history and for different reasons. Diamond V Mills, Markel, X-Rite and Revere Copper Products were in business for decades before starting to export. Lake Shore Cryotronics, Brock Solutions and DALSA started to export almost from inception. Their high-technology niche products or services and small domestic markets probably played a role in their becoming exporters so early.

Diamond V, Markel and Revere faced stagnant US markets and hoped to expand sales by exporting. Diamond V made its earliest export sales in response to unsolicited orders, but it soon developed a ten-year plan to increase international sales from 20 per cent to 50 per cent of its total sales. Revere and Markel followed current customers abroad, and Revere currently watches its current domestic customers for signs of moving offshore. X-Rite saw an opportunity to grow through international sales and seized it. Diamond V and X-Rite relied on Gold Key Service of the US Commercial Service[2] for market studies and help in identifying prospective distributors and customers.

The companies vary considerably in their initial mode of entry into a foreign market, and in the mode they used in subsequent market entries. Markel used an export agent to start selling internationally, but it switched to manufacturing representatives after 15 years so that it could communicate directly with its customers. Lake Shore generally enters new foreign markets with a direct sales force and then switches to distributors after a year. A direct sales force can only be used effectively in small markets because complexity increases quickly as markets grow. Distributors are easier to manage than a direct sale force because they know their territories well, and their career development and compensation are easier to manage. This assumes careful initial selection of distributors, monitoring their performance and assigning a territory that is appropriate in size and complexity. In contrast, X-Rite starts with distributors but switches to a direct sales force if the business supports it. The company's direct presence is needed because customers need pre-sale and after-sale support. X-Rite may buy a local distributor or develop a new sales and service team with temporary help from an ex-patriot from US headquarters.

Entry modes also vary by country. Diamond V gives exclusive rights to distributors in the EU, but has wholly owned subsidiaries in China and Mexico that do everything but manufacture products. Markel uses independent local manufacturing reps who sell and service a few large customers per country (mainly in the EU). Revere searches for distributors who sell non-competing products to the same customers that are targets of Revere. Diamond V and Markel have warehouses in the EU because their customers require frequent, small batch deliveries. Brock Solutions sells services rather than products, which it integrates by using multinational virtual teams that can deliver solutions easily across international borders.

The five US companies sell most of their products in US dollars, and those with distributors leave currency transactions to them. The EU is often an exception. For example, Markel sells its products (mostly to the EU) in euros. Its sales have increased considerably since 2003 because of the weak US dollar. Markel also hedges its currency risk by negotiating three-year price contracts that are matched with equivalent length contracts with its suppliers. Markel also assumes duty and regulatory risk by selling its product at delivered duty-paid prices.

Regulatory issues are a common challenge for these exporters. Diamond V faces uncertainty as to whether a country will classify its product as a food additive or a pharmaceutical. The latter classification requires payment of a higher duty. Diamond V hired a full-time person to deal with these issues. Lake Shore's distributors help it to deal with different electrical codes, plugs and standards. Brock Solutions says its customers take care of its regulatory issues. Most manufacturing companies must deal with Waste Electrical and Electronic Equipment (WEEE) and Reduction of Hazardous Substances (RoHS) directives from the EU that eliminated lead solder and other materials from their exported products after July 2006.

Companies face integration issues as their export sales grow, especially with increases in the number of countries served. These issues include how to gain economies across diverse platforms, integrate domestic and foreign operations, create a common brand identity worldwide, and conduct business in multiple currencies. X-Rite integrated order fulfilment, financial reporting and customer management onto a single platform. It now coordinates simultaneous new product development launches that include digital displays and user manuals in ten languages. Lake Shore introduced an enterprise resource planning (ERP) system that tracks warranty issues, customer needs and complaints. It relies on its dealers in each country or region to translate user manuals. Markel uses its ERP system to process orders and invoices in local currencies.

Exporting success depends heavily on selecting the right people as distributors, manufacturing representatives or direct sales employees, and motivating and training them to sell the company's products in foreign markets. Lake Shore looks for entrepreneurial personalities who run SME distributor businesses in their home countries. Diamond V seeks people who speak at least two languages. Even if they do not speak these languages fluently, this experience tends to make them more culturally sensitive. Distributors need as much attention as regular employees through constant communication, e-mails and training to make sure that everyone has the same knowledge and achieves the same technical level. The culture of each country is different, so the approach may need to vary. X-Rite brings all foreign-based employees together once a year for common budget meetings. Each business unit also has an Intranet-based 'chat room' that employees can visit to post questions, read answers and see updates. X-Rite uses a culture survey to assess its success in creating a common culture.

Employee and customer diversity increases as internationalization proceeds. Lake Shore and Dalsa have a high number of foreign-born employees in their home offices. Diamond V hosts international days to celebrate diversity. Lake Shore and Diamond V prominently display the flags of their customers in their offices and plants.

Manuel Rosales, Associate Administrator for International Trade in the US Small Business Administration, discussed the key challenges that small businesses face when considering international trade and what the SBA can do to help SMEs to meet them. These challenges include fear of foreign laws, regulations and language, complacency in light of a large domestic market, requisite knowledge of logistics, packaging, standards, prices, limited time to acquire knowledge, lack of foreign contacts and limited financial resources. The SBA has many excellent people and programmes to address each of these challenges. These include consultation, training, making foreign contacts and loan guarantees.

Markos Tambakeras, Executive Chairman to the Board of Directors of Kennametal Inc., emphasized that manufacturing still contributes significantly to GDP, employment and exports, but it faces domestic structural disadvantages that are unrelated to labour costs and exporting obstacles. These obstacles can be surmounted by allowing US firms fair access to foreign capital markets and requiring trading partners to adhere to transparent operating rules and common ethics and standards. US manufacturing output has increased considerably since the North American Free Trade Agreement (NAFTA) was implemented, and the recently enacted Central American-Dominican Republic Free Trade Agreement (CAFTA-DR) promises to continue this trend. China's membership in the World Trade Organization (WTO) puts the US in a much better position to hold

China accountable to WTO standards and to influence its trading behaviour. SMEs can contribute significantly to US export growth as they account for 97 per cent of all exporting firms, and two-thirds of them export to only one foreign market.

## NOTES

1. Forward citations are citations that a particular patent receives from subsequent patents. Subsequent patents list the earlier patent as 'prior art'.
2. The US Commercial Service is the trade promotion arm of the International Trade Administration and helps US small and medium-sized businesses to grow international sales. The Gold Key Service provides SMEs with one-on-one appointments with pre-screened potential agents, distributors, sales representatives, association and government contacts, licensing or joint venture partners, and other strategic business partners in targeted export markets.

PART I

Innovation and Competitive Advantage

# 2. Exploring the reach of innovation-related cooperation in small firms

**Mark Freel**

## INTRODUCTION

One can scarcely doubt the increasing popularity of network- or cooperation-based models of innovation and economic development. While there have been occasional dissenting voices (for example, Appold, 1995; Love and Roper, 2001) and some words of caution (for example, Oerlemans et al., 1998; Freel, 2003) studies have, on the whole, been confirmatory. That is, cooperation typically affects innovation activities positively, in terms both of the propensity to innovate and of the intensity of innovation (Arndt and Sternberg, 2000). This observation has, in turn, had considerable influence upon industrial policy (Huggins, 2001). Bougrain and Haudeville (2002), for instance, note a clear and growing preference for network promotion policies over those which provide direct financial assistance (at least within the OECD). However this rush to policy masks considerable enduring ignorance.

Remarkably, while a commendable amount of energy has been expended on establishing the link between cooperation and innovation, it is only relatively recently that researchers have begun to ask 'who cooperates for innovation and why?' (Tether, 2002). Accordingly, though one may be confident, in very general terms, that networking is frequently positively associated with 'innovativeness',[1] our understanding of the characteristics and motivations of cooperators is noticeably less assured (Fritsch and Lukas, 2001). This, of course, is not to suggest that we know nothing. Indeed, a steady stream of recent articles has begun to provide some of the answers (for example, Fritsch and Lukas, 2001; Bayona et al., 2001; Tether, 2002; Miotti and Sachwald, 2003). However these studies have been marked by a narrowness of focus, which serves to limit generalizability, and an insensitivity to the central feature in popular expositions of innovation networks. That is, they have been concerned with R&D, and not innovation, and have been essentially aspatial. The former is a concern because it is liable to capture only a small proportion of technical change activity (Patel and Pavitt, 1994). However the latter is perhaps more worrying still: a fundamental tenet of many networking models is the suggestion that 'proximity matters'. And, while there has been a growing recognition that proximity is not simply a spatial phenomenon (Boschma, 2005), the presumed importance of geography continues to loom large. The issue, as Howells (1999) records, is that 'Studies indicate to a lesser or greater extent a typical distance decay function in communication' (p. 83). This apparent lacuna is the focus for the present chapter.

Drawing upon data from a sample of 1345 small firms, the analysis begins by identifying only those firms involved in innovation-related cooperation. The concern is not with the differences between cooperators and non-cooperators, but with discriminating between those firms engaged in local (intraregional) networks only and those whose networks are more spatially extended. The present author touched upon this issue in a previous paper (Freel, 2003), observing, inter alia and rather prosaically, that firm size and export intensity were positively associated with the spatial reach of networks. However, in this earlier paper, no distinction was made between the various innovation partners. Yet, just as the characteristics of cooperators (relative to non-cooperators) have been shown to vary systematically by innovation partner (Tether, 2002), so one might anticipate systematic differences, along the same lines, in the factors associated with the spatial reach of cooperation. Accordingly, the paper distinguishes between cooperation with customer, suppliers and competitors. Scope also exists to comment upon cooperation with universities, service firms and the public sector – though, on the whole and for a variety of reasons, these tend to be more spatially concentrated.

## BACKGROUND

The starting point for this chapter is an item of (relatively recent) academic orthodoxy: the view that 'interactive learning and collective entrepreneurship are fundamental to the process of innovation' (Lundvall, 1992, p. 9). Since innovation involves the cumulative acquisition of new knowledge, or the novel recombination of existing knowledge, innovation is essentially concerned with learning. Learning, in its turn, is largely a social process and, as such, will involve at least two actors.

From this, and for a variety of more and less convincing reasons (see Freel and Harrison, 2006), the interactivity of the innovation process has been taken to signal not merely iterations and collaborations involving individuals within a given (innovating) firm, but also the importance of inter-firm linkages. John Donne is frequently, and perhaps inappropriately, paraphrased to the effect that 'no firm is an island' (for example, Oerlemans and Meeus, 2001). The traditional view of innovation as a linear process enacted, wholly or largely, by a single firm is thought atypical at best (Rothwell, 1994). While one is occasionally anxious about this seemingly casual leap from 'interactivity' to 'inter-firm', there does appear to be evidence of an increasing division of innovative labour and general agreement that innovation activity is 'becoming increasingly distributed, as fewer firms are able to "go it alone" in technological development' (Tether, 2002, p. 947).

Accordingly, for present purposes, the importance of innovation-related inter-firm cooperation is taken as given. Rather, my concern begins with the tendency to privilege 'local' ties. Much of the current interest in innovation networks has drawn impetus from developments in a variety of related literatures; most obviously: new industrial districts (Brusco, 1982; Becattini, 1978, 1990); innovative milieux (Maillat, 2001); new industrial spaces (Scott, 1988); spatial systems of innovation (Freeman, 1987; Lundvall, 1992; Nelson, 1993); and clusters (Porter, 1990). These literatures define innovation networks, to a greater extent, spatially. That is, they

> emphasise the spatial organisations of the market by different players (firms essentially), the inter-relation between these players and, eventually, the diffusion of economic growth from a given set of players to the rest of the geographic area. (Andréosso-O'Callaghan, 2000, pp. 70–71)

In many respects, a local territorial focus is entirely reasonable. Discussions are often framed in terms of 'common social culture' and 'industrial atmosphere' (for example, Bianchi, 1998). And, while one might wonder about the extent to which this represents 'old wine in new bottles' (Harrison, 1992), such trust-creating mechanisms and local specialization may sensibly provide the basis for innovation networking. However one can set against this the regularity with which empirical studies record a higher incidence of extraregional cooperation relative to intraregional cooperation (for example, Freel, 2000; Arndt and Sternberg, 2000; Kaufmann and Tödtling, 2000). From these it is clear that innovation networks may extend more or less spatially. Understanding the respective roles of, and motivations for, local and extralocal networks becomes important. In this light, it is difficult not to sympathize with the view that the bulk of existing empirical work has tended to 'fetishize' the former at the expense of the latter (Amin and Cohendet, 1999): 'focussing on processes and conventions *within* clusters, rather than the transfer of critical knowledges through extra-local connections' (Bunnell and Coe, 2001, p. 578). Or, at the very least, trying to understand the circumstances under which they may be more or less appropriate or achievable.

To this end, and in addition to the influence of what may be termed 'social proximities' (Boschma, 2005), it is common to view the relative embeddedness of innovation networks as a function of characteristics of the knowledge involved. For example, a large body of literature has evolved which takes correlations between meso-level R&D expenditure (as a measure of accumulated specialist knowledge) and innovation outputs and implies micro-level interactions[2] (for example, Jaffe et al., 1993; Feldman, 1994; Audretsch and Feldman, 1996; see Oerlemans, Buys and Pretorius, 2001; Cappellin, 2004). Central to this line of argument is the contention that successful innovation relies upon gaining access to external (tacit) knowledge, rather than (codified) information (Rothwell, 1991). While the ICT revolution allows information to be transferred over great distances at relatively low cost, the efficiency and efficacy of knowledge transfer continues to revolve around face-to-face contacts, naturally facilitated by spatial proximity (Romijn and Albu, 2002). In these terms, the importance of space is thought to 'reflect the linguistic and geographic constraints imposed by person-embodied exchanges and transfers of tacit knowledge' (Patel and Pavitt, 2000, p. 218).

Unfortunately reliance upon the role of tacit knowledge in explaining the spatial distribution of innovation networks raises a number of concerns, not least of which is that the distinction between knowledge types is unlikely to be very clear in practice (Breschi and Lissoni, 2001). However, perhaps more importantly for current purposes, the argument seems most often to be used to explain the clustering of innovation networks involving high-technology, science-based firms. Yet science-based knowledge tends towards relative codifiability. At the risk of oversimplification, technological development in many science-based areas draws on *know-why* knowledge rather than *know-how* knowledge (Johnson and Lundvall, 2001). By and large, the former lends itself to more ready codification than the latter. Accordingly, if transfers of tacit knowledge are the basis for the geographic clustering of innovation networks, one would expect these to be most evident in sectors where *know-how* (acquired through learning by doing) provides the platform for (probably incremental) technological development. High-technology sectors are not the ones which spring most readily to mind. This is over and above a general sympathy with the view that the pervasiveness of inherently tacit knowledge is somewhat overstated (Cowan et al., 2000).

As such, Lundvall (1992), by highlighting the role of complexity, may provide a stronger basis for understanding why innovation networks can be more or less spatially constrained. In this view, the complexity of innovation activities is the mechanism which induces firms to search for external resources. The subsequent transfer of knowledge between organizations may be thought of as a process of 'learning by interacting', as distinct from 'learning by doing' or 'learning by using'. Consequently 'the more complex the learning process, the more interactions it probably requires' (Johnson and Lundvall, 1993, p. 75) and, presumably, the more important spatial proximity becomes in facilitating frequent direct interaction (Freel, 2003). Importantly, complexity is concerned with process and is not synonymous with 'radicalness' or 'novelty' of outputs (Oerlemans et al., 2001).

Of course, the tendency to cooperation and the geography of ensuing relationships are unlikely to be simple functions of knowledge characteristics and learning processes. Rather both are also likely to be contingent upon the availability and location of resources. To this end, a common preliminary observation is to note that 'firms must have resources to get resources' (Eisenhardt and Schoonhaven, 1996, p. 137). Rothwell and Dodgson (1991, p. 131), for instance, suggest that 'the most important factors determining an SME's propensity and ability to access external sources of technology are *internal* to the firm'. This is often framed in terms of the 'absorptive capacity' thesis (classically Cohen and Levinthal, 1989, 1990). That is, a firm's ability to identify, evaluate and utilize external knowledge is, to a greater extent, a function of the level of its prior related knowledge, that is, its 'absorptive capacity'. Recent empirical evidence suggests that the conduct of internal R&D,[3] as a key constituent of absorptive capacity, positively correlates with the propensity to cooperate (for example, Fritsch and Lukas, 2001; Bayona et al., 2001; Tether, 2002). Moreover, other repositories of absorptive capacity, such as technical employees, have also been shown to stimulate external collaboration (Rothwell and Dodgson, 1991). On this basis, it does not seem unreasonable to speculate that a more developed absorptive capacity may allow firms to identify cognitively proximate (Nooteboom, 1999) knowledge and information at greater geographical remove.

While having some resources is generally thought to improve a firm's ability to cooperate (and to identify cooperative partners), not having others (or, at least, such a perception) must also be a prerequisite for collaboration. This is clearly recognized in the *milieux innovateurs* literature (for example, Aydalot and Keeble, 1988). Maillat (1991), for instance, argues that the local production environment is largely unimportant to the innovation processes of incremental innovators. In such instances, the necessary resources can usually be found within the firm. However radical innovations frequently require access to external resources and these, in turn, are commonly found 'locally'. The contention that external resources are liable to be sourced locally is made with reference to the importance of social proximities to effective cooperation and their essential immobility. Cappellin (2004, p. 216) captures the gist well: 'In a world of freely moving capital and increasingly freely moving people, it is only social capital that remains tied to specific locations.' This may well be, more or less, correct. However it is difficult to shake the suspicion that the influence of social proximity (and, hence, spatial proximity) on innovation networking has been overstated. Again Cappellin (2004) sums up well:

> geographic distance, which is related to transport and communications technologies, is less
> important as an obstacle to international cooperation when organisational and technological

distance is limited, as occurs between firms which operate in the same technological sector or between countries which have traditions, norms and institutions in common.

The various roles played by 'organizational', 'institutional' and 'technological' proximities (Kirat and Lung, 1999) often appear neglected in the rush to (re)discover the importance of 'being there' (Gertler, 1995). Yet, if one allows for relative organizational or technological proximities (such as are likely to exist between buyers and suppliers and between competitors), there seems less reason, *ceteris paribus*, to insist upon the importance of spatial proximity. Indeed, one might expect firms engaged in relatively complex innovation processes to be more likely to have geographically extended networks, as the local environment proves to be inadequate as a source of specialized or unusual resources (Oerlemans et al., 1998). Grotz and Braun (1997, p. 549) for instance, find that 'local subcontractors mainly perform low-level production operations', while the 'more crucial and innovation-oriented ties are very often national or international in character'.

Finally, beyond issues of innovation strategies and resources, there is the reassuringly simple view that the spatial distribution of innovation-related collaborations is likely to be largely a function of the spatial distribution of market relations and of firm age and firm size. Certainly there is evidence to suggest that smaller firms, younger firms and non-exporters are liable to be more locally embedded than are their larger, older and exporting peers (Freel, 2003; Arndt and Sternberg, 2000; Kaufmann and Tödtling, 2000). This, in turn, might suggest that integration within local innovation networks indicates either resource limitations, which confine search processes, or development stage, which sees the firm serve a mainly, perhaps initially, localized market. Either way, the features of a firm's innovation process or the pervasiveness of some local 'institutional' innovation system may have limited influence on the spatial distribution of cooperative partners.

However, irrespective of the merits of the various theses, what is clear is that, while there is now a corpus of literature addressing knowledge networks on the local (primarily regional) scale, there has been far less consideration of extraregional networks (Bunnell and Coe, 2001). Indeed, as Malecki et al. (1999) note, this emphasis on local linkages has resulted in a corresponding neglect of the critical role of non-local networks. Yet, in the absence of a supportive local milieu, firms must rely on national and international networks of customers, suppliers and other third parties for access to technology (Asheim and Isaksen, 2002). Moreover, though positive accounts dominate, there is some recognition that a purely inward-looking innovation system runs the risk of functional and cognitive 'lock-in' and the vulnerability this entails: retarding the development of both firms and regions (Grabher, 1993; Hassink and Shin, 2005). In other words, local knowledge networks are not inevitably good. Identifying the respective motives and characteristics of firms engaged in local and non-local networks is a useful foundation for understanding the circumstances in which they may be more or less appropriate. A contribution to a better understanding of these issues is the aim here.

## DATA

The analysis draws on data from a large-scale survey of small and medium-sized enterprises (SMEs) in 'Northern Britain'.[4] This parent sample was drawn in a similar manner to the successful Cambridge studies (see SBRC, 1992; CBR, 1996, 1998, 2000, 2004) and was designed, in large part, to address limitations in the spatial coverage of these earlier studies. Fuller details of the sample and of the survey methodology can be found elsewhere (for example, Freel and Harrison, 2006). However, for present purposes, it is important to note that, in common with the Cambridge studies, the sample frame used in constructing the database was the Dun and Bradstreet UK Marketing Database (D&B). This database is known to underrepresent single-person self-employed, sole proprietors and partnerships, in comparison to the overall enterprise sector, and to overrepresent expanding firms in search of finance (Bullock and Hughes, 2000). Accordingly one obvious consequence of using this database is the likely underrepresentation of the smallest firms. In the context of the present chapter, the main effect of this skew is likely to be an overestimate of population levels of innovation, networking, R&D expenditure, and so on. However, when this caveat is borne in mind (that is, that the survey did not seek to represent, in any isomorphic manner, the notional population), the legitimacy of the subsequent analyses should not be compromised.

In limited detail, 5200 manufacturing firms and 7472 business service firms were surveyed, providing 597 and 748 useable responses, respectively (response rates of 11.5 per cent and 10 per cent). Though the response rates are a little disappointing, the sample appears statistically reliable. That is, from an SME manufacturing population of approximately 15 180 firms, the 597 responses represent a 3.9 per cent sampling error at the 95 per cent confidence level. For business services, given an approximate SME population of 40 555 firms, the 748 responses represent a 3.5 per cent sampling error at the 95 per cent confidence level. In most survey research, error levels typically lie between 2 and 6 per cent, with 95 per cent confidence limits (Oerlemans, Meeus and Boekema, 2001).

With regard to the sectoral distribution of sample firms, Table 2.1 records the relevant data by narrative descriptors at the two-digit (in the case of manufacturing) and four-digit (in the case of business services) SIC(92) level. The distributions are broadly representative of the populations of 'Northern British' business services and manufacturers. Importantly manufacturing activity in the survey regions is biased towards lower-technology sectors than the UK average. Indeed the data indicate an oversurveying of textile and clothing firms and firms involved in the manufacture of wood and paper products (SIC (92) Divisions 17–19 and 20–21, respectively) relative to the pertinent population. The decision to oversurvey firms in the identified sectors was made with reference to recognized regional industrial clusters (DTI, 2001). While stratification of the sample in this manner will inevitably distort aggregate observations, as before, one does not anticipate that the analyses presented below will be greatly compromised.

Beyond these general characteristics, the subset of specific interest here is those firms who had engaged in innovation-related cooperation. To this end, firms were asked whether they had cooperated 'with other firms or organisations for innovation related activities (including marketing, training, etc.) and/or technology transfer during the last 3 years'. Firms were also asked to signal the spatial scale at which cooperation took place. Figure 2.1 presents these data, with firms classed by the highest spatial level for each potential innovation partner. Thus, though firms may have cooperated with both 'local' and 'international' customers, they will be categorized as 'international' only. The concern is with distinguishing between firms integrated within extralocal networks and those solely engaged in local networks.

*Table 2.1    Sectoral distribution of sample firms*

| Service sectors | (%) |
| --- | --- |
| Hardware consultancy | 0.9 |
| Software consultancy | 9.4 |
| Data processing | 1.4 |
| Other computer | 6.6 |
| Research (NSE) | 3.4 |
| Architectural, engineering, etc. | 25.2 |
| Accounting, etc. | 11.5 |
| Advertising | 3.9 |
| Other business activities necessary | 37.7 |
| | (n=748) |

| Manufacturing sectors | (%) |
| --- | --- |
| Food & beverages | 14.6 |
| Textiles/leather | 13.7 |
| Wood/paper | 10.9 |
| Publishing & printing | 4.2 |
| Chemicals/rubber & plastics | 10.1 |
| Metals/metal fabrication | 18.1 |
| Machinery & equipment necessary | 10.1 |
| Electrical machinery/instruments | 9.5 |
| Transport vehicles/equipment | 3.0 |
| Furniture | 5.9 |
| | (n=597) |

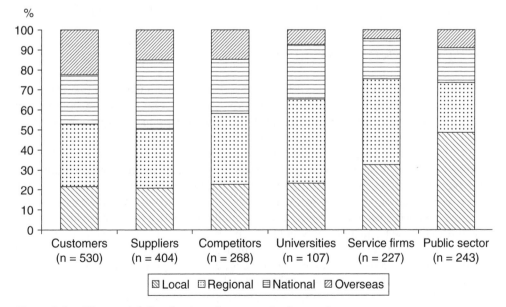

*Figure 2.1    The spatial distribution of cooperative innovation*

As the data in Figure 2.1 indicate, value chain linkages are the most common by some margin. Moreover, for customer and supplier cooperation, there appears to be a, more or less, even split between intraregional and extraregional collaborations. In addition, though competitor collaborations show signs of a tentative subregional bias, over 40 per cent of recorded competitor linkages are extraregional. In contrast, cooperative ventures involving universities, service firms and public sector agencies exhibit a marked tendency to be located within the same region as the focal firm. This final observation is as anticipated. For instance, other studies have shown research institutions to have a disproportionately high share of intraregional linkages when compared to other cooperation partners (Sternberg, 1999). 'To a much greater extent than commonly realized, university research programmes are not undifferentiated parts of a national innovation system broadly defined, but rather are keyed into particular technologies and particular industries' (Nelson, 2000, p. 13), often in particular locales. Similarly, given their largely local remits, one would expect cooperation with public sector agencies or service firms frequently to be characterized by spatial proximity. In light of these patterns, the current investigation is restricted to consideration of customer, supplier and competitor cooperation. This focus has the ancillary benefit of filtering the likely influences or organizational or technological proximities. As noted, these are likely to be greater between firms operating in the same technological sector (Cappellin, 2004). That is, one may anticipate a relatively high degree of technological and organizational proximity to exist between competitors and between customers and suppliers. This is less likely to be the case where extra-industry partners are concerned. Finally, for the purposes of analysis, the four spatial levels have been collapsed into two: intraregional and extraregional. Though they are often shaped by political expediency, it is fashionable to view 'the region as increasingly the level at which innovation is produced' (Lundvall and Borrás, 1997, p. 39). Moreover, within Europe at least, the region is increasingly the level at which innovation policy is enacted. Scotland and the North East are two of the UK's 14 NUTS1[5] regions.

## METHODS AND MEASUREMENT

Estimating the characteristics associated with extraregional cooperation takes the form of three multivariate regression equations (for customers, suppliers and competitors, respectively). Given the binary nature of the dependent variables (cooperative ventures were either with extraregional partners or not) logits are suggested. Logit equations allow one to compare those firms engaged in extraregional innovation networks with those involved solely in local networks, and to estimate which of the measured independent variables (Table 2.2) exhibit a systematic influence on the propensity to cooperate with a given type of extraregional partner. On the whole, the models seem to have a number of satisfactory properties. For instance, tests for multicollinearity (using correlation matrices and multiway frequency analysis (Tabachnick and Fidell, 2001)) give no cause for concern. Moreover, as the data in Table 2.2 indicate, the models appear reasonable predictors of the propensity for extraregional cooperation – in all instances, significantly improving upon constant only prediction at the 1 per cent level.

The models incorporate a number of variables intended to proxy many of the supposed influences on spatial proximity discussed in earlier sections. For instance, inclusion of

*Table 2.2    Variables used in the analysis*

| Variable | Description | Link |
|---|---|---|
| Age | Binary dummy variables for firm age in 2001; a score of 1 signifies that the firm is older than 5 years | + |
| Size | Natural log of the number of full-time employees in 2001 | + |
| Manufacturing | Dummy variable denoting sector classification; manufacturing = 1, otherwise business services | + |
| QSEs | Proportion of workforce classed as technologists or scientists | + |
| Technicians | Proportion of workforce classed as technicians | + |
| R&D expenditure | Dummy variables denoting R&D expenditure as a proportion of sales turnover; categories are 1–10% and >10%; no R&D spend is treated as the reference group | − |
| Larger competitors | Proportion of self-identified 'serious competitors' who are larger than the firm | + |
| Overseas competitors | Proportion of self-identified 'serious competitors' who are based outside the UK | + |
| Cluster | Binary dummy indicating membership of an industrial cluster as identified by the Department of Trade and Industry (DTI, 2001) | − |
| Customer dependency | Dummy customer dependency variable; >49% of turnover from largest 5; customer = 1, otherwise = 0 | + |
| Skill barrier | Factor score from 10 item question detailing 'factors hindering innovative activity' (see Appendix 2A.1) | + |
| Financial barrier | Factor score from 10 item question detailing 'factors hindering innovative activity' (see Appendix 2A.1) | + |
| Proactivity | Factor score from 8 item question detailing 'main reason for introducing' innovations (see Appendix 2A.2) | + |
| Reactivity | Factor score from 8 item question detailing 'main reason for introducing' innovations (see Appendix 2A.2) | − |

variables measuring firm age, firm size, the size distribution of competitors (as a proxy for market power considerations) and the extent of overseas competition (as a proxy for engagement in international markets) should allow one to identify the marginal effect of issues over and above these obvious structural concerns. Similarly, given the traditional view of services as local or parochial[6] (Fuchs, 1968), the models also control for macro-sectoral variations. Beyond these, internal R&D expenditure is considered an indicator of both the complexity of innovation processes and the development of absorptive capacity. Along the same lines, proportionate employment of qualified scientists and engineers (QSEs) and technicians further signals the extent of internal knowledge bases and absorptive capacity. In contrast, the scale of perceived barriers to innovation (in terms of both finance and skills) may be thought of as denoting weaknesses in internal resources as a necessary trigger to seeking external resources. Location within a designated cluster acts as a surrogate measure of local environmental munificence. In other words, one would imagine that specialist suppliers, competent competitors and demanding local customers would be present within the cluster (Porter, 1990) making extraregional cooperation less necessary. Moreover the degree of customer dependency (the extent to which a limited number of customers account for a large proportion of total sales) is included in the model. The interest is primarily with its effect on customer cooperation. However, to the extent that 'close and stable relationships with customers are positively associated with (a) supplier relations, (b) product innovation, and (c) process innovation' (Bengtsson and Sölvell, 2004, p. 232), customer dependency is more generally of interest.

Finally, one would anticipate that a firm's objectives in innovating would influence not only their propensity to cooperate (Bayona et al., 2001) but also the spatial distribution of cooperative relationships. Firms collaborate, not only to gain access to technological knowledge, but also to gain access to sales abilities, market information or new markets (Teece, 1992). One of the obvious implications of Grotz and Braun's (1997, p. 550) study is that local ties may be important for 'low profile interactions [and] general innovation consultancies', while for high-profile technology transfer and joint product development 'spatial proximity is irrelevant'. The current study incorporates two measures of stimuli to innovation: relative proactivity and reactivity. Here the index of proactivity is driven by factors such as new market penetration and diversification. Reactivity, in contrast, relates primarily to the role of standardization and legislation in stimulating innovation (see Freel, 2005).

Importantly, the analysis explores a number of potential influences on the reach of innovation-related cooperation. Accordingly, it is difficult to develop a series of simple, comprehensive and testable, hypotheses. Rather, the earlier discussions imply several, occasionally countervailing, possible effects. Indeed, I anticipate that the influence of any given variable may vary by innovation partner (that is, whether the cooperation is with a customer, a supplier or a competitor). However, in very general terms, and as a 'rough guide', the third column in Table 2.2 indicates a priori expectations.

## ANALYSIS AND DISCUSSION

Turning to the details of the analysis and, in the first instance, to the 'control' variables, these do not perform wholly as anticipated (see Table 2.3). Certainly, in all instances, perceptions of larger competition (of market power concerns) are positively associated with extraregional cooperation. Similarly, operating in international markets is positively associated with extraregional cooperation with customers and competitors. Indeed, the absence of an equivalent relationship relating to supplier cooperation may also be as expected. There is certainly empirical precedent. Oerlemans, Buys and Pretorius (2001, p. 71), for instance, observe that 'the regional orientation of firms is far more important for localised ties with buyers than suppliers', particularly where one measures that orientation by means of geographical features of sales markets.[7]

Likewise, the influence of the macro-sector variable is, more or less, in line with expectations. Manufacturers are significantly more likely to have recorded extraregional customer and supplier cooperative ventures than were their business service peers. That this does not appear to hold for the marginal influence on extraregional competitor cooperation may initially seem remarkable. However there is reason to suspect that this observation reflects issues of relative appropriability and imitability (Gallouj, 2002; Tether and Hipp, 2002) and is related, in turn, to the varying influence of R&D expenditure (discussed below).

*Table 2.3   Logit models of the probability of engaging in extraregional cooperation*

| Independent variables | Cooperation partner | | |
|---|---|---|---|
| | Customer | Supplier | Competitor |
| Log size | 0.010 (0.006) | 0.098 (0.535) | 0.351 (3.715)[b] |
| Age | 0.515 (1.690) | −0.306 (0.617) | 1.005 (3.143)[c] |
| Manufacturing | 0.785 (5.744)[b] | 0.774 (5.132)[b] | 0.278 (0.340) |
| QSEs (%) | 1.034 (1.326) | 1.893 (3.537)[c] | 0.607 (0.183) |
| Technicians (%) | 0.975 (1.381) | 3.056 (6.414)[a] | 0.432 (0.126) |
| R&D (greater than 10%) | 1.647 (5.719)[b] | 0.072 (0.009) | −1.349 (2.761)[c] |
| R&D (1–10%) | 0.755 (6.589)[a] | 0.250 (0.635) | 0.531 (1.406) |
| Larger competitors | 0.778 (3.380)[c] | 0.998 (5.294)[c] | 1.415 (4.622)[b] |
| Overseas competitors | 1.397 (6.444)[a] | 0.331 (0.575) | 2.875 (8.515)[a] |
| Cluster | −0.725 (5.679)[b] | −0.017 (0.003) | −0.907 (3.738)[b] |
| Customer dependency | 0.503 (3.157)[c] | −0.468 (2.375) | 0.631 (2.420) |
| Skill barrier score | −0.116 (0.704) | −0.069 (0.206) | 0.098 (0.210) |
| Finance barrier score | −0.193 (1.960) | −0.128 (0.721) | −0.348 (2.840)[c] |
| Proactivity score | 0.338 (5.076)[b] | 0.203 (1.462) | 0.120 (0.278) |
| Reactivity score | −0.123 (0.888) | −0.192 (1.623) | −0.009 (0.003) |
| Constant | −1.232 (4.522) | −1.671 (8.076) | −2.041 (5.614) |
| Nagelkerke $R^2$ | 0.252 | 0.180 | 0.317 |
| −2 Log-likelihood | 308.171 | 273.498 | 159.903 |
| $^d\chi^2$ | 55.050[a] | 32.076[a] | 39.112[a] |
| N | 408 | 323 | 228 |
| Classification improvement | 16.7% | 10% | 16.5% |

*Notes:*
Figures in parenthesis are Wald $\chi^2$ test statistics; [a] significant at 1% level; [b] significant at 5% level; [c] significant at 10% level; [d] full model versus constant only model.

More remarkable is the lack of significant correlations between firm size and age and both customer and supplier cooperation. On this basis, one is tempted to support the contention that the general comprehension of small and young firms as highly dependent upon the local industrial milieu requires modification (Asheim and Isaksen, 2002, p. 13). When one controls for a variety of other variables, size and age do not seem to strongly influence the spatial distribution of innovation networks – at least those involving customers and suppliers. That older and larger firms are more likely to have engaged in innovation-related cooperative ventures with extraregional competitors may, again, say something about appropriability and corresponding issues of trust and power. Alternatively, it may simply reflect higher search and management (agency) costs, which require more developed resources.

Beyond these, some interesting patterns emerge. For instance, the data provide little support for the central proposition that 'the more knowledge intensive the innovative activities are, the greater the necessity of spatial proximity' (Arndt and Sternberg, 2000, p. 480). Indeed the supposition that more complex innovation (proxied here by R&D expenditure) implies greater reliance upon local networks is supported for innovative ties with competitors only. And, here, one is tempted to argue that this reflects heightened appropriability concerns, greater scope for free riding and associated difficulties in developing trust. As Nooteboom (1994) notes, successful cooperation requires trust in both the competence and the disinterestedness of partners. While competitors are likely to be highly competent, their disinterestedness is probably less assured. In this way, spatial proximity, facilitating frequent face-to-face contact, may allow easier development of the necessary interpersonal trust. Of course, it may also afford greater opportunity for monitoring the actions of partners. This may be thought to echo Sternberg's (1999, p. 534) observation: 'in reference to contacts with competitors . . . it is less frequently believed that spatial proximity will become irrelevant in the future, suggesting that frequent personal contacts cannot be replaced via the new communications technologies'.

In the case of customer cooperation, and in stark contrast to expectations, innovation complexity is positively associated with extraregional cooperation. One might see this as validation of the absorptive capacity thesis: as a more developed absorptive capacity expands the spatial reach of search activities and subsequent cooperation. Alternatively, relatively R&D-intensive small firms may be thought to possess a degree of technology-based global market advantage of the kind implied by traditional monopolistic theory (see Keeble et al., 1998). The greater reach of their innovation networks with customers merely reflects their relative specialization. On the whole, while this latter argument is rather more prosaic, it is also more convincing.

In contrast, one may be a little more confident when suggesting absorptive capacity influences on the propensity to cooperate with extraregional suppliers. In this instance, there is no significant relationship between R&D expenditure and extraregional cooperation. However the proportionate employment of both QSEs and technicians positively correlates with engagement in these more distant networks. Qualified employees are likely to retain and maintain networks of experts and expertise on which their firms may draw. The importance of such networks was clearly set out in the original work on absorptive capacity:

> Critical knowledge . . . includes awareness of where useful complementary expertise resides within and outside the organisation. This sort of knowledge can be knowledge of who knows what, who can help with what problem, or who can exploit new information. (Cohen and Levinthal, 1990, p. 133)

In addition, the effect of cluster membership is also essentially in line with expectations. That is, firms located in industrial clusters were significantly less likely to have recorded an extraregional cooperative relationship with either competitors or customers. Clearly, suitable local partners are more readily available. However, given concerns over (particularly) cognitive lock-ins (Grabher, 1993), one need not construe this as inevitably optimistic. Indeed the current data suggest that intraregional customer cooperation, for instance, is likely to revolve around less complex or radical innovations. On a different note, that clustered firms are not as reliant upon local suppliers is perhaps more remarkable. However it is possible that local suppliers are generally a source of more regular, but less specialized, forms of inputs. Accordingly, in acquiring less common expertise, firms must reach further afield. In Lublinski's (2003) work on the German aeronautical industry, for instance, he notes that both cluster and non-cluster firms consider local suppliers to be less specialized than distant suppliers.

Finally, neither motivations nor perceptions of barriers to innovation greatly influence the spatial reach of cooperation. Exceptions include the relationship between customer cooperation and 'proactivity' and between competitor cooperation and financial barriers. In the former instance, this is likely to be a function of the extent to which the 'proactivity' variable describes the influence of market considerations. Firms whose innovation strategy is driven by a determination to expand market share or diversify the business were significantly more likely to have engaged in extraregional customer cooperation.

As regards the association between perceptions of financial constraints to innovation and competitor cooperation, this may simply reflect the sorts of resource issues touched upon in relation to firm size and age. And, in this vein, the generally negative signs on the barriers coefficients may hint at the greater resources required for distant cooperation. However, while perceived constraints may influence the propensity to cooperate (Bayona et al., 2001), there is little evidence that it influences the location of cooperative partners.

## CONCLUDING REMARKS

Many studies begin from the assumption that intraregional linkages are more important for innovation processes in small firms than are extraregional linkages (Sternberg, 1999). The dominant view holds that innovation, in contrast to many other value-adding activities, remains tied to specific locations (Ernst, 2005). While markets, production and finance have become increasingly geographically dispersed, innovation has not been subject to the same degree of internationalization (Patel and Pavitt, 1991). However there is growing evidence that a central feature of the internationalization process of small firms is the gradual extension, from subnational to international levels, of those relationships of trust and cooperation that were common initially within local clusters alone (Cappellin, 2004). For the small firm sector as a whole, innovation-oriented relationships, and weak ties generally, are usually far less spatially restricted than is normally assumed (Grotz and Braun, 1997). Indeed access to extraregional networks is frequently more important, especially for technology-based firms. Accordingly, a wholly, or largely, inward-looking innovation system should give cause for concern.

Given these concerns, this chapter has sought to contribute to a better understanding of the characteristics and motivations of small firms engaged in extraregional innovation networks. Though the approach taken and the specific results differ, in very general terms the observations echo Oerlemans, Buys and Pretorius (2001, p. 72):

> spatial embeddedness is sensitive to features of innovative activity and even differs depending on the position of the innovator firm: being a user in a relationship with a producer (supplier) or being a producer in a relationship with a buyer (user) [and, one might add, being in a relationship with competitors].

Perhaps most notably, the frequent assertion that more complex forms of innovation are likely to be more reliant upon local ties is supported only for innovation networks involving competitors. For suppliers and, in particular, customers, there is evidence that technological sophistication correlates with greater reach. This resonates with the internationalization literature, which seems to suggest that 'internationalist' small firms (where this term implies more than exporting) are more innovative and more research-focused than their 'nationalist' peers. Importantly, signalling such associations must merely be preliminary. Further work is required to establish the mechanisms underpinning these relationships, though one may speculate more or less fruitfully. Moreover, to the extent that the results suggest sensitivity to local specialization, one might anticipate that the balance between intraregional and extraregional networks will vary across the space economy. However, this, again, requires further study.

## NOTES

1. Though, in practice the statement would be couched in conditional terms.
2. Or, at least, has allowed others to do so.
3. The extent of internal R&D may also usefully proxy the 'complexity' of the innovation process (Tether, 2002).
4. For the present purposes, 'Northern Britain' encompasses Scotland and the Northern English counties of Northumberland, County Durham, Tyne and Wear, Teesside and Cumbria.
5. Nomenclature of Territorial Units for Statistics.
6. While the increasing internationalization of some service activities may serve to attenuate the strength of this observation, 'it should be recognised that the "reach" and diffusion of many services, particularly more sophisticated services, remains partial' (Howells, 2000, p. 18).
7. Unremarkably, these authors do note that a higher regional purchase ratio increases the probability of localized ties to suppliers, although the influence is less than regional sales on the localization of customer networks.

## REFERENCES

Amin, A. and P. Cohendet (1999), 'Learning and adaptation in decentralised business networks', *Environment and Planning D: Society and Space*, **17**(1), 87–104.

Andréosso-O'Callaghan, B. (2000), 'Territory, research and technology linkages – is the Shannon region a propitious local system of innovation?', *Entrepreneurship and Regional Development* **12**(1), 69–87.

Appold, S. (1995), 'Agglomeration, interorganizational networks, and competitive performance in the US metal working sector', *Economic Geography*, **71**(1), 27–54.

Arndt, O. and R. Sternberg (2000), 'Do manufacturing firms profit from intraregional innovation linkages? An empirical based answer', *European Planning Studies*, **8**(4), 465–85.

Asheim, B. and A. Isaksen (2002), 'Regional innovation systems: the integration of local sticky and global ubiquitous knowledge', *Journal of Technology Transfer*, **27**(1), 77–86.

Audretsch, D. and M. Feldman (1996), 'R&D spillovers and the geography of innovation and production', *American Economic Review*, **86**(3), 630–40.

Aydalot, P. and D. Keeble (eds) (1988), *High Technology Industry and Innovative Environments: The European Experience*, London: Routledge.

Bayona, C., T. García-Marco and E. Huerta (2001), 'Firms' motivations for cooperative R&D: an empirical analysis of Spanish firms', *Research Policy*, **30**(8), 1289–308.

Becattini, G. (1978), 'The development of light industry in Tuscany', *Economic Notes* (2–3), 53–78.

Becattini, G. (1990), 'The Marshallian industrial district as a socio-economic notion', in F. Pyke, G. Becattini and W. Sengenberger (eds), *Industrial Districts and Inter-Firm Co-operation in Italy*, Geneva: International Institute for Labour Studies.

Bengtsson, M. and O. Sölvell (2004), 'Climate of competition, clusters and innovative performance', *Scandinavian Journal of Management*, **20**(3), 225–44.

Bianchi, G. (1998), 'Requiem for the Third Italy? Rise and fall of a too successful concept', *Entrepreneurship and Regional Development*, **10**(1), 93–116.

Boschma, R.A. (2005), 'Proximity and innovation. A critical assessment', *Regional Studies*, **39**(1), 61–74.

Bougrain, F. and B. Haudeville (2002), 'Innovation, collaboration and SMEs' internal research capacities', *Research Policy*, **31**(5), 735–48.

Breschi, S. and F. Lissoni (2001), 'Localised knowledge spillovers versus innovative milieux: knowledge "tacitness" reconsidered', *Papers in Regional Science*, **80**(3), 255–73.

Brusco, S. (1982), 'The Emilian model: productive decentralisation and social integration', *Cambridge Journal of Economics*, **6**(2), 167–84.

Bullock, A. and A. Hughes (2000), 'The survey method, the SME panel database and sample attrition', *British Enterprise in Transition*, ESRC Centre of Business Research, University of Cambridge.

Bunnell, T. and N. Coe (2001), 'Spaces and scales of innovation', *Progress in Human Geography*, **25**(4), 569–89.

Cappellin, R. (2004), 'International knowledge and innovation networks for European integration, cohesion and enlargement', *International Social Science Journal*, **56**(180), 207–25.

CBR (1996), 'The changing state of British enterprise', ESRC Centre of Business Research, University of Cambridge.

CBR (1998), 'Enterprise Britain', ESRC Centre of Business Research, University of Cambridge.

CBR (2000), 'British enterprise in transition', ESRC Centre of Business Research, University of Cambridge.

CBR (2004), 'Enterprise challenged', Department of Applied Economics, University of Cambridge.

Cohen, W. and D. Levinthal (1989), 'Innovation and learning: the two faces of R&D', *The Economic Journal*, **99**(397), 569–96.

Cohen, W. and D. Levinthal (1990), 'Absorptive capacity: a new perspective on learning and innovation', *Administrative Science Quarterly*, **35**(1), 128–52.

Cowan, R., P. David and D.Foray (2000), 'The explicit economics of knowledge codification and tacitness', *Industrial & Corporate Change*, **9**(2), 211–53.

DTI (Department of Trade and Industry) (2001), *Business Clusters in the UK: A First Assessment*, London: DTI.

Eisenhardt, K. and C. Schoonhaven (1996), 'Resource-based view of strategic alliance formation: strategic and social effects in entrepreneurial firms', *Organization Science*, **7**(2), 136–50.

Ernst, D. (2005), 'Complexity and internationalisation of innovation – why is chip design moving to Asia?', *International Journal of Innovation Management*, **9**(1), 47–73.

Feldman, M. (1994), 'Knowledge complementarity and innovation', *Small Business Economics*, **6**(5), 363–72.

Freel, M. (2000), 'External linkages and product innovation in small manufacturing firms', *Entrepreneurship and Regional Development*, **12**(3), 245–66.

Freel, M. (2003), 'Sectoral patterns of small firm innovation, networking and proximity', *Research Policy*, **32**(5), 751–70.

Freel, M. (2005), 'Perceived environmental uncertainty and innovation in small firms', *Small Business Economics*, **25**, 49–64.

Freel, M. and R. Harrison (2006), 'Innovation and cooperation in the small firm sector: evidence from "Northern Britain"', *Regional Studies*, **40**(4), 289–305.

Freeman, C. (1987), *Technology Policy and Economic Performance: Lessons from Japan*, London: Pinter Publishers.

Fritsch, M. and R. Lukas (2001), 'Who cooperates on R&D?', *Research Policy*, **30**(2), 297–312.

Fuchs, V. (1968), *The Service Economy*, New York: NBER-Columbia University Press.

Gallouj, F. (2002), 'Innovation in services and the attendant old and new myths', *Journal of Socio-Economics*, **31**(2), 137–54.

Gertler, M.S. (1995), 'Being there: proximity, organization, and culture in the development and adoption of advanced manufacturing technologies', *Economic Geography*, **71**(1), 1–27.

Grabher G. (1993), 'The weakness of strong ties; the lock-in of regional development in the Ruhr area', in G. Grabher (ed.), *The Embedded Firm: on the Socioeconomics of Industrial Networks*, London: Routledge, pp. 255–77.

Grotz, R. and B. Braun (1997), 'Territorial or trans-national networking: spatial aspects of technology-oriented co-operation within German mechanical engineering industry', *Regional Studies*, **31**(6), 545–57.

Harrison, B. (1992), 'Industrial districts: old wine in new bottles?', *Regional Studies*, **26**(5), 469–83.

Hassink, R. and D.-H. Shin (2005), 'Guest editorial: the restructuring of old industrial areas in Europe and Asia', *Environment and Planning A*, **37**(4), 571–80.

Howells, J. (1999), 'Regional systems of innovation?', in D. Archibugi, J. Howells and J. Michie (eds), *Innovation Policy in a Global Economy*, Cambridge: Cambridge University Press, pp. 67–93.

Howells, J. (2000), 'Innovation and services: new conceptual frameworks', CRIC discussion paper 38, University of Manchester.

Huggins, R. (2001), 'Inter-firm network policies and firm performance: evaluating the impact of initiatives in the United Kingdom', *Research Policy*, **30**(3), 443–58.

Jaffe, A., M. Trajtenberg and R. Henderson (1993), 'Geographical localization of knowledge spillovers as evidenced by patent citations', *Quarterly Journal of Economics*, **108**(3), 577–98.

Johnson, B. and B. Lundvall (1993), 'Catching-up and institutional learning under post-socialism', in J.J. Hausner, B. Jessop and K. Neilsen (eds), *Institutional Frameworks of Market Economies*, Aldershot: Avebury, pp. 68–86.

Johnson, B. and B.A. Lundvall (2001), 'Why all this fuss about codified and tacit knowledge?', DRUID Winter Conference, 18–20 January.

Kaufmann, A. and F. Tödtling (2000), 'Systems of innovation in traditional industrial regions: the case of Styria in a comparative perspective', *Regional Studies*, **34**(1), 29–40.

Keeble, D., C. Lawson, H. Lawton Smith, B. Moore and F. Wilkinson (1998), 'Internationalisation processes, networking and local embeddedness in technology-intensive small firms', *Small Business Economics*, **11**(4), 327–42.

Kirat, T. and Y. Lung (1999), 'Innovation and proximity: territories as loci of collective learning', *European Urban and Regional Studies*, **6**(1), 27–38.

Love, J. and S. Roper (2001), 'Location and network effects on innovation success: evidence for UK, German and Irish manufacturing plants', *Research Policy*, **30**(4), 643–62.

Lublinski, A. (2003), 'Does geographic proximity matter? Evidence from clustered and non-clustered aeronautic firms in Germany', *Regional Studies*, **37**(5), 453–67.

Lundvall, B. (ed.) (1992), *National Systems of Innovation: Towards a Theory of Innovation and Interactive Learning*, London: Pinter Publishers.

Lundvall, B.-Å. and S. Borrás (1997), 'Innovation policy in the globalising learning economy', TSER Programme, European Commission, Brussels.

Maillat, D. (1991), 'The innovation process and the role of the milieu', in E.M. Bergman, G. Maier and F. Tödtling (eds), *Regions Reconsidered – Economic Networks, Innovation and Local Development in Industrialised Countries*, London: Mansell Publishing.

Maillat D. (2001), 'Territory and innovation: the role of the milieu', in G. Sweeney (ed.), *Innovation, Economic Progress and the Quality of Life*, Cheltenham, UK and Northampton, MA, USA: Edward Elgar, pp. 137–43.

Malecki, E.J., P. Oinas and S.O. Park (1999), 'On technology and development', in E.J. Malecki and P. Oinas (eds), *Making connections: Technological Learning and Regional Economic Change*, Aldershot, UK: Ashgate, pp. 261–75.

Miotti, L. and F. Sachwald (2003), 'Co-operative R&D: why and with whom? An integrated framework of analysis', *Research Policy*, **32**(8), 1481–500.

Nelson, R. (ed.) (1993), *National Innovation Systems: A Comparative Analysis*, New York: Oxford University Press.

Nelson, R. (2000), 'National innovation systems', in Z. Acs (ed.), *Regional Innovation, Knowledge and Global Change*, London: Pinter Publishers, pp. 11–26.

Nooteboom, B. (1994), 'Innovation and diffusion in small firms: theory and evidence', *Small Business Economics*, **6**(5), 327–47.

Nooteboom, B. (1999), 'Innovation and inter-firm linkages: new implications for policy', *Research Policy*, **28**(8), 793–805.

Oerlemans, L. and M. Meeus (2001), 'R&D cooperation in a transaction cost perspective', *Review of Industrial Organisation*, **18**(1), 77–90.

Oerlemans, L., A. Buys and M. Pretorius (2001), 'Research design for the South African innovation survey 2001', ECIS, WP 01.02, Technical University of Eindhoven.

Oerlemans, L., M. Meeus and F. Boekema (1998), 'Do networks matter for innovation? The usefulness of the economic network approach in analysing innovation', *Tijdschrift voor Economische en Sociale Geografie*, **89**(3), 298–309.

Oerlemans, L., M. Meeus and F. Boekema (2001), 'On the spatial embeddedness of innovation networks: an exploration of the proximity effect', *Tijdschrift voor Economische en Sociale Geografie*, **92**(1), 60–75.

Patel, P. and K. Pavitt (1991), 'Large firms in the production of the world's technology: an important case of non-globalisation', *Journal of International Business Studies*, **22**(1), 1–21.

Patel, P. and K. Pavitt (1994), 'The continuing, widespread (and neglected) importance of improvements in mechanical technologies', *Research Policy*, **23**(5), 533–45.

Patel, P. and K. Pavitt (2000), 'National systems of innovation under strain: the internationalisation of corporate R&D', in R.Barrell, G. Mason and M. O'Mahoney (eds), *Productivity, Innovation and Economic Performance*, Cambridge: Cambridge University Press.

Porter, M.E. (1990), *The Competitive Advantage of Nations*, London: Macmillan.

Romijn, H. and M. Albu (2002), 'Innovation, networking and proximity: lessons from small high technology firms in the UK', *Regional Studies*, **36**(1), 81–6.

Rothwell, R. (1991), 'External networking and innovation in small and medium-sized manufacturing firms', *Technovation*, **11**(2), 93–112.

Rothwell, R. (1994), 'Towards the fifth-generation innovation process', *International Marketing Review*, **11**(1), 7–31.

Rothwell, R. and M. Dodgson (1991), 'External linkages and innovation in small and medium-sized enterprises', *R&D Management*, **21**(2), 125–37.

SBRC (1992), 'The state of British enterprise', Department of Applied Economics, University of Cambridge.

Scott, A. (1988), *New Industrial Spaces*, London: Pion Ltd.

Sternberg, R. (1999), 'Innovative linkages and proximity: empirical results from recent surveys of small and medium sized firms in German regions', *Regional Studies*, **33**(6), 529–40.

Tabachnick, B. and L. Fidell (2001), *Using Multivariate Statistics*, 4th edn, Needham Heights, MA: Pearson Education.

Teece, D. (1992), 'Competition, cooperation and innovation', *Journal of Economic Behaviour and Organization*, **18**(1), 1–25.

Tether, B. (2002), 'Who cooperates for innovation and why? An empirical analysis', *Research Policy*, **31**(6), 947–68.

Tether, B. and C. Hipp (2002), 'Knowledge intensive, technical and other services: patterns of competitiveness and innovation compared', *Technology Analysis and Strategic Management*, **14**(2), 163–82.

## APPENDICES

*Appendix 2A.1    Factor analysis of barriers to innovation items*

| Item | Factor 1: knowledge | Factor 2: finance | $\bar{x}$ | $\sigma$ |
|---|---|---|---|---|
| Access to technological skills | **0.769** | −0.071 | 2.248 | 1.322 |
| Access to marketing skills | **0.609** | 0.308 | 2.244 | 1.297 |
| Access to management skills | **0.602** | 0.313 | 2.075 | 1.194 |
| Access to finance skills | 0.462 | **0.534** | 1.841 | 1.147 |
| Access to debt finance | 0.125 | **0.839** | 1.674 | 1.119 |
| Access to equity finance | 0.093 | **0.827** | 1.556 | 1.071 |
| Access to grants | 0.250 | **0.608** | 2.201 | 1.407 |
| Access to appropriate information/advice | **0.701** | 0.206 | 2.239 | 1.263 |
| Access to suitable partners | **0.597** | 0.192 | 1.743 | 1.139 |
| Access to specialist equipment/facilities | **0.634** | 0.172 | 1.847 | 1.193 |
| Eigenvalues | 2.875 | 2.349 | | |
| Percentage of total variance explained | 28.75 | 23.49 | | |
| N = 561 | | | | |

*Notes:*
Factor loadings greater than or equal to ± 0.50 (boldface) are significant.
PCA with Varimax rotation.

Respondents were asked to rank on a scale of 1–5 (1=not important and 5=crucial) the extent to which the above items hindered their innovative activity during the three-year period covered by the study.

*Appendix 2A.2    Factor analysis of stimuli to innovation items*

| Item | Factor 1: proactive | Factor 2: reactive | $\bar{x}$ | $\sigma$ |
|---|---|---|---|---|
| To comply with legislation/regulation | 0.018 | **0.859** | 2.022 | 1.290 |
| To respond to competition | **0.634** | 0.293 | 2.898 | 1.321 |
| To meet a specific customer request | 0.352 | 0.012 | 3.397 | 2.560 |
| To enter a new market | **0.770** | −0.035 | 2.805 | 1.531 |
| To diversify the business | **0.734** | 0.054 | 2.860 | 1.515 |
| To maintain sales revenue/market share | **0.749** | 0.202 | 3.069 | 1.461 |
| To increase sales revenue/market share | **0.792** | 0.115 | 3.243 | 1.439 |
| As a result of standardization (e.g. BS, ISO) | 0.167 | **0.801** | 1.601 | 0.976 |
| Eigenvalues | 2.874 | 1.532 | | |
| Percentage of total variance explained | 35.92 | 19.04 | | |
| N = 549 | | | | |

*Notes:*
Factor loadings greater than or equal to ± 0.50 (boldface) are significant.
PCA with Varimax rotation.

Respondents were asked to rank on a scale of 1–5 (1=not important and 5=crucial) the main reasons for introducing new or improved products and/or processes during the three-year period covered by the study.

# 3. Innovation, productivity and growth: an analysis of Irish data

**James H. Love and Stephen Roper**

## INTRODUCTION

Innovation is now widely understood as an evolutionary process, strongly conditioned by a firm's institutional, locational and market context (Nelson and Winter, 1982). An innovation event (such as the introduction of a new product or process), however, represents the end of a process of knowledge sourcing, coordination and codification. It also represents the beginning of a process of value added generation which, subject to market and appropriability conditions, may result in an improvement in the performance of the innovating business and also perhaps (through spillovers) improvements in the performance of core-lated or colocated firms. In this chapter, following recent studies by Crépon et al. (1998), Lööf and Heshmati (2001, 2002) and Love and Roper (2001a), we specify and begin to test a new integrative model of the causal links in this process of knowledge sourcing, coordination and exploitation and its relationship to enhanced business performance.

The main novelty of the chapter is empirical in that we use a new panel data set to trace the use of knowledge from its *development* (either in-house or externally sourced), through its *application* in the process of innovation, and finally to the *exploitation* of innovation in subsequent business performance. Our focus is therefore on three groups of issues:

a.  From where do firms assemble the bundle of knowledge necessary for innovation? What roles do in-house R&D, supply-chain collaboration and non-supply-chain collaboration play in firms' knowledge sourcing activities? How are these activities interrelated?
b.  How do the characteristics of the enterprise, including its own knowledge and managerial resources, shape organizations' ability to acquire and coordinate the knowledge necessary for innovation?
c.  How do the characteristics of the enterprise and its operating environment influence the organization's ability to appropriate economic value from its knowledge base and innovation activity?

The second section of the chapter defines our conceptual approach to addressing these questions, developing a model of the process of knowledge sourcing, coordination and exploitation (KSCE). Developing the model is largely an integrative endeavour, drawing on the literatures on the make or buy decision in R&D, the innovation production function and other studies which have considered innovation and business performance. The third section describes our data and empirical approach. The data are taken from a new panel data set of Irish plants' innovation activity over the 1991–2002 period. The fourth section reports the main empirical analysis and the last section concludes with a summary and final remarks.

## CONCEPTUAL FOUNDATIONS

Underlying our analysis is an evolutionary perspective on the innovation process of knowledge sourcing, coordination and exploitation. At the level of the individual enterprise this sees the innovation process as influenced strongly by the dynamic (internal) capabilities of enterprises (Teece et al., 1997), by the extent and richness of firms' boundary-spanning networks (Conway, 1995; Oerlemans et al., 1998) as well as the cultural norms, markets and the presence of colocated firms and other organizations (for example, universities, government research laboratories) which comprise the innovation system.

The causal process underlying our analysis begins with firms' knowledge sourcing and generation activities. As Veugelers and Cassiman (1999, p. 64) remark, however, 'Technology sourcing strategies have not been well explored in the theoretical literature and the empirical evidence remains to a large extent anecdotal.' At the level of the firm, conceptual models typically see external knowledge sourcing as a substitute for internal knowledge creation (that is, the classic make or buy decision) giving firms the ability to obtain specialist knowledge and/or accelerate knowledge acquisition. Such alternatives have, until recently, however, only been poorly reflected in the empirical literature, with Crépon et al. (1998) and Lööf and Heshmati (2001, 2002) implicitly assuming that undertaking R&D provides a unique route through which a firm may acquire the knowledge on which to base its innovation activities. This assumption is contradicted by much recent evidence, however, which stresses the importance for innovation of knowledge flows which span the boundaries of individual businesses creating 'extended enterprises' and providing the basis for competition between supply chains. At the level of the individual business too, inter-company networks (for example, Oerlemans et al., 1998) and intra-group knowledge transfers (for example, Love and Roper, 2001a) have been shown to have positive effects on innovation outputs.

Here we distinguish three routes by which firms can source or generate knowledge: by undertaking R&D (the standard 'make' option), by developing partnerships with other firms in the supply chain (one 'buy' option), or by developing partnerships with organizations outside the supply chain (another 'buy' option). To reflect firms' internal decision process and their environment we therefore relate the intensity of knowledge sourcing activity to expected post-innovation margins, the market position of the firm and a range of indicators relating to the strength of firms' internal resource base. This suggests that investments by firm $i$ in knowledge sourcing through R&D ($RKS_i$), supply chain collaboration ($SCKS_i$) and non supply-chain collaboration ($XSCKS_i$) may be represented by equations of the following form:

$$RKS_i = \gamma_{10} + \gamma_{11}\pi_i^e + \gamma_{12}MPOS_i + \gamma_{13}RBASE_i + \varepsilon_1,$$

$$SCKS_i = \gamma_{20} + \gamma_{21}\pi_i^e + \gamma_{22}MPOS_i + \gamma_{23}RBASE_i + \varepsilon_2,$$

$$XSCKS_i = \gamma_{30} + \gamma_{22}\pi_i^e + \gamma_{32}MPOS_i + \gamma_{33}RBASE_i + \varepsilon_3, \tag{3.1}$$

where $\pi^e_i$ is the expected level of post-innovation returns, $MPOS_i$ is a group of variables representing the market position of the firm, and $RBASE_i$ is a group of variables reflecting the strength of the firm's internal resource base.

The inclusion of variables to represent the market position of the firm (MPOS) is intended to reflect issues of appropriation and potential Schumpeterian or monopoly effects related to plant size. Crépon et al. (1998), for example, in their model for R&D investment, include measures of firms' market share and diversification. Indicators of business size (and size squared) are also included by Crépon et al. (1998), Lööf and Heshmati (2001, 2002) and Love and Roper (2001a) to reflect potential scale effects. The characteristics of the internal resource base of the business are less well represented in Crépon et al. (1998) and Lööf and Heshmati (2001, 2002) although both include a measure of the quality of firms' workforce. In their knowledge sourcing equations, Love and Roper (2001a) also include measures relating to the nature of firms' production activities and the organization of any R&D being undertaken in-house.

If firms' expectations about post-innovation returns are rational, that is, they involve no systematic errors, and we regard:

$$\pi_i = \beta_0 + \beta_1 MPOS_i + \beta_2 RBASE_i + \eta_i, \tag{3.2}$$

we can substitute for expected post-innovation returns in equation (3.1) to obtain reduced-form knowledge sourcing equations:

$$RKS_i = \theta_{10} + \theta_{12} MPOS_i + \theta_{13} RBASE_i + \lambda_1,$$

$$SCKS_i = \theta_{20} + \theta_{22} MPOS_i + \theta_{23} RBASE_i + \lambda_2,$$

$$NSCKS_i = \theta_{30} + \theta_{32} MPOS_i + \theta_{33} RBASE_i + \lambda_3, \tag{3.3}$$

where, for example, $\theta_{12} = \gamma_{12} + \gamma_{11}\beta_1.$

Knowledge sourced through R&D, supply-chain or non-supply-chain collaboration will then be coordinated into a form which can be commercially exploited, innovation. This involves relating innovation outputs to the inputs to the innovation process, that is, the knowledge or innovation production function (Geroski, 1990; Harris and Trainor, 1995):

$$INNOV_i = g\,(RKS_i, SCKS_i, NSCKS_i, MPOS, RBASE), \tag{3.4}$$

where we allow for the possibility that firms' market position and resource base may influence the efficiency of their knowledge coordination activities.

The final link in the causal chain is that from innovation to business performance. Following Crépon et al. (1998) and Lööf and Heshmati (2001, 2002) we approach this by estimating an innovation-augmented production function, with the form of the equation depending on the specific business performance indicator being examined. Crépon et al. (1998) and Lööf and Heshmati (2001, 2002) for example, focus on productivity and productivity growth, while Roper and Love (2002a, 2002b) focus on export performance. Depending on the performance measure being considered we also allow for possible links to the plant's market position (MPOS) and internal resource base (RBASE). Crépon et al.

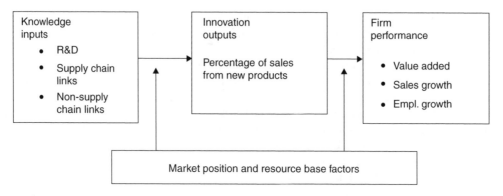

*Figure 3.1    Diagrammatic model*

(1998), for example, include the skill composition of the business which they argue reflects the differences in the efficiency of skilled relative to unskilled labour (p. 123). Thus business performance ($BPERF_i$) is given by

$$BPERF_i = h(INNOV_i, MPOS_i, RBASE_i) \qquad (3.5)$$

The complete KSCE model will then consist of the largely recursive system of equations (3.3), (3.4) and (3.5). In diagrammatic terms, the above set of equations can be represented as in Figure 3.1.

## DATA AND METHODS

Our empirical analysis is based on data from the Irish Innovation Panel (IIP) which provides information on knowledge use, innovation and the performance of manufacturing plants throughout the Republic of Ireland and Northern Ireland over the period 1991–2002. The IIP comprises four linked surveys conducted using similar survey methodologies and questionnaires with common questions. Each survey covers the innovation activities of manufacturing plants with ten or more employees over a three-year period (Roper et al., 1996; Roper and Hewitt-Dundas, 1998; Roper and Anderson, 2000; Roper et al., 2003). Each wave of the IIP was undertaken by post using a sampling frame provided by the economic development agencies in Northern Ireland and the Republic of Ireland. The initial survey, undertaken between October 1994 and February 1995, related to plants' innovation activity over the 1991–93 period, and achieved a response rate of 38.2 per cent (Roper et al., 1996; Roper and Hewitt-Dundas, 1998, Table A1.3). The second survey was conducted between November 1996 and March 1997, covered plants' innovation activity during the 1994–96 period, and had a response rate of 32.9 per cent (Roper and Hewitt-Dundas, 1998). The third survey covering the 1997–99 period was undertaken between October 1999 and January 2000 and achieved an overall response rate of 32.8 per cent (Roper and Anderson, 2000). The fourth survey was undertaken between November 2002 and May 2003 and achieved an overall response rate of 34.1 per cent (Roper et al., 2003).

For this preliminary analysis we use only the second, third and fourth survey results which relate to the period 1994–2002, a period over which both the Irish and Northern Ireland economies grew rapidly. In Ireland, export volume growth averaged 12–15 per cent per annum during this period, compared to around 4–6 per cent from Northern Ireland. Average real GDP growth from 1991 to 2000 in Ireland was 7.1 per cent per annum, compared to 2.7 per cent in Northern Ireland.[1] Much speculation has surrounded the causes of the 'Celtic Tiger' phenomenon in Ireland (for example, Sweeney, 1998; Barry, 1999; Murphy, 2000) with the general consensus focusing on the vital role of inward investment and the growth of the externally owned, high-tech sector (for example, McCarthy, 1999; Ruane and Görg, 1997; Roper and Frenkel, 2000).[2] Other factors have also been implicated, however, as explanations for differential trade performance. Barry and Bradley (1997), for example, emphasize the importance of market orientation and industrial sector to the success of the Irish economy. For Northern Ireland, while the evidence suggests that political conditions did have a negative effect on investment in Northern Ireland's manufacturing sector, this was more than compensated by the positive effect of higher industrial subsidies and the attractiveness of Northern Ireland as a production location for companies seeking to emigrate from southern regions of the UK. The net result was that manufacturing employment and investment in Northern Ireland was actually sustained at a higher level than that in the UK as a whole over the 1971–96 period (Fielding, 2003, p. 514), although, as Harris et al. (2002) and Roper and Hewitt-Dundas (2001) point out, the effects of government assistance on productivity in Northern Ireland were less positive.

In this context, we focus in the current chapter on the innovation production function and the process which links innovation to business performance, that is, with equations (3.4) and (3.5) above.[3] The remainder of this section deals with the independent and dependent variables used in the estimation, and the estimation techniques used.

The innovation production function (equation 3.4) requires measures of knowledge sourcing activity, and of plants' market position and resource base. Measuring the intensity of firms' knowledge sourcing through R&D is relatively straightforward with standard indicators (used by Crépon et al., 1998; Lööf and Heshmati, 2001, 2002; Love and Roper, 2001a), measuring R&D employment relative to total employment (Table 3.1). Measuring knowledge sourcing through firms' supply-chain and non-supply-chain innovation linkages is more experimental, and here we follow Love and Roper (1999, 2001a) who develop scores for the extent of firms' external contacts. More specifically, we construct scores for each plant's knowledge sourcing through supply-chain and non-supply-chain collaboration based on the number of types of organization with which the firm is undertaking collaborative innovation activity. For example, we identify five types of potential supply-chain partners (customers, suppliers, competitors, other group companies and joint ventures): plants undertaking innovation collaboration with three of these types of partner 'score' 60 per cent; plants collaborating with all five types of partner score 100 per cent, and so on. Reflecting both those plants with no supply chain links and those with links, the average value of the supply chain collaboration variable for the whole sample was 18.33 (Table 3.1).[4] Non-supply-chain linkages are constructed in a similar way, using links with four types of possible partners (consultancies, universities, government bodies and industry research establishments). Again, reflecting both those

*Table 3.1   Descriptive statistics*

| | Northern Ireland | | Republic of Ireland | | Whole sample | |
|---|---|---|---|---|---|---|
| | Mean | s.d. | Mean | s.d. | Mean | s.d. |
| *Innovation and performance indicators* | | | | | | |
| Innovation success (%) | 13.31 | 21.54 | 16.51 | 23.70 | 15.13 | 22.84 |
| Process innovation | 0.51 | 0.50 | 0.59 | 0.49 | 0.57 | 0.50 |
| Gross profit margin | 0.17 | 0.38 | 0.17 | 0.90 | 0.17 | 0.73 |
| Value added per employee (log) | 3.35 | 0.71 | 3.57 | 0.81 | 3.48 | 0.77 |
| Sales growth (%) | 29.82 | 58.52 | 44.27 | 112.75 | 38.20 | 94.09 |
| Employment growth (%) | 15.61 | 46.64 | 23.24 | 59.47 | 20.03 | 54.57 |
| *Knowledge-sourcing activities* | | | | | | |
| R&D intensity | 2.35 | 5.37 | 2.96 | 10.69 | 2.71 | 8.91 |
| Supply-chain collaboration | 16.47 | 25.35 | 19.70 | 26.11 | 18.33 | 25.84 |
| Non-supply-chain collaboration | 10.83 | 23.13 | 13.92 | 25.59 | 12.61 | 24.61 |
| *Market position indicators* | | | | | | |
| Employment | 110.13 | 400.06 | 125.67 | 263.58 | 119.18 | 327.63 |
| Plant vintage (years) | 35.26 | 32.06 | 31.02 | 28.00 | 32.47 | 29.51 |
| Production mainly one-offs | 0.18 | 0.38 | 0.16 | 0.37 | 0.17 | 0.38 |
| Production mainly small batches | 0.41 | 0.49 | 0.39 | 0.49 | 0.40 | 0.49 |
| Production mainly large batches | 0.28 | 0.45 | 0.30 | 0.46 | 0.29 | 0.46 |
| *Resource indicators* | | | | | | |
| Part of multi-plant operation | 0.37 | 0.48 | 0.53 | 0.50 | 0.47 | 0.50 |
| Externally owned | 0.28 | 0.45 | 0.39 | 0.49 | 0.34 | 0.47 |
| Workforce with degree (%) | 7.56 | 10.48 | 9.71 | 12.25 | 8.82 | 11.60 |
| Workforce with no qualifications (%) | 49.77 | 32.60 | 48.35 | 31.84 | 48.94 | 32.16 |
| R&D in group | 0.16 | 0.36 | 0.27 | 0.44 | 0.22 | 0.42 |
| Govt assistance for product development | 0.23 | 0.42 | 0.26 | 0.44 | 0.25 | 0.43 |
| Capital investment | 0.06 | 0.11 | 0.07 | 0.16 | 0.07 | 0.14 |
| Export sales (%) | 16.48 | 27.39 | 31.24 | 36.93 | 25.03 | 34.04 |

firms with and without linkages, the average value of this variable was 12.61 for the whole sample (Table 3.1).[5]

Market position or organizational context indicators include size variables (employment) and dummy variable indicators of the plants' form of production activity. The strength of each plant's internal resource base is proxied by a variety of measures, including whether or not the plant is part of a multi-plant group, whether it is externally owned and whether there is any R&D relevant to the plant carried out elsewhere within the group. These measures of intra-group resources have proved important in previous research on innovation (Love et al., 1996; Love and Roper, 1999, 2001a). Indicators of labour and capital inputs are also included (percentage of workforce with a degree and percentage with no qualifications; capital investment relative to turnover). Finally, a measure of whether the plant had received any government assistance for product development during the survey period is included.

In the business performance estimations (equation 3.5), a very similar set of market position and plant resource indicator variables is used,[6] and the knowledge sourcing measures are replaced by the measure of innovation success (that is, the dependent variable from equation 3.4). In both equations industry dummies at the two-digit level are included.

The estimators used in the econometric analysis are governed by the panel and by the characteristics of the dependent variables. The structure of the IIP permits a recursive rather than simultaneous approach to be adopted, in line with the KSCE model, because, where the performance indicators in equation (3.5) relate to year $n$, the innovation indicator relates to the three-year period $n$-2 to $n$ inclusive. The innovation production function reflects the effectiveness with which knowledge inputs are translated into innovative outputs. Innovation success is defined as the percentage of sales derived from products newly introduced or updated in the previous three years. Process innovation, used alongside innovation success in the performance equations, is a dummy variable taking value one if the firm introduced any new or improved processes over the previous three years. This is a value censored at 0 and 100, and thus Tobit is an appropriate estimator.[7] In equation (3.5) we consider three indicators of business performance, one relating to productivity (value added per employee) and two relating to growth over the previous three years (sales and employment growth, respectively). Linear estimation is used for equation (3.5).

## RESULTS OF ESTIMATION

### Innovation Success

The results of the fixed-effects Tobit model are shown in Table 3.2. Two alternative estimations are presented. The first includes a dummy variable for plants in Northern Ireland to check for differences between the Irish and Northern Irish subsamples. This dummy is statistically insignificant, and is removed in the second estimation.[8]

All three knowledge-sourcing activities have a strongly positive effect on innovation success, with supply-chain collaboration dominating non-supply-chain collaboration effects. This reflects the findings of other studies which have emphasized the importance of boundary-spanning networks for innovation (Oerlemans et al., 1998; Love and Roper, 2001b). At first sight, the positive sign on all three coefficients appears to suggest that there is a complementary rather than substitute relationship between the three knowledge-sourcing activities. However the introduction of cross-product variables somewhat qualifies this. The positive impact of both supply-chain and non-supply-chain linkages on innovation is reduced in the presence of R&D, although the size of the effect is small, and having both forms of collaborative activity in tandem also slightly reduces the positive impact of each separately. Overall, therefore, the results of the knowledge-sourcing variables suggest that it pays to gain access both to internal and to external knowledge sources for innovation, but at the margin there is some degree of substitutability between them.

The market position indicators suggest that little significant difference is evident in innovation success between different employment size bands. Relative to plants undertaking continuous production, those mainly producing large batches are relatively

*Innovation and competitive advantage*

*Table 3.2 Fixed effects Tobit model of innovation success (marginal effects)*

| Dependent variable | Innovation success | | Innovation success | |
|---|---|---|---|---|
| | Coefficient | t-ratio | Coefficient | t-ratio |
| *Knowledge-sourcing activities* | | | | |
| R&D intensity | 1.386 | 7.519 | 1.450 | 7.861 |
| Supply-chain collaboration | 0.414 | 9.179 | 0.429 | 9.801 |
| Non-supply-chain collaboration | 0.160 | 2.819 | 0.155 | 2.689 |
| Non-supply-chain collab. with R&D | −0.012 | −2.176 | −0.012 | −2.146 |
| Supply-chain collab. with R&D | −0.018 | −3.171 | −0.018 | −3.229 |
| Supply-chain collab. with non-supply-chain collab. | −0.004 | −3.586 | −0.004 | −3.505 |
| *Market position* | | | | |
| Employment 50–99 | 2.357 | 1.305 | 2.431 | 1.306 |
| Employment 100–249 | −1.294 | −0.676 | −1.445 | −0.729 |
| Employment 250+ | −3.400 | −1.358 | −3.569 | −1.379 |
| Plant vintage (years) | −0.033 | −1.220 | −0.034 | −1.229 |
| Production mainly one-offs | −6.602 | −3.695 | −6.683 | −3.624 |
| Production mainly small batches | 2.002 | 1.543 | 2.063 | 1.548 |
| Production mainly large batches | 5.856 | 3.924 | 6.084 | 4.000 |
| *Resource indicators* | | | | |
| Part of multi-plant operation | 3.959 | 1.902 | 4.446 | 2.093 |
| Externally owned | −2.818 | −1.317 | −2.569 | −1.176 |
| Workforce with degree (%) | −0.046 | −0.676 | −0.056 | −0.814 |
| Workforce with no qualifications (%) | −0.079 | −3.710 | −0.081 | −3.638 |
| R&D in group | 1.837 | 0.953 | | |
| Govt assistance for product development | 6.144 | 4.014 | 6.304 | 4.049 |
| Capital investment per employee | 0.076 | 2.211 | 0.082 | 2.343 |
| *Northern Ireland plant* | 2.185 | 0.889 | | |
| *Sectoral indicators* | | | | |
| Food, drink and tobacco | 2.767 | 1.239 | 3.049 | 1.328 |
| Textiles and clothing | 9.715 | 3.501 | 10.155 | 3.589 |
| Wood and wood products | −2.831 | −0.874 | −2.591 | −0.774 |
| Paper and printing | −10.061 | −2.878 | −10.281 | −2.837 |
| Chemicals | 0.953 | 0.288 | 0.929 | 0.272 |
| Metals and metal fabrication | 2.335 | 0.945 | 2.459 | 0.967 |
| Mechanical engineering | 13.547 | 4.556 | 13.888 | 4.669 |
| Electrical and optical equipment | 8.419 | 3.291 | 8.744 | 3.364 |
| Transport equipment | −1.999 | −0.505 | −2.067 | −0.505 |
| N | 1052 | | 1052 | |
| Log-L | −4101.65 | | −4102.22 | |

successful innovators, while those with one-off production methods are relatively less 'successful'. There is also no evidence of any 'learning' effect with respect to plant vintage, something which might have been expected if innovation was the type of cumulative causation process envisaged in the Schumpeter Mark II model. This latter finding reflects the results of other recent studies which have emphasized the lack of persistence of innovation across different populations of companies and pointed instead to a polarized distribution of non-innovative and strongly innovative companies (for example, Malerba et al., 1997; Cefis and Orsenigo, 2001).

A range of indicators of plants' resource base also prove important in determining the efficiency with which plants translate knowledge inputs into innovation success. Being part of a multi-plant operation has a substantial positive effect, which may, of course, be yet another facet of knowledge-sourcing activity, especially where knowledge is tacit and there may be reasons to fear dissipation of property rights. However the fact that there is no effect arising from having access to group R&D weakens the knowledge-sourcing argument, and indicates that the advantages of group membership may reflect the financial support which groups can provide, or some other advantage which is not directly R&D/innovation-based. Perhaps surprisingly, the proportion of graduates in the workforce has no effect on innovation success. This does not indicate, however, that the qualifications issue is unimportant; the significantly negative coefficient on the proportion of the workforce with no qualifications suggests that mid-level qualifications such as apprenticeship or other firm/sectoral-level training may be an important determinant of innovation success, a factor emphasized previously in Ireland–Germany skill comparisons (for example, Roper and Hoffman, 1993).

Unsurprisingly both capital investment and having received government financial assistance for product development have a strong positive association with innovation success. The capital investment effect may suggest that investment leads to innovation, or maybe because plants which introduce new products require capital investment as they gear up for production. The positive effect of the policy dummy is reassuring but requires some care in interpretation (Greene, 1997, p. 982). In particular, the coefficient will give an unbiased indication of the effect of grant support only if support is randomly distributed across the population of plants. Where there is any element of selection in the award of grants the coefficients on the grant dummy will reflect the combination of 'assistance' and 'selection' effects. For example, if product development assistance was aimed at firms which were more likely to be successful innovators even without assistance, the coefficient will overestimate the true assistance effect.[9]

**Productivity and Growth**

Here we are concerned with the impact of the innovation success measure and of the market position and resource indicators on the three performance variables defined earlier (Table 3.3). A key issue is the differential effect of product innovation success and process change on productivity and growth.

Following a range of alternative tests, LM tests suggested the validity of a simple approach based on OLS, possibly reflecting the short and relatively unbalanced nature of the panel. Perhaps unsurprisingly, given both the different nature of the dependent variables and the heterogeneity in performance exhibited within the panel of manufacturing

*Table 3.3    OLS regression models of performance*

| Dependent variable | Value added per employee (log) | | Sales growth | | Employment growth | |
|---|---|---|---|---|---|---|
| | Coeff. | t-ratio | Coeff. | t-ratio | Coeff. | t-ratio |
| *Innovation success* | −0.002 | −3.535 | 0.334 | 7.218 | 0.205 | 6.888 |
| *Process innovation* | 0.055 | 1.946 | 9.164 | 4.481 | 6.930 | 5.240 |
| *Market position* | | | | | | |
| Employment 50–99 | 0.020 | 0.570 | 1.722 | 0.680 | 0.793 | 0.487 |
| Employment 100–249 | 0.057 | 1.421 | −3.947 | −1.379 | −0.311 | −0.168 |
| Employment 250+ | 0.074 | 1.374 | −3.914 | −1.034 | −1.762 | −0.727 |
| Plant vintage (years) | 0.001 | 2.758 | −0.199 | −5.914 | −0.161 | −7.452 |
| Production mainly one-offs | −0.056 | −1.538 | −0.404 | −0.151 | −2.166 | −1.256 |
| Production mainly small batches | −0.068 | −2.503 | −0.714 | −0.360 | 2.313 | 1.814 |
| Production mainly large batches | −0.014 | −0.468 | −1.516 | −0.702 | −0.800 | −0.576 |
| *Resource indicators* | | | | | | |
| Part of multi-plant operation | 0.301 | 7.296 | −7.156 | −2.390 | −6.696 | −3.516 |
| Externally owned | 0.021 | 0.479 | −1.149 | −0.361 | 1.526 | 0.750 |
| Capital investment per employee | 0.004 | 4.419 | 0.059 | 0.991 | 0.099 | 2.419 |
| Workforce with degree (%) | 0.009 | 5.441 | 0.458 | 4.216 | 0.208 | 3.001 |
| Workforce with no qualifications (%) | 0.000 | −1.107 | 0.019 | 0.574 | 0.008 | 0.397 |
| Export sales (%) | 0.001 | 1.595 | −0.078 | −2.251 | −0.034 | −1.522 |
| *Northern Ireland plant* | −0.098 | −3.609 | −3.796 | −1.901 | −2.053 | −1.595 |
| *Sectoral indicators* | | | | | | |
| Food, drink and tobacco | 0.057 | 1.274 | −3.688 | −1.145 | −0.267 | −0.129 |
| Textiles and clothing | −0.302 | −5.659 | −9.685 | −2.541 | −2.985 | −1.218 |
| Wood and wood products | −0.032 | −0.501 | −5.674 | −1.175 | 2.107 | 0.686 |
| Paper and printing | 0.059 | 1.031 | −3.160 | −0.748 | 3.556 | 1.304 |
| Chemicals | 0.333 | 4.951 | −5.061 | −1.130 | −1.689 | −0.586 |
| Metals and metal fabrication | 0.063 | 1.298 | 0.751 | 0.209 | 5.461 | 2.346 |
| Mechanical engineering | 0.003 | 0.057 | −3.007 | −0.734 | 0.813 | 0.310 |
| Electrical and optical equipment | −0.167 | −3.290 | −0.272 | −0.072 | 1.455 | 0.598 |
| Transport equipment | 0.031 | 0.405 | 10.248 | 1.785 | 10.101 | 2.729 |
| Constant | 3.266 | 60.870 | 29.153 | 7.615 | 11.500 | 4.600 |
| N | 1588 | | 1639 | | 1645 | |
| Adj R sqrd | 0.227 | | 0.109 | | 0.123 | |
| s.d.e(i) | 0.517 | | 38.049 | | 24.510 | |
| F( ..) | 19.69 | | 9.04 | | 10.42 | |

plants (Table 3.2), there is a substantial variation in both the explanatory power of the equations and in the effects of individual variables.[10]

The first striking result in the performance models is the positive impact of product innovation success on growth and the effect of process innovation on both growth and productivity. In the growth equations the innovation success indicator is positive and significant for sales and employment growth. The effect of product innovation success on productivity is more complex, with a negative and significant effect. This result, which has been noted elsewhere (Freel and Robson, 2004) we interpret as a disruption effect. For example, the introduction of new products to a plant may disrupt production and reduce productivity, an effect which is also suggested by the negative productivity effects of one-off and small batch production. Alternatively the negative productivity effect of innovation success may be explained by a product life cycle type of effect. In this scenario, newly introduced products are initially produced inefficiently with negative productivity consequences before becoming established and the focus of process innovations is to improve productive efficiency.

Indicators of market position are, in general, fairly weakly defined in the performance models. Employment size has little significant impact on growth but has a weakly positive effect on productivity: larger plants tend to have higher productivity than their smaller counterparts. Plant vintage is positive with respect to productivity, and strongly negative with respect to sales and employment growth; that is, young plants grow quickly and (perhaps as a result) have lower productivity than their older counterparts.

The resource indicators reveal an interesting pattern of results. Although being part of a multi-plant group is helpful for innovative success (see Table 3.2) and for productivity, it has a negative effect on growth. Thus being part of a multi-plant group helps innovation success, and innovation leads to growth, but this is offset by a strong negative effect of multi-plant operation on growth. This may suggest that, while they benefit in terms of innovation output and productivity, plants which are part of a group are ultimately constrained in their growth by the corporate policies of the parent organizations. As might be expected, having a well-qualified workforce also strongly aids growth and productivity. Capital investment shows an extremely strong positive effect on productivity but has a weaker growth effect (see Table 3.3).

While exporting has a positive effect on productivity,[11] it also has what at first seems to be a somewhat counterintuitive negative influence on sales growth during the 1990s. The implication is that Irish plants with a stronger export orientation grew more slowly than those with a stronger domestic orientation over this period. This is just what we would expect, however, given the relative growth rates of the Irish 'Celtic Tiger' economy during the 1990s and the markedly slower growth of the EU which forms the main export market for Irish manufacturers.

## DISCUSSION AND CONCLUSIONS

Based on data for Irish manufacturing firms we here provide further support for the importance of external knowledge sources for innovation. In-house R&D is very important for innovation success, and supply-chain collaboration dominates non-supply-chain collaboration. In addition, however, we find evidence of substitutability between these knowledge-sourcing activities in contrast to other studies which largely suggest a pattern of complementarity. In addition to these knowledge-sourcing variables, we find strong evidence that innovation success (measured by the percentage of sales derived from new products), depends on plants' organizational context, skills, capital investment and the receipt of government grant assistance for product development.

Innovation success is, in turn, shown to have strong positive effects on business growth measured in terms both of sales and of employment. The impact of innovation on productivity is more complex, however, with product innovation reducing productivity. Two explanations for this latter effect are discussed. First, it may simply reflect the disruption caused to production by the introduction of new products. Secondly, it may be related to product life cycle, and reflect an initial period of inefficient and small-scale production before more efficient mass production begins. By contrast, process innovation unambiguously improves both productivity and growth.

Our analysis (very much part of a continuing project)[12] adds to the growing literature on the relationship between innovation and business performance. It also focuses attention on the knowledge flows which shape and determine the innovation process and the importance of firms' internal resources and market position in determining the efficiency of firms' knowledge coordination and exploitation activities. For example, while there is little evidence that plant size has a significant effect either on innovation success or on subsequent performance, it is clear that being part of a multiplant operation has a significant and subtle impact both on innovation and on productivity and growth. Interestingly this effect seems to arise not directly from group R&D, but from access to the wider (financial or personnel) resources which group operations may afford. There is also some suggestion of a link between exporting, innovation and performance, although the possible endogeneity of these effects is beyond the scope of the present chapter.

Drawing firm policy conclusions from this preliminary analysis is difficult but a number of points are worth highlighting. First, our analysis again emphasizes the importance of boundary-spanning links for innovation success. Policy measures to support collaboration are therefore likely to have positive innovation benefits, as are those designed to strengthen firms' internal R&D capability. Second, skill levels emerge as important both in terms of shaping firms' innovation success and in their ability to exploit that innovation and achieve either more rapid growth or higher productivity. Measures to promote skill development are therefore likely to be doubly effective in increasing wealth creation both by promoting innovation and by increasing the effectiveness with which innovation activity is commercially exploited. Different skill mixes appear important, however, for innovation and exploitation: innovation seems to depend strongly on intermediate skills, while graduate employment has a stronger impact on subsequent exploitation. Third, grant support for product development has a strong positive effect on innovation success, suggesting the potential value of such intervention.

## ACKNOWLEDGEMENTS

We are grateful to Gerald Susman, Mark Freel, Irene Petrick and other participants at the Klein Symposium for detailed and constructive comments on this chapter. Members of the Department of Industrial Economics and Strategy, Copenhagen Business School and participants at EARIE 2005 in Oporto also provided comments on earlier versions. We also acknowledge the financial support of the ESRC under award RES-000-22-0729.

# NOTES

1. Sources: Ireland, GDP volume growth average measure, Table 3.1, Budgetary and Economic Statistics, March 2001, Department of Finance; Northern Ireland, NIERC/OEF Regional Economic Outlook, Spring 2001.
2. Murphy (2000) describes the situation as follows: 'Ireland's transformation, one primarily caused by multinationals, was facilitated by the phenomenon of globalisation . . . Globalisation enabled Ireland to move from the periphery towards the centre of the new global economy. Now Ireland is the second largest exporter of packaged software in the world after the US . . . From having virtually no major export industries (Guinness and Irish whiskey representing two exceptions) Ireland has become a significant platform for US high-tech companies competing in the European market' (p. 4).
3. Consideration of the full recursive KSCE is the subject of current research.
4. The actual proportions of firms in the sample with each type of supply-chain linkage were as follows: to other group companies, 21.4 per cent; to clients, 27.2 per cent; to suppliers, 28.6 per cent; to competitors, 7.1 per cent; and to joint ventures 7.2 per cent. For non-supply chain links the proportions were: consultants, 18.9 per cent; government, 7.7 per cent; universities, 15.3 per cent; industry labs 8.2 per cent and private labs 5.2 per cent.
5. Note that the supply-chain and non-supply-chain scores measure extent or scope of knowledge sources, rather than intensity or depth. This, of course, means that in the econometric analysis the coefficients on R&D intensity cannot be directly compared with those of the other linkages in terms of overall effects.
6. The only difference is that the 'R&D in group' and 'government assistance' variables in equation (3.4) are replaced in equation (3.5) by a measure of export sales.
7. An alternative estimator is fractional logit regression (Papke and Wooldridge, 1996). However previous analysis which we have carried out suggests that, in practice, the signs and significance levels obtained using the fractional response model are very similar to those obtained using Tobit (Roper et al., 2005).
8. This estimation also removes the 'group R&D' variable, which always proved highly insignificant.
9. Separately identifying the selection and assistance effects requires a different estimation approach to that adopted here. See Maddala (1993, pp. 257–90) for a general discussion of the issue and Roper and Hewitt-Dundas (2001) for an application.
10. The number of observations for the estimations in Table 3.3 is greater than in Table 3.2 because not all respondents gave details of supply-chain and non-supply-chain linkages.
11. The literature suggests, however, that the direction of causality may actually be reversed; that is, high-productivity firms become exporters. See, for example, Bernard and Jensen (1999).
12. The next steps in the research programme are to estimate knowledge-sourcing models and consider the potential for alternative innovation output indicators.

# REFERENCES

Barry, F. (1999), *Understanding Ireland's Economic Growth*, London: Macmillan.

Barry, F. and J. Bradley (1997), 'FDI and trade: the Irish host-country experience', *Economic Journal*, **107** (November), 1798–811.

Bernard, A.B. and J.B. Jensen (1999), 'Exceptional export performance: cause, effect, or both?', *Journal of International Economics*, **47**(1), 1–25.

Cefis, E. and L. Orsenigo (2001), 'The persistence of innovative activities; a cross country and cross-sectors comparative analysis', *Research Policy*, **30**(7), 1139–58.

Conway, S. (1995), 'Informal boundary-spanning communications in the innovation process: an empirical study', *Technology Analysis & Strategic Management*, **7**(2), 327–42.

Crépon, B., E. Duguet and J. Mairesse (1998), 'Research, innovation and productivity: an econometric analysis at the firm level', *Economics of Innovation and New Technology*, **7**, 115–58.

Fielding, D. (2003), 'Investment, employment and political conflict in Northern Ireland', *Oxford Economic Papers*, **55**(3), 512–35.

Freel, M. and P.A. Robson (2004), 'Small firm innovation, growth and performance', *International Small Business Journal*, **22**(6), 561–75.

Geroski, P.A. (1990), 'Innovation, technological opportunity, and market structure', *Oxford Economic Papers*, **42**(3), 586–602.

Greene, W.H. (1997), *Econometric Analysis*, New York: Macmillan.

Harris, R.I.D. and M. Trainor (1995), 'Innovations and R&D in Northern Ireland manufacturing: a Schumpeterian approach', *Regional Studies*, **29**(7), 593–604.

Harris, R.I.D., M. Trainor, S. Roper and M. Hart (2002), 'Evaluation of the effectiveness of financial assistance to industry', Final Report to Department of Enterprise Trade and Investment, Belfast.

Lööf, H. and A. Heshmati (2001), 'On the relationship between innovation and performance: a sensitivity analysis', SSE/EFI working paper no. 446, Stockholm School of Economics.

Lööf, H. and A. Heshmati (2002), 'Knowledge capital and performance heterogeneity: a firm level innovation study', *International Journal of Production Economics*, **76**(1), 61–85.

Love, J.H. and S. Roper (1999), 'The determinants of innovation: R&D, technology transfer and networking effects', *Review of Industrial Organization*, **15**(1), 43–64.

Love, J.H. and S. Roper (2001a), 'Location and network effects on innovation success: evidence for UK, German and Irish manufacturing plants', *Research Policy*, **30**(4), 643–61.

Love, J.H. and S. Roper (2001b), 'Outsourcing in the innovation process: locational and strategic determinants', *Papers in Regional Science*, **80**(3), 317–36.

Love, J.H., B. Ashcroft and S. Dunlop (1996), 'Corporate structure, ownership and the likelihood of innovation', *Applied Economics*, **28**(6), 737–46.

McCarthy, J. (1999), 'Foreign direct investment: an overview', Central Bank of Ireland, Autumn, 55–65.

Maddala, G. (1993), *Limited Dependent and Qualitative Variables in Econometrics*, New York: Cambridge University Press.

Malerba, F., L. Orsenigo and P. Peretto (1997), 'Persistence of innovative activities, sectoral patterns of innovation and international technological specialisation', *International Journal of Industrial Organisation*, **15**(6), 801–26.

Murphy, A.E. (2000), 'The Celtic tiger – an analysis of Ireland's economic growth performance', Robert Schuman Centre for Advanced Studies EUI working paper 2000/16.

Nelson, R.R. and S.G. Winter (1982), *An Evolutionary Theory of Economic Change*, Cambridge, MA: Harvard University Press.

Oerlemans, L.A.G., M.T.H. Meus and F.W.M. Boekema (1998), 'Do networks matter for innovation? The usefulness of the economic network approach in analysing innovation', *Tijdschrift voor Economische en Sociale Geografie*, **89**(3), 298–309.

Papke, L.E. and J.M. Wooldridge (1996), 'Econometric methods for fractional response variables with an application to 401(k) plan participation rates', *Journal of Applied Econometrics*, **11**(6), 619–32.

Roper, S. and J. Anderson (2000), 'Innovation and e-commerce – a cross-border comparison of Irish manufacturing plants', Northern Ireland Economic Research Centre (NIERC), Research Report 17, Belfast.

Roper, S. and A. Frenkel (2000), 'Different paths to success? The electronics industry in Israel and Ireland', *Environment and Planning: C*, **18**, 651–65.

Roper, S. and N. Hewitt-Dundas (1998), 'Innovation, networks and the diffusion of manufacturing best practice', Northern Ireland Economic Research Centre (NIERC), Research Report 14 (April), Belfast.

Roper, S. and N. Hewitt-Dundas (2001), 'Grant assistance and small firm development in Northern Ireland and the Republic of Ireland', *Scottish Journal of Political Economy*, **48**(1), 99–117.

Roper, S. and H. Hofmann (1993), 'Training and competitiveness – a matched plant comparison of companies in Northern Ireland and Germany', Northern Ireland Economic Research Centre, Research Report 11, Belfast.

Roper, S. and J.H. Love (2002a), 'Innovation and export performance: evidence from UK and German manufacturing plants', *Research Policy*, **31**(7), 1087–102.

Roper, S. and J.H. Love (2002b), 'Innovation and export propensity: panel evidence for Irish firms', working paper, Belfast, NIERC.

Roper, S., N. Hewitt-Dundas and M. Savage (2003), 'Innovation, best practice adoption and innovation networks – a comparison of Northern Ireland and the Republic of Ireland' (December), InnovationLab (Ireland) Ltd, Belfast.

Roper, S., J.H. Love and D. Añon Hígon (2005), 'The determinants of export performance: evidence for manufacturing plants in Ireland and Northern Ireland', mimeo, Aston Business School, Birmingham, UK.

Roper, S., B. Ashcroft, J.H. Love, S. Dunlop, K. Vogler-Ludwig and H. Hofmann (1996), 'Product innovation and development in UK, German and Irish manufacturing firms', NIERC/Fraser of Allander Institute.

Ruane, F. and H. Görg (1997), 'The impact of foreign direct investment on sectoral adjustment in the Irish economy', *National Institute Economic Review*, 2(160), 76–86.

Sweeney, P. (1998), *The Celtic Tiger – Ireland's Economic Miracle Explained*, Dublin: Oak Tree Press.

Teece, D.J., G. Pisano and A. Shuen (1997), 'Dynamic capabilities and strategic management', *Strategic Management Journal*, **18**(7), 509–33.

Veugelers, R. and B. Cassiman (1999), 'Make and buy in innovation strategies: evidence from Belgian manufacturing firms', *Research Policy*, **28**(1), 63–80.

# 4. Innovation strategies and manufacturing practices: insights from the 2005 Georgia Manufacturing Survey

**Jan Youtie and Philip Shapira**

## INTRODUCTION

In a globalized market environment, the competitiveness of manufacturing, which we understand as the ability to make and sell products while maintaining or increasing real income, is influenced by many factors, including the growth of productivity and the exchange rate. This chapter focuses on the role and extent of innovation as a basis for sustaining manufacturing competitiveness. It was Schumpeter (1934) who prompted the modern argument that innovation was important to firm survival across business cycles. The importance of innovation to manufacturing competitiveness has received renewed attention in US policy making through studies conducted by the Council on Competitiveness (2004) and the National Academies (National Research Council, 2005) as well as through the introduction of the proposed National Innovation Act of 2005 (US Congress, 2005).

Innovation encompasses steps and activities involved in the introduction and deployment of new or improved ideas within and between companies. Innovation has been viewed as the entire process through which knowledge is created and used to develop new or improved goods and services that are disseminated into the market. It contrasts with invention, where ideas are first developed but not yet transformed into practical and marketable use (Fagerberg, 2004).

Within the domain of innovation, it is useful to distinguish between firms with an explicit strategy to compete through innovation and firms that do not emphasize innovation as a major business strategy (although they may, from time to time, introduce new products, processes, or methods). The OECD's *Oslo Manual* notes that the starting point of innovation in a firm is its strategic orientation: decisions about what types of markets the firm will serve and how innovative it will be (OECD, 1995). The manual suggests that firms may be categorized according to the type of innovation they adopt to compete for customer sales in the market.

Much of the current interest in innovation in the context of firm strategy is founded on the work of Michael Porter (1980), who argued that innovation may be considered a core competency for strategic advance. It is driven by industrial structure but also influenced by firms' actions in their desire to hold offensive or defensive positions within this structure. He identified two types of strategies that a firm may use in applying this competence: low cost or differentiation through quality, marketing and customer segmentation.

Williamson (1991) similarly echoed the duality of these strategic positions using the terms 'strategizing' versus 'economizing'. Spanos and Lioukas (2001) developed a model demonstrating that these two positions are complementary rather than mutually exclusive relative to firm performance.

Emerging from this literature on competitive advantage is the position that innovation can be considered a core competency for strategic advantage, while the firm applies this competency in pursuit of various strategies such as low cost, high quality or combinations. However, if this is the case, the line of reasoning could be extended in such a way that any strategy could be viewed as innovative. Addressing this quandary is a further body of research which has examined whether there is a separate innovation dimension that comprises its own distinct firm strategy. For example, firms may compete by being a first mover or through the use of technology and these could be perceived of as using innovation as a strategy to gain competitive advantage (Lieberman and Montgomery, 1988; Hitt and Brynjolfsson, 1996). There is some support for this latter stance in research that has built on Porter's work to investigate bundles of strategies. Miller and Toulouse (1986) identified four bundles of strategies including separate innovation and marketing factors in addition to cost leadership. In a survey of nearly 200 small manufacturers, Chaganti et al. (1989) uncovered strategies such as innovativeness, quality and product scope, as well as a cost leadership strategy. Carter et al. (1994) differentiated strategic dimensions and archetypes into six categories: market response, technology, product offerings, firm location, service offerings and pricing. Much of this work has used factor analysis to measure firm strategy, under the guise that strategy is a latent attribute that can be best identified from a series of observable questions about it.

Strategy is most effective to the degree that it stimulates firm actions. In this study we examine firm actions using a framework which defines innovation in terms of the introduction of technologically new or significantly improved products, process, organizational methods and systems, and marketing methods and systems. We draw upon analogous innovation measurement concepts used by Community Innovation Surveys (CIS) in Europe and elsewhere (see, for example, European Commission, 2004). Additionally we also take into account related arguments about how to understand contemporary forms of innovation. The OECD's *Oslo Manual* indicates that innovation can be supported by technological activities such as research on new products and through non-technological innovations related to softer areas such as deriving new product concepts, engaging in marketing and customer relationships, monitoring competitors' capabilities, using consultants, purchasing information, buying engineering skills, investing in equipment or software systems, investing in new skills training, reorganizing production systems and managing product quality (OECD, 1997, pp. 36–7; Jaramillo, Lugones and Salazar, 2001). The OECD manual originally focused its definition on technologically new or significantly improved product or process innovations. These definitions were criticized for being too production-oriented. As a consequence, the manual also considered the category of 'non-technological innovations' which can include organizational, management and marketing innovations (OECD, 1997, p. 117).

Using these definitions, Wengel and Shapira (2004) depict an innovation spectrum which distinguishes innovation focus (product or process) from innovation forms (material or immaterial). The resulting matrix includes product innovation, process innovation (for example, improved technologies, techniques or informatics), organizational innovations (for example, teamwork, supply-chain management, networks) and service innovations (for example, value-added service offerings). Rouvinen (2002) further finds that product and process innovation cannot be treated as homogeneous because they are driven by different factors. Process innovation is oriented around capital-embodied technologies, whereas product innovation is based to a greater degree on disembodied knowledge-based capabilities.

It has also been acknowledged that there are sectoral differences in innovations and the propensity to innovate (OECD, 2000). Indeed Pavitt (1984) originally distinguished between four general industrial sectors based on the technological and innovation trajectories they adopted. Supplier-dominated firms, in traditional agricultural and textiles industries, were deemed to be most affected by suppliers of machinery, equipment and other inputs. Scale-intensive firms, found in bulk materials and automotive industries, employed product and process innovations in tandem through incremental changes informed by, for example, internal engineering departments. Specialized suppliers were in high-tech instruments, and machinery industries that focus on product innovation for use by other sectors. Science-based firms in chemical and pharmaceutical industries employed internal R&D and relationships with academic researchers to develop product innovations and the new processes to develop these products. Subsequently differences in the adoption of innovation-related practices have been examined by firm size and spatial linkages, as well as by sector (Shapira and Rephann, 1996; Cohen, Levin and Mowery, 1987; Acs and Audretsch, 1991; Rosenfeld, 1992).

Yet, while research has highlighted the role of firm strategy, innovation practices and firm characteristics, quantitative studies have not always identified a straight line relationship between innovation and firm performance factors. Smallbone et al. (2003) found that innovation was associated with sales growth but not necessarily profitability. Christensen (1997) explained that disruptive innovations do not necessarily have near-term returns for the companies that discover them. This experience is borne out at the firm level. Companies are concerned about the risks associated with competition based on innovation (Rouse, 2005). Innovation and change can seem risky for manufacturers, particularly for small and mid-sized enterprises (SMEs). Negative impacts from transformational change can mean the end of the firm itself. Thus the typical response for SMEs to address risk is product standardization, mass production and application of lean production principles. This approach enables cost advantages and economies of scale and offers an alternative to innovation-based competition. Managing costs is one of the major drivers of any manufacturing business, although satisfying customer needs through lowering costs may not be sufficient to ensure survival in the long run.

An additional series of studies has arisen to examine how certain types of innovations serve a mediating role between company attributes and performance. Vincent et al. (2004) conducted a meta-analysis of 83 studies to examine factors that mediate organizational innovation and firm performance. Using generalized least squares, the authors found that organizational innovation is related to higher firm performance. They also tested various measurement considerations associated with innovation. Dichotomous measures of innovation were found to have a dampening effect, and industry context matters. Krishnan and Ulrich (2001) and Brown and Eisenhardt (1995) have found that product innovations have different correlates and impacts in different contextual settings, different stages of the product life cycle (new market introduction versus mature stage) and whether the product is completely new to the market or new to the firm but a repositioning or copy of an existing good or service.

Our analysis aims to probe further the interface between firm strategy and practices associated with innovation in manufacturing. We use a data set on innovation in manufacturing in the state of Georgia, as described in the next section. We seek to bridge and extend the available literature by examining how innovation practices are combined with firm strategies in clusters of differentiated approaches. With regard to strategy, in support of Chaganti et al. (1989) and Carter et al. (1994), it is anticipated that innovation would appear as a distinct strategy to compete in the market for sales from either low cost or quality, even in the context of Georgia manufacturing, which is not commonly viewed as a region of innovation. Turning to the strategy-practice link, strategy is expected to mediate the introduction of new or significantly improved products, processes and organizational and marketing approaches. In particular, innovation-based strategies are expected to stimulate product introductions. Quality-based strategies are anticipated to mediate process and organizational introductions. Using a probit analysis, the results will show that innovation emerges as an opposing strategy to low cost along a common dimension rather than a different strategy. Quality in turn surfaces as a separate factor, thus supporting the Porter strategy dichotomy. The data further show that strategy does have some influence on the introduction of new or significantly improved products, processes and organizational and marketing approaches. However, this influence occurs only through the innovation–low cost dimension and it does so quite closely in all four types of innovation. The quality dimension does not appear to significantly mediate new or improved introductions of these approaches. The chapter will conclude with a discussion of these findings and implications for further research.

## MANUFACTURING IN GEORGIA

Georgia is the ninth-largest US state by population and among the fastest-growing, emblematic of the American Sunbelt region's rapid expansion. Recent business and job growth has mostly occurred in the services industry. Still, approximately 10 000 manufacturers did business in Georgia in 2004 (Georgia Department of Labor, 2005). Of these establishments, 98 per cent were small and medium-sized (SMEs). Some 450 000 employees worked in manufacturing establishments, accounting for 14 per cent of private sector employment in the state and 14 per cent of gross state product. Georgia lost more than 110 000 employees in manufacturing from December 1998 to December 2004, or about 20 per cent of its industrial workforce in the recent economic downturn. However labour productivity in the state's manufacturing sector has continued to grow: it increased by 20 per cent between 1998 and 2002, and overall output in manufacturing is thus little changed.[1]

Georgia is not typically viewed as a leading location for innovation in manufacturing. The state does have a growing high technology sector, but – with the exception of aerospace manufacturing – mostly in knowledge-based services such as software publishing, telecommunications and Internet services. By number of establishments, Georgia's manufacturing sector is quite diverse. However, by employment distribution, much of the state's industrial base is in traditional resource-based sectors such as food processing, textiles, and pulp and paper. These three industries accounted for 42 per cent of manu-facturing jobs in the state in 2003 and more than half of rural Georgia's industrial base. In addition, the US South is known as a region of branch plants and in Georgia more than 40 per cent of the manufacturers are branch plants. Private sector research and development (R&D) is relatively lower in Georgia than in the rest of the country. Although Georgia ranked ninth in population in 2001, it ranked 24th in the level of industrial R&D (US National Science Foundation, 2002). The industrial make-up of Georgia's industry accounts for some of this lower ranking. The ratio of R&D perform-ance as a percentage of net sales nationally for Georgia's three traditional industries rel-ative to all manufacturers in 2001 was 0.14 (food), 0.22 (textiles) and 0.31 (wood products).[2]

## Method

The Georgia Manufacturing Survey is conducted by Georgia Tech's Enterprise Innovation Institute and the Georgia Tech School of Public Policy every two-to-three years to identify needs, understand trends in strategy and adoption of technologies and techniques, assess use of programmes to assist manufacturers, and define benchmarks.[3] The survey is mailed to manufacturing establishments with ten or more employees and weighted to reflect the industry–employment size distribution of firms as reported in the Georgia Department of Labor's ES-202 database. Data presented in this chapter are based on analysis of 653 manufacturing establishments responding to the 2005 Georgia Manufacturing Survey (see also Youtie et al., 2005).

To examine the existence of a separate innovation dimension, a factor analysis has been conducted using principal components extraction of rankings of firm strategic ori-entation. The identification of new or significantly improved products, processes, orga-nizational and marketing introductions was measured in the survey using wording comparable to that employed in the CIS surveys. The extent to which firm strategy medi-ates the introduction of new or significantly improved products, processes, organiza-tional and marketing approaches, presented here, is a probit analysis which includes controls for firm attributes typically found in previous studies, such as, facility employ-ment size and wages, single establishment versus branch facility, year manufacturing first started at this location, and location in an urban versus non-urban area. Wald tests of the extent to which separate regressions are required to capture industry effects are pre-sented.

## Results

In the Georgia Manufacturing Survey, we sought to distinguish firms by their strategic orientation, so as to better understand the context within which specific innovations were introduced. The survey thus included a series of questions that asked manufacturers to rank six factors from one (highest importance) to six (lowest importance) according to the way the facility competes in the market place for sales. The six strategies were low price, high quality, innovation/new technology, quick delivery, adapting to customer needs, and value-added customer and product services (Table 4.1). We have asked this question in prior surveys, which enables us to identify trends in strategic orientation.

*Table 4.1   Importance of factors competing in the marketplace for sales, by respondent characteristics*

| Number of employees | Low price | High quality | Innovation | Quick delivery | Adapting to customer needs | Value-added services |
|---|---|---|---|---|---|---|
| Mean ranking* | 3.6 | 1.9 | 4.3 | 3.0 | 3.4 | 3.9 |
| Standard deviation | 1.9 | 1.2 | 1.6 | 1.4 | 1.5 | 1.6 |
| % ranking strategy as number 1** | 19.9 | 52.3 | 7.6 | 12.6 | 14.4 | 10.0 |
| 10 – 19 | 15.6 | 54.8 | 7.5 | 17.8 | 20.6 | 12.6 |
| 20 – 99 | 21.6 | 51.0 | 7.1 | 11.0 | 11.8 | 9.0 |
| 100 or more | 22.4 | 51.3 | 8.7 | 8.8 | 11.1 | 8.2 |
| *Industry* | | | | | | |
| Food, textiles, apparel | 27.8 | 50.8 | 2.3 | 10.9 | 13.6 | 6.9 |
| Nonmetallic materials | 16.7 | 52.6 | 7.2 | 14.8 | 13.9 | 12.5 |
| Metals, machinery | 19.6 | 50.9 | 7.7 | 13.8 | 17.2 | 6.4 |
| Electr., transportation | 19.7 | 53.7 | 17.9 | 11.2 | 9.6 | 6.7 |
| Science-based | 15.7 | 56.9 | 11.8 | 5.9 | 17.7 | 17.7 |

*Notes:*
\* 1=highest priority, 6=lowest priority.
\** Sums to more than 100 because some respondents picked more than one strategy as their top one.

*Source:* Georgia Manufacturing Survey (2005), weighted responses from 625 establishments.

More than half of Georgia manufacturers chose quality of service as their primary factor in competing for customer sales. Low price was a primary competitive factor for 20 per cent of Georgia manufacturers. Adapting to customers' needs was cited by 14 per cent of the manufacturers, followed by quick delivery at 12 per cent and value-added services at 10 per cent. Innovation/new techniques constituted a top competitive factor for the fewest manufacturers (less than 8 per cent).

Since 2001, the percentage of respondents competing for sales primarily based on low price declined from 27 per cent in 2002 to less than 20 per cent in 2005. It is unknown whether this fall-off in firms competing primarily through low price is a result of past low-price manufacturers having gone out of business, or whether more Georgia manufacturers are migrating away from competition oriented solely toward low price. The percentage of firms competing for sales primarily through quick delivery stayed about the same, while the prioritization of other factors increased slightly from 2002 levels.

Manufacturing establishments of all sizes (small, medium and large, by number of employees) were apt to compete for sales primarily through high quality. Medium-sized and large manufacturers were slightly more likely to compete for sales through low price than were small firms. Small manufacturers also were more apt to say that quick delivery, customization or value-added services was a primary strategy for them than were their larger counterparts. The percentage of firms competing for sales through innovation-oriented strategies did not vary much by size.

By industrial sector, establishments across all industries favoured high quality as a primary sales strategy.[4] Food/textile/apparel/leather firms were the most apt to respond that low price was their primary strategy for competing for sales in the market. Respondents in the materials and metals/machinery groups were about average in terms of their distribution across the various primary strategies. One would expect that science-based industries would have the highest percentage of firms competing for sales primarily through innovation and technology. Although this was true (12 per cent among science-based firms versus 8 per cent across all respondents), manufacturers in the electronics/electrical/transportation group actually had the highest percentage of respondents (18 per cent) saying they compete primarily through innovation. Compared with other sectors, science-based firms were most apt to say that they compete by offering value-added services.

We employed principal components analysis in an exploratory manner to understand these underlying dimensions of strategy. Commonalities captured from 25 per cent to 77 per cent of the variance in each of the items. Two factors, which explain nearly half of the total variance, were extracted.[5] These factors have been interpreted on the basis of high loadings in the rotated matrix (see Table 4.2). The first factor counterposes low price and innovation. They are essentially polar ends of the dimension. This factor tends to bundle innovation, value-added services and adapting to customer needs. Low price is most closely associated with quick delivery strategies within this dimension. The second factor reflects a high quality strategic focus, with adapting to customer needs and value-added services showing opposite loadings. We saved the factor scores associated with these three dimensions as separate variables for further analysis of firm performance.

In addition to firm strategy, the survey also asked manufacturers to report on the introduction in their facility of product, process, organizational or marketing approaches in the 2002 to 2004 period. These introductions were defined to be new or significantly improved from the perspective of the facility but not necessarily the sector or market. This relatively broader definition parallels definitions found in OECD innovation guidelines and CIS surveys.

A majority of Georgia manufacturers were found to have introduced a new or significantly improved product (56 per cent), organizational (52 per cent) or process (48 per cent)

*Table 4.2   Principal components factor analysis with Varimax rotation: two-factor solution*

| Questionnaire items | 1 | 2 | Commonality |
|---|---|---|---|
| Low price | **−0.82** | 0.02 | 0.67 |
| High quality | 0.34 | **0.81** | 0.77 |
| Innovation/new technology | **0.62** | 0.04 | 0.39 |
| Quick delivery | −0.49 | 0.10 | 0.25 |
| Adapting to customer needs | 0.42 | −0.49 | 0.41 |
| Value-added services | 0.44 | −0.48 | 0.42 |
| Percentage of variance | 30.3% | 18.2% | |

*Note:*   Numbers in bold have factor loadings of more than 0.50.

*Source:*   Georgia Manufacturing Survey (2005), weighted responses from 625 establishments.

innovation to their facility. Marketing innovations were less common, having been introduced by fewer than 30 per cent of survey respondents. By facility employment size, larger
manufacturing establishments were more apt to have introduced product, process or organizational innovations than were smaller establishments. However marketing innovations were almost as common among smaller manufacturers as among larger ones
(see Table 4.3). By industry, science-based establishments were most likely to have introduced product, process or marketing innovations, although product introductions were
twice as common among science-based firms as marketing introductions. Electrical/elec-
tronic/ transportation firms had a slightly higher percentage of firms that had introduced
organizational innovations than did science-based firms, but their product and marketing
innovation rates were lower. The metals and machinery and materials groups' introductions of innovations were at lower levels than for science-based firms, especially product
innovations. The food/textile/apparel/leather group was least likely to have introduced
process or organizational innovation. Interestingly new marketing introductions
accounted for a bigger proportion of food/textile/apparel/leather industry innovations
than was the case with the other groups.

The relationship between strategy and the introduction of new or significantly improved
products, processes, organizational or marketing approaches was explored through probit
analyses. The dependent variable was the presence or absence of these product, process,
organizational and marketing introductions. The probability of new or significantly
improved introductions in each of these four areas was assessed through four different
probit regressions.

Based on the aforementioned studies that emphasized the importance of industrial
context, consideration was given to the way to handle industry group: in separate regressions

*Table 4.3    Percentage of manufacturing establishments that introduced new or
significantly improved products/services, processes, organizational methods,
or marketing methods into their facility in the period 2002–04*

| | Introduced New or Significantly Improved | | | |
| --- | --- | --- | --- | --- |
| | Products | Processes | Organizational methods | Marketing methods |
| All Respondents | 56.3 | 48.2 | 51.5 | 29.6 |
| *Employment* | | | | |
| 10–19 | 49.4 | 32.9 | 37.0 | 28.0 |
| 20–99 | 57.2 | 50.7 | 52.6 | 29.0 |
| 100 or more | 64.4 | 64.4 | 69.8 | 33.2 |
| *Industry* | | | | |
| Food, textiles, apparel | 51.7 | 39.1 | 41.8 | 32.4 |
| Nonmetallic materials | 54.4 | 49.8 | 53.0 | 27.1 |
| Metals, machinery | 51.7 | 47.2 | 52.1 | 27.9 |
| Elect., transportation | 63.8 | 53.2 | 60.6 | 29.1 |
| Science-based | 80.4 | 60.8 | 58.8 | 39.2 |

*Source:*   Georgia Manufacturing Survey (2005), weighted responses from 653 establishments.

*Table 4.4    Probit analysis of product, process, organizational, and marketing introductions, 2002–04, as a function of strategy*

| | Introduced New or Significantly Improved | | | |
| | Products | Processes | Organizational methods | Marketing methods |
| --- | --- | --- | --- | --- |
| Innov. strategy | 0.267 | 0.171 | 0.211 | 0.272 |
| | (0.071)** | (0.068)* | (0.070)** | (0.072)** |
| Quality strategy | 0.008 | 0.010 | −0.104 | −0.051 |
| | (0.069) | (0.070) | (0.069) | (0.070) |
| Food-text | −0.563 | −0.586 | −0.161 | −0.111 |
| | (0.324) | (0.310) | (0.311) | (0.304) |
| Materials | −0.464 | −0.175 | 0.183 | −0.192 |
| | (0.300) | (0.277) | (0.280) | (0.276) |
| Metals, mach. | −0.546 | −0.263 | 0.171 | −0.269 |
| | (0.306) | (0.282) | (0.287) | (0.282) |
| Electronics | −0.539 | −0.090 | 0.021 | −0.280 |
| | (0.347) | (0.327) | (0.326) | (0.333) |
| Single estab. | −0.126 | −0.055 | −0.370 | 0.027 |
| | (0.147) | (0.146) | (0.150)* | (0.150) |
| Year began | 0.007 | 0.003 | 0.008 | 0.002 |
| | (0.004)* | (0.004) | (0.003)* | (0.004) |
| Urban | 0.209 | 0.247 | 0.266 | −0.094 |
| | (0.155) | (0.155) | (0.155) | (0.160) |
| Employees, 2002 | 0.001 | 0.002 | 0.002 | 0.000 |
| | (0.001) | (0.001)** | (0.001)** | (0.000) |
| Avg. wage, 2002 | 0.000 | −0.000 | −0.000 | 0.000 |
| | (0.000) | (0.000) | (0.000) | (0.000) |
| Constant | −14.150 | −5.037 | −16.055 | −4.845 |
| | (6.974)* | (7.002) | (6.903)* | (7.644) |
| Observations | 402 | 402 | 402 | 402 |
| Pseudo R-sq. | 0.076 | 0.062 | 0.077 | 0.043 |

*Notes:*   Robust standard errors in parentheses; * significant at 5% level, ** significant at 1% level.

or a pooled analysis. Wald tests were employed to indicate whether industry-related coefficients were significantly different to warrant the calculation of separate regressions for each industry group or whether they could be combined. In all four regressions, the tests showed that the industry coefficients were not significantly different (product introductions, $p > 0.46$; process introductions, $p > 0.20$; organizational introductions, $p > 0.44$; marketing introductions, $p > 0.85$). Thus industry effects are represented in the probit analyses through dummy variables in a main equation. We also included controls for facility employment size and wages, location in an urban area, single establishment versus branch facility, and year manufacturing first began at the facility.

Table 4.4 shows the results of these analyses. The innovation-negative low price factor was found to have a significant and positive association with all four types of introductions: product, process, organizational and marketing approaches. An innovation-negative low price strategy was likely to increase the probability of a new product introduction as expected. In addition, this strategy was also more likely to be associated with new process, new organizational and new marketing introductions. The relationship between the innovation-negative low price strategy was not as strong in the case of new or significantly improved process innovation, although it was still significant. The same was not found for the quality strategy dimension. A quality strategy was not necessarily more likely to have an impact on the probability of new product, process, organizational or marketing strategies.

## CONCLUSION

This analysis focused on the role of strategy in mediating new or significantly improved manufacturing practices. The initial focus was on the measurement of strategy itself. The survey's prioritization of factors in competing for sales found that innovation/new technology yielded a small percentage of manufacturing establishments, giving this factor their highest prioritization. A possible reason for the low number of respondents who considered their firm's strategy to be innovation was that they did not use this term to describe their strategy. Perhaps they were innovative but would describe what they do differently. Although this may be true at the margins, it does appear that the concept of innovation/new technology measures a perspective that is distinct from (and opposed to) low price.

At the outset, it was expected that there would be multiple bundles of strategies that distinguish innovation from low price and from quality. Instead the analysis showed that innovation was counterpoised to low price but along the same strategic dimension, one that was distinct from high quality. One reason for this was that there were a small number of observable items in the survey, which inevitably leads to smaller numbers of dimensions. Further research could continue investigation of the nature of multidimensionality in firm strategy.

Other studies suggest that industry context matters. It was expected that would be the case, but it was not found that there were sufficient differences across industry groups to require separate models. However it is possible that strategy and introduction of new or significantly improved technologies, approaches, methods and systems are secondary technologies and techniques that cut across broad product areas rather than being tied to specific industries.

Product, process, organizational and marketing introductions were expected to be mediated by strategy in diverse ways. However probit modelling indicated that strategies defined by an innovation-negative–low price axis were positively associated with these introductions, but in a similar way regardless of whether the introduction dealt with product, process, organizational or marketing. The key distinction seems to be between companies that compete on innovation and those that compete on price, rather than on the kinds of innovations that companies introduce. Quality-based strategies did not significantly mediate any of these introductions. One explanation for this finding regarding quality-based strategies may relate to the high proportion of manufacturers that consider quality to be their top method for competing for sales. At the same time, firms that compete on quality were also less likely to be associated with strategies related to adapting to customer needs or delivering value-added services. Quality and lean production practices have become more commonplace in the global manufacturing environment. As a result, it may be that quality has become a necessary condition to compete in today's economy, and firms can survive – at least for now – by primarily emphasizing this aspect. In a larger sense, it seems that Georgia (like other parts of the US South) is attractive today as a location for lean and quality-based manufacturing production, just as low cost was the leading attraction for manufacturers in the region for much of the twentieth century.

Our study demonstrates that innovation-based strategies are associated with the introduction of new products, processes, and organizational and marketing approaches. Despite this finding, many Georgia manufacturers continue to compete using a variety of business strategies oriented around low price and basic quality. In the short term (as in the period covered by our data), they are able to survive by lowering prices and offering basic quality. We doubt, however, that this is an effective strategy for the long term. In Georgia, manufacturing as a whole has relatively weaker innovation performance than that of many other states, with smaller and traditional industries contributing to this weakness. In this context, policy and programmatic initiatives should continue to place emphasis on stimulating manufacturers to be more aware of the importance of long-term investments in innovation.

## ACKNOWLEDGEMENTS

An earlier version of this chapter was prepared for the Third Klein Symposium on the Management of Technology, 12–14 October 2005, Smeal College of Business, Pennsylvania State University, University Park, Pennsylvania, USA. This version of the chapter has benefited from comments provided by Gerald Susman, Terrence Guay, Paul Swamidass and other symposium participants. We also gratefully acknowledge suggestions received from Andrea Fernandez-Ribas and assistance with data analysis provided by Ajay Bhaskarabhatla and Li Tang. The Georgia Manufacturing Survey 2005 received sponsorship from the Georgia Manufacturing Extension Partnership and the Georgia Tech Center for Paper Business and Industry Studies.

## NOTES

1.  Authors' calculation based on gross state product data from the US Bureau of Economic Analysis and employment data from the US Bureau of Labor Statistics.
2.  National Science Foundation/Division of Science Resources Statistics, Survey of Industrial Research and Development (2001), Table A-20.
3.  For more information on the Georgia Manufacturing survey, see http://www.cherry.gatech.edu/survey.
4.  We adapt Pavitt (1984) to classify major manufacturing sectors in Georgia (see Youtie et al., 2005).
5.  We also explored a three-factor solution, but it did not appear to add substantial further explanatory power, and review of a scree plot did not illustrate a marked change in slope.

## REFERENCES

Acs, Z. and D. Audretsch (1991), 'R&D, firm size, and innovative activity', in Z. Acs and D. Audretsch (eds), *Innovation and Technological Change: An International Comparison*, New York: Harvester Wheatsheaf.

Brown, S.L. and K.M. Eisenhardt (1995), 'Product development: past research, present findings, and future directions', *Academy of Management Review*, **20**(2), 343–78.

Carter, N.M., T.M. Stearns, P.D. Reynolds and B.A. Miller (1994), 'New venture strategies: theory development with an empirical base', *Strategic Management Journal*, **15**(1), 21–41.

Chaganti, R., R. Chaganti and V. Mahajan (1989), 'Profitable small business strategies under different types of competition', *Entrepreneurship Theory and Practice*, **13**(3), 21–35.

Christensen, C. (1997), *The Innovator's Dilemma: When New Technologies Cause Great Firms to Fail*, Boston, MA: Harvard University Press.

Cohen W., R. Levin and D. Mowery (1987), 'Firm size and R&D intensity: a re-examination', *Journal of Industrial Economics*, **35**(4), 543–63.

Council on Competitiveness (December 2004), *Innovate America*, Washington, DC: Council on Competitiveness.

European Commission (2004), *Innovation in Europe – Results for the EU, Iceland, and Norway (Data 1998–2001)*, Luxembourg: Office for Official Publications of the European Communities.

Fagerberg, J. (2004), 'Innovation: a guide to the literature', in J. Fagerberg, D.C. Mowery and R. Nelson (eds), *The Oxford Handbook of Innovation*, Oxford, UK: Oxford University Press.

Georgia Department of Labor (2005), *Covered Employment and Wages*, May 2003, Atlanta, GA: Georgia Department of Labor.

Hitt, L. and E. Brynjolfsson (1996), 'Productivity, profit and consumer welfare: three different measures of information technology's value', *MIS Quarterly*, **20**(2), 121–42.

Jaramillo H., G. Lugones and M. Salazar (2001), 'Bogota manual: standardisation of indicators of technological innovation in Latin American and Caribbean countries'.

Krishnan, V. and K. Ulrich (2001), 'Product development decisions: a review of the literature', *Management Science*, **47**(1), 1–21.

Lieberman, M. and D. Montgomery (1988), 'First mover advantages', *Strategic Management Journal*, **9**(special issue, Summer), 41–58.

Miller, D. and J.M. Toulouse (1986), 'Strategy, structure, CEO personality and performance in small firms', *American Journal of Small Business*, **10**(3), 47–62.

National Research Council (2005), *Rising above the Gathering Storm: Energizing and Employing America for a Brighter Economic Future*, Washington, DC: National Academies Press.

OECD (1995), 'The measurement of scientific and technological activities, proposed guidelines for collecting and interpreting technological innovation data', *Oslo Manual*, 2nd edn, DSTI, OECD/European Commission Eurostat, Paris, 31 December.

OECD (1997), 'Proposed guidelines for collecting and interpreting technological innovation data', Oslo Manual, Eurostat.

OECD (2000), *Final Report: Measuring and Reporting Intellectual Capital: Experience, Issues, and Prospects*, Paris: OECD.

Pavitt, K. (1984), 'Sectoral patterns of technical change: towards a taxonomy and a theory', *Research Policy*, **13**(6), 343–73.

Porter, M. (1980), *Competitive Strategy*, New York: The Free Press.

Porter, M. (1990), *The Competitive Advantage of Nations*, London: Macmillan.

Rosenfeld, S. (1992), 'Competitive manufacturing: new strategies for regional development', Center for Urban Policy Research, New Brunswick, NJ.

Rouse, W. (2005), 'Enterprises as systems: essential challenges and approaches to transformation', *Systems Engineering*, **8**(2), 138–50.

Rouvinen, P. (2002), 'Characteristics of product and process innovations: some evidence from the Finnish innovation survey', *Applied Economics Letters*, **9**(9), 575–80.

Schumpeter, J. (1934), *The Theory of Economic Development*, Cambridge, MA: Harvard University Press.

Shapira, P. and T. Rephann (1996), 'The adoption of new technology in West Virginia: implications for manufacturing modernization policies', *Environment and Planning C: Government and Policy*, **14**(4), 431–50.

Smallbone D., D. North, S. Roper and I. Vickers (2003), 'Innovation and the use of technology in manufacturing plants and SMEs: an interregional comparison', *Environment and Planning C: Government and Policy*, **21**(1), 37–52.

Spanos, Y.E. and S. Lioukas (2001), 'An examination into the causal logic of rent generation: contrasting Porter's competitive strategy framework and the resource-based perspective', *Strategic Management Journal*, **22**(10), 907–34.

US Congress, Senate (2005), National Innovation Act of 2005, 109th Congress, S.2109, 15 December (URL: http://thomas.loc.gov/cgi-bin/bdquery/z?d109:s 2109).

US National Science Foundation (January 2002), 'Survey of industrial research and development', National Science Foundation, Division of Science Resources Statistics, Washington, DC (URL: http://www.nsf.gov/statistics/nsf05305/htmstart.htm).

Vincent, L.H., S.G. Bharadwaj and G.N. Challagalla (2004), 'Does innovation mediate firm performance? A meta-analysis of determinants and consequences of organizational innovation', Georgia Institute of Technology, Atlanta, GA.

Wengel, J. and P. Shapira, P. (2004), 'Machine tools: the remaking of a traditional sectoral innovation system', in F. Malerba (ed.), *Sectoral Systems of Innovation: Concepts, Issues and Analyses of Six Major Sectors in Europe*, Cambridge, UK: Cambridge University Press, pp. 243–86.

Williamson, O.E. (1991), 'Strategizing, economizing, and economic organization', *Strategic Management Journal*, **12**(Winter special issue), 75–94.

Youtie, J., P. Shapira, J. Slanina, J. Wang and J. Zhang (2005), 'Innovation in manufacturing: needs, practices, and performance in Georgia, 2002–2005', GaMEP Evaluation Working Paper E200502, Georgia Tech Policy Project on Industrial Modernization, Georgia Institute of Technology, Atlanta, GA.

# PART II

# Network Dynamics

# 5. Economies of speed: a conceptual framework to describe network effectiveness

## Irene J. Petrick and Carleen Maitland

## INTRODUCTION

While small to medium-sized enterprises (SMEs) are frequently involved in supply networks, it is rare that one acts as the lead firm in a network; rather they are often responding to the demands of others. However this is not to imply that SMEs should take a passive role in networks. Instead we argue that they should actively assess networks for their ability both to compete effectively against other networks and to provide an opportunity for the SME to add relational capabilities.

Such assessments will require an understanding of the complex relationships between information capture, sharing and innovation as these lead to competitive advantage. Firms have been described as leveraging economies of scale and/or economies of scope to reap competitive advantage. *Economies of speed* (Ito and Rose, 2004) add yet another competitive dimension, one that applies particularly well to networks of companies competing against one another. Economies of speed, which emphasize the benefits of rapid innovation and product delivery, capture the multidimensional aspects of knowledge creation and sharing as they relate to the collective ability of a network to learn or develop new knowledge and then to translate that knowledge into intellectual capital that can be embodied in an innovation in a more efficient and effective manner (Burt, 1992).

Our conceptual framework borrows from social capital theory (Kogut and Zander, 1992) that describes the way that intellectual capital and the underlying social structure that supports its development yield organizational advantage (Nahapiet and Ghoshal, 1998). Here we extend these constructs to a network environment to better describe successful practices of individual companies as they relate to increasing the effectiveness of the network.

Thus our premise is that an effective network is one that not only develops but also shares knowledge and does so in a way that it can be used quickly to the benefit of all members. Our model, which reflects this premise, in turn provides a basis for analysing network effectiveness. From the SME perspective, an understanding of network effectiveness will help SMEs gain an increased share of the network value. This is particularly relevant as SMEs struggle to adapt to globalization challenges.

In addition to passively analysing the networks, this information can also be used to enable SMEs to make significant contributions to the network, through their unique local technical and cultural knowledge. Such linkages may provide valuable knowledge to the larger network and offer the SME an opportunity to provide localized knowledge that the lead firm might not possess. Such knowledge may actually enable networks of smaller companies to compete more effectively with multinational companies.

In the following pages we describe the concepts and develop a model of network effectiveness. We begin with a discussion of the essential concepts and subsequently propose a model. We then consider that model through the lens of globalization and its influence on situational awareness. Next we apply the model to assess the implications of industry sector differences. The chapter concludes with a discussion of the findings for SMEs.

## ESSENTIAL CONCEPTS

### What is a Network?

We define a network as a collection of firms working toward a common *broadly defined* goal where the activities of the network participants are supported by multiple administrative arrangements, often between subsets of the network membership. From a supply chain perspective in the twenty-first century, these networked firms might compare to a vertically integrated multinational company, replacing the vertical intra-firm linkages with inter-firm linkages. Though we believe that many of the network linkages will favour vertical linkages (a transfer of information, goods or services from one firm to another), we acknowledge that in the case of collaborative development, the linkages may be horizontal as well.

Networks can be distinguished from individual dyad pairs (Nohria, 1992) in that the network involves multiple linkages which are often supported by formal and informal communication, information sharing, collaboration and joint or coordinated production practices.

In a supplier network such as we conceive, firms will seek to optimize their individual advantage, and only the most successful networks balance individual and collective or network advantage (Jones et al., 1998). However, whereas constellations (Gomes-Casseres, 1997) achieve such balance through formal and inclusive operating rules and contracts that attempt to articulate shared goals, in our conceptualization of a network, where not all members are bound by the same administrative agreement, such comprehensive agreements do not exist. In point of fact, a successful network is one that can balance individual firm goals with network goals without such overarching agreements between all members (Lee, 2004).

Our definition of a network emphasizes individual firm choices concerning participation. This should be contrasted to supplier networks where equity and influence/governance is shared. In this later type of network, the lead firm exerts influence not only through its own practice, but through its partial ownership stake. Such networks are distinctly different from our conceptualization of a set of independent firms choosing to act in a symbiotic manner.

Regardless of whether we are speaking of a network, a strategic alliance or a constellation, however, for SMEs they all present a common problem: how does an individual member garner its share of the value from the network's ability to compete more effectively than its rivals, thus accruing economic rent? In other words, how can an SME operating within a network achieve growth commensurate with or exceeding the network's growth? Related to this, how can a firm operating within the network keep others from acting opportunistically (Doz, Hamel and Prahalad, 1989) for their own benefit rather than for the network's benefit?

## Social Capital as it Supports the Creation of Knowledge

Important to answering these questions concerning a SME's participation in a network is the concept of social capital. Nahapiet and Ghoshal (1998, p. 243) describe social capital as the 'sum of the actual and potential resources embedded within, available through, and derived from the network of relationships possessed by an individual or social unit'. These scholars describe three aspects of social capital: structural, relational and cognitive. Structural and relational social capital describes communication patterns and norms, whereas cognitive social capital describes formal mechanisms and tools to capture, transfer and re-use information. All three are relevant to network effectiveness.

- The structural dimension of social capital refers to the overall pattern of connections between actors, including who you reach and how you reach them. This network configuration has been described in terms such as density, connectivity and hierarchy. This dimension describes the overall pattern of connections between actors. From a network effectiveness perspective, we would expect to see different strategies operating in dense centralized networks of firms on the one hand, compared to more loosely coupled dispersed networks of firms.
- The relational dimension of social capital focuses on the personal relationships that people have, particularly as they relate to assets that are created and leveraged by those personal relationships. This dimension is differentiated from the structural dimension as it relates to the personal relationships that evolve through a history of interactions. From a network effectiveness perspective, we would anticipate that dispersed nodes in the network might have access to very different actors, and that the personal relationships that evolve might be substantially different. This is particularly relevant in geographically dispersed networks.
- The cognitive dimension of social capital refers to resources that provide shared representations, and thus create shared meaning between participants. From a knowledge creation and sharing perspective, the cognitive dimension of social capital is particularly important to innovation and value creation across networks of autonomous but interdependent firms. The more diverse the domain expertise within the network, the greater the likelihood that the network can sense important and relevant information, particularly as it relates to technology evolution and the potential for innovation.

Social capital creates a framework to improve the efficiency of actions, thus reducing the cost of transactions. However, unlike a transaction cost economics perspective (Williamson, 1981), a social capital analysis employs a multi-transaction assessment, which considers learning costs (Ring, 1996) and coordination costs (Gulati and Singh, 1998). As market uncertainty increases, the costs of learning and coordination rise. Moreover, as market uncertainty increases, the need to reach out to external entities to provide valuable information rises. Increased uncertainty should favour firms that possess unique knowledge.

Our interest in social capital is its basis for the development of network-based knowledge, both explicit and tacit (Polanyi, 1967). In networks, as well as within individuals and firms, explicit knowledge is codified, captured and transferred easily. This is in contrast to tacit knowledge, which is a shared understanding often related to the expertise of an individual or firm, that is not easily transferred. Nelson and Winter (1982) argue that tacit knowledge in an organization is different from tacit knowledge of the individuals within the organization, and we extend that same argument to a network. The tacit knowledge that a network possesses cannot be reduced to the tacit knowledge of its individual members. A further parsing of knowledge dimensions helps to explain why this is the case.

**Knowledge Typologies and their Relation to Economies of Speed**

Spender (1996) decomposes explicit and tacit knowledge into the following four classifications: conscious knowledge (facts, figures and frameworks that can be stored and retrieved); automatic knowledge (theoretical and practical knowledge that people possess thanks to their unique skills); objectified knowledge (distributed knowledge that can be put into a common framework, thus expanding the use of facts and figures by the relationships between these facts and figures); and collective knowledge (knowledge that is fundamentally embedded in the organization's practices and which is sustained by interactions). In the context of a network, a key distinction between the four types is the ability to capture and/or transfer.

One key to network effectiveness is the ability to use tacit knowledge to understand and expand explicit knowledge (creation), and furthermore to transfer this newly created knowledge (creating objectified knowledge) to others who can understand it and who have the strategic experience to make use of it.

While this process of knowledge creation and transfer may be considered a feat in and of itself, increasing time pressure across all industries demands that the process happen quickly. However, in doing so, care must be taken to identify only relevant information, as processing superfluous information slows the process. Extending the argument, if we apply the concept of economies of speed to the process of *careful* knowledge creation and transfer, we assert that an efficient and effective network should engage in the following process: first, identify relevant information; second, identify the 'right' expert or set of experts to assess the value of the information due to the situational awareness possessed by the expert(s), and, third, develop a collective strategy for action.

Whereas SMEs in a network can play an active role in all three of these steps, we contend that it is in the second step that their unique contribution to situational awareness can make a significant contribution. Situational awareness is the ability of the individual or group to assess incoming information in light of the current environment, and to determine how that information might in itself alter the environment; its presence within the individual or group has been linked to performance outcomes (Endsley, 1995). Situational awareness helps an individual or group determine the relevance of incoming information through a deep understanding of the critical elements of that information. From an innovation perspective, situational awareness is important for individuals and their associated collaborators in areas such as coordinating complex tasks, establishing mutual confidence, drawing attention to scientific details, developing a working understanding of new concepts and synthesizing results into new knowledge (Sonnenwald, Maglaughlin and Whitton, 2004). Situational awareness in an individual is enabled by tacit knowledge since situational awareness evolves as the result of an individual's preexisting knowledge and cognitive processing skills (Salas, Prince, Baker and Shresta, 1995). Teams (and thus networks) can possess situational awareness when there is overlap of each member's situational awareness to create an interwoven situational awareness (Sonnenwald and Pierce, 2000). Team situational awareness is facilitated by behaviours that allow knowledge to be developed and maintained (Salas et al., 1995).

The relationship between knowledge and situational awareness is further illuminated in Table 5.1, in which Spender's typology (1996) is applied to distinguish knowledge residing in firms and networks. Consequently, Table 5.1 also demonstrates the way that each type of knowledge contributes to situational awareness, thus improving network effectiveness and efficiency.

Thus the two types of knowledge particularly relevant to networks are objectified knowledge and collective knowledge. Objectified knowledge shared between members of an organization or across organizations is a goal of many companies, and has received a great deal of attention in the technology development arena in the area of strategic roadmapping (Petrick and Echols, 2004; Petrick and Provance, 2005) and R&D management effectiveness (Gupta, Wilemon and Atuahene-Gima, 2000).

Collective knowledge is the most difficult to replicate and often yields significant competitive advantage. Collective knowledge helps to explain why, for example, companies cannot replicate Toyota's production system with the same level of success. In this example, collective knowledge adds to the organization's tacit knowledge through repeated use of explicit and tacit knowledge, thus building an additional experiential

*Table 5.1   Firm and network knowledge typologies*

| | Firm | Network |
|---|---|---|
| Explicit | *Conscious knowledge*: facts, figures, drawings and other renderings that the individual within a firm can create or know, and retrieve intact at a later time | *Objectified*: facts, figures, drawings and other renderings that an individual can create or know and which can be put into a common framework to expand the use of that information by the network, including the relationships between the facts and figures |
| | → Exchange | |
| Tacit | *Automatic*: expertise and skill-based understanding possessed by an individual within the firm that enables him or her to recognize and value relevant information, derived from the individual's situational awareness | *Collective*: knowledge which is embedded in practices and which is sustained through interactions; collective knowledge helps to build and is enhanced by situational awareness |
| | Continuous → dialogue | |

capability. The Toyota example also demonstrates the way that collective knowledge works in a network as the Toyota production system involves both Toyota and its suppliers working in a collaborative (networked) manner.

We assert that it is the early and continual sharing of knowledge that is a primary distinguishing factor between more successful and less successful networks, particularly in the creation of intellectual capital and the development of innovation. One major reason for firms interacting with suppliers or customers is to gain access to critical knowledge (Rungtusanatham et al., 2003). Lorenzoni and Lipparini (1999) further this argument by noting that it is not just access to critical knowledge that yields competitive advantage, it is the ability to integrate knowledge residing within and outside the firm's boundary that is a distinctive organizational capability. Their work suggests that, within a supply chain, a firm can concentrate on its core competencies if it has developed multiple formal and informal ties to achieve knowledge access and transfer. Moreover a firm within the network can benefit from increased awareness of the needs of its customers' customers, and the requirements of its suppliers' suppliers (Horvath, 2001).

Figure 5.1 summarizes our argument thus far. On the left side of this figure (Capture & Creation), the firm uses its conscious and automatic knowledge to capture or create knowledge. These enable the firm to develop its situational awareness which, in turn, enables the firm to assess the value of the captured or created knowledge (Assessment & Exchange). Here the firm's employees can determine whether the knowledge is useful to the firm only, in which case the firm adds the knowledge to its conscious knowledge. If the knowledge is useful to the network, through exchange it can be objectified to build network situational awareness. Network situation awareness only leads to network effectiveness if one or more nodes in the network can formulate strategic plans that take advantage of this knowledge, thus building intellectual capital (Action & Coordination). Decisions must be made about these strategic plans and, once a series of actions is chosen by one or more network nodes, these must be coordinated. Coordination facilitates network efficiency. Together network effectiveness and efficiency combine to provide economies of speed for the network, which ultimately yields competitive advantage.

An individual firm within the network gains economic value if it is one of the nodes chosen for some type of action that yields economic rent. In a supply network, for example, firm action might include design, development, manufacturing, distribution or support. Economic rent may accrue to a single firm for one or more of these activities or, if firms are collaborating, it may accrue to more than one firm. The individual firm also gains from the network's activities as the firm builds its social capital through repeated interactions with other network members (Spekman, Spear and Kamauff, 2002). Such social capital adds to the firm's resource capabilities over time. The learning that can happen within a network suggests a proactive role for individual firm relational management in effective networks.

## GLOBAL INFLUENCES ON SITUATIONAL AWARENESS

### Local and International Firms

Globalization in manufacturing supplier networks offers both challenges and opportunities. Medcof (1997) developed a classification of firm location and activity that offers

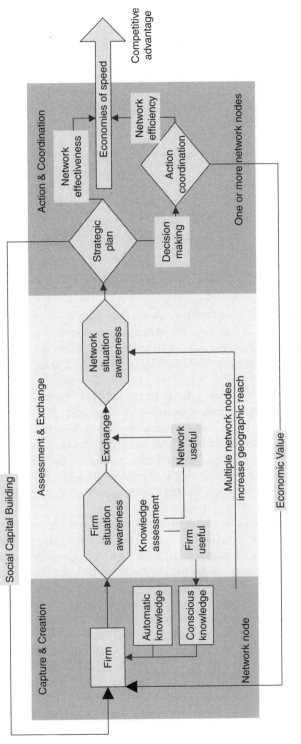

*Figure 5.1  The role of situational awareness in firm and network effectiveness*

a framework for better understanding these challenges and opportunities. The eight-level classification includes local research units, local development units, local market-ing support units, local manufacturing support units, international research units, international development units, international marketing support units and interna-tional manufacturing support units. Medcof uses the words 'local' and 'international' in a way that has value for our discussion of network effectiveness. Local units are those firms that are located geographically closer to the network's focal point, while those considered 'international' are geographically located in a far-flung region relative to the network's focal point. Those companies considered 'local' might be expected to have a transportation cost advantage, but would be expected to add little unique information with respect to market knowledge. Conversely those companies considered 'interna-tional' might be expected to have unique access to market knowledge and technology knowledge that may not be available to the majority of the network. Multinational corporations have long been known to take advantage of these international units to gain access to important market and scientific knowledge (Medcof, 2001; Cho and Lee, 2004; Lu and Beamish, 2004).

## Globalization Enhances Network Effectiveness by Building Social Capital

Motwani, Larson and Ahuja (1998) propose that global supply chain management enables corporations to leverage diversity in the international environment by exploiting regional differences, and there is evidence to suggest that firms do, indeed, seek partners who provide the best opportunity for learning, regardless of their location (Narula and Hagedoorn, 1999).

To be successful at innovation, the firm or network must create a product that delights the market (Mascarenhas, Kesavan and Bernacchi, 2004). 'Delight' embodies two concepts: the product has features that are tailored to the specific market, and the product has features that outperform competitor offerings on a performance/price basis. Networks seeking to offer products outside of their focal region must gain knowledge about more far-flung market dimensions. By adding network members who are more geographically dispersed, the network gains insight into other regions' market needs.

Performance/price issues affect both product features and processes that might manu-facture these features at a lower cost. Thus the technical knowledge needed to address this aspect of 'delight' requires the network to be aware of emerging technology solutions for both product features and manufacturing methods. As product complexity increases, the ability of any one firm to be aware of all new developments that might be germane declines. Heterogeneity of firms within the network increases the social capital of the network as individual network members possess different skills, assets and technical cap-abilities. Combining this with geographic reach, networks which have one or more geo-graphically dispersed nodes should have access to emerging knowledge that the focal members might not.

Etemad (2004) suggests that SMEs possess their own strong social networks, including family networks, that cannot be easily replicated. This is a unique aspect of social capital that, if leveraged to create automatic knowledge, can strengthen the SMEs' capabilities, making the SME more appealing to supply networks.

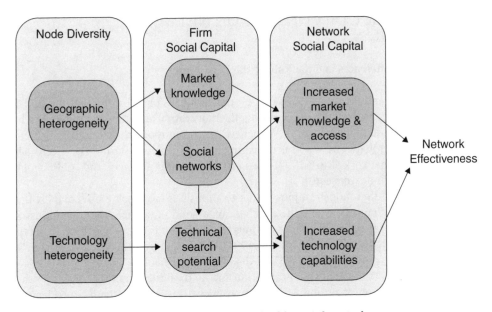

*Figure 5.2    Geographic and technical diversity builds social capital*

Figure 5.2 highlights the role that node diversity plays in building social capital unique to the firm and thus desirable for the network. A firm that is geographically dispersed from the network focal point (geographic heterogeneity) brings unique access to markets and social networks and, because the firm is located in a different region, that firm has unique knowledge about customs, norms and other factors that might not be readily available to those outside that region.

When a firm possesses technical capabilities that are different from the network and is geographically dispersed from the network focal point, that firm's unique technical capabilities and social network combine to enhance its technical search potential. Such a firm builds the network's social capabilities when added to the network, thus increasing the likelihood that the network is effective in creating innovations that might yield competitive advantage.

Crucial to achieving the benefits proposed in Figure 5.2 are the formal and informal communication channels that network members employ to exchange information and coordinate activity. Hitt, Lee and Yucel (2002) argue that the culture in Asian countries makes Asian companies more likely to focus on building social capital thanks to the business focus on relationships. Hagedoorn and Schakenraad (1994) suggest that larger firms are more likely to be able to take advantage of geographically dispersed partners, particularly related to technology development, than their smaller counterparts. These authors suggest that this is true partly owing to the lack of smaller firm experience in the international arena. We argue, however, that, as smaller firms develop social capital through repeated interactions with larger, more globally connected network partners, they should be able to enhance their ability to leverage geographically dispersed knowledge for firm and network benefit.

# THE INFLUENCE OF CONTEXT ON NETWORK EFFECTIVENESS

## Industry Sector Differences and the Role of the Lead Firm

Madhavan, Koka and Prescott (1998) suggest that, whereas past research has focused on the way networks constrain and shape action, the more important question might be what factors constrain and shape networks. We believe that one important distinguishing factor that constrains and shapes networks is the competitive dynamic of the industry sector. An efficient–effective network (Burt, 1992) must attract the right partners, and 'right' will be tightly coupled to industry sector.

It must be noted that industrial purchasing relationships are much more complex than consumer market channels, where the purchase of a good or service from one industrial concern by another may involve joint activities that transcend the specific good or service (Monczka, Petersen, Handfield and Ragatz, 1998). Industrial buyers may be concerned with such aspects of the product quality and on-time delivery, the ability of the good or service to add to the flexibility of the buyer's production flow, or the flexibility of the buyer's product design. Modularization of an industrial end-product helps increase the independence of supplier design and manufacturing activities, while also enabling suppliers to play a more dominant role in product innovation at the component level (Veloso and Fixson, 2001).

Technology development is one area where the strategic character of inter-firm relationships is as important as the transactional (Hagedoorn, 1993). Here the longer-term value of the inter-firm linkage lies in the way that the development influences the market position of the end-product seller, thus influencing the position of the network participants relative to firms in an alternative network.

## Industry Sector Competitive Dynamics and Supplier Roles

The relative importance of declining costs, increasing quality, decreasing cycle time and innovation varies across sectors. Because of increased product complexity, within supplier networks, individual firms are likely to have greater impacts on the quality, cost, technology and delivery of a buying company's own products and services (Handfield, Drause, Scannell and Monczka, 2000).

The importance of supplier-based components and subassemblies to the final end-product extends the normal transaction model view of supplier decisions into a much more strategic view of supplier selection and relationship management. Laseter and Ramdas (2002, p. 108) identify four unique clusters of supplier product type:

1. Critical systems that are high-cost and have high complexity;
2. Simple differentiators that are moderately costly with low complexity;
3. Hidden components that are low-cost, low-complexity components; and
4. Invisible components that are moderately costly and moderately complex.

Types (1) and (2) help to differentiate the buyer's products in the market. Types (3) and (4), on the other hand, while important to the buyer's product, are not clearly evident to end users and so do not directly impact the buyer's product in the marketplace.

Interestingly Laseter and Ramdas's (2002) work identifies two aspects of the importance of a supplier product. First, their clusters identify the impact that the supplier product might have on the end consumer perception (differentiating/non-differentiating to buyer product). Second, they highlight the interface complexity between the supplier component or subassembly and the buyer's product. Their work refines our understanding of two critical aspects of supplier influence which Porter's work further elucidates.

Power and influence in a supply network rests with the firm or firms that can direct innovation, determine cost targets and/or enforce production schedules on other players in the chain. Porter (1998, p. 29) suggests six ways that suppliers (and by extension in this chapter, supplier networks) can gain influence:

1.  The supplier or supplier network is large relative to a more fragmented buyer base. Here the supplier can exert influence over prices, quality and terms;
2.  The supplier or supplier network produces an item for which there are few, if any substitutes;
3.  The supplier or supplier network is selling to a buyer sector that makes up only a small fraction of its total sales. Thus the buyer represents only a small percentage of the supplier/supplier group's sales;
4.  The supplier or supplier network's input to the buyer's business is strategic. Such would be the case where the supplier/supplier group product helps to differentiate the buyer's product in the marketplace;
5.  The supplier or supplier network possesses a differentiated product for which the buyer would incur switching costs if it chooses to substitute another group's product. High switching costs act as a disincentive to the buyer to consider alternatives;
6.  The supplier or supplier network poses a credible threat to forward integration in the value chain, thus invading the buyer's traditional market space and competing head-on with the buyer.

Conversely, claims Porter, buyers have power if purchases can be concentrated in large volumes and if the items purchased are non-differentiated and of low overall value to the end-product's cost. In an industry where the end-customer is price-sensitive, there is downward pressure across the supply network to reduce the price/performance ratio over time. When end-customers are price-insensitive, firms within the supplier network have an incentive to innovate since they do not face the same downward cost pressures.

For the purposes of this discussion, we distil industry sector differences into three basic competitive strategies, based on the end-customer preferences: low cost, differentiation based on product features, or differentiation based on product mix. In a low-cost industry sector, larger size companies have an advantage as economies of scale dictate that fixed assets spread over an increasingly large volume provide competitive advantage as individual piece costs decline. Such competition relies on the interchangeability of one firm's product for another – a commodity-type market. On the other hand, firms that compete on the basis of differentiation deal with end-customers who do not perceive individual firms as having equally substitutable products, and these customers see value in product features, brand consistency or other reputational attributes.

We suggest a third type of sector competition based on differentiation: product diversity. Economies of scope drive this type of competition, where an end-customer values a firm with a larger and more diverse set of products more highly than a firm with a smaller or more focused set of products. This type of product mix differentiation is evident in the health care and home building product industries as customers seek 'one stop shopping' rather than multiple contacts with more niche suppliers, as evidenced by the emergence of intermediary sellers in health care and big box retailers such as Home Depot, Lowes and B&Q in home building products (Petrick, Purdum and Young, 2004).

**Centrality and Centralization to Describe Firm Influence**

Research suggests that sourcing strategies are not randomly adopted, nor do they remain constant over the range of industry sectors (Heriot and Kulkarni, 2001). Choosing network participants on the basis of dynamics of industry competition suggests that company centrality (Madhavan et al., 1998) will differ across sectors. Centrality is a measure of firm importance based on the number of firms interacting with a single firm. A company with more linkages is said to be more central to a network than a company with fewer linking firms. Firms possessing unique capabilities that help to differentiate a product in the customer's view will be more important to a network than those firms whose contributions to the product, though necessary, do not drive customer perception. A firm with such unique capabilities would be in higher demand as a network participant. In the medical devices industry, for example, smaller innovative companies can frequently command a larger share of the end-product's value thanks to their possession of unique intellectual property that is an enabler of the end-product. Here innovation power resides with the firms that can develop unique technical capabilities. Also in this industry, smaller firms have begun to join together into horizontal alliances within the network to bundle their resources and capabilities into higher value products that are then purchased by OEM assemblers (Petrick et al., 2004).

Centralization, a distinct concept from centrality, which is a firm measure, helps to define the relative power distribution across a network (Freeman, 1979). In a highly centralized network, one or only a few firms will have multiple contacts with other network firms, with a high number of the network firms having only limited numbers of contacts. Centralization helps explain the dominance of OEM practices in networks where the OEM is the primary organizer of the network. In a centralized network, the firm that has the highest centrality can be expected to exert more influence than other firms in the network, and conversely a decentralized network may contain several firms with high centrality measures.

For example, the commercial aeroplane industry is characterized by four main players: Boeing and Airbus at the larger end of the commercial airliner scale, and Bombardier and Embraer at the smaller regional jet scale. Commercial aeroplanes tend to be a differentiated product, with the end-customer preferences driving product feature development. Within this industry, the OEM is a large-scale systems integrator, a firm that chooses to rely on its supplier network for a large portion of its components and subassemblies. Here the OEM determines end-product configuration, interacts with designers across the supplier network and is the final assembler and the interface to the end-consumer. Supplier networks to the major OEM tend to adopt OEM approaches. This is particularly true with the airframe structural components which would be unique to the individual aeroplane configuration, and is less true with respect to electronics, which might be used across not only aeroplanes, but outside the commercial aeroplane industry. Modular design helps to create this component independence, giving suppliers more room to manoeuvre within and across multiple networks.

OEM supremacy is also the case in the automotive industry, where OEM design and assembly practices guide activities of tier 1, 2 and 3 suppliers, as well as those of distributors. Here the automotive industry OEMs hold economic power in an industry that is heavily cost-driven. Both GM and Ford are also large-scale system integrators, relying heavily on their suppliers for components and subassemblies. Suppliers in GM or Ford networks are driven by the low-cost strategy, with GM beginning to seek cost reductions on a part-by-part basis (Hawkins, 2005). In fact, though GM and Ford rely heavily on suppliers for parts, the relationships between the OEMs and their suppliers are often hostile, with reverse auctions and last-minute supplier shifts commonplace (Liker and Choi, 2004).

Networks within the same industry sector can choose to compete in slightly different ways, strengthening our argument for the importance of social capital to help describe economies of speed in networks. Interestingly, whereas GM and Ford are pushing cost reduction strategies onto their networks, Toyota is combining a cost reduction strategy with an emphasis on leveraging innovation throughout its network (Okamura, 2005). Suppliers who are critical to Toyota because they possess unique innovation capabilities may be valued less highly by GM or Ford. Toyota's *kiretsu* type of network arrangement encourages firms to invest in technical capabilities that benefit the network (Gilson and Roe, 1993; Granovetter, 1985).

Toyota takes the management of its network one step further, encouraging its suppliers to develop capabilities that help to make each individual company perform better. Toyota works with its suppliers to help these companies retool and fine-tune their operations (Dyer and Hatch, 2004), posting large gains for both the network and for individual members within the network. Toyota embraces a *kyohokai* approach to knowledge sharing that focuses on sharing of explicit knowledge among participants. As participants become more adept at sharing this knowledge, the network begins to build collective knowledge, strengthening network capabilities through the process of sharing. In other words, through extensive and continuous sharing, Toyota and its supplier network have created a shared situational awareness that enables the network to respond more effectively to its environment. We noted earlier, however, that networks that are based in whole or in part on shared equity and governance exhibit a degree of coordination of behaviour that is beyond what we might otherwise expect among autonomous but interdependent firms.

Thus there are two ways that a firm within a network might gain a preferred position, and these are related to the network's structure: (1) if the network itself is highly centralized through either OEM low-cost strategies or distributor differentiation by product mix strategies, then the firm or small number of central firms within that network dominates network practices and influences the practices of other network members; conversely, (2) if the network must compete in a differentiated product manner, then the firm or small number of firms possessing unique capabilities and resources can determine its own course, in cooperation with network members, but not necessarily dominated by another network member.

# CONCLUSIONS

Underlying our discussion is our belief that network effectiveness and efficiency produce economies of speed that yield competitive advantage for one network compared to another. With respect to supplier networks, the ability to capture and exchange knowledge is rooted in the firm's and the network's social capital. More successful networks can use social capital to develop knowledge in support of innovation. We note, however, that only when the firm can continue to develop its own capabilities through interactions with the network does the firm build both economic value and social capital. Figure 5.3 summarizes this logic, and highlights the way that industry structure centralizes influence to one or several firms within the network, and the way that globalization may have a mitigating effect to help geographically dispersed firms gain influence. We note that globalization can have a positive impact on non-lead firm influence in differentiated competition, but that the existence of globally available substitute products actually strengthens the influence of the lead OEM firm(s) in situations of low-cost competition.

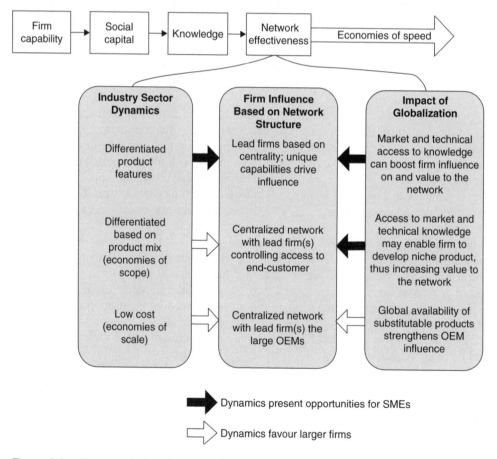

*Figure 5.3    Sector and globalization influences on SME opportunities and constraints within the network*

From an innovation standpoint where intellectual capital is valued (differentiated competition), the ability of a firm that is globally dispersed from the focus of the network to gain access to different market and technical knowledge may increase that firm's influence on the network or may help to mitigate the influence that the larger (centralized) firm(s) exert. From a social capital perspective, the geographically dispersed firm may increase the ability of the network to enhance its situational awareness, thus adding to its economies of speed.

Thus SMEs competing in a global environment should seek network opportunities where unique SME social capital is valued by the network members. In cases where the SME cannot choose, it should at least be aware of these issues. If choice is possible, in return these SMEs can build knowledge through the social capital of the network. SME learning will be critical to achieving an increase in influence within the network. The SME must view the interactions with network partners as a learning opportunity and should not concentrate solely on the short-term value of a particular contract or transaction. Instead SMEs must take a strategic view of their participation in the network, first by selecting the network in which they wish to participate, and then, once a participant, in seeking out other network members with complementary assets. The network's social capital can only yield SME benefits through repeated and long-term interactions.

# REFERENCES

Burt, R.S. (1992), *Structural Holes: The Social Structure of Competition*, Cambridge, MA: Harvard University Press.

Cho, K.R. and J. Lee (2004), 'Firm characteristics and MNC's intra-network knowledge sharing', *Management International Review*, **44**(4), 435–55.

Doz,Y., G. Hamel and C.K. Prahalad (1989), 'Cooperate with your competitors and win', *Harvard Business Review*, **67**(1), 133–9.

Dyer, J.H. and N.W. Hatch (2004), 'Using supplier networks to learn faster', *MIT Sloan Management Review*, **45**(3), 57–63.

Endsley, M.R. (1995), 'Toward a theory of situation awareness in dynamic systems', *Human Factors*, **37**(1), 32–64.

Etemad, H. (2004), 'Internationalization of small and medium-sized enterprises: a grounded theoretical framework and an overview', *Canadian Journal of Administrative Sciences*, **21**(1), 1–21.

Freeman, L. (1979), 'Centrality in social networks: conceptual clarification', *Social Networks*, **1**, 215–39.

Gilson, R.J. and M.J. Roe (1993), 'Understanding the Japanese keiretsu: overlaps between corporate governance and industrial organization', *The Yale Law Journal*, **102**(4), 871–906.

Gomes-Casseres, B. (1997), 'Alliance strategies of small firms', *Small Business Economics*, **9**(1), 33–44.

Gulati, R. and H. Singh (1998), 'The architecture of cooperation: managing coordination costs and appropriation concerns in strategic alliances', *Administrative Science Quarterly*, **43**(4), 781–814.

Granovetter, M.S. (1985), 'Economic action and social structure: the problem of embeddedness', *American Journal of Sociology*, **91**(3), 481–510.

Gupta, A.K., D. Wilemon and K. Atuahene-Gima (2000), 'Excelling in R&D', *Research Technology Management*, **43**(3), 52–8.

Hagedoorn, J.H. (1993), 'Understanding the rationale of strategic technology partnering: interorganizational modes of cooperation and sectoral differences', *Strategic Management Journal*, **14**, 371–85.

Hagedoorn, J.H. and J. Schakenraad (1994), 'The effect of strategic technology alliances on company performance', *Strategic Management Journal*, **15**(4), 291–311.

Handfield, R.B., D.R. Drause, T.V. Scannell and R.M. Monczka (2000), 'Avoid the pitfalls in supplier development', *Sloan Management Review*, **41**(2), 37–49.

Hawkins, L., Jr. (2005), 'GM announces cost-cutting plan', *Wall Street Journal*, 23 September, p. A6.

Heriot, K.C. and S.P. Kulkarni (2001), 'The use of intermediate sourcing strategies', *Journal of Supply Chain Management*, **37**(1), 18–26.

Hitt, M.A., H-U. Lee and E. Yucel (2002), 'The importance of social capital to the management of multinational enterprises: relational networks among Asian and Western firms', *Asia Pacific Journal of Management*, **19**(2,3), 353.

Horvath, L. (2001), 'Collaboration: the key to value creation in supply chain management', *Supply Chain Management*, **6**(5), 205–7.

Ito, K. and E.L. Rose (2004), 'An emerging structure of corporations', *Multinational Business Review*, **12**(3), 63–84.

Jones, C., W. Hesterly, K. Fladmoe-Lindquist and S. Borgatti (1998), 'Professional service constellations: how strategies and capabilities influence collaborative stability and change', *Organization Science*, **9**(3), 396–409.

Kogut, B. and U. Zander (1992), 'Knowledge of the firm, combinative capabilities and the replication of technology', *Organization Science*, **3**(3), 383–97.

Laseter, T.M. and K. Ramdas (2002), 'Product types and supplier roles in product development: an exploratory analysis', *IEEE Transactions on Engineering Management*, **4**(2), 107–18.

Lee, H.L. (2004), 'The triple-A supply chain', *Harvard Business Review*, **82**(10), 102–12.

Liker, J.K. and T.Y. Choi (2004), 'Building deep supplier relationships', *Harvard Business Review*, **82**(12), 104–13.

Lorenzoni, G. and A. Lipparini (1999), 'The leveraging of interfirm relationships as a distinctive organizational capability: a longitudinal study', *Strategic Management Journal*, **20**(4), 317–38.

Lu, J.W. and P.W. Beamish (2004), 'Network development and firm performance: a field study of internalizing Japanese firms', *Multinational Business Review*, **12**(3), 41–61.

Madhavan, R., B.R. Koka and J.E. Prescott (1998), 'Networks in transition: how industry events (re)shape interfirm relationships', *Strategic Management Journal*, **19**(5), 439–59.

Mascarenhas, O.A., R. Kesavan and M. Bernacchi (2004), 'Customer value-chain involvement for co-creating customer delight', *The Journal of Consumer Marketing*, Santa Barbara, **21**(7), 486.

Medcof, J.W. (1997), 'A taxonomy of internationally dispersed technology units and its application to management issues', *R&D Management*, **27**(2), 301–18.

Medcof, J.W. (2001), 'Resourced-based strategy and managerial power in networks of internationally dispersed technology units', *Strategic Management Journal*, **22**(11), 999–1054.

Monczka, R.M., K.J. Petersen, R.B. Handfield and G.L. Ragatz (1998), 'Success factors in strategic supplier alliances: the buying company perspective', *Decision Sciences*, **29**(3) 553–77.

Motwani, J., L.Larson and S. Ahuja (1998), 'Managing a global supply chain partnership', *Logistics Information Management*, **11**(6), 349–54.

Nahapiet, J. and S. Ghoshal (1998), 'Social capital, intellectual capital, and the organizational advantage', *Academy of Management Review*, **23**(2), 242–66.

Narula, R. and J. Hagedoorn (1999), 'Innovating through strategic alliances: moving towards international partnerships and contractual agreements', *Technovation*, **19**(5), 283–94.

Nelson, R.R. and S.G. Winter (1982), *An Evolutionary Theory of Economic Change*, Boston, MA: Belknap Press of Harvard University Press.

Nohria, N. (1992), 'Information and search in the creation of new business ventures', in N. Nohria and R.G. Eccles (eds), *Networks and Organizations: Structure, Form and Action*, Boston, MA: Harvard University Press, pp. 240–61.

Okamura, A. (2005), 'Beyond the keiretsu', *Automotive Design & Production*, **117**(9), 20–22.

Petrick, I.J. and A.E. Echols (2004), 'Technology roadmapping in review: a tool for making sustainable new product development decisions', *Technological Forecasting and Social Change*, **71**(1–2), 81–100.

Petrick, I.J. and M. Provance (2005), 'Roadmapping as a mitigator of uncertainty in strategic technology choice', *International Journal of Technology Intelligence and Planning*, **1**(2), 171–84.

Petrick, I.J., S. Purdum and R.R. Young (2004), 'Impact of supply chain decisions on small to mid size manufacturers', Final Report to the National Institutes for Standards and Technology, Penn State University.

Polanyi, M. (1967), *The Tacit Dimension*, London: Routledge and Kegan Paul.

Porter, M.E. (1998), *On Competition*, Cambridge, MA: Harvard University Press.

Ring, P.S. (1996), 'Fragile and resilient trust and their roles in economic exchange', *Business and Society*, **35**(2), 148–75.

Rungtusanatham, M., F. Salvador, C. Forza and T.Y. Choi (2003), 'Supply-chain linkages and operational performance: a resource-based-view perspective', *International Journal of Operations & Production Management*, **23**(9), 1084–100.

Salas, E., C. Prince, D.P. Baker and L. Shresta (1995), 'Situation awareness in team performance: implications for measurement and training', *Human Factors*, **37**(1), 123–36.

Sonnenwald, D.H. and L.G. Pierce (2000), 'Information behavior in dynamic group work contexts: interwoven situation awareness, dense social networks and contested collaboration in command and control', *Information Processing and Management*, **36**(3), 461–79.

Sonnenwald, D.H., K.L. Maglaughlin and M.C. Whitton (2004), 'Designing to support situation awareness across distances: an example for a scientific collaboratory', *Information Processing and Management*, **40**(6), 989–1011.

Spekman, R.E., J. Spear and J. Kamauff (2002), 'Supply chain competency: learning as a key component', *Supply Chain Management: An International Journal*, **7**(1), 41–55.

Spender, J.-C. (1996), 'Making knowledge the basis of a dynamic theory of the firm', *Strategic Management Journal*, **17**(S2), 45–62.

Veloso, F. and S. Fixson (2001), 'Make-buy decisions in the auto industry: new perspectives on the role of the supplier as innovator', *Technological Forecasting and Social Change*, **67**(June), 239–57.

Williamson, O.E. (1981), 'The economics of organization: the transaction cost approach', *American Journal of Sociology*, **87**(3), 548–77.

# 6. Sourcing of innovation as trendsetting in the imaging sector: a comparison between large MNEs and SMEs

## Johannes M. Pennings and Gino Cattani

Photography appears to be an easy activity; in fact it is a varied and ambiguous process in which the only common denominator among its practitioners is in the instrument.

(Henri Cartier-Bresson)

## INTRODUCTION

A major challenge for representing the evolution of an industry or market involves its multi-level nature in a wide range of disciplines. Industry boundaries are difficult to pinpoint, their onset or demise even less so. Industry evolution can be understood through the lens of biology (for example, Hannan and Freeman, 1984; Levinthal, 1997; Cattani, 2005), industrial and institutional economics (Dosi, 1982; Nelson and Winter, 1982; Klepper, 2002), entrepreneurship (for example, Schumpeter, 1934; Aldrich, 2000), institutional theory (for example, DiMaggio and Powell, 1983; North, 1990) and history (for example, Chandler, 1962; Mokyr, 1990; Murmann, 2003). Evolutionary trajectories and their disruptive transitions have been conceived as being triggered by managerial or entrepreneurial decision making (for a review, see Hill and Rothaermel, 2003); regulatory fiat (for example, Rosenkopf and Tushman, 1998) or collusive conduct (for example, Rosenbloom and Cusumano, 1987); cognitive and cultural inertia (Christensen, 1997), perhaps in combination with firm selection, whether internal (for example, Burgelman, 1994) or external (for example, Hannan and Freeman, 1984) to the organization; and national context conditions (for example, Landes, 1969).

An exploration of the factors that induce directionality in industry evolution with disruptive or discontinuous changes motivated this chapter. Most sectors comprise numerous agents such as individuals, regulators, firms and clusters of firms in the form of associations, cartels and consortia. As a result, the boundaries of what defines an industry are often difficult to identify. The reliance of SIC codes and other efforts at identifying sector boundaries is most tenuous, although industries so defined continue to be the most prevalent setting (or sample) for conducting studies in industrial organization (for example, Gollop and Monahan, 1991; Patel and Pavitt, 1994) and strategic management (for example, Montgomery and Wernerfelt, 1988). The implied boundaries are blurry rather than sharp, putative boundary sharpness often being assumed in industrial organization economics, with conventional focus on categories like Standard Industrial Clarification (SIC) notwithstanding (for a discussion, see also Silverman, 1999).

Mapping changes that might be either endogenous (for example, by the conduct of incumbents and/or their spin-offs) or exogenous (for example, through the role of new entrants or regulators within such domains) is therefore fraught with many difficulties. In this chapter, we present a new attempt at documenting industry or sector evolution. We do so by focusing on imaging, confining ourselves to its most recent decades (1975–2005) during which it has witnessed a dramatic paradigm shift, with concomitant transformations across the globe and among various value chains including still and movie images, photocopying, lithography and distribution to equipment for image capturing, editing and publishing.

We confine ourselves to the most recent decades of what might be called the photographic sector and explore the innovative productivity of firms as individual and collective agents of change. We present some trends of six firms that were selected to fit the frame of reference of this book (that is, small and medium-sized companies in different parts of the world contrasted with three large firms). We include also some large firms as stalwarts of the imaging sector to indicate how they mediate the bundling of complementary knowledge towards emerging dominant designs. The design of this exploration is therefore multi-level, considering the interaction between firms and their sector. In other words, the concern is with firms' mediation through a patent-based network as a result of which their knowledge base becomes connected or marginalized. We examine their innovative sourcing by tracing the volume (that is, patent counts) and the impact (that is, citations received from other firms) of their patenting activity over time. We do so by contrasting some large 'chemical' incumbents (Kodak and Fuji) with medium (Adobe) and small (Indigo and Interactive Pictures) firms. We also include Sony as an electronic incumbent whose knowledge legacy might be less susceptible to destruction by the paradigm shift. By varying the size to include small- and medium-sized (SME) firms across the globe, the study might hint at the combinative role of old and new knowledge as the sector converges towards new dominant designs.

## THEORY

The evolution of an industry, market or sector can be articulated by the successive dominant designs to which firms subscribe (for example, Abernathy and Utterback, 1978; Utterback, 1994). We believe that the imaging sector constitutes an attractive setting for mapping successive paradigms. Furthermore its boundaries are rather fluid such that inclusion of firms, their knowledge base and the conversion of that knowledge base into products or components has been subject to important discontinuities. Finally, its subfields are constantly rearranged into new and modified configurations.

The rise and fall of industry standards (paradigms or dominant designs) in a given sector coincide with evolving sets of firms, whose fortunes rise and decline with the dominant design to which their current legacy is attached. The death of a dominant design, for example the microprocessor or 35 MM camera, triggers waves of bankruptcies, as illustrated by Braun and MacDonald's (1978) study of the semiconductor or Christensen's (1997) study of the disk drive industry.

Firms play a significant role in driving their collective evolution. By their combinative capabilities firms might bundle knowledge and thus produce new products or components that become crucial in the emergence of new products. Other firms might be more prone to consolidating and institutionalizing bundled knowledge and the associated products through their networking with other firms. In other words, a dominant design might be crafted through the combination or integration of previously loosely coupled knowledge and become legitimized or widely accepted through the participation of firms into an emergent dominant design. Such firms' role is framed in terms of *brokerage* or *closure* (compare Burt, 2005). As 'broker' the firm combines the disparate knowledge of peers, while firms that forge the acceptance of newly-integrated knowledge into emergent paradigms do so through their embeddedness in critical locations.

The old dominant design becomes partially or completely replaced through regulatory intervention, substitution and network effects of new products or services whose price-adjusted quality outperforms predecessors, or through the erosion of established social order, as enunciated by institutional schools in economics and sociology. The sector then tips towards a new era, displacing many of its incumbents while accommodating new entrants (for example, Lee and Song, 2006). The above-mentioned issue of sector boundaries complicates any theorizing or empirical research on market or industry evolution and firm conduct because products are inherently hierarchical, with designs being part of a larger architecture while they themselves can often be decomposed into smaller parts or complements (Simon, 1962; Schilling, 2000). The hierarchical architecture of products maps onto the configuration of firms and their (sub)sectors. The implication is that substitution and complementarity challenge the quest for any analysis regarding industry evolution and the evolving role of firms which are complementary in their contribution. Markets are often sequentially or hierarchically arrayed from raw materials to end products locking producers of peripheral components into dependency of dominant component producers, such as the microprocessor within desktop computing where far-reaching modularity is paramount (Ethiraj and Levinthal, 2004).

Such complexity is often illustrated by the sector producing the various stereo equipment components (speakers, amplifiers, MP3) and the clusters of firms that participate in the design, production, marketing and sales of such components. In line with this argument, Schilling (2000) examines modularity and system-level integration both within and between firm interoperability and what she calls 'combinationability'. Yet we need some articulation of boundaries to circumscribe a sector which, as we will see shortly, can be done operationally by an implicit self-definition of the sector – in this study, the imaging industry through the patent citations patterns of their firms. It is the conduct of firms at the intersection of evolving boundaries that is at the core of our inquiry regarding sector evolution and the associated rise and fall of dominant designs. The presumption is that the more or less chequered integration of knowledge among subfields engenders the rise of new knowledge which subsequently becomes solidified into coherent bodies of new knowledge and organized around the architecture of a new dominant design.

## Firms and Evolution of their Sector

Firms constitute the elements of a (strategic) group, a community of knowledge or practice and produce dynamics which they not only affect but also are affected by: whence the argument that multi-level designs are required for tracing evolutionary trajectories. Patents belong to classes and subclasses, whose stock is generated by individuals and the firms that employ them, which can be mapped through the networks that tie them together. Patent citations constitute a form of organizational social capital. Each patent can be read as an announcement to an audience as selected by the firm or its patent examiner. As asset, such an implicit network conveys (according to Bourdieu and Wacquant, 1992) resources, actual or virtual, that accrue to a firm by virtue of possessing a lasting network of more or less institutionalized relationships as embodied in documented knowledge flows.

Social capital thus construed entails minimal levels of cognitive awareness, unlike individuals as sentient actors engaged in exchange relationships. Network relationships are largely assumed, based on the interconnectedness imputed to citation patterns. The diminished awareness does not detract from the connections between observable flows of research that we assume to embody an evolving institutional, shared and normative context and represent a clustering of firms as repositories of knowledge, which is continuously assembled and disassembled and eventually becomes further bundled through the creation of industry associations, regulatory oversight, and heightened merger and acquisition (M&A) activity and joint ventures.

A firm tends towards 'brokerage' (Burt, 2005) to the extent that it produces greater knowledge variability through inter-firm *combinative* behaviours. Combinative flows have been attributed to firms, whence their innovative achievements through the knowledge management arrangements that are so common in firms today, but we should be equally observant of the synthesis of knowledge across firms. Patent citations amount to bridges that span pools of knowledge between firms. According to Burt, firms (as any other actor – whether individual or higher social aggregate) can be viewed as potential mediators in integrating divergent networks. But he advances the term 'constraint' to describe the condition where an actor is unencumbered or confined in navigating through its sector. When overembedded, any interaction with a contact (often called 'alter') might have repercussions on contiguous relationships, thus constraining the focal actor. In contrast, when such an actor is connected with alters who, among themselves, are minimally connected, or who are separated by 'structural holes', the focal actor becomes inoculated against their pressures and is relatively unconstrained. Opportunities for brokerage abound. Burt proposes a so-called 'constraint score' for identifying the topography of firms or other classes of actors such as people or patents within the network. In the present case we generate patent-citations derived $C_{ij}$ scores, which are computed as follows:

$$C_{ij} = (p_{ij} + \Sigma_q p_{iq} p_{qj})^2 \quad \text{for } q \neq ij,$$

where $p_{ij}$ is the proportion of firm *i*'s patenting link with firm *j* [$p_{ij}$ is equal to $z_{ij}/\Sigma_q z_{iq}$ with $z_{ij}$ measuring the zero to one citation strength between firm *i* and firm *j*]. The total amount that is between parentheses represents the proportion of firm *i* citations towards firm *j* whether directly or indirectly through firm *q*. The sum of the squared proportions $\Sigma_j c_{ij}$ is the citation network constraint score, *C*. Computational details are provided in Burt (1992). Firms that are positioned in more constrained networks span fewer structural holes and therefore their performance (for example, ability to innovate but also the quality of their innovations) typically has a negative association with network constraint. While the firms as actors thus construed do not represent the sentient actors in contact, advice or trust networks (see Krackhardt and Hanson, 1993), we can nevertheless represent firms in citation networks as mediators or consolidators between other firms in their quest to push knowledge frontiers.

Patents and their citations represent information on inter-firm networking and inform the firms' role in crafting and consolidating knowledge in their sector. We therefore examine a small set of organizations that differ in size and geographic location to investigate this role. These firms might differ in their embeddedness in the sector, depending on what other firms they cite in their patenting activities. If strongly embedded, they are less likely to perform in some combinative capacity and less likely to drive the evolution in the sector.

The imaging sector appears eminently suited for such an inquiry, not only because it shifted from being chemically based to being electronically based, but also because imaging entails the novel bundling of disparate products and their underlying knowledge, ranging from storage, distribution, editing and other functions. This sector is rife with strategic groups, the bridges between which might play a critical role in grasping sectoral evolution. Their evolutionary significance is traced by assessing the firm's impact as inferred from its forward citations (see below).

**Patents and Patent Classes**

Many sectors can be decomposed into subfields, and in fact the literature on strategic groups (for example, Hatten and Hatten, 1987; Barney and Hoskisson, 1990; Porac, Thomas and Baden-Fuller, 1989; Porac and Thomas, 1990; Porac et al., 1995; Peteraf and Shanley, 1997) suggests a certain amount of discontentment with prevailing arbitrary classifications such as the SIC code and other commonly used categories such as those illustrated by *Fortune* magazine and census categories used in the EU or Japan. The unbundling and bundling of subfields is a phenomenon of considerable interest, with patent classes and their subclasses becoming a prominent method for documenting trajectories among sectors, however narrowly delineated. Capturing knowledge flows within and between sector-defined fields becomes feasible when examining patents through their backward and forward citations, and constitutes the input for a methodology for tracing the pathway of innovative trajectories in the imaging sector since 1975. The flows intersect to engender new paradigms and might become consolidated, depending on type and number of firms and their clientele joining the bandwagon.

Data on patents and patent citations lend themselves to the delineation of a sector, partly because patents are quite explicit regarding the application for a product or service, and patent citations convey new claims that set them apart from 'prior art' and its claims. Patents, as classified into classes and subclasses, allow also a more or less institutionalized demarcation of knowledge fields and the claims (possible applications) that are associated with them. Patents document new, non-obvious inventions and assign rights to their owner, usually a corporation, with so-called 'claims', that is, attributes of the invention over which the firm, or inventor, exercises sole property rights. Patents typically cite other patents and publications to differentiate the new claims from those that fall under prior art. Mapping patents and their citations will thus implicitly produce a more or less bounded field that might be classified as a sector. Some authors have gone so far as to explore the concordance between patent and standard industrial classes (compare Silverman, 1999).

The connection between a patent and its prior art amounts to forms of networking between platforms of knowledge. Depending on whether prior art falls within the narrow scope of the new patent or is historically more remote, this would suggest an opportunity for tracing the degree of continuity of innovations. The innovation literature is replete with notions of incremental, continuous versus radical, frame-breaking discontinuities (for example, Abernathy and Utterback, 1978; Tushman and Anderson, 1986; Anderson and Tushman, 1990; Mokyr, 1990). When viewed in the context of patenting, radical innovations signal the observable evolution of a sector. As indicated before, innovations depend not only on their articulation by novel art, but also the growing acceptance of that novel art in its diffusion throughout the sector. As we will observe, some firms are important agents of change while others act to consolidate their sector into a coherent and well-synthesized cluster with one or a few standards.

We examine patents and the connections among them through citations so that firms can stand on the proverbial shoulders of other firms. As patents and their owners converge (for example, Jaffe et al., 1993), through R&D outputs and their relationships with those of others, webs of knowledge can be constructed in terms of backward and forward citations. When patents cite other patents, they acknowledge their dependence on prior art, including home-grown art, often described as 'self-citations'. By contrast, forward citations reveal the impact that a firm's patenting activity has on peer firms' innovative output. When the intensity of citations declines, the focal firm's intellectual property (IP) stock shows sign of decay and ipso facto diminished importance.

The patents as knowledge-codified output become embedded in a knowledge network that can be aggregated to the level of the inventor or the firm that employs her. Firms can thus be placed in a web based on patent citations fanning backward into the past or forward into the future, and reveal themselves as knowledge reservoirs. A firm might cite patents that are more or less remotely removed from its legacy. When remote, the firm is sometimes viewed as behaving in an 'explorative' rather than 'exploitative' manner (March, 1991). Self-cited patents or patents close to their legacy amount to a deepening and consolidation of proprietary knowledge and might constitute the pinnacle of entrenchment and exploitation (Rosenkopf and Nerkar, 2001). Backward citations reveal the extent to which a firm bundles other firms' knowledge; this is particularly critical when other firms' knowledge remains fragmented and unconsolidated. This notion of bundling or combining other firms' knowledge or intellectual property is central in brokering knowledge evolution. A multi-level approach to sector evolution is, therefore, desirable. Likewise, it is of considerable interest to contrast the role of large versus small- and medium-sized enterprises (SMEs) when tracing the sector evolution over time. SMEs are not encumbered with asset legacy and might be disproportionately influential in shaping the new paradigm.

## EMPIRICAL ANALYSIS

### The Imaging Sector

Imaging is one of many sectors that have gone through numerous paradigm shifts. A vast literature exists already on industrial evolution and technological paradigms (for example,

Abernathy and Utterback, 1978; Sahal, 1985; Utterback, 1994; Klepper, 1997; Christensen, 1997). The innovation literature is replete with research on successive paradigms, the demise of incumbents, the waves of creative destruction and the entrepreneurial activity that rides on them (for example, Dosi, 1982). In many sectors, the prevailing trajectories are not neatly bounded, nor do we observe the emergence of a singular design, although it is tempting to represent the history of an industry in terms of a linear process culminating in peaks and valleys. It would also be tempting to envision such an imagery in the imaging industry. Rather paradigms are embedded in various architectures or represent the architectures as such (Henderson and Clark, 1990; Baldwin and Clark, 2000): compare film, photography, xerography and scanning.

This setting has been evolving over the last three decades, although imaging, of course, has been a central feature since the onset of recordable or accessible civilization from Lascaux and beyond. Imaging comprises many components, bundled in architectures such as movie screens, photocopies, picture albums or magnetic resonance imaging (MRI). It comprises artifacts, production and delivery systems, regulations, standard-setting agreements and behaviours. Significant inventions dating from the earlier part of the nineteenth century include the glass-plated images of Daguerre in 1837 and the fax machine in 1838. We confine ourselves to the more recent disruptive change associated with the rise of optical telecommunications and semiconductor technology, and cover the period 1975–2005.

Imaging as a technology, market, use function or complement to other products and services has undergone many transformations during the last 30 years, with most noticeable the electronic creation, storage and duplication of images as a discontinuous innovation from chemically-based photography. Many domains within imaging, such as studios, film production and movie screens, are still firmly anchored in the chemical regime, while advertising and medical imaging have become more firmly entrenched in microelectronics. Yet, even within electronic domains, we observe the retention of components (or so-called 'complementary assets') that become bundled with ingredients of the new regime, a phenomenon well-illustrated in Tripsas (1997)'s study of the typesetting industry, with its successive paradigms. Incumbents, associated with a dying dominant design, might possess complementary assets which become bundled with chunks of knowledge that are associated with a new paradigm: in the Tripsas example, the font library of some diehard typesetters entering the postscript era.

How do sectors evolve if they cannot neatly fit into an imagery of successive paradigms with *peaks* and *valleys* as is so common in the literature of industry evolution? The imaging sector is highly differentiated into classes such as film, medical imaging, photocopying or photography, and embodies clusters of firms and their suppliers and customers who overlap, intersect, diverge and converge, making this sector highly complex, 'rugged' or multi-peak and ill-bounded. It is generally assumed that sectors evolve through periods of reorientation and innovation (Normann, 1977), eras of consolidation and ferment, or competency enhancing and destroying periods of innovations (for example, Tushman and Anderson, 1986; Anderson and Tushman, 1990).

Yet, as the Tripsas (1997) study demonstrates, we have ample evidence that elements of the old paradigm combine with elements of the new, while other parts are discarded; but also that a sector with fluid boundaries, and multiple performance peaks, manifests the existence of chunks of old knowledge which become bundled with elements of the new design. The death of firms need not entail the total loss of their legacy and this often becomes acquired by or transferred to new generations of firms (Nelson and Winter, 1982; Winter, 1994). The rise of a new (dominant) design retains elements of the old design or the sector might contain numerous domains whose coexistence defies simple announcements of a new arrival, as is often insinuated with the emergence of the digital camera. Ultimately we need to consider both brokerage and cohesion, eventually to provide closure on the evolutionary trajectory of the sector (compare Fleming et al., 2005).

## Background

Originating in the early 1980s with the release of the first commercial digital cameras by, among other firms, Eikonix and Mavica, the digital imaging sector has matured over the years with participants entering from computing, electronics and photography. The sector has also seen considerable M&A and alliance activity, beginning with Kodak's acquisition of Eikonix in 1984 and going on to the recent series of technology consortia between computing and photography firms. We therefore view this arena as having great potential for describing and explaining evolutionary patterns in market, product and technology (see Box 6.1, with a brief historical overview, at the end of the chapter).

## Trends in Inter-firm IP Activity

The patenting activity of incumbents shows a clear trend away from chemical to electronic imaging technology. Many incumbents have abandoned their chemical legacy and moved into microelectronics, although some firms, such as Polaroid and Agfa-Geveart, are facing bankruptcy or, like Zeiss Ikon, have already exited the sector. Kodak claims to be an industry leader in both chemical and electronic knowledge accumulation, and is the frontrunner in patenting activity among imaging firms. However, whether patenting pre-eminence translates into being a trendsetter remains to be seen.

Fowler and Jeon (2005) have constructed legal trajectories, distinguishing between 'authorities' which are legal rulings or 'opinions' cited by many other decisions and 'hubs' which are opinions that cite other opinions, resulting in each case becoming rated as authority and opinion. The results allowed these authors to reveal the decay and ascendancy of strings of Supreme Court decisions that enjoy a certain prominence based on forward citations with the implication that its embedded position is becoming the most salient within a window of time.

In the spirit of such research traditions we likewise try to identify small or large (and US, EU or Japanese) firms that enjoy a certain level of 'authority'; that is, firms that have become trendsetters in the imaging sector based on their ability to function as a 'hub' or broker. The status of broker is based on the linkages among its cited patents and differs therefore in important respects from other network studies that rely on centrality, *betweenness* and other network measures as indicated by UCINET and similar network software packages. Note that we focus on firms or assignees as brokers when mapping the evolution of the sector, much less so individuals or their 'art' unless that individual is a firm rather than an employed inventor.

Backward citations signal the extent to which a firm is cast in a brokerage role. Drawing on his previous work, as well as that on the presence of small worlds (Watts,1999), Burt

(2005) has recently suggested that a firm's network might be interpreted as placing the firm in an intermediary position between other firms. The firm's ability to be an intermediary hinges on the extent to which it bridges other firms and their knowledge. If both the focal firm and its 'alters' are well-connected, that firm displays diminished intermediation capacity and becomes more entrenched into a clique where it and its peers have access to the same resources and become highly subject to conformity pressures.

The implication is that imaging firms, acting as brokers, are more likely to ignite new waves of innovative activity and to become more prominent in their IP status; that is, to be a central rather than a peripheral player. The trendsetting towards a new paradigm is inferred from the extent to which forward citations reveal that firm's impact. In the imaging sector, IP decays rapidly as inferred from comparatively sharp drops in forward citation rates, but important differences in hazard rates among firms can be observed.

In the exploratory analysis we carried out, we constructed for each firm a score in the imaging 'sector' (it would be tenuous to define a patent-derived domain or sector as market or industry, hence our preference for 'sector') based on its connections to other firms as derived from backward and forward citations. A firm that becomes connected to other firms that among themselves remain less connected will be rated more strongly as a broker and its network will then have the character of a brokerage. If, however, the firms are well-connected, both directly and even more so indirectly, their network acquires the character of 'closure'. The software for obtaining such metrics is provided in Burt (2005). We surmised that broker firms are more prominent in shaping the evolution in the imaging sector, as indicated by two possible outcomes: (1) the volume of a firm's patenting activity as captured by the number of patents filed in a given year; and (2) the impact of a firm's patenting activity, as captured by the number of future citations received from other firms' patents.

We hypothesize that firms will accumulate more valuable patents and enjoy more impact if they emerge as brokers. Whether firms are trendsetters depends very much on whether they are at the basis of some trend, or whether they solidify a trend – an issue that is hard to resolve in a limited set of case studies. Tripsas (1997) argues that some firms dominate the architecture and let other firms provide the building blocks. Apple provides the architecture that surrounds its music retail device, together with the iPod eco-system, while other firms provide the elements that become attached to iPod. In imaging, such architectural configuration and associated leadership have not yet been established.

## DATA

The information to explore the role of firms in driving industry evolution came from the United States Patent Office (USPTO), made accessible through NBER (Hall, Jaffe and Trajtenberg, 2001). The patents backward and future citations were made available through Micropatent, an on-line readable database. We limited ourselves to six cases, differing in size and geographic location with variable membership in the sector (that is, incumbents or start-ups). They serve as illustrative cases for documenting the evolution in the imaging sector. The firms we focus on are Adobe, Kodak, Fuji, Indigo, Interactive Pictures and Sony (see Table 6.1). These firms vary significantly with respect to their geo-

*Table 6.1   Selected firms in the imaging sector*

| Firm name | Location | Size |
|---|---|---|
| Sony | Japan | Large |
| Fuji | Japan | Large |
| Kodak | US | Large |
| Indigo | EU | Small |
| Adobe | US | Medium |
| Interactive Picture | US | Small |

graphical location (US, Japan or EU) and size, but also patenting activity and the number of years over which they patented in the imaging sector. These firms thus represent a good cross-section of the imaging sector during the past 30 years. A follow-up paper (Pennings and Cattani, 2006) examines the sector with over 19 000 firms during a 30-year window in its entirety and captures the sector-wide effects of a firm's patenting activity.

As described before, we ascertained their degree of 'brokerage–closure' by determining the extent to which these firms are constrained in their network, which we extracted from their patenting activity and citations to other firms in earlier years. For each firm we computed the number of patents filed (and subsequently granted) in a given year in the chemical and digital technological fields, respectively. While Kodak, Fuji and Sony have spanned the two eras, the other firms are essentially digital companies and did not enter until after the digital period had begun. Comparing these firms in the context of digital imaging gives us the opportunity to evaluate the influence of a firm's legacy on its subsequent inventive efforts.

**Variables**

**Performance measure: patent counts and patent impact**
In our preliminary inquiry, we measured the performance of our subset of firms in technological terms using patent counts and patent future citations from other firms to estimate the value of a firm's innovative output. The first variable, patent counts, measures a firm's R&D productivity as the number of patents filed by that firm in a given year in the chemical and digital domains, respectively. We first measured performance in technological terms by using patent counts on the premise that patents 'are directly related to innovativeness, they represent an externally validated measure of technological novelty, and they confer property rights on the assignee and therefore have economic significance' (Ahuja, 2000, p. 433).

We also look at the impact of a firm's patenting activity as indicated by how often a firm's patents are cited in the future. Strong citation indictors also tend to be positively correlated with firm sales, profits and stock prices (see Narin et al., 2001). For all patents the sample firms filed over the study period in both the chemical and digital domains we collected future citations up to April 2004 from Micropatents. Since patents filed in earlier years are exposed to the risk of being cited by subsequent patents for a longer period, we compared patents only to those filed during the same year and restricted the analysis to the period 1975–2000. As a result, on average, the focal patents have remained at risk of being cited for at least four years. For each patent, we counted all future citations received until April 2004, net of a firm's self-citations. While self-citations measure the extent to which a firm builds upon its previous R&D efforts, citations from other firms more objectively estimate the actual relevance of a firm's patents.

Following Trajtenberg (1990a, 1990b), our performance measure estimates the average impact of a firm's patenting activity and was computed as the ratio between the number of citations that all patents filed by (and then granted to) firm $i$ (1, . . ., 6) in year $t$ (1975, . . ., 2000) received in subsequent years (until year 2004) from patents filed in imaging by other firms, and the number of patents the focal firm filed in the same year. Regardless of their quality, on average recent patents are less frequently cited than older patents simply because they have been exposed to the risk of being cited for a shorter period. To make the comparison possible, we used different citations windows by computing the ratio (or average patent impact) for future citations received within four to five years after the focal patents were issued, but the results did not change significantly.[1]

In the present chapter, we confine ourselves to simply plotting the constraint measure against yearly patent counts and patent impact, respectively, on the premise that the volume of a firm's patenting activity as well as the impact of its patents inform about the ability of this firm to set the trend in the imaging sector. More specifically, we expect our constraint measure to display an inverse relationship with both outcome and performance measures. As firms come to look more like closures than brokers their patent productivity and the impact of their patents will decline; but the opposite holds true when firms' network is richer in structural holes and thus they enjoy more opportunities for innovation.

This expectation is rooted in an increasingly large body of empirical evidence on the effect of structural holes on innovation. According to Burt's (1992) classic argument, for instance, nodes in a network rich in structural holes should be expected to have better access to novel information from remote parts of the network and exploit that information to their advantage. This in turn would result in better conditions for generating innovative outcomes (Burt, 2004). Consistent with this reasoning, Zaheer and Bell (2005) demonstrated that mutual fund companies with many structural holes are more likely to be recognized as innovative by appropriate industry observers. Similarly, earlier evidence from McEvily and Zaheer (1999) indicates that the presence of structural holes in a firm's advice network is beneficial for the acquisition of innovative capabilities.

## PRELIMINARY RESULTS

We present a small subset of exploratory findings in Figures 6.1a to 6.3b. Although the results of the analysis do not lend themselves to any generalization, they nevertheless provide evidence supporting the hypothesized relationship between brokerage (measured in terms of constraint) and innovation, more precisely patent counts and patent impact.

Figures 6.1a and 6.1b display the trend lines of the constraint measure for Kodak, Sony and Fuji, in chemical and digital, respectively. We distinguished between digital and chemical to establish more accurately how the structural position of three incumbent firms varies over time under the old (chemical) and the new (digital) technological paradigm but also to gauge how the very same firms affected the industry on the basis of their commitment to

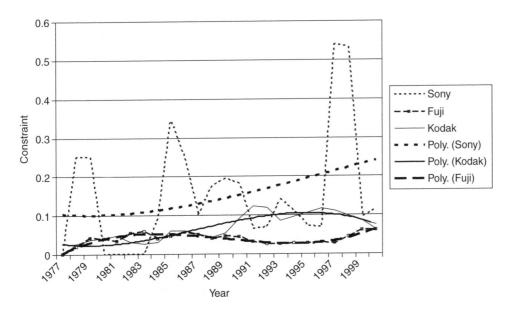

*Figure 6.1a    Trend lines for brokerage (constraint) – three leading chemical firms*

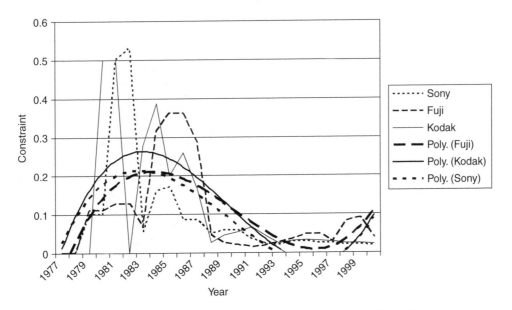

*Figure 6.1b    Trend lines for brokerage (constraint) – three leading digital firms*

the old (chemical know-how) and the new (digital know-how) technology. To render a smoother visual display of their evolutionary trajectory we added to the original plotted lines three fitted lines. The changes in brokerage of the three leading firms are presented through interpolation of its values over time using a polynomial function, as indicated by the bold lines. We included Sony also as 'chemical' as this firm aggressively accumulated intellectual property in imaging prior to the arrival of digital technology.

The figures clearly show how the network position of each firm – in particular, the presence of structural holes in their network – varies over time. However, while the constraint measure for the three firms seems to have gone up in the case of chemical, the same measure seems to have gone up and down over time in the case of digital. As implied before, we are presuming that shifts in patenting activity and patent impact are induced by changes in the firms' brokerage behaviour. Since we estimated the extent to which a firm is a broker by using Burt's constraint measure, in Figures 6.1a and 6.1b we should interpret a downward (upward) moving line as indicating an increase (decrease) in the firm's brokerage position.

Figures 6.2a to 6.3b list the chemical and digital trend lines for Kodak only.[2] We used in fact Kodak as an example to illustrate the relationship between a firm's structural position, as captured by Burt's constraint measure, and its ability to innovate in terms both of number of innovations (patent counts) and of quality of the innovative output (patent impact). It is worth noting that we created the figures after lagging the constraint measures by one year to account for the fact that a firm's structural position is very unlikely to have a contemporaneous effect on its patenting activity. An innovation may take time, often years, to materialize. Given the scale difference between the constraint measure and the patent count and average patent impact measures, we rescaled the vertical axis on the right side of each diagram with respect to constraint measure. Again we determined more precisely the trend lines between brokerage (constraint) and patent counts, on the one hand, and brokerage (constraint) and patent impact, on the other, by interpolating their values using a polynomial function. We did so for both chemical and digital.

The expected inverse relationship between constraint and patent counts and patent impact is only partially confirmed in the case of chemical (Figures 6.2a and 6.2b): an increase in the level of constraint (and thereby a decline in the number of structural holes in Kodak's network) seems to have depressed the average quality (impact) of their innovations (patents) but not the ability to generate an innovative output (patent counts). By contrast, the relationship turned out to be as expected in the case of digital (Figures 6.3a and 6.3b). The observed pattern suggests that an increase (decrease) in the constraint measure reduces (raises) the number of patents filed and their impact. Putting it differently, a firm with many structural holes is in a more favourable position to innovate as well as to generate innovations of greater impact. A closer look at the trend lines for Kodak reveals how its network position in more recent years has been characterized by fewer structural holes, as captured by the increase in the constraint measure. However, while a drop in the number of structural holes does not seem to have jeopardized Kodak's ability to innovate, the quality of its innovations (that is, their subsequent impact) has declined in more recent years.

The medium-sized and two small-sized firms (Adobe, and Indigo and Interactive Pictures, respectively) were deemed to press for new products and components and to be cast in a more disruptive role in the sector. The two small firms are only associated with the paradigm breaking stage of the sector. The three major firms, Kodak, Fuji and Sony, figured prominently in both what might be called the chemical and digital imaging eras. While this label is highly deceptive as many firms were attached to electronic or electrical, mechanical, optical and kindred platforms of knowledge, those existing before 1985 were

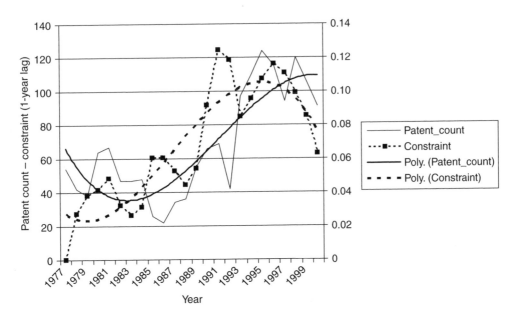

*Figure 6.2a   Kodak trend lines regarding brokerage and chemical patent count*

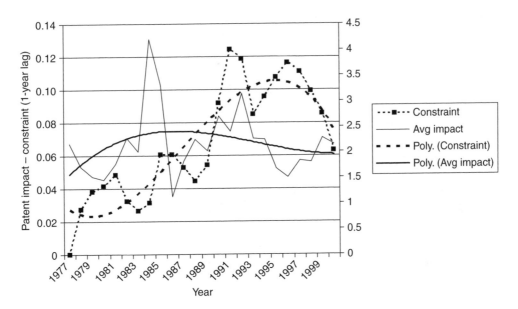

*Figure 6.2b   Kodak trend lines regarding brokerage and chemical patent impact*

largely attached to film and paper. The medium-sized firm Adobe, in the 1990s also an SME, and the two SMEs (Indigo was acquired by HP when it had grown to a level of over 500 employees) are digital players and, given their chemical-destroying role as well as small size, cannot be readily included in this type of analysis. However all three new

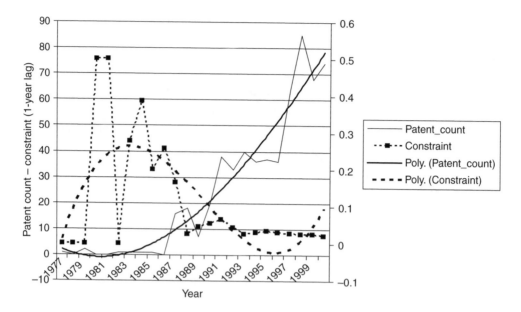

*Figure 6.3a   Kodak trend lines regarding brokerage and digital patent count*

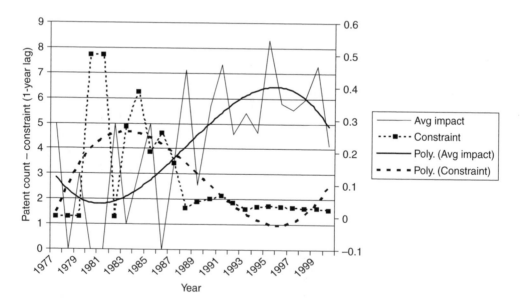

*Figure 6.3b   Kodak trend lines regarding brokerage and digital patent impact*

entrants to the digital sector are left censored and emerged instantly as 'brokers' and contributed significantly to the bundling of disparate pools of knowledge in the sector.
Ironically the SMEs show a rapid decline in brokerage following their creation, suggesting some initial advantage that dissipates after a 'honeymoon period'. One possible

explanation for this pattern is that those single inventions or a cluster of initial inventions draw on patents associated with different patent classes that propel a start-up into becoming an IP (intellectual property) broker, but that appeal shrinks shortly after. A honeymoon period has also been observed in the studies of entrepreneurship (for example, Brüderl and Schlüssler, 1990).

In the present study, the short trend lines do not provide sufficient information for the expected inverse relationship between constraint, and patent counts and patent impact among SMEs. Ideally we need to complement such network data on intellectual property with information on other types such as strategic alliances and social networks.

## CONCLUSIONS

This chapter presents an exploratory and preliminary study on patenting activity of firms in the evolving imaging sector during the period 1975–2005. We have tried to show that firms, whether entrepreneurial or established, US, EU or from Japan, whose patent citation activity points to a brokering role enjoy a greater impact on subsequent R&D activity, as indicated by the volume of their patenting activity and overall patent impact. Although the sector exhibits growing cohesion as the firms become increasingly constrained, high levels of closure do not preclude brokerage opportunities. As a result, some more central firms can still find opportunities to fill unexploited gaps and benefit accordingly. A firm's network position, and in particular the presence of many or just a few structural holes, varies over time and so does the firm's role as a broker. This variation is largely the result of the behaviour (that is, patenting activity) of other firms. More data and data analysis are required, however, to explore further the consistency of this pattern and delve more deeply into the underlying causal mechanisms.

In the results, we tried to depict six firms in terms of brokerage (constraint). While networks comprise firms with ties that are more or less strong (Granovetter, 1973), brokerage exists when a firm bridges other, more or less unconnected, firms. To capture the notion of cohesion or closure, within a patent citation network, we could suggest that, if a firm's inter-firm network ties are small in number, such knowledge-based ties are 'strong'. Such strong and closed ties make connections to divergent networks less likely. On the opposite side of the spectrum, a firm with weak ties between itself and peer firms resides in a patent-derived network that is non-exclusionary and exhibits bridges among firms with divergent IP.

During the break-up of conventional photography, firms with an 'insular' patenting portfolio – that is, consisting of self-cited patents or patents of peers such as those belonging to its strategic group or community of knowledge – will generate innovations of inferior quality. The implication is that firms with open citation networks stand to break newer ground, to set the stage for new technology platforms, in short to become prominent in crafting new product-market designs.

Our preliminary results indicate an overall decline among the six cases (though we report only the results for Kodak) in the degree of brokerage and a corresponding increase in the degree of closure, which is partly the result of higher levels of connectedness among firms within the industry over time. The most compelling result is that incumbents (imaging firms present before the transition towards digital technology) witness a decline in innovative impact together with concomitant, if not somewhat delayed or diminished, brokerage and increased closure.

By contrast, the two small SMEs and Adobe are new entrants, and by implication played no role during the chemical stage of the sector's evolution. They emerged as brokers enjoying an initial spike in the impact they had on the sector. Their patenting reflected high initial levels of brokerage but, after a honeymoon period, their brokerage tapered off, and so did their impact and patent count score, suggesting that these medium and small enterprises (SMEs) are initially disproportionately influential but rather soon move from being a trendsetter to becoming more of a 'follower' or 'conformist.' SMEs that emerge as brokers with commensurate high impact are attractive acquisition candidates for larger firms that seek to capitalize on their initial influence in the sector. SMEs seem to leave the sector through M&A if their brokerage renders them influential. However, more data on the differential role of large versus SMEs are needed before we can fully represent their unique role in shaping the evolution of a sector or market: for example, the role of the firms' strategists in negotiating strategic alliances and even full merger and acquisitions. SMEs might leave a sector through bankruptcy, but also because they are acquired. Firms like CISCO have grown by acquisition of SMEs whose intellectual property becomes inserted into the firm after acquisition. Ideally we also need to differentiate between SMEs that leave the sector prematurely, as Indigo did when it was acquired by Hewlett Packard, and SMEs that preserve their independence and move on to remain a lasting trendsetter, as Adobe did. Similarly we need data for a longer time period to trace an SME like Adobe which evolved from its honeymoon period towards a successful mid-sized firm and is emerging as one of the lead players in imaging software. A standard such as the well-known Acrobat™ is still elusive in 2006, whether as a component of imaging or as a catalyst or leading component in the ultimate 'dominant design'.

In conclusion, we would like to emphasize that, despite their many useful applications, patent data exhibit some shortcomings as well. While patents have been increasingly used as a measure of firm knowledge, and citations as knowledge networks, they do not fully measure a firm's overall base of experience. For instance, even though reference to prior art (that is, citations to patents by other firms) has been a core methodology in research on social, organizational and geographic pathways of knowledge flows, citations made by patent examiners have not been separated from citations made by inventors (Alcacer and Gittelman, 2006). Focusing on a single industry, as in this chapter, where patents are important for appropriating returns to R&D, might significantly reduce the effect of this problem, which is on the contrary compounded in studies comparing knowledge flows across very different industries. Of course, similar problems afflict most empirical measures, especially those measuring intangibles such as skills and knowledge.

The results so far do not reveal anything about the relative prominence of firms in driving the innovative trajectory in the sector. To represent such a comprehensive trend we need to include all firms in the sector (over 19 000 firms in our data set). Such an analysis might also expose multiple dominant designs. While imaging involves the image in all its shapes and forms, including still photographs, movies and diagnostics, its complements such as its capture, distribution and use functions, are used in widely divergent settings such as consumer electronics, military intelligence, medical diagnostics, entertainment and the arts. Any of these ill-bounded areas might acquire its own unique dominant design, suggesting that the imaging sector is a multi-peaked landscape. Although the objective of depicting that landscape as well as understanding its dynamics is elusive, it is worth pursuing.

## ACKNOWLEDGEMENTS

We thank Dasapich Thongnopnua and Le Truong (School of Engineering and Applied Science at the University of Pennsylvania) for their outstanding data management assistance; Micropatent for providing data on patents, including forward and backward citations, in a highly readable format; and the Mack Center at the Wharton School of the University of Pennsylvania for financially supporting this research in progress.

## NOTES

1. As discussed in Hall et al. (2001), an alternative approach would be to use the so-called fixed-effects' method where the citations received by the patents the focal firms filed in a given year are divided by a discount factor computed as the industry average impact. The discount factor is estimated by including all patents filed in the relevant classes/subclasses by any type of assignee (whether a public or a private firm, an academic institution or an individual inventor), not just the sample firms, and computing the average impact of all these patents for each year. As a result, the yearly average patent impact for each firm will be corrected by the average patent impact at the industry level for the chemical and digital domains, respectively. The results of the analysis (available from the authors on request) are consistent with those presented here.
2. The results of the analysis for the other two firms, though not reported here, are available from the authors on request.

## REFERENCES

Abernathy, W.J. and J. Utterback (1978), 'Patterns of industrial innovation', *Technology Review*, **50**(7), 40–47.
Ahuja, G. (2000), 'Collaboration networks, structural holes, and innovation: a longitudinal study', *Administrative Science Quarterly*, **45**(3), 425–55.
Alcacer, J. and M. Gittelman (2006), 'How do you know what you know? Patent examiners and generations of patent citations', *Review of Economics and Statistics*, forthcoming.
Aldrich, H.A. (2000), *Organizations Evolving*, Thousand Oaks, CA: Sage.
Anderson, P. and M. Tushman (1990), 'Technological discontinuities and dominant designs: a cyclical model of technological change', *Administrative Science Quarterly*, **35**(4), 604–33.
Baldwin, C.Y. and K.B. Clark (2000), *Design Rules: The Power of Modularity*, Cambridge, MA: MIT University Press.
Barney, J.B. and R.E. Hoskisson (1990), 'Strategic groups: untested assertions and research proposals', *Managerial & Decision Economics*, **11**(3), 187–98.
Bourdieu, P. and L.J.D. Wacquant (1992), *An Invitation to Reflexive Sociology*, Chicago: University of Chicago Press.
Braun, E. and S. MacDonald (1978), *Revolution in Miniature*, Cambridge, UK: Cambridge University Press.
Brüderl, J. and R. Schlüssler (1990), 'Organizational mortality: the liability of newness and adolescence', *Administrative Science Quarterly*, **35**(3), 530–47.
Burgelman, R.A. (1994), 'Fading memories: a process theory of strategic business exit in dynamic environments', *Administrative Science Quarterly*, **39**(1), 24–56.
Burt, R.S. (1992), *Structural Holes*, Cambridge, MA: Harvard University Press.
Burt, R.S. (2004), 'Structural holes and good ideas', *American Journal of Sociology*, **110**(2), 349–99.

Burt, R.S. (2005), *Brokerage and Closure: An Introduction to Social Capital*, Oxford, UK: Oxford University Press.

Cattani, G. (2005), 'Pre-adaptation, firm heterogeneity, and technological performance: a study on the evolution of fiber optics, 1970–1995', *Organization Science*, **16**(6), 563–80.

Chandler, A.D.J. (1962), *Strategy and Structure: Chapters in the History of the American Industrial Enterprise*, Cambridge, MA: MIT Press.

Christensen, C.M. (1997), *The Innovator's Dilemma: When New Technologies Cause Great Firms to Fail*, Boston, MA: Harvard Business School Press.

DiMaggio, P.J. and W.W. Powell (1983), 'The iron cage revisited: institutional isomorphism and collective rationality in organizational fields', *American Sociological Review*, **48**(2), 147–60.

Dosi, G. (1982), 'Technological paradigms and technological trajectories: a suggested interpretation of the determinants and directions of technical change', *Research Policy*, **11**(3), 147–62.

Ethiraj, S. and D.A. Levinthal (2004), 'Modularity, innovation in complex systems', *Management Science*, **50**(2), 159–73.

Fleming, L., S. Mingo and D. Chen (2005), 'Brokerage versus cohesion and collaborative creativity: an evolutionary resolution', working paper, Harvard Business School.

Fowler, J.H. and S. Jeon (2005), 'The authority of Supreme Court precedent: a network analysis', working paper, University of California Davis, CA.

Gollop, F.M. and J.L. Monahan (1991), 'A generalized index of diversification: trends in U.S. manufacturing', *Review of Economics and Statistics*, **73**(2), 318–30.

Granovetter, M. (1973), 'The strength of weak ties', *American Journal of Sociology*, **78**(May), 1360–79.

Hall, B.H., A.B. Jaffe and M. Trajtenberg (2001), 'The NBER patent citations data file: lessons, insights and methodological tools', NBER working paper series no. 8498, Cambridge, MA.

Hannan, M.T. and J.H. Freeman (1984), 'Structural inertia and organizational change', *American Sociological Review*, **49**(2), 149–64.

Hatten, K.J. and M.L. Hatten (1987), 'Strategic groups, asymmetrical mobility barriers and contestability', *Strategic Management Journal*, **8**(4), 329–42.

Henderson, R.M. and K.B. Clark (1990), 'Architectural innovation: the reconfiguration of existing product technologies and the failure of established firms', *Administrative Science Quarterly*, **35**(1), 9–30.

Hill, C.W. and F.T. Rothaermel (2003), 'The performance of incumbent firms in the face of radical technological innovation', *Academy of Management Review*, **28**(2), 257–74.

Jaffe, A.B., M. Trajtenberg and R.M. Henderson (1993), 'Geographic localization of knowledge spillovers as evidenced by patent citations', *Quarterly Journal of Economics*, **108**(3), 577–98.

Klepper, S. (1997), 'Industry life cycle', *Industrial and Corporate Change*, **6**(1), 145–81.

Klepper, S. (2002), 'The capabilities of new firms and the evolution of the US automobile industry', *Industrial and Corporate Change*, **11**(4), 645–65.

Krackhardt, D. and J.R. Hanson (1993), 'Informal networks: the company behind the charts', *Harvard Business Review*, July/August, 104–11.

Landes, D.S. (1969), *The Unbound Prometheus: Technological Change and Industrial Development in Western Europe from 1750 to the Present*, Cambridge, MA: Cambridge University Press.

Lee, J. and J. Song (2006), 'Incompatible entry in small-world networks', *Management Science*, forthcoming.

Levinthal, D.A. (1997), 'Adaptation on rugged landscapes', *Management Science*, **43**(7), 934–50.

March, J.G. (1991), 'Exploration and exploitation in organizational learning', *Organization Science*, **2**(1), 71–87.

McEvily, B. and A. Zaheer (1999), 'Bridging ties: a source of firm heterogeneity in competitive capabilities', *Strategic Management Journal*, **20**(12), 1133–56.

Mokyr, J. (1990), 'Punctuated equilibria and technological progress', *The American Economic Review*, **80**(2), 350–54.

Montgomery, C.A. and B. Wernerfelt (1988), 'Diversification, ricardian rents and Tobin's q', *RAND Journal of Economics*, **19**(4), 623–32.

Murmann, P. (2003), *Knowledge and Competitive Advantage. The Co-evolution of Firms, Technology, and National Institutions in the Synthetic Dye Industry*, Cambridge, UK: Cambridge University Press.

Narin, F., P. Thomas and A. Breitzman (2001), 'Using patent indicators to predict stock portfolio performance', in B. Berman (ed.), *From Ideas to Assets: Investing Wisely in Intellectual Property*, New York: John Wiley & Sons, pp. 293–308.

Nelson, R.R. and S.G. Winter (1982), *An Evolutionary Theory of Economic Change*, Cambridge, MA: Belknap Press.

Normann, R. (1977), *Management for Growth*, New York: Wiley.

North, D.C. (1990), *Institutions, Institutional Change and Economic Performance*, Cambridge, UK: Cambridge University Press.

Patel, P. and K. Pavitt (1994), 'Uneven (and divergent) technological accumulation among advanced countries: evidence and freamework of explanation', *Industrial and Corporate Change*, 3(3), 759–87.

Pennings, J.M. and G. Cattani (2006), 'Paradigm shifts: the case of brokerage and closure in the imaging sector', working paper, the Wharton School, University of Pennsylvania.

Peteraf, M. and M. Shanley (1997), 'Getting to know you: a theory of strategic group identity', *Strategic Management Journal*, **18**, Summer, 165–86.

Porac J.F. and H. Thomas (1990), 'Taxonomic mental models in competitor definition', *Academy of Management Review*, **15**(2), 224–40.

Porac, J.F., H. Thomas and C. Baden-Fuller (1989), 'Competitive groups as cognitive communities: the case of Scottish knitwear manufacturers', *Journal of Management Studies*, **26**(4), 397–416.

Porac, J.F., H. Thomas, F. Wilson, D. Paton and H. Kanfer (1995), 'Rivalry and the industry model of the Scottish knitwear producers', *Administrative Science Quarterly*, **40**(2), 203–27.

Rosenbloom, R.S. and M.A. Cusumano (1987), 'Technological pioneering and competitive advantage: the birth of the VCR industry', *California Management Review*, Summer, **29**(4), 56–76.

Rosenkopf, L. and A. Nerkar (2001), 'Beyond local search: boundary-spanning, exploration, and the impact in the optical disk industry', *Strategic Management Journal*, **22**(4), 287–306.

Rosenkopf, L. and M.L. Tushman (1998), 'The coevolution of community networks and technology: lessons from the flight simulation industry', *Industrial and Corporate Change*, **7**(2), 311–46.

Sahal, D. (1985), 'Technological guideposts and innovation avenues', *Research Policy*, **14**(2), 61–82.

Schilling, M.A. (2000), 'Towards a general modular systems theory and its application to inter-firm product modularity', *Academy of Management Review*, **25**(2), 312–34.

Schumpeter, J.A. (1934), *The Theory of Economic Development*, Cambridge, MA: Harvard University Press.

Silverman, B.S. (1999), 'Technological resources and the direction of corporate diversification: toward an integration of the resource-based view and transaction cost economics', *Management Science*, **45**(8), 1109–24.

Simon, H.A. (1962), 'The architecture of complexity: hierarchic systems', *Proceedings of the American Philosophical Society*, **106**(December), 467–82.

Trajtenberg, M. (1990a), 'A penny for your quotes: patent citations and the value of innovations', *RAND Journal of Economics*, **21**(1), 172–87.

Trajtenberg, M. (1990b), *Economic Analysis of Product Innovation*, Cambridge, MA: Harvard University Press.

Tripsas, M. (1997), 'Unraveling the process of creative destruction: complementary assets and incumbent survival in the typesetter industry', *Strategic Management Journal*, **18**(Summer Special Issue), 119–42.

Tushman, M.L. and P. Anderson (1986), 'Technological discontinuities and organizational environments', *Administrative Science Quarterly*, **31**(3), 439–65.

Utterback, J.M. (1994), *Mastering the Dynamics of Innovation*, Boston, MA: Harvard Business School Press.

Watts, D. (1999), *Small Worlds: The Dynamics of Networks between Order and Randomness*, Princeton, NJ: Princeton University Press.

Winter, S.G. (1994), 'Organizing for continuous improvement: evolutionary theory meets the quality revolution', in J.A.C. Baum and J.V. Singh (eds), *Evolutionary Dynamics of Organizations*, New York: Oxford University Press.

Zaheer, A. and G.G. Bell (2005), 'Benefiting from network position: firm capabilities, structural holes, and performance', *Strategic Management Journal*, **26**(9), 809–25.

BOX 6.1    IMAGING: A BRIEF HISTORY AND AN OVERVIEW
           OF THE TECHNOLOGY FROM CHEMICAL TO
           ELECTRONIC ENGINEERING

Electronically-based imaging is gradually replacing chemically-based imaging. The key element of the latter is silver halide which, when interacting with light waves, becomes transformed into an image and can be transmitted from film to paper, or projected onto some other medium such as a screen. Digital or electronic imaging entails devices that take pictures and develop those using electrons instead of film and then transmit, store and process these images electronically, as if they were files of data, unlike silver halide-based imaging where the film and paper are covered by a layer of silver embedded substrates. NASA developed digital imaging technology in the early 1970s for its space programme; this technology was closely tied to computer technology and, as costs of computer processing fell, the technology began diffusing into other areas. From the realm of consumer electronics, the development of video cameras had an impact on the way initial digital cameras were configured. Video technology had already shown that it was possible to dispense with film, though that industry remained rooted in analog technology until the late 1980s. Prior to 1990, the usage of digital photography was largely restricted to a few scientific (medicine and satellite imaging) and commercial (publishing and real estate marketing) applications. The primary advantages of this technology were the ability to manipulate and edit pictures on computers and the ease and speed of development, storage, recall and transmission. With decreasing costs and increasing functionality in many of the component technologies of digital imaging, particularly semiconductors, computer hardware and software, it has since been making steady inroads into conventional, silver halide-based film-based imaging, as well as spawning new products and services.

Historically, digital imaging is an arena which contains participants from multiple industries, including its progenitor the chemically-based, silver halide photographic industry with the major players of Kodak, Agfa, Polaroid and Fuji, to whom digital imaging represents a competence-destroying innovation. Another group of firms came from the consumer electronics industry (e.g., Panasonic), and typically attempted to leverage their experience with video cameras into digital imaging, particularly in the early stages of digital imaging. Yet another group of firms originated in the graphic arts and printing industry (e.g., Scitex) which had pioneered the use of electronic scanning. Finally, there were entrants from the computer hardware, software and semiconductor industries (e.g. Intel, Hewlett Packard) as digital cameras began to be accepted as computer peripherals. Digital imaging today draws on technological competencies from the semiconductor and electronics industries, computer hardware and software industries, and conventional film-based imaging industries. An enumeration of the components of a standard digital camera illustrates this.

The basic image-capture technology is based on the CCD (Charge Capture Device) sensor, which serves the function of converting light energy into a digital data file. The CCD technology has remained virtually dominant until recently, when CMOS' (Combined Metal Oxide Semiconductor)-based technology has begun to replace it; sensors using CMOS sensors are about ten times as energy-efficient as CCDs, and cost substantially less. The earliest versions of digital cameras did not have any storage device, thus severely constraining the portability of the instrument as it meant attachment via cables to a computer. Today, there are two major competing formats for the storage of digital photo files: removable PCMIA cards and micro drives. These are removable media, which effectively function like a roll of film. The file format in which the digital images are transferred to a computer, and then undergo further manipulation, is another critical aspect of the digital camera industry. Today, there are competing alternatives available for the format in which digital imaging files can be stored, as well as for the software used to manipulate and use these data image files. Finally, there is a microprocessor chip, which controls the operation of the camera. Its key metric is speed (and size). In addition, most present-day digital cameras have an LCD display, and a lithium battery to meet the power requirements. Related components of the architecture are printers, computers and other visual display devices. In 2003, sales of digital cameras exceeded sales of silver halide-based or analog cameras, but movie production and screens continued to be closely tied to silver halide.

PART III

Technology and Enhanced Capabilities

# 7. The fastest growing SMEs in Canada: their strategies, e-commerce and network practices

**Hamid Etemad**

## INTRODUCTION

This chapter's focus is on the growth of smaller firms in general and the rapid internationalization of such firms in particular. The popular belief is that the firms' fast growth is attributable to the presence, if not the abundance, of exceptional resources and potent capabilities enabling the formulation and implementation of dynamic strategies, including the utilization of collaborative advantages (Kanter, 1994; Gomes-Casseres, 1996, 1997; Yoshino and Rangan, 1995; Gulati, 1995). This includes the influences of resource-, strategy- and network-related advantages (Katz and Shapiro, 1985, 1994). When entrepreneurial initiatives, intellectual property and management expertise are viewed as resources, this common belief is consistent with the resource-based view of the firm (Barney, 1991; Nelson and Winter, 1982; Grant, 1991, 1996; Wernerfelt, 1984). When management learns and evolves rapidly over time to increase corporate capabilities, this will also be consistent with the concept of learning organizations (Nonaka, 1994; Nonaka and Tackeuchi, 1995; Argyris and Schön, 1978, 1996; Schön, 1973) and the behavioural theories of the firm (Cohen and Cyert, 1965; Cyert and March, 1963). When the management succeeds in improving upon the fit between its response and the environment, its strategic efficiency improves even further. This resonates well with the formation of dynamic strategies (Teece, Pisano and Shuen, 1997). However, when small firms recognize their own resource and strategic limitations and join forces with other firms, the consequent strategic direction is consistent with collaborative advantages (Kanter, 1994) associated with alliances and networks (Doz, 1996; Hakansson and Snehota, 1989; Katz and Shapiro, 1985, 1994; Overby and Min, 2001; Yoshino and Rangan, 1995; Gulati, 1995).

Although these theories explain much of a firm's growth and evolution over time, most of the smaller firms suffer from constrained resources, relatively inexperienced management and austere operating systems that cannot support rapid growth by deployment of potent resources, learning through networking or dynamically formulating a strategy, especially at the early stages of their existence. This suggests that the resource-based view (RBV) or the network-based view (NBV) alone (that is, each at the time and separately) is incapable of accounting for the rapid and sustained growth of smaller firms.

The above discrepancies suggest two possibilities: either (i) the small rapidly-growing firms differ from others in the population of typical firms, or (ii) they use different growth-enabling mechanisms and processes to support their rapid growth. Although both possibilities merit intense examination, as they elucidate on the state of the extant theory and on the process of rapid growth of smaller firms, this chapter focuses on the latter.

Two aspects of this research are noteworthy. First, the focal SMEs' fast growth rate may enable us to observe a compressed version of a potentially long process in a short span of time. Such shorter time periods would allow us to study the phenomenon through a cross-sectional methodology (for example, conducting a rich and in-depth set of interviews), thus avoiding a longer longitudinal study that would expose the study to the inherent hazards of long and drawn-out research. Second, the smaller size of the firms facilitates access to the true architects and decision makers of the firms, which avoids problems associated with multiple informants, fading memories and a lack of supporting corporate documentation. Naturally the in-depth pertinent information could only be collected from a small number of such firms in order to discriminate successfully between the source, impact and the nature of the influential forces, including those related to resources and networks, among others.[1]

## OBJECTIVE AND SCOPE OF THE CHAPTER

The primary objective of this chapter is twofold: (i) to examine the impact of various theoretical traditions in terms of distinguishing their corresponding patterns on the phenomenon of rapid growth in small and medium-size enterprises,[2] and (ii) to explore the possibility that the Internet and Internet-based technologies (IBTs) may have introduced the enabling capabilities that can potentially act directly (similar to resources) in facilitating network arrangements (similar to catalytic agents) to create or augment advantages in these firms.

### The Structure of the Chapter

Following this introduction, two plausible scenarios characterizing the resource-based and the network-based views of the firm will be presented. A discussion of methodology, sample population and in-depth interviews will follow. In light of the findings, a discussion of each scenario is presented next and the conclusions and implications are presented last.

## PLAUSIBLE SCENARIOS

Although the above theoretical foundations are neither exclusive nor exhaustive, their potent impact on small firm's growth, individually or collectively, can give rise to many possibilities. Naturally, not all such possibilities are feasible or correspond to promising outcomes. Furthermore, a detailed examination of many potentially feasible possibilities may be beyond the scope of a research project. Given the compression of time in rapid growth, we must also be cognizant of the differential impact of these possibilities exerting a pattern of influence (on focal enterprises) simultaneously or sequentially over time.

Etemad (2004) suggests that the influential forces (or factors) in the extant theory fall into three broad categories of *push, pull* and *interactive* forces. A typical pattern is the confluence of all three with one or two of the forces playing more dominant roles. For example, a firm's initial growth, and internationalization, may start with the influence of 'push' forces, such as an entrepreneurial drive, innovative ideas, intellectual property or a potentially exploitable resource pushing the firm forward. An enabling environment may enhance a firm's advantage(s) and expedite growth. Similarly, the 'pull' forces, accommodated by the enabling environment, pave the road and pull the firm to growth through the various barriers and thus further enhance the growth of a firm. For example, a firm's membership in a network of international distributors may facilitate the international expansion of a firm (that would remain domestic, otherwise). The confluence of these forces is depicted schematically in Figure 7.1. However, it is the absorptive capacity (Cohen and Levinthal, 1990) that mediates the firm's response to the interactive confluence of all forces (regardless of the type, the origin and the respective sequence of their influences) and propels the new enterprise forward. These influences can easily increase a firm's growth rate and expedite the firm's frontiers forward into the larger and richer international markets and even create born globals (Oviatt and McDougall, 1994, 1995).[3]

Therefore a plausible scenario must contain a logical sequence, or combination, of the three families of forces exerting influence sequentially, or in tandem, throughout the evolutionary phases of a growing enterprise. Although a complex set of forces may be influential in each phase, we assume an orderly process in building two polar and plausible scenarios, each more intensively reliant on one of the received theoretical traditions than on the others to further inform the research. In so doing, each scenario can, therefore, be viewed as an

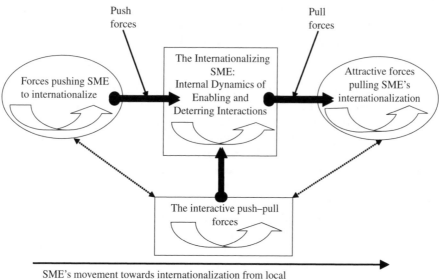

*Note:* The evolutionary process of each construct due to, for example, bench marking, experimentation and learning, among the other self-renewal processes, is represented by a feedback arrow within each construct (revised version, adopted from Etemad, 2004).

*Figure 7.1   Simplified depictions of forces in SMEs' internationalization combined with continual feedback reflecting learning*

archetype for introducing a distinct pattern of influences. The recognition of such patterns may better inform the research, with diagnostic measures capable of detecting the presence, if not the dominance, of the influential forces. Each scenario may then distinguish its forces and influence from others and hold important lessons for firms that aspire to follow those patterns in order to grow and evolve. While each of these scenarios articulates a pattern of growth and evolution, they can collectively specify the diversity of growth patterns.[4] Methodologically, the constituent characteristics of a pattern can serve as diagnostic tools and point to the dominance of a scenario to which the pattern belongs. This suggests that each scenario can be broken down to a sequence of observable milestones, each highlighting an integral part of the pattern. Naturally the detection of such patterns can point to dominance of that scenario. The two distinct scenarios, where a theoretical tradition plays a dominating role in each, are outlined below.

## A Resource-intensive Scenario

In this scenario, the impact of resources dominates the pattern of influences in a typical firm's various states of development, consistent with the resource-based view of the firm. If the origin and the nature of the influence are ignored, growth can be viewed as resource-based, which is tantamount to considering all influential forces (for example, pull, push and interactive) as conveyors of resources to the firm over time (regardless of the nature and the source of the influence and the respective way in which they materialize and influence the firm's growth path). Naturally the process of resource acquisition and exploitation may not follow a strictly linear process. It may also vary over time and across firms. However this scenario proposes that firms possess resources and the impact of such resources dominates all other factors in growth and internationalization phases.

### Typical examples

At the conceptual level, a typical example is the case of a resource-rich firm empowering the commercialization of a portfolio of intellectual property or properties. These intellectual properties (IPs) may have been in the commercial domain (or even in the public domain in the case of patents) for some time, but not adequately commercialized owing to the lack of resources. The financial resources and the backing of the resource-rich firm can provide the necessary resources to accelerate the commercialization. The *push force* of such enabling resources may also shorten the developmental time or solve some of the difficult technical problems. Such problems plague the growth of small firms and cannot be resolved without external and supportive resources. The various rounds of venture capital financing at the start-up phases of a new enterprise are also typical examples of financial resources. However, most of such financial resources become instrumental in acquiring or developing other potent resources and capabilities.

The celebrated case of MIPS, a start-up company in Silicon Valley that changed the face of computing, is an insightful example (Gomes-Casseres, 1996). With its introduction of RISC (reduced instruction set computation) chips, against all the adverse forces of the established computer industry based on CISC (complex instruction set computation), MIPS was an entrepreneurial start-up that all industry experts considered improbable. MIPS received massive financial support from an unlikely source, Kubota, a large, rich international firm in construction and earth-removal equipment based in Japan, which wanted to diversify at the time. The push force of Kubota's financial resources removed hitherto insurmountable barriers. It also led to MIPS' rapid growth and the acceptance of its design as the dominant standard in the industry. The industry was composed of giant chip makers, such as Hitachi, IBM, Intel, Motorola, Sun and Toshiba, among others, who fought to preserve their established positions or to make their own designs the industry's dominant standard. MIPS' truly impressive growth challenged the prevailing wisdom at the time. Although other resources, including massive intellectual property (IP), knowledge-intensive initiatives and tremendous human capital, were also involved, the dominant force behind MIPS was the financial backing of Kubota, without which other required capabilities and resources could not be acquired and the early rapid progress would not have been possible. Once the dominant standard was reluctantly accepted by the industry, MIPS was forced to build a worldwide coalition of more than 140 firms for using and also distributing its RISC-based systems against the entrenched rival standard (the CISC-based). In fact, MIPS' evolutionary growth, beyond the early stages, could be viewed as network-enabled growth. This points to the evolving confluence of influential forces over the life cycle of a growing firm, which is challenging the heavy (if not the exclusive) reliance of each of the received theoretical traditions in favour of their own propositions to the exclusion of others. Similarly, this is a vivid case example of an evolutionary pattern, where the initial push force merged with, and eventually turned into, a *pull force* in later phases of firm growth and expansion. It is such confluence of forces that affect the growth of firms as they evolve over time.

**A Network-intensive Scenario**

This scenario relates to cases where the impact of network-related advantages dominates a typical firm's evolutionary path. At the conceptual level, one can, for example, envision membership in a resource-rich network of individuals, firms and public institutions as the necessary constituent (especially in strong and tightly-knit networks), or at least as a catalyst, for acquiring the necessary resources and capabilities. Such membership provides for easier access to, as opposed to outright ownership of, the required resources for launching a project, for example, a start-up firm to realize the project. Similarly the initial start-up may be followed by a supply agreement (such as an OEM supply agreement by a network member) to ensure progress beyond start-up and pave the way for further growth. The initial membership may also provide connection to related networks to gain access to other capabilities through joint members. These related networks can be tapped for complementary advantages. The joint membership is usually mediated by the network bridges, such as the initial joint members in both the initial and the related networks, which can support the firm's further growth beyond the reaches of the initial network. Similarly previous membership of a network, or a new membership of a related network (for example, through the connections of the other members), may facilitate access to new buyers and suppliers domestically and globally and also enable further growth, regardless of their location. Similarly, internationalization may also occur through membership in networks with worldwide reach that can provide easier access to buyers and suppliers in the international markets. Therefore internationalization can be realized more easily and rapidly than otherwise if the required network connections are already in place when the firm wishes to pursue such a progressive expansion phase.

**An example**

A typical spin-off in a large firm can be viewed as an example of the above scenario, whereby an existing company invites the *internal champion* of a novel idea (or firm's intellectual property) to set up a new firm (to be called the 'spun-off' firm) with adequate provisions for access to scientists, knowledge, know-how and other intraorganizational resources in order to commercialize the designated IP successfully (for example, under-developed R&D results) in the start-up phase. The noteworthy point is the importance of the champion's intra-firm network connections. Not only are these connections necessary for setting up and transferring the IP smoothly to the newly spun-off firm, they are also bound to facilitate access to the required resources, capabilities and competences, without which the emerging firm could not start. Similarly, thanks to its network connections, the new firm can provide badly needed resources and capabilities by drawing upon the parent firm's own network, whereby the necessary requirements are loaned or transferred to the newly spun-off firm. In satisfying its own internal needs, the parent firm may issue an outsourcing contract in favour of the newly spun-off firm (to meet the parent company's needs), which may provide the new firm with the stability of a guaranteed demand, decreased risk and uncertainty. These are the enabling, if not the necessary, conditions for any start-up to get over the difficult problems of financing developmental costs (of the initial R&D), staffing, sourcing, production and especially selling its final products in the early phases of its life cycle. Of pivotal importance are the intra-firm network connections, to which the champion(s) already belong(s), and from which he can draw network-based resources (or advantages) at least in the initial and difficult stages of its growth path. Although resources must eventually be utilized, it is the initial membership of the network (the intra-organization network of firms and its people) that provides access to them and energizes the start-up and the subsequent growth processes. Therefore a typical spin-off firm can be viewed as a practical manifestation of forces emanating from network-dominant influences facilitating access to the necessary resources, strategies, supply contracts and even sowing the seeds of an interorganizational network between the parent and the spun-off firms later on, regardless of the eventual ownership. It can, therefore, be convincingly argued that membership in the parent's (or other) networks removes costly barriers and makes further evolution and progress possible at lower cost. It should be noted that in such spin-off case examples, the new firm is not required to focus on raising external funds, before all other tasks, in order to possess the required resources and capabilities. Rather the network connections provided those resources.

Theoretically the possibility of easier access to the network's enabling resources and capabilities (as opposed to acquiring them independently) encourages the firm to search for and to join the pertinent network, which permits the firm to gain access to network resources for deploying them, regardless of its initial network membership. In the context of Figure 7.1, while the initial network resources make the firm's establishment possible, network membership can then *pull* the new firm through the difficult start-up stages and further expedite its growth. Naturally, when there is a need to contact the members of other desired networks, a network bridge (Coleman, 1988) must be established. A bridging relationship can be then cultivated through effective communication with those who reside in the target network(s) beyond the firm's own initial network. The initial network may be the entrepreneur's own social network (Granovetter, 1973; Coleman, 1988; Burt, 1997) or the champion's corporate network. Network bridges may parallel weak links to other networks (Granovetter, 1985). Such network expansions further elevate the firm's (or the champion's) profile within its prevailing environment and thus increase the firm's attractiveness to other buyer and supplier networks (consistent with the network theory), which enable further expansion and growth.

Therefore the initial *pull* forces of a network can draw upon the network-centred resources and advantages and transform a young firm into a networking organization capable of gaining incremental competitive advantages through further exploitation of other links in a web of networks and alliances. Consequently a portfolio of the necessary collaborative (and mostly temporal) advantages could be converted to competitive (or strategic) arsenals for launching the firm onto successively higher stages of a typical growth and expansion, including internationalization, over time. In the context of Figure 7.1, the pull forces associated with network-intensive forces enable the firm to attain the necessary resources to *push* the firm's expansion forward. Accordingly, by measuring intensity in each of the above scenarios, one can point to the relative dominance of operating forces.

## THE SAMPLE AND THE METHODOLOGY

The sample consists of 15 rapidly growing SMEs. Their selective characteristics are highlighted in Table 7.1. They were drawn from the 2003 list of the 'Top 100 Fastest Growing Firms in Canada'. This list is formed, ranked and published on an annual basis and is available publicly (see http://www.profitguide.com). Fast growth is defined in terms of average growth of sales over a five-year period – in this case, from 1998 to 2002 (inclusive). This five-year averaging smoothes temporary fluctuations and spikes in the growth rates and points to a trend line for at least five years.[5]

**General Characteristics of the 2003 Top 100 Fastest Growing Firms in Canada**

These firms have been growing very fast over the five-year range of the rankings (1998–2002). The fastest growing firm in the list achieved a five-year cumulative rate of

*Table 7.1   The selective characteristics of the top 100 fastest growing firms in Canada on the 2003 profit 100 list*

| Sales | Average sales | $47.6mn |
|---|---|---|
|  | Median sales | $8.7mn |
| Number of employees | Average number of employees | 258 |
|  | Median number of employees | 50 |
| Internationalization | Number of exporting firms | 76 |
|  | Average exports as % of sales | 48% |
| Growth | Average | 1976% |
| R&D as per cent revenue | Average | 7.2% |
|  | Median | 3.0% |
| Employee training as per cent revenue | Average | 1.43% |
|  | Median | 1.00% |

*Source:*   www.profitguide.com.

16 298 per cent (growing more than 16-fold) and the slowest growing firm on the list attained a respectable five-year cumulative rate of 552 per cent. The average five-year cumulative rate is reported as 1976 per cent. These firms are younger, more agile and efficient (Evans, 2002) than their counterparts. On average, they employ 258 employees (with the median of 50 employees) for the list as a whole. While the average revenue is $47.6 million (with the median for the list as a whole at $8.7 million), they spend an average of 7.2 per cent of their revenue on research and development (R&D) and 1.43 per cent on employee training and retraining (medians are about 3 per cent and 1 per cent, respectively). In spite of their youth, however, 76 of them (or 76 per cent) are exporters and the average export as a percentage of revenue is 48 per cent. Some of them generate close to all of their revenues from abroad. One company is active in 111 countries, while most of them are focused primarily on NAFTA countries. Additional pertinent information about these 15 interviewed firms is provided in Table 7.2.

**The Interview Process**

In order to capture the rich details and discriminate among factors and their impacts, semi-structured and in-depth interviews with the principal(s) of the focal firms were conducted over three weeks in April 2004. Typical length of an interview was over an hour. All interviews were tape-recorded and fully transcribed. Interviews were carefully pre-arranged with the executive in charge, or the best-informed person in the firm, to obtain the most reliable information. The willingness of corporate officers to respond to this research's request and provide us with open and candid answers played a crucial role in selecting who would be included in the sample of the focal firms. The scheduling of these interviews was based strictly on the interviewees' convenience in order to attain their utmost attention, maximal information and cooperation without the customary corporate disruptions and time pressures. We offered anonymity and confidentiality in order to attain full cooperation and detailed information, which allowed us to record all the interviews. However interviewees were also informed that the interview would be recorded for increasing reliability and facilitating an undisturbed flow of information. At times, the interview process took a few telephone calls to develop a clear picture of a particular situation. In the event of unclear response, or responses, follow-up interview(s) were arranged to clarify the topic(s) in question. The follow-up interviews were also recorded and the initial points in question were amended and clarified immediately after the follow-up interviews. At least two analysts read each interview transcript to avoid potential misrepresentation or misunderstanding. Their consensus forms the information on which this research is based.

**The Interview Protocol**

These interviews followed an interview protocol consisting of 25 broad questions. These questions and the interview protocol followed all the recommendations and precautions for prudent qualitative research (Eisenhardt, 1989; Yin, 1984). They were designed as guidelines to ensure the collection of the most pertinent, reliable and necessary information in a conducive context in order to create opportunities for additional voluntary comments by the firms' principals. Background research from public sources informed the

*Table 7.2    Selected characteristics of the 15 interviewed rapidly growing firms*

| Firm | Type of products | Year of establishment | Number of employees | 5-year growth rate (%) | City and province | International as percentage of revenues |
|---|---|---|---|---|---|---|
| A | Fuel cell and testing equipment | 1995 | 242 | 16 298 | Mississauga, Ontario | 99 |
| B | Computers manufacture and franchise retailer | 1997 | 57 | 4349 | Richmond B.C. | 0 |
| C | Airport solar lighting | 1994 | 50 | 3669 | Victoria B.C. | 85 (in 110 countries) |
| D | Computer game developer | 1990 | 102 | 2970 | Montreal, Quebec | 100 |
| E | Dental services | 1996 | 280 | 2570 | Vancouver, B.C. | 80 |
| F | Financing medical care and procedures | 1996 | 23 | 2431 | Vancouver B.C. | 0 |
| G | Financial and insurance services | 1905 | 405 | 1583 | High River, Alberta | 0 |
| H | Nursing agency and homecare | 1988 | 175 | 1513 | Toronto Ontario | 0 |
| I | Pharmaceuticals & biomaterials | 1992 | 62 | 1502 | Vancouver B.C. | 100 |
| J | Educational products for children | 1997 | 8 | 991 | Montreal Quebec | 74 |
| K | Olive oil producer and distributor | 1993 | 3 | 935 | St Laurent, Quebec | 45 |
| L | Manufacturer of ice blankets | 1993 | 63 | 641 | Delta, B.C. | 82 |
| M | Sporting surfaces | 1989 | 86 | 638 | Fonthill, Ontario | 76 |
| N | Vision correction | 1993 | 1000 | 626 | Mississauga, Ontario | 97 |
| O | Business service for executives | 1996 | 17 | 566 | Calgary, Alberta | 0 |

interviewer and the interview process. This information was used to put the interviewee at ease and to create an encouraging interview environment. The protocol also allowed the interviewer to invite further comments and to expand the possibility for further elaboration beyond the immediate topic at hand.

More than one-third of the questions had some reiterative feature and related to previous or future questions for obtaining either confirmatory information (to check discrepancies) and/or to extract different perspectives on the topic in order to develop further depth and to increase reliability. The interviewer was instructed to be careful about the reiterative aspects and also to take note of any contentious topic about which the respondent was either hesitant or vague in his answers. Retrospectively, the interview protocol served as the initial list of topics of interest, which led to open-ended dialogues and follow-up informal conversations at the end of the formal questions.

## Discussions of Scenarios in Light of Findings

Following the formulation of the two polar scenarios earlier, this section will discuss them in relation to the findings.

### First scenario: the impact of the resource-based view of the firm

The common belief is that practically all firms accumulate and deploy resources. This belief is consistent with the resource-based view (RBV) of the firm (Barney, 1991; Nelson and Winter, 1982; Grant, 1991, 1996; Wernerfelt, 1984). The resource-based view of the firm also maintains that more potent resources lead to differentially higher growth and expansion. It characterizes potency in terms of a range of characteristics, including *valuable, inimitable, rare and not-substitutable*. Although most of the smaller firms, especially at the early stages of their lives, are relatively resource-poor (as they are building up their equity and accumulating resources), they possess some form of intellectual property (IP), mostly in the form of knowledge and information. The entrepreneurial characteristics of these firms (which may be viewed as a resource) can also further compensate for the initial shortage of their own conventional resources. One of the prominent characteristics of IP in general, and knowledge as a resource in particular, is that they are time-sensitive and have a limited shelf-life (as manifested in patents, copyrights and trademarks).[6] This suggests that they should be commercialized as fast as possible, and on a larger and broader scale than other conventional resources, in order to realize their full potential in a shorter time than other conventional resources. Without exception, all of the firms in the sample had some documented IP in general and some of them were also knowledge-intensive as well.

As the Internet and IBTs, including e-commerce technologies and processes, can enhance a firm's reach and expedite deployment of IP on a broader scale than conventional means, it is logical to view them as complementary resources that make faster and broader deployments possible. In relation to IP, IBTs and e-commerce processes have emerged as potent resources in their own right. Their acquisition and deployment offers a firm a range of incremental capabilities similar to those associated with other complementary resources. Consider, for example, that they can augment and enhance the firm's communication processes with internal and external agents, save time and reduce uncertainty due to lack of information, enhance the quest for competitiveness and play instrumental roles in the continual struggle of smaller firms for gaining incremental market share. Therefore, the Internet and IBTs, including e-commerce technologies, are viewed here as a resource.

Similar to the other resources, the access to, and deployment of, these technologies does not necessarily mean that the firm is automatically enabled to achieve certain objectives better than the others and to attain incremental competitive gains. On the other hand, however, the realization of the firm's potential depends on how they are deployed and incorporated into the firm's overall strategy for growth. Accordingly, we will discuss the various ways in which such technologies can at least augment a firm's strategies as complementary (and thus further enabling) resources that can even originate new avenues for growth and internationalization.

### Increased and improved information handling as a complementary resource

As reviewed briefly earlier, intensive and continual communication may have a positive impact on growth and internationalization. Etemad (1999), for example, characterizes a typical international transaction in terms of an eightfold flow, the nature of most of which could be viewed as sequential communications. These flows mainly provide information, helping firms to organize their marketing efforts, especially in international markets. They are as follows:

1.  An outbound flow of information and communication from the firm. Usually this originates from the producer/supplier and is directed to potential buyers (for example, through advertising and communication in the form of one-to-one or one-to-many,[7] or establishing an informative and interactive website);
2.  An inbound inquiry for acquiring further information or knowledge by potential buyers in reaction to the initial communication. Generally, this is a reactive stimulus-response that can become interactive and eventually result in a successful transaction when the firm responds satisfactorily by transmission of additional information, requiring a follow-up;
3.  An outbound response providing the requested information, terms and so on, which is usually done by transmission of documents outlining the pertinent, or requested, information by sending the documents through fax or e-mail, or by posting them on a website;
4.  An inbound financial flow as payment for consummating the transaction (when the potential buyer is so disposed, which depends on the efficacy of communication in terms of the above three flows); and thus requiring
5.  An outbound shipment of goods, or delivery of service; along with
6.  An outbound transfer of legal title and other entitlements through the transmission of actual title, warrantees, instructions and so on (that is, in documentary or in equivalent digital information format, parts of which can be posted on a website for selected downloads by the buyer); followed by
7.  An outbound request for confirmation of receipt and information feedback regarding satisfaction with what was sent; and
8.  An inbound flow of acknowledgment followed by an outward flow of follow-up(s), news bulletins and so on to ensure continued satisfaction with the current transaction and to influence future potential transactions.

A cursory examination indicates that the above characterization portrays the nature of a typical information-intensive transaction and is very well-suited for adoption to on-line transmission and communication. Except for the physical shipment of goods (when they are not in digital forms), all other flows either are in the form of pure information or have a very high information content. Relatively expensive, uncertain and time-consuming efforts, such as international travel, long-distance telephones and letters, handled the initial phases of communication in the past, prior to the intensive deployment of the

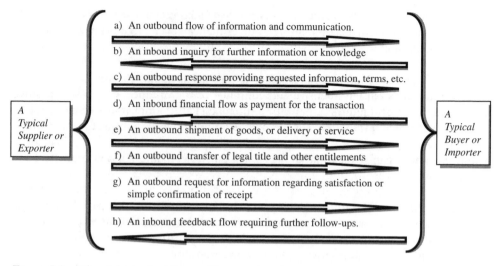

*Figure 7.2    The eight typical flows of international transactions*

Internet and IBTs. The uncertain aspects of the early communication alone could take time, money and effort, which most of the smaller firms can ill-afford. In contrast, the Internet and IBTs can routinize these affairs economically and effectively over time, thus saving time, money and effort just as any efficient resource is expected to do.[8] Furthermore most of the IBTs and e-commerce technologies require almost no intervention by managers, which allows their time to be devoted to more important and non-routine aspects. Figure 7.2 depicts the above flows schematically. Even when physical shipment is involved, the digital version of the shipment-related documents and information is also transmitted through the Internet. Accordingly, the access to the Internet and deployment of its technological capabilities can act as any other resource or capability with highly potent impact.

**Typical examples**
Although we observed some variations in the overall use of the above-defined flows, many of the focal companies used most, if not all, of the flows extensively. At least five of the firms involved in design of computer games, educational programmes and financial services used all of the eight flows intensively (8/8). Even the shipping of computer games and training packages went electronically, mostly through their websites (using file transfer protocols). One medium-sized firm with sales in more than 110 countries told us that most of their transactions (except for shipping of their physical products, that is, solar equipment and lighting) were handled through their website and e-commerce. This particular company has a very informative website and is capable of handling all their transactions on-line. Most of their routine and information-intensive flows were conducted on-line, including the first three and the last three flows (that is, a minimum of 6/8). Regarding flows falling under the general category of communication for request for, or acquisition of, information[9] (for example, at least five of the eight flows – the first three and the last two flows), on-line communication served the purpose, but actual documents followed to confirm and reconfirm the information.

Overall the findings of this research point to the positive impact of increased communication on faster internationalization due to the Internet, thus resulting in improved information handling and efficient communication as the Internet-based communications can be very detailed, are less costly and in many respects less time-consuming.[10] The respondents consistently referred to the improvements in communications as having a positive impact on internationalization thanks to ease of information handling in one form or a combination of forms. These findings also resonate with the critical role of information in general, and the Internet-based technologies assisting information transmission and communication in particular, in reducing perceived on-line transactions costs (Anderson and Coughlan, 1987; Berthon, Pitt and Watson, 1996; Klein, Frazier and Roth, 1990; Klein, 1989).

Although the cost of Internet-based communication has decreased dramatically, our findings point to the increased costs of international transactions owing to their added complexity, which require more effective communication, detailed information and follow-up, for which the Internet is well-suited. Without exceptions, all firms in our sample indicated that e-mail and other forms of Internet-based communication technologies, including their presence on the world-wide web (WWW), served as pivotal instruments in the success of their business models. This finding is very consistent with the extant literature on the subject (for example, see Peterson, Balasubramanian and Bronnenberg, 1997; Dutta, Kwan and Segev, 1998; Dutta and Segev, 1999; Dutta and Biren, 2001; Geiger and Martin, 1999; Hamill, 1997; Hamill and Gregory, 1997; Lituchy and Rail, 1999; Overby and Min, 2001; Quelch and Klein, 1996).

While an e-commerce-enabled website can handle almost all aspects of an international transaction (except for the shipping or delivery of non-digital goods and services), e-mail alone holds the potential of handling all information-related flows easily and quickly (but not necessarily very effectively). However a simple website can automate and thus facilitate all outbound information flows, as highlighted in Figure 7.2 and discussed earlier. Some respondents pointed to the power of complementing e-mail communication with a simple website (for example, 'brochure-ware'). Others pointed to their use of e-commerce-enabled websites with more powerful and customer-friendly procedures than mere communication through e-mails, one response at a time. Naturally, such websites can initiate unsolicited inquiry and facilitate, and even substitute for, the early phases of potential transactions (consisting of the first four flows). Regarding further coordination, a large portion of these rapidly growing firms indicated that they communicated intensively by e-mails at all levels of their supply and value chains, including those with the suppliers and buyers. Most of these firms' e-mail systems were integral parts of their presence on the web and website, to provide a consistent and coherent picture of the firm (although this is not technically necessary).

Some firms indicated that they created their websites to initiate, complement and even facilitate communication at first (both inward and outward), but this has become an 'integral resource in managing international sales'. This is a clear indication that, even without e-commerce capabilities, a website had begun to serve as a source (or resource) for (i) outward transmission of information in various forms (for example, from one-to-many potential clients), (ii) inward and outward facilitation of routine communication, (iii) provision and receipt of financial information, (iv) delivery tracking in the case of non-digital goods, and (v) full delivery for fully-digitized goods and services. This finding is very consistent with the earlier discussion and with Figure 7.2.

In the absence of the Internet and IBTs, the above processes would have required staff and resources, which are not abundant in smaller firms. Without exception, all rapidly growing small firms have an active website, but not all are e-commerce-enabled. Most firms used the Internet as a communication resource through e-mails, e-marketing for potential sales (by postings announcements on the website to advertise, provide information, cultivate new contacts and develop fresh leads) as well as collecting business intelligence and benchmarking against other competitors, among others. The e-commerce-enabled websites capable of consummating transactions were viewed as more powerful and also as parallel sales channels.

**The Level of Support for the First Scenario**

The overall analysis and findings of this research are very supportive of the first scenario in terms of characterizing the firm's initial IP, especially when complemented by the Internet and its associated technologies, as resources with potent influences on rapidly growing firms' growth and internationalization. However, we did not find strong support for equating mere presence on the Internet with internationalization: that is, 'Internetization' is not equal to 'internationalization'. This suggests that the Internet can play a complementary or catalytic role in increasing the awareness of (or openness to) transforming the firm's initial orientation towards international markets and thereby stimulating internationalization; but it is not causing internationalization on its own. It further suggests that the IBTs and e-commerce technologies are also viewed as complementary resources that can augment other resources and thus hold the potential of enhancing growth and expansion.

**Second Scenario: The Impact of the Network-based View of the Firm**

In answering questions regarding the importance of the Internet and its potential impact on the firm and on its rapid growth in comparison with any other capability, all the respondents strongly agreed with the variants of the statement that, without Internet-based technologies and processes, they could not conduct their business globally, nor could they have grown as fast as they had already. In order to explore the topic further, the interviewer briefly outlined several variants of scenarios outlined earlier and put brief 'what if' questions within the scenario to the respondents. For example, the interviewer suggested: if the focal company could be divided into various constituents, which of those components could be outsourced; and which one would be most dependent on e-mails, the Internet and the web-based technologies for accomplishing their respective tasks? Communications for coordination (both the inbound and outbound), including those related to production and marketing, turned out to be the top two candidates in terms of perceived importance that could not be outsourced. A confirmatory follow-up question asked about the importance of the e-mail and Internet-based facilities to various constituent functions of the value net. The answers corroborated the response to the previous two questions. The important role of production-related communications (those related to the supply chain) was also reaffirmed as critical and thus added to the previous list.

# THE SCOPE AND REACH OF THE INTERNET-BASED FACILITIES

Without exception, the respondents pointed to the small size of the Canadian market as compared to the size of the US and other markets in the world. These firms found communication with clients (buyers, suppliers and third parties all over the world) as both necessary and enabling to their rapid growth. Some sold directly worldwide and some sold indirectly through third parties. We learned that the third parties (worldwide distribution network or regional marketing companies) would provide local representation in terms of the required support, adaptation and technical services. However all the respondents pointed to the importance of global clients to their growth and would not feel restricted to their home market because of the global reach of the Internet. This points either to prior overall international orientation or to an early transformation of the orientation from local to international and possibly global. It also suggests that the IBTs and e-commerce strategies may have played influential roles in that evolution. Although these findings resonate with the extant theories of internationalization (see, for example, Johanson and Vahlne, 1977; Buckley and Casson, 1976; Dunning, 1980, 1988), it is difficult to attribute rapid growth rates and internationalization to IBTs and e-commerce processes exclusively. It is equally difficult to view IBTs and e-commerce processes as network instruments, or as resources, each to the exclusion of the other. The firms in our sample viewed them as complementary resources that would facilitate networking and better communication, which could in turn stimulate growth and expansion.[11] We learned that the deployment of various Internet-centred facilities that can stimulate internationalization (in different possible forms) is viewed as enabling capabilities without much concern for whether they fall in resource-based or in network-based categories. Our findings provide support for viewing the Internet and IBTs, including e-commerce processes, as facilitators of international transactions.

## The Economic and Strategic Advantages of the Network Membership

The economic and strategic benefits of a network are the integral parts of the second scenario and can be attributed in part to proximity in the real spaces (such as, industrial clusters) and in virtual spaces (that is, virtual electronic networks – VENs). The extant literature suggests that young firms are attracted to regional or industrial clusters for a host of primary reasons (for example, Anderson, 1994; Enright, 1996; Markusen, 1996). For example, industrial clusters offer a conducive and competitive environment for younger firms thanks to the close proximities in their settings. Such proximities provide them with easier access to resources, especially when their products and services relate to the overall supply/value chains and activities of the other firms in the region, and those of the regional cluster as a whole.[12] A deeper examination suggests that the economics of proximity in the supply chain space can provide most benefits of the regional clusters, including (i) the economics of agglomeration (Marshall, 1949), (ii) easier access, and (iii) more effective learning (Argyris and Schön, 1978, 1996; Nonaka, 1994; Nonaka and Tackeuchi, 1995; Schön, 1973) in the cluster, and also (iv) networking advantages (for example, Katz and Shapiro, 1985, 1994; Yoris and Kaufmann, 2001; Wynne et al., 2000). Some of these advantages are more important in most cases than the economies associated with shorter geographical proximities (or distances), especially when the ratio of value to mass (for products) and ratio of value to elapsed time to delivery (for services) are relatively high.[13] Such proximities would also permit the firm to seek other firms with complementary goods and services and thereby add incremental value to their mutual supply/value chains in a shorter time, offering them synergistic features (Etemad, 2003a, 2003b) in terms of incremental value along and across their value chains. This suggests that, if the costs of communication and transactions in supply/value chains can be controlled, most of the benefits of regional clusters can accrue to the members of efficiently run supply/value chains.

Thus we expected to find support for a combination of cluster membership and the intensive deployment of the Internet and the Internet-based communication as influential factors in the fast growth of the young firms beyond domestic markets. Stated differently, network membership, defined in terms of proximities within the supply net space, regardless of the space within which the network would be situated, should be influential in increasing the smaller firm's growth rates. Naturally, when the Internet and Internet-based technologies enable small firms to attain rich benefits due to their virtual proximity at much lower cost and without limitations of moving into particular regions (for example, proximity in a functional space through the Internet and IBTs as opposed to geographical proximity), they should logically lead to the enhancement of these firms' growth rates even further.

This line of theorizing was supported by our in-depth interviews. While the focal firms did not appear to be explicit members of regional clusters, they did use the Internet and Internet-based technologies intensively to enforce their membership in their respective value nets; but these networks turned out to be cyberspace-based clusters. Our findings suggest that rapidly growing firms had become active players in their Internet-connected value nets, to which they belonged and contributed, or from which they benefited. Therefore they were only proximate in the cyberspace due to the Internet, IBTs and e-commerce models, as discussed earlier. This suggests that the virtual electronic networks (VENs) may have augmented, and even in some cases replaced, conventional networks without diminishing network benefits.

## CONCLUDING REMARKS AND IMPLICATIONS

This chapter reports on the first phase in a multi-phase research programme. The findings and the analysis of results point to the rapidly growing firms' acute sense of entrepreneurial intuition supporting the challenges facing them. Although this topic is one of the main pillars of young and small entrepreneurial firms, we did not view it as critical to our study because all the firms have already attained rapid growth over the past five-year period, if not longer. However, we attributed much of their rapid growth to either the resource-based (RBV) or the network-based (NBV) view of their activities.

This research's support for both families of scenarios, portraying the resource-based view and the network-based view of the firm, as discussed earlier, point to a more comprehensive and eclectic theory of the firm at work than those portrayed by either views or their related variants. The strong support for the resource-based view of the firm can be easily attributed to the presence of intellectual property (evidenced by high R&D

expenditures, as reported in Table 7.2), among the other resources representing push forces, in these rapidly growing firms. The richer and larger international markets may have acted as the *pull forces* in attracting firms to these markets. As noted earlier, such markets provide much larger benefits than domestic markets, regardless of the latter's size. In addition, for highly specialized products, domestic markets are not large enough to support sustained growth and expansion. The presence of such attractions accounts for the difference between success and demise of these smaller firms, especially in the earlier stage of their life cycle. Naturally, successful penetration of these markets makes faster growth and early internationalization possible.

The resource-based view was further confirmed with the emergence of the Internet and its associated technologies, perceived as an enabling resource. However these technologies turned out to be the pivotal instruments in providing easier access to international markets than the conventional methods as well enhancing the formation of networks (the focus of the second scenario). This suggests that the use of the Internet and e-commerce technologies may have brought the two views of the firm closer together. This argument opens new, but complementary, avenues for viewing the economic and strategic aspects of the firm that neither view alone would easily accommodate.

We attribute many of the additional insights to the interactive nature of the chosen methodology enabling us to explore the topics in-depth and as openly as possible. These insights turned out to be very helpful as they painted a much fuller and clearer picture than would be obtained by using another methodology, such as a questionnaire. The in-depth interviews, with many redundancies and reiterative teaser questions inviting the interviewees to comment at length on the topics at hand, provided us with a much clearer picture of smaller firms' growth strategies and their daily challenges. It also exposed us to problems not envisioned before and forced us to rethink the underlying forces beyond the extant theory and to examine our view in a slightly different light.

The concept of formulating two alternative polar scenarios served as an umbrella for guiding the interview protocol design and informing the research. It also helped to place responses in a proper context in search of the dominant patterns, but also forced us to think through the confluence of different forces (as opposed to one or the other set of forces) influencing those growth patterns. Overall, we found more agreement and concordance with the pattern of growth characterized by a combination of the resource-centred and the network-centred scenarios than with each of them alone. In that light, the coordinating, mediating and connecting roles of the Internet and Internet-based technologies became increasingly clear, if not overwhelming.

Collectively, the above discussion, findings and corresponding analysis suggest the implications considered in the next subsection.

### Communication and the Rapid Growth of Smaller Firms

Our theoretical discussion and the analysis of in-depth interviews resonate very strongly with the theoretical traditions underlying this research. They all converge on the critical role of information and communication in coordinating with partners for the access to, and the deployment of, necessary resources. In the absence of regional clusters to attract smaller firms, the formation of virtual electronic networks (VENs) turned out to be a powerful substitute and only feasible through the Internet and IBTs, including e-commerce, along and across the supply/value chain. Our findings strongly confirm that the smaller rapidly growing firms have been joining such virtual clusters, which offered them, among other things, the concept of 'e-proximity'. This proximity appears to have replicated the advantages of cluster membership for smaller rapidly growing firms, as they had become active members of their own VENs supporting their supply chain and value nets.

Our findings, complemented by analytical discussions, confirm that small younger firms should not shy away from maximal selective information disclosure, and even transparency, to reduce the risks associated with relative paucity of information or perceived structural uncertainty (for example, the possibility of demise) on the part of their actual and potential buyers and suppliers. Almost all rapidly growing firms in our sample had an active and rich presence on the Internet, and they stated that the Internet and e-commerce technologies played critical roles in all aspects of their growth and internationalization. They even referred to them as 'competitive requirements'. Obviously, these firms have been collecting competitive intelligence to adjust their own competitive and strategic profile in the rapidly changing world of globalization. This may have also stimulated their desire to become rapidly growing organizations. By implication, the smaller and younger firms should ensure that their potential international buyers, suppliers and clientéle will have access to as much easily accessible and objectively verifiable information as those in domestic markets to override their perceived fears. Naturally, a dynamic, up-to-date, interactive and even multilingual presence on the Internet can help to allay such possible suspicions and fears significantly.

**Information handling and rapid growth of smaller firms**
Information handling and transmission of requisite information emerged as one of the necessary conditions for attaining rapid growth in the rapidly changing environment facing these smaller firms. The theoretical discussions supporting the findings of this chapter point to the positive impact of effective coordination in terms of effective communication and information handling in support of rapid growth. Without exception, all the members of this study's sample suggested that they used Internet and Internet-based technologies intensively in order to manage optimally their respective information handling, communication and coordination of their various functions with different clienteles, which in turn enabled them to avoid unnecessary losses of opportunities, time and resources, thus stimulating their rapid growth in spite of size and resource adversities.

In summary, our research findings suggest that the experience of rapidly growing smaller firms in Canada merits the close attention of scholars, practitioners and policy makers. The shortcomings of the extant theory regarding these firms challenge scholars to seek further clarity in the received theory. As discussed earlier, this research offers strong support for an eclectic view of rapidly growing firms' activities as opposed to those of either the RBV or the NBV. The rapid growth of these firms, against the background of intensive global competition, size and resource adversities, offers practical lessons to practitioners and managers of small and large firms alike. Our findings suggest that these firms may have combined their own resources, complementary technologies and network resources for attaining their fullest potentials in order to enable their rapid growth. Accordingly, such strategic combinations merit further attention. On the public policy side, the absence of incremental incentives, beyond those available to the general population of firms, suggests that the impact of these firms is not fully understood by policy makers. Logically, additional support for these firms may return handsome benefits in terms of employment, tax revenues and wealth creation.

## ACKNOWLEDGEMENT

An earlier version of this chapter was presented at the Klein Symposium at Pennsylvania State University, University Park, Pennsylvania, USA, 12–14 October 2005. This revised version has benefited from the comments and questions of other scholars in the symposium. The author wishes to thank Dr Gerald Susman, the Robert and Judith Klein Professor of Management, for his in-depth review, detailed comments and insightful suggestions for revising this chapter.

## NOTES

1. Regardless of the nature and structure of the networks (that is, real or virtual) that firms may have used, this research questioned whether the Internet and Internet-related technologies may have created a new landscape in cyber space with composite advantages over which the rapidly growing small firms operate. The review of findings suggests that in fact such a new landscape may be emerging, if it has not emerged already.
2. The initial objective of the research, as stated earlier, was to assess three broad families of relationships, namely: (i) the impact of the Internet on the internationalization processes, (ii) the potential role of e-commerce technologies in changing the orientation of a rapidly growing small enterprise during the growth period, and (iii) the extent of adoption and the corresponding impact of using pervasive Internet-based communication technologies (and processes) on the membership in clusters, as well as cluster formation, as an intermediate step towards internationalization. However this research agenda evolved as research progressed.
3. Born globals are defined as firms whose international sales achieve a substantive portion (usually 25 per cent) of their revenues in a short period (usually less that three years) from their initial public offering (IPOs) (Oviatt and McDougall, 1994, 1995).
4. We suggest that the pattern recognition can serve as a powerful tool in informing the early inclination in terms of a heavier reliance on, for example, push forces, even though the firm's evolutionary growth path may evolve and transcend that pattern over time.
5. It is noteworthy that some of these firms have been on the list of the 'Top 100 Fastest Growing Firms in Canada' for more than one year).
6. The useful life of a patent, for example, is limited to about 15 years, although a patent is granted for 21 years.
7. Generally, electronic version of communication takes the following patterns:

   a. direct one-to-one communication: sending selected e-mails and communicating through the Internet (or its counterparts in interactive websites),
   b. direct one-to-many communications: the transmission of e-mails to lists and list servers,
   c. indirect one-to-one communications: the posting of interactive 'News Bulletins' through relevant news groups and other target media, and
   d. indirect one-to-many communications: the posting of interactive 'News Bulletins' on multiple servers and websites or advertising through the Internet by instruments such as Banners and reciprocal cooperative arrangements by partners.

8. However, in order to take a full advantage of these on-line resources, a firm must realize that their transactions must be adapted to the Internet for on-line engagement and IBTs are capable of handling most, if not all, aspects of their typical transactions.
9. The actual use of the eight flows varies with the type of product, firm and potential customers. It ranged from the low of 4/8 to the high of 8/8 with average use of the eight flows being clearly above 50 per cent.
10. The Internet and e-commerce technologies allowed for an easy transformation of one-to-one communication to one-to-many and many-to-many through the information presented on the website, thus increasing the pace of information dissemination to stimulate internationalization. For further discussion, see note 9, above.

11.  The term 'complementary resource' was used by many respondents to characterize the IBTs and e-commerce processes. We have adopted this term to refer to a potent resource with diverse capabilities that can augment others in achieving ends that would otherwise be difficult or impossible to attain – networking in this case.
12.  This relatedness facilitates their existence in the cluster, allows the younger firm to connect with other firms that can benefit from the young firm's portfolio of goods and services for stimulating their mutual growth. In turn, this connectedness benefits the small firm as well.
13.  Practically all high-technology and knowledge-intensive goods and services have either a very high ratio of value to mass (for products) and value to elapsed time to deliver (for services) or even both when life cycles are dramatically shortened.

# REFERENCES

Anderson, E. and A.T. Coughlan (1987), 'International market entry and expansion via independent or integrated channels of distribution', *Journal of Marketing*, **51**(1), 71–82.
Anderson, G. (1994), 'Industry clustering for economic development', *Economic Development Review*, **12**(2), 26–32.
Argyris, C. and D. Schön (1978), *Organizational Learning: A Theory of Action Perspective*, Reading, MA: Addison-Wesley.
Argyris, C. and D. Schön (1996), *Organizational Learning II: Theory, Method and Practice*, Reading, MA: Addison-Wesley.
Barney, J. (1991), 'Firm resources and competitive advantage', *Journal of Management*, **17**(1), 99–120.
Berthon, P., L. Pitt and R. Watson (1996), 'Marketing communications and the world wide web', *Business Horizons*, **39**(5), 24–31.
Buckley, P.J. and M. Casson (1976), *The Future of the Multinational Enterprise*, London: Holmes and Meier.
Burt, R. (1997), 'The contingent value of social capital', *Administrative Science Quarterly*, **42**(2), 339–65.
Cohen, K.J. and R.M. Cyert (1965), *The Theory of the Firm: Resource Allocation in a Market Economy*, Englewood Cliffs, NJ: Prentice-Hall.
Cohen, W. and D. Levinthal (1990), 'Absorptive capacity: a new perspective on learning and innovation', *Administrative Science Quarterly*, **35**(1), 128–52.
Coleman, S.J. (1988), 'Social capital in creation of human capital', *The American Journal of Sociology*, **94** (Supplement), S95–S120.
Cyert, R.M. and J.G. March (1963), *A Behavioral Theory of the Firm*, Englewood Cliffs, NJ: Prentice-Hall.
Doz, Y.L. (1996), 'The evolution of cooperation in strategic alliances: initial conditions or learning processes?', *Strategic Management Journal*, **17**(Special Issue), 55–83.
Dunning, J.H. (1980), 'Toward an eclectic theory of international production: empirical tests', *Journal of International Business Studies*, **11**(1), 9–31.
Dunning, J.H. (1988), 'The eclectic paradigm of international production: a restatement and some possible extensions', *Journal of International Business Studies*, **19**(1), 1–31.
Dutta, S. and B. Biren (2001), 'Business transformation on the internet: results of the 2000 survey', *European Management Journal*, **19**(5), 449–62.
Dutta, S. and A. Segev (1999), 'Business transformation on the Internet', *European Management Journal*, **17**(5), 466–76.
Dutta, S., S. Kwan and A. Segev (1998), 'Business transformation in electronic commerce: a study of sectoral and regional trends', *European Management Journal*, **16**(5), 540–51.
Eisenhardt, K.M. (1989), 'Building theory from case study research', *Academy of Management Review*, **14**(4), 532–50.
Enright, M.J. (1996), 'Regional clusters and economic development: a research agenda', in U. Staber, N.V. Schaefer and B. Sharma (eds), *Business Networks: Prospects for Regional Development*, Berlin, New York: Walter de Gruyter & Co, pp. 190–213.
Etemad, H. (1999), 'Globalization and small and medium-sized enterprises: search for potent strategies', *Global Focus*, (formerly *Business and Contemporary World*), **11**(3), Summer, 85–105.

Etemad, H. (2003a), 'Managing relations: the essence of international entrepreneurship', in H. Etemad, and R. Wright (eds), *Globalization and Entrepreneurship: Policy and Strategy Perspectives*, Cheltenham, UK and Northampton, MA, USA: Edward Elgar Publishing.

Etemad, H. (2003b), 'Marshalling relations: the enduring essence of international entrepreneurship', in L.P. Dana (ed.), *Handbook of International Entrepreneurship*, Cheltenham, UK and Northampton, MA, USA: Edward Elgar Publishing.

Etemad, H. (2004), 'Internationalization of small and medium-sized enterprises: a grounded theoretical framework and an overview', *Canadian Journal of Administrative Sciences*, 21(1), 1–22.

Evans, N.D. (2002), *Business Agility, Strategies for Gaining Competitive Advantage through Mobile Business Solutions*, Upper Saddle River, US: Prentice-Hall.

Geiger, S. and S. Martin (1999), 'The internet as a relationship marketing tool – some evidence from Irish companies', *Irish Marketing Review*, 12(2), 24–36.

Gomes-Casseres, B. (1996), *The Alliance Revolution: The New Shape of Business Rivalry*, Cambridge, MA: Harvard University Press.

Gomes-Casseres, B. (1997), 'Alliance strategies of small firms', *Small Business Economics*, 9(1), 33–44.

Granovetter, M. (1973), 'The strength of weak ties', *American Journal of Sociology*, 78(6), 1360–80.

Granovetter, M. (1985), 'Economic action and social structure: the problem of embeddedness', *American Journal of Sociology*, 91(3), 481–510.

Grant R.M. (1991), 'The resource-based theory of competitive advantage: implications for strategy formulation', *California Management Review*, 33(3), 114–35.

Grant, R.M. (1996), 'Toward a knowledge-based theory of the firm', *Strategic Management Journal*, 17(Winter Special Issue), 109–22.

Gulati, R. (1995), 'Does familiarity breed trust? The implications of repeated ties for contractual choice in alliances', *Academy of Management Review*, 38(1), 85–112.

Hakansson, H. and I. Snehota (1989), 'No business is an island: the network concept of business strategy', *Scandinavian Journal of Management*, 4(3), 187–200.

Hamill, J. (1997), 'The internet and international marketing', *International Marketing Review*, 14(5), 300–323.

Hamill, J. and K. Gregory (1997), 'Internet marketing in the internationalisation of UK SMEs', *Journal of Marketing Management*, 13(1–3), 9–28.

Johanson, J. and J.-E. Vahlne (1977), 'The internationalization process of the firm – four Swedish case studies', *Journal of Management Studies*, 12(3), 305–22.

Kanter, E.M. (1994), 'Collaborative advantage: the art of alliances', *Harvard Business Review*, 72(4), 96–108.

Katz, M.L. and C. Shapiro (1985), 'Network externalities, competition and compatibility', *The American Economic Review*, 75(3), 424–40.

Katz, M.L. and C. Shapiro (1994), 'Systems competition and network effects', *Journal of Economic Perspectives*, 8(2), 93–115.

Klein, S. (1989), 'A transaction cost explanation of vertical control in international markets', *Journal of the Academy of Marketing Science*, 17(3), 253–60.

Klein, S., G. Frazier and V.J. Roth (1990), 'A transaction cost analysis model of channel integration in international markets', *Journal of Marketing Research*, 27(2), 196–208.

Lituchy, T.R. and A. Rail (1999), 'Bed and breakfasts, small inns and the internet: the impact of technology on the globalization of small businesses', *Journal of International Marketing*, 8(2), 86–97.

Markusen, A. (1996), 'Sticky places in slippery space: a typology of industrial districts', *Economic Geography*, 72(3), 293–313.

Marshall, A. (1949), *Principles of Economics*, London: Macmillan.

Nelson, R.R. and S.G. Winter (1982), *An Evolutionary Theory of Economic Change*, Cambridge, MA: University Press.

Nonaka I. (1994), 'A dynamic theory of organizational knowledge creation', *Organization Science*, 5(1), 14–37.

Nonaka, I. and H. Takeuchi (1995), *The Knowledge-Creating Company*, New York and Oxford: Oxford University Press.

Overby, J.W. and S. Min (2001), 'International supply chain management in an internet environment: a network-oriented approach to internationalization', *International Marketing Review*, **18**(4), 392–420.

Oviatt, B. and P. McDougall (1994), 'Toward a theory of international new ventures', *Journal of International Business Studies*, **25**(1), 45–64.

Oviatt, B. and P. McDougall (1995), 'Global start-ups: entrepreneurs on a worldwide stage', *Academy of Management Executive*, **9**(2), 30–44.

Peterson, R.A., S. Balasubramanian and B.J. Bronnenberg (1997), 'Exploring the implication of the internet for consumers', *Journal of the Academy of Marketing Science*, **25**(4), 329–46.

Quelch, J.A. and L.R. Klein (1996), 'The internet and international marketing', *Sloan Management Review*, **37**(3), 60–76.

Schön, D.A. (1973), *Beyond the Stable State*, Harmondsworth: Penguin.

Teece, D.J., G. Pisano and A. Shuen (1997), 'Dynamic capabilities and strategic management', *Strategic Management Journal*, **18**(7), 509–33.

Wernerfelt, B. (1984), 'A resource-based view of the firm', *Strategic Management Journal*, **5**(2), 171–80.

Wynne, C., P. Berthon, L. Pitt, M. Ewing and J. Napoli (2000), 'The impact of the internet on the distribution value chain: the case of the South African tourism industry', *International Marketing Review*, **18**(4), 420–31.

Yin, R. (1984), *Case Study Research: Design and Methods*, Beverly Hills, CA: Sage.

Yoris, A.A. and R.J. Kaufmann (2001), 'Should we wait? Network externalities, compatibility, and electronic billing adoption', *Journal of Management Information Systems*, **18**(2), 47–63.

Yoshino, M. and V.S. Rangan (1995), *Strategic Alliances: An Entrepreneurial Approach to Globalization*, Boston: Harvard Business School Press.

# 8. Knowledge and capabilities in subcontractors' evolution: the Italian case

**Roberto Grandinetti, Andrea Furlan and Arnaldo Camuffo**

## INTRODUCTION AND THEORETICAL BACKGROUND

The Italian industrial system is known worldwide for its high degree of fragmentation, its organization around geographically coupled supply systems (industrial districts) and the prevalence of small and medium-sized firms, vertically specialized in one or a few phases of a supply chain (Sabel and Piore, 1984; Porter, 1990). Traditionally Italian subcontractors have prospered in such 'protected', semi-closed environments, embedded in well defined geographical clusters. They have relied on a few, main, co-located customers and such 'quasi-captive' demand has usually saturated their production capacity and shaped their capabilities. Furthermore social embeddedness and geographical proximity have facilitated the development of relational contracts, knowledge diffusion and mutual learning between buyers and suppliers. Within this context, subcontractors usually have not grown and have become highly specialized in single production stages.

Challenged by globalization and new technologies, in recent years these production systems have often lost their competitive edge and undergone major structural and strategic changes, partly losing their historical peculiarities (Berger and Locke, 2001; Grandinetti and Bortoluzzi, 2004).

Firstly, increasing competition from producers located in low-cost countries and ever new, more powerful information and communication technologies have reduced the importance of geographical proximity as a competitive advantage factor. Secondly, globalization and the related risks call for financial structures and managerial capabilities not easily accessible and adoptable by district firms, which are mostly undercapitalized, family-owned and family-run businesses.

Finally, while manufacturing, built on a heritage of craftsmanship and skilled labour, has historically been district firms' core competence, marketing and design capabilities have been neglected and are underdeveloped. Now that innovation and internationalization are key success factors, competencies other than manufacturing efficiency and flexibility have become critical.

In the attempt to address at least some of these structural weaknesses, district firms are changing (Camuffo, 2003). On the one hand, the largest firms, usually assemblers/buyers located in the downstream sections of supply chains, have changed sourcing policies, reducing their dependence on their local suppliers' bases, actively seeking low-cost sources in such emerging areas as East Europe and East Asia and establishing direct access to global markets even with autonomous distribution networks. On the other hand, some of the small and medium-sized suppliers have also tried to carve out a new role within global supply chains, diversifying their businesses, moving from subcontracting to direct business, and reducing their level of symbiosis with a few, local main customers.

But only some of these firms have been able to change and adapt. This wide variation in strategies, structures and behaviours derives from the capabilities the subcontractors have been able to develop as well as from the type of buyer–supplier relationships they are into. And, for the reasons briefly described above, they especially need to develop appropriate design and marketing capabilities (Esposito and Raffa, 1994).

In this chapter, we classify Italian subcontractors in terms of their design and marketing capabilities and we investigate how these capabilities coevolve over time. Our theoretical framework follows Olsen and Ellram's (1997) intuition that subcontractors' diversity and evolution are derived from the capabilities they are able to develop as well as from the type of buyer–supplier relationships they are into. Such intuition puts together two different perspectives on suppliers' segmentation and development that draw upon a variety of managerial and economic disciplines. A first perspective takes a static approach and aims to classify suppliers on the basis of variables like industry, size, product/market scope, technology and various performance and relational attributes. Classifying suppliers into types and tiers, among other things, helps customers to prioritize and differentiate supply management practices (Kraljic, 1983; Dyer et al., 1998; Petroni and Panciroli, 2002; Camuffo et al., 2004). A second perspective takes a dynamic approach and aims to identify models of suppliers' evolution, disentangling the factors shaping such transformation and providing directions to guide it (Zanoni, 1992; Esposito and Raffa, 1994; Lamming, 1993; Helper and Kiehl, 2004).

In this chapter we blend these two perspectives by studying the case of Italian subcontractors. Firstly, we apply cluster analysis to a sample of 417 North East Italian subcontractors to explore whether (and to what extent) Italian subcontractors differ and can be classified on the basis of their design and marketing capabilities (next section). Secondly, using this classification as a baseline, we analyse data from ten in-depth subcontractors' case studies, to develop a model of the way subcontractors' capabilities coevolve over time (third section). The fourth section discusses the findings and provides some theoretical and policy implications.

## CLUSTERING ITALIAN SUBCONTRACTORS

### Data and Variables

As part of a broader research project on the evolution of Italian subcontracting relationships conducted in 2003 and 2004, we used an online questionnaire survey to gather a wide array of data regarding, among other aspects, the marketing and design capabilities of subcontractors located in Friuli-Venezia Giulia, in the North East of Italy. The data source is the Regional Centre for Subcontracting of Friuli Venezia Giulia, an agency within the Pordenone Chamber of Commerce. We gathered data on 417 firms, operating in several industries. Even if the subcontractors involved in the research are located only in the Region of Friuli Venezia Giulia, the data set is fairly representative of the Italian subcontracting system as a whole.

Our intent is to provide a segmentation of subcontractors on the basis of their design and marketing capabilities; that is, to identify clusters of subcontractors that share a similar profile as concerns basic marketing and design capabilities. The database includes several variables that can be used to measure subcontractors' design and marketing capabilities. In order to select the variables subjected to cluster analysis we followed the criteria suggested by Chiu et al. (2001). Firstly, we limited the range of measures to only a few and accurate ones. Secondly, we excluded the variables that are strongly correlated.

**Construct 1: Marketing Capabilities**

Marketing capabilities relate to the ability of the subcontractor to monitor the market, to seek and identify new opportunities and market niches, to develop interactive relationships with its customers and to adopt customer relationship management (CRM) practices. The last two types of capabilities are often indicated as 'relational capabilities' in the industrial marketing literature (Hakansson and Snehota, 1995). This literature maintains that marketing capabilities positively affect the subcontractor's ability (a) to diversify its customers' portfolio; and (b) to internationalize its sales. Thus we use the degree of diversification of the customers' portfolio and the degree of internationalization of revenues as proxies for marketing capabilities. More specifically, we use two variables to capture subcontractors' marketing capabilities (MC): the degree of diversification of the customers' portfolio (CPD) and the degree of internationalization of the subcontractor's sales (SI). We use the number of customers served by each subcontractor during the last fiscal year (the data set provides the following ranges of customers: 1–2; 3–5; 6–9; 10–19; 20–49; >50) as the measure for the first variable. We use only the unweighed number of customers rather than the proportion of the main customers on the subcontractors' total sales, for two reasons. Firstly, at the early stages of evolution, subcontractors typically have a few customers, each accounting for a high proportion of total sales (for example, in the cases of spin-offs, subcontractors have only one customer, the originating firm). As subcontractors evolve, the number of customers increases and the proportion of each customer's sales to subcontractors' total sales usually decreases. Secondly, since each customer represents a source of knowledge regardless of the proportion of its sales to subcontractors' total sales, the larger the number of customers the more opportunities for subcontractors to learn (Hakansson and Snehota, 1995). We use the percentage of export sales on total revenues as the measure for the second variable.

**Construct 2: Design Capabilities**

Design capabilities (DC) relate to the ability to develop autonomously products/services that meet the client's requirements. The use of computer-aided design (CAD) systems to design new products is our measure of subcontractors' design capabilities. We choose this measure for reasons strictly connected to the peculiarities of the Italian subcontracting system. Firstly, other measures of design capabilities suggested by the literature, such as the presence of appropriate product development systems (Liu and White, 1997; Wynstra et al., 1999; Petroni and Panciroli, 2002) do not seem appropriate in the case of small and medium-sized businesses like those included in the analysed sample (35 per cent of the firms has fewer than ten employees and 88.5 per cent of the firms has fewer than 50 employees).

Secondly, the implementation of CAD systems seems to be a clear and unequivocal signal of the presence, in the subcontractor's organization, of specific design capabilities. Interestingly we observe that (a) of 173 subcontractors that claim to have autonomous design capabilities, 162 (94 per cent) have implemented a CAD system; (b) of 244 subcontractors that claim to have no autonomous DC, 14 subcontractors (6 per cent) have implemented a CAD system. Given the fact that firms that claim to have or not have autonomous DC may have overestimated or underestimated their DC, we considered the adoption of CAD as a more conservative and accurate measure of autonomous DC.

## CLUSTER ANALYSIS

Cluster analysis techniques have already been used to analyse supplier relations (Bensaou and Venkatraman, 1995). Using SPSS, we apply two-step cluster analysis, based on the aggregation algorithm proposed by Chiu et al. (2001), to our data (the three variables, CPD, SI, DC, used as measures for the two constructs defining subcontractors' design and marketing capabilities). We choose this procedure because: (a) it allows dealing with variables that have a different nature (in our case CPD is an ordinal variable, SI is a continuous variable and DC is a dichotomous variable); (b) it provides an effective and efficient way for identifying outliers (Chiu et al., 2001).

The two-step procedure proposes the number of clusters on the basis of a subprocedure that uses the Bayes Information Criterion and the variation of the distance between the clusters (Ketchen and Shook, 1996). The procedure uses a distance measure based on the log-likelihood function to assign each firm to its cluster. It automatically excludes 33 firms (7.9 per cent of the sample) as outliers that cannot be aggregated to any of the clusters. Table 8.1 provides a summary of the sample characteristics by industry and size.

Applying this procedure to our data we identify four clusters (Table 8.2 summarizes the profile of each cluster):

A-type subcontractors: *developed subcontractors* (n = 93, 24.2 per cent of the sample). They show the highest percentage of exports in total sales (23.7 per cent) with a diversified customers' portfolio (all the firms have more than 50 customers). Almost all subcontractors (94 per cent) adopt a CAD system.
B-type subcontractors: *developing subcontractors* (n =77, 20.1 per cent of the sample). They have a lower propensity to export than developed subcontractors (12.2 per cent is the average percentage of export in total sales) and a less diversified customers' portfolio (the customer range with the highest frequency is 20–49, with almost 55 per cent of the subcontractors). However all the developing subcontractors have adopted a CAD system.
C-type subcontractors: *question mark subcontractors* (n=123, 32 per cent of the sample). These subcontractors do not have autonomous design capabilities (none of them uses a CAD system), present a low propensity to export (6.7 per cent is the average percentage of exports in total sales) but show a certain degree of diversification of the customer portfolio (approximately 39 per cent of the subcontractors fall into the 20–49 customer range).

*Table 8.1    The sample composition*

| Industry | Subcontractor size (number of employees) | | | | | |
|---|---|---|---|---|---|---|
| | 1–9 | 10–19 | 20–49 | 50–99 | >100 | Total |
| Electronics | 6 | 4 | 4 | 1 | 2 | 17 |
| | % 35.3 | 23.5 | 23.5 | 5.9 | 11.8 | 100 |
| Mechanics | 68 | 56 | 49 | 16 | 10 | 199 |
| | % 34.2 | 28.1 | 24.6 | 8.0 | 5.0 | 100 |
| Rubber & Plastics | 13 | 9 | 10 | 1 | 4 | 37 |
| | % 35.1 | 24.3 | 27.1 | 2.7 | 10.8 | 100 |
| Furniture | 33 | 42 | 25 | 5 | 3 | 108 |
| | % 30.6 | 38.9 | 23.1 | 4.6 | 2.8 | 100 |
| Apparel | 15 | 4 | 0 | 1 | 0 | 20 |
| | % 75.0 | 20.0 | 0.0 | 5.0 | 0.0 | 100 |
| Textiles | 5 | 3 | 3 | 1 | 1 | 13 |
| | % 38.4 | 23.1 | 23.1 | 7.7 | 7.7 | 100 |
| Total | 140 | 118 | 91 | 25 | 20 | 394 |
| | % 35.5 | 29.9 | 23.1 | 6.4 | 5.1 | 100 |

*Table 8.2    Cluster analysis summary*

| Clusters | % export on total sales (SI) | Number of customers (CPD) (mode and %) | CAD system (DC) (%) |
|---|---|---|---|
| A (n=93) | 23.7 | 50 or more (100) | Yes (94.9) |
| B (n=77) | 12.2 | 20–49 (54.7) | Yes (100) |
| C (n=123) | 6.7 | 20–49 (38.9) | No (100) |
| D (n=91) | 6.0 | 1–9 (40.7) | No (100) |

D-type subcontractors: *traditional subcontractors* (n=91, 23.7 per cent of the sample). They have a low propensity to export (6 per cent is the average percentage of export on total sales), a limited customer portfolio (40.9 per cent of the subcontractors have from one to nine customers) and no design capabilities (no subcontractors employ a CAD system).

In order to provide a crisper characterization of the clusters, we also calculated, for each of them, further descriptive statistics on other variables (that is, subcontractors' characteristics) of related interest. These variables and data, presented in Table 8.3, also come from the online questionnaire survey. They confirm the results of the cluster analysis, providing further evidence that the more developed the subcontractor is, the more valuable its relational and technological capital is.

First of all, the first two types of subcontractors are, on average, larger than the others. This seems to suggest that there are some scale effects involved due either to technological indivisibilities and threshold effects in marketing or, alternatively, to complementarities among these activities. Moreover, the average proportion of sales coming from exclusive, customer-dedicated shop floor activities to total sales is smaller for developed and developing subcontractors. The presence of exclusive, customer-dedicated shop floor activities is

*Table 8.3   Clusters' profiles*

| Clusters | Modal size (%) | % sales from shop floor activities | APT (%) | Patents | Proprietary technology | Certified quality |
|---|---|---|---|---|---|---|
| Developed subcontractors | 20–49 (36) | 26 | 30 (32) | 14 (15%) | 36 (39%) | 31 (33%) |
| Developing subcontractors | 20–49 (26) | 36 | 23 (30) | 10 (13%) | 22 (29%) | 24 (31%) |
| Question mark subcontractors | 10–19 (41) | 47 | 20 (16) | 5 (4%) | 16 (13%) | 17 (13%) |
| Traditional subcontractors | 1–9 (39) | 51 | 10 (11) | 5 (5%) | 15 (16%) | 7 (8%) |

a typical feature of the traditional subcontracting relationship, with subcontractors treated as mere 'external' capacity, as a buffer against demand fluctuations, as a pure contractual extension of the customer manufacturing activities. Conversely the use of advanced production technologies (APT) such as flexible automation is significantly higher for developed and developing subcontractors than for traditional and question mark subcontractors. Other variables, such as the ownership of patents and proprietary technologies, as well as quality certification, confirm the presence of significant differences among the four clusters, and suggest that developed and developing subcontractors possess a wider set of capabilities.

Summarizing, we identify four types of subcontractors which are diverse in terms of marketing and design capability endowment. The following step is to investigate whether there is any dynamic relationship between design and marketing capabilities that would help explain subcontractors' evolution and, more specifically, the transition from one type to another. The following section addresses this research question and proposes a model of subcontractors' evolution.

## ITALIAN SUBCONTRACTORS' EVOLUTION: AN EXPLORATORY STUDY

### Methodology and Data Collection

Using our cluster analysis as a starting point, we also want to assess some of the dynamics in Italian supply systems, exploring a typical evolutionary pattern for subcontractors. Thus we conducted ten in-depth case studies of subcontractors selected among those included in the sample used in the cluster analysis. As usual in case study research (Yin, 1984; Eisenhardt, 1989), we did not choose the research sample randomly but theoretically. We picked subcontractors belonging to different industries and different clusters (seven developed subcontractors, two developing subcontractors and one question mark subcontractor).

As suggested by Ellram (1996) and Voss et al. (2002), we collected information through semi-structured interviews, guided by a common case study protocol purposely designed after reviewing the relevant literature, and based on discussions with several top managers

*Table 8.4   The case studies*

| Stage of evolution | Funded | Industry | Sales (million €) | Emp. | CAD | No. cust. | % of export | Advanced production technologies (APT) |
|---|---|---|---|---|---|---|---|---|
| Developed | 1979 | Furniture | 4.994 | 150 | Yes | >100 | 20 | Automated handling (AH), FMS, CNC, CAM |
| Question mark | 1956 | Furniture | 7.105 | 88 | No | >150 | 5 | FMS, automated handling, CNC |
| Developed | 1972 | Mec. | 40.762 | 351 | Yes | 20 | 70 | FMS, EDI, ERP |
| Developed | 1990 | Mec. | 4.573 | 50 | Yes | >200 | 10 | FMS, CNC, CAM |
| Developed | 1978 | Mec. | 2.861 | 80 | Yes | 300 | 75 | EDI, AH, FMS, DNC, CAM |
| Developed | 1985 | Mec. | 4.132 | 37 | Yes | >100 | 15 | EDI, AH, FMS, CNC, CAM |
| Developed | 1952 | Mec. | 4 | 35 | Yes | >500 | 50 | EDI, CNC |
| Developing | 1980 | Plastics | 1.70 | 40 | Yes | 100 | 5 | EDI, CAM, Robots, Moldflow |
| Developed | 1950 | Rubber | 19.192 | 440 | Yes | >100 | 55 | FMS, CNC, CAM |
| Developed | 1969 | Plastics | 44.802 | 130 | Yes | >50 | 25 | FMS, CNC, CAM |

*Notes:*
AH – Automated Handling.
CAM – Computer-aided Manufacturing.
CNC – Computer Numerically Controlled.
EDI – Electronic Data Interchange.
ERP – Enterprise Resource Planning.
FMS – Flexible Manufacturing Systems.

of subcontracting firms. For each case study, we interviewed the CEO and top managers of the firm. The interviews focused on the evolution process of each subcontractor (from foundation/inception to present time). In all, we interviewed 18 persons, with each interview lasting approximately two hours. The interviews were taped and transcribed. The transcripts were then used for the subsequent within-case and cross-case analysis. Table 8.4 reports some key data about the ten analysed subcontractors.

Our research protocol is divided into three sections. The first section addresses the evolution process of the subcontractors from the point of view of their design and marketing

*Table 8.5    Examples of questions of the research protocol*

| Section | Questions |
|---|---|
| Section one: subcontractors' capabilities evolution | How have your design and marketing functions evolved over time (i.e., organizational structure, equipment used, people employed)? How have your customers changed over time (i.e., their number, identity, location)? |
| | How have the relationships with your main customers evolved over time (e.g., adoption of co-development/CRM/JIT practices)? |
| | When did you introduce a CAD system? When did you start to use the CAD for designing new products? |
| | Since your foundation, have you developed any patent? |
| | Are there any other capabilities (beyond design and marketing capabilities) that have been relevant for the evolution of your firm? |
| Section two: the drivers of the evolution | What are the reasons (i.e., external or internal factors) that have triggered the evolution of the capabilities identified in the previous section? |
| | What led you to develop the capabilities identified in the previous section? |
| Section three: the investments for the evolution | What investment in tangible, intangible and organizational resources have you made to face the challenges identified in the previous section? |
| | What are the investments in tangible, intangible and organizational resources that have supported the evolution of your capabilities? |
| | Does the evolution of the capabilities affect such investments? |

capabilities (given the sampling procedure, we were sure that each of the subcontractors had already undergone a partial or total evolution process from the standpoint of these two capabilities). This part of the research protocol contains specific questions related to explicit research constructs (design and marketing capabilities). However the section also includes a more general question aimed at investigating whether there are other unspecified capabilities involved in the evolution of subcontractors (see Table 8.5).

The second section investigates what triggers the evolution of the capabilities with questions analysing both external and internal factors. The third section analyses what investments subcontractors undertake to face the challenges identified in the previous section. We adopt a broad definition of investment, as any effort of the firm to increase its tangible, intangible and organizational resources. Table 8.5 provides examples of questions for each section of the research protocol.

**A model of subcontracting evolution**
From the cross-analysis of the case studies and after a series of iterative cycles of data gathering (Westbrook, 1995) we build an interpretative framework (Figure 8.1) that explains subcontractors' evolution (owing to space constraints, we do not report the

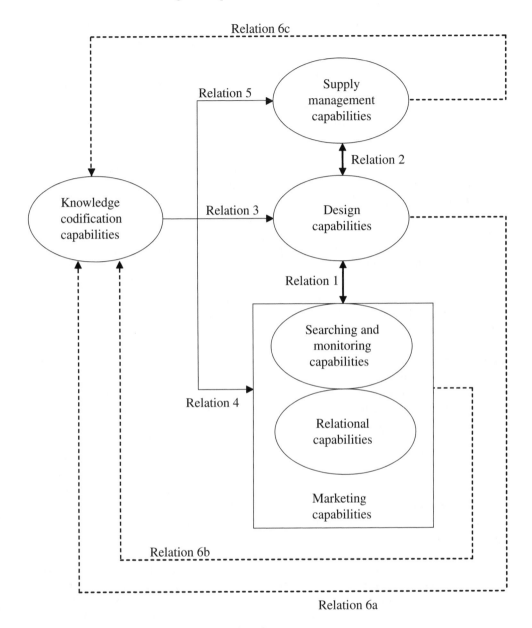

*Figure 8.1   A model of subcontractors' evolution*

longitudinal within-case analysis of each of the subcontractors). This framework was developed using the information gathered during the interviews.

   Firstly, the answers to the questions of the first section of the interview confirm that design and marketing capabilities (the first two research constructs of the framework) are crucial for the evolution of the subcontractor. Moreover the analysis highlights that there is a bidirectional dynamic relationship between design capabilities and marketing capabilities (relation 1). On the one hand, it emerges that better design capabilities improve the subcontractor's ability to approach the market proactively and represent the prerequisite for buyer–supplier codevelopment practices. For example, several interviewees point out that shorter development times and lower design costs widen subcontractors' market potential, allowing them to reach more prospective customers, thus abandoning the local approach that typically characterizes traditional subcontractors. On the other hand, the development of marketing capabilities grants access to technological knowledge from customers (Dyer and Singh, 1998), thus enhancing the subcontractor's design capabilities. For example, one of the interviewees claims that fulfilling customers' requirements in terms of quality, safety and legal standards enriches the subcontractor's ability to develop autonomously products/services that meet the requirements of other potential customers.

The thematic analysis of the answers to the last question of the first section of the interview leads us to identify the third research construct of the framework corresponding to a different kind of capability: supply management, that is, the ability (a) to design the upstream supply chain, (b) to select suppliers with the required capabilities, and (c) to develop satisfactory supply relationships (in terms of purchased goods costs and quality, service level, delivery lead times and flexibility) (Fine, 1998). Several interviewees claim that supply management capabilities are important in the subcontractors' evolution because they positively affect their design capabilities. For example, engaging in collaborative practices with suppliers (for example, co-development, target costing, residential engineers) facilitates the acquisition and development of technological knowledge that enhances the ability to develop new and more suitable products. Moreover interviews show that, as subcontractors improve their design capabilities, they also refine their ability to allocate design tasks efficiently within and outside their organizational boundaries. From this evidence, we infer that a bidirectional dynamic relation exists between supply management and design capabilities (relation 2).

The answers to the second section of the interview highlight that one reason why subcontractors evolve is the need and the willingness to avoid the risk and reduce the dependence on their current position in the environment. For example, some subcontractors maintain that they started to change when they fully recognized the risk of relying on a few local customers facing ever stronger global competition. Others claim that the transformation process was initially aimed at reducing their technological dependence on their main customers.

As for the third section of the interview, the interviewees provide several examples of different kinds of investments in tangible, intangible and organizational resources. Some managers suggest that investments in marketing information systems allow them to better track the relationships with main customers, thus supporting the adoption of CRM practices. Others maintain that the introduction of an Enterprise Resource Planning (ERP) grounded the improvement of the operations coordination with suppliers. Others claim that the development of technical archives improved the performance of their design activities. Despite their differences, these investments have the common nature of concerning people and technologies needed to develop written tools such as manuals, blueprints, procedures, spreadsheets, decision support teams and software. As a matter of fact, these investments underlie the ability to codify a firm's understandings of the performance implications of internal routines. Following Zollo and Winter (2002),[1] we call these capabilities 'knowledge codification capabilities' (the fourth research construct of our framework). Indeed all the interviews confirm that the main driver of subcontractors' evolution is the codification of at least part of their tacit technical and commercial knowledge. These codification capabilities are a sort of meta-capability in that they support the evolution of all the other capabilities involved in our framework. In other words, it is knowledge codification that drives subcontractors' evolution from less developed stages (D and C subcontractor types in our cluster analysis) to more developed ones (B and A subcontractor types in our cluster analysis). Knowledge codification widens subcontractors' relational capabilities because they permit them to 'establish conversations' with non-local actors. Also it allows developing self-awareness about the knowledge, routines and relationships the firm has. This, in turn, makes such capital replicable or, at least applicable to different business situations at negligible costs; and it prevents its underutilization. Finally, being able to codify knowledge represents a necessary condition to structure an autonomous R&D function and introduce Total Quality Management (TQM) and quality certification (Bénézech et al., 2001).

The interviews clearly show a tight relationship between knowledge codification capabilities and the other capabilities of the framework.[2] Firstly, knowledge codification capabilities constitute the ground on which design capabilities are developed (relation 3). For example, one manager argues that the possibility of retrieving drawings or design elements from electronic archives facilitates autonomous new product development, shortening lead times and reducing design costs. Secondly, being able to codify knowledge means being able to set up marketing information systems which support market searching and monitoring capabilities and facilitate the establishment of non-passive relationships with key customers (relation 4). For example, several subcontractors maintain that such cross-firm activities as root cause problem solving, just in time delivery, target costing pricing and total quality management require the adoption of standard interfaces of communication between the parties. Finally, knowledge codification capabilities have a positive impact on supply management capabilities (relation 5). For example, one of the interviewees said that the possibility of acquiring and systematically updating market data on the cost of raw materials and components supports such processes as vendor rating and suppliers' development.

As for the evolution of knowledge codification capabilities, interviews suggest that they are exogenous to the model. Our cross-case analysis shows that investments in knowledge codification capabilities are usually caused by organizational and managerial discontinuities (such as managerial turnover, strategies breakthrough, entrepreneurial succession, financial crisis, change in governance or stakeholders, and new requirements of the main customers).[3] For example, in one case of a subcontractor operating in high precision mechanics, the introduction of an ERP system was compelled by Magneti Marelli and Bosch, the two largest customers of the firm. In another case, a subcontractor of electrical components for photocopying machines introduced ISO 9001 standards when the son of the founder took over the firm. These managerial and organizational discontinuities remove the hurdles, typical of small family-owned businesses, which obstruct the processes of formalization, the structuring of the organization into specialized functions, and the delegation of authority that are associated with knowledge codification processes.

However some interviews highlight that there can be some feedback relationships between design, marketing and supply management capabilities and knowledge codification capabilities (relations 6a, 6b and 6c). For example, the adoption of reporting software in sales (knowledge codification) allowed the salesforce to update the marketing information system daily, thus enhancing marketing capabilities of the firm. After the introduction of the software, the salesforce suggested several modifications of the software to make it more suitable to the specificities of the customers (for example, a new record for the customers' operations layouts). In other cases, the introduction of CAD reinforced knowledge codification through the software with which it is associated. These feedback relations, however, seem to have a different nature from the other causal relations of the model, in that they have to be accompanied by other factors (such as the actual willingness to reinforce knowledge codification capabilities) in order to produce their effects. In the previous example, the salesmen's suggestions did not produce any modifications of the software because top management considered them too expensive from an organizational standpoint. Because of this different nature, we represented these feedback relations graphically by dashed arrows in Figure 8.1.

## DISCUSSION AND CONCLUSION

Our empirical analysis leads to two main results. Firstly, it provides a classification of Italian subcontractors on the basis of their design and marketing capabilities. Secondly, it proposes a model to understand and predict subcontractors' evolution. From these findings we can derive some important theoretical, managerial and policy implications.

As for the first point, our cluster analysis supports theory predictions and confirms our understanding of the Italian context: subcontractors differ in terms of design and marketing capabilities, and they can be meaningfully classified accordingly. As for the second point, a cross-case analysis of ten case studies allowed us to build a theoretical framework to explain subcontractors' evolution. The framework defines the capabilities subcontractors need to develop and how these capabilities should interact in order to allow the transition from less to more developed evolutionary stages. More specifically, our framework identifies knowledge codification as the fundamental capability that drives subcontractors' evolution. This capability supports three other capabilities, those of supply management, design and marketing. These characterize subcontractors' transformation, reinforce one another and need to align over time. On the whole, our findings are consistent with the resource-based view of the firm, and suggest that longitudinal case studies help to understand firms' dynamics (Teece et al., 1997; Lorenzoni and Lipparini, 1999) and processes of new knowledge creation (Kotabe et al., 2003). Furthermore supply management capabilities surprisingly emerge as core subcontractors' capabilities. The ability to manage supply networks is crucial not only for leading firms in clusters (such as assemblers or product designers) (Lorenzoni and Baden-Fuller, 1995; Lorenzoni and Lipparini, 1999), but also, although from a different perspective, for subcontractors. In fact, many of the developed (A-type) subcontractors do outsource relevant activities to second-tier suppliers and manage a supply network of numerous suppliers at different levels. These subcontractors leverage on the complementary knowledge (Roper and Crone, 2003) of assemblers or upper-tier suppliers and coordinate supply chains where knowledge is fragmented over a variety of actors.

Knowledge codification capabilities constitute a sort of logical antecedent and organizational prerequisite of subcontractors' evolution. They contribute to the creation of new knowledge in the form of new design, marketing and supply management capabilities. They also foster the creation of new knowledge since they enhance within-organization knowledge sharing (Un and Cuervo-Cazurra, 2004), promote new communication protocols and organizational routines, and contribute to creating a common knowledge base (Arrow, 1974; Grant, 1996) that makes it possible for individuals to understand each other. From this standpoint our study supports the view that knowledge codification is intimately related to the concept of dynamic capabilities in that it is a deliberate process of learning and one of the mechanisms involved in the creation and evolution of dynamic capabilities (Zollo and Winter, 2002).

Finally our evolutionary model has policy implications, too. Firstly, government agencies and business associations can act as facilitators of subcontractors' knowledge codification. For example, training programmes that specifically support ISO 9000 certification are welcome, since these standards represent a code (that is, common language) that might be used within firms to enhance knowledge codification (Bénézech et al., 2001). Secondly, public institutions should focus their policies on the upstream (subcontractors) stages of supply chains, rather than, as they often do, on downstream stages. Policies aimed at the improvement of design and marketing capabilities of upstream suppliers would be more effective and innovative than the support usually given to downstream firms (for example, consortia aimed at creating 'industrial district' brands). Indeed, these programmes may improve firm performance in the short term but, according to our model, they do not sustain long-term competitiveness as they do not create the conditions for effective knowledge codification.

Beyond its implications, this study can also be useful in generating further conceptual and empirical research. Firstly, future research may refine subcontractors' classification, articulating the four clusters we identified. Secondly, our framework for subcontractors' evolution should be tested on large-scale databases through quantitative research. Thirdly, more accurate measures of subcontractors' capabilities should be conceived and tested. Finally, given that knowledge codification is a sort of fundamental dynamic capability, it is worth conducting more in-depth research about how this capability originates.

## NOTES

1.  The nature of knowledge codification and its relationships with the concept of dynamic capability is still somewhat problematic (Dosi, Nelson and Winter, 2000). Following Eisenhardt and Martin (2000) and Zollo and Winter (2002), we assume an intimate relationship between the two.
2.  From our data it is impossible to establish a general chronological sequence of relationships between knowledge codification capabilities and the other three. As a matter of fact, some investments in knowledge codification capabilities have initially affected marketing capabilities, other design capabilities and other supply management capabilities (see the examples in the text). We also have cases in which an investment in knowledge codification capabilities has simultaneously affected all three of the other capabilities. For example, the introduction of an ERP or the ISO 9001 standards (that are examples of knowledge codification capabilities because they entail codification of a firm's understanding of the performance implications of internal routines in written tools such as manuals, blueprints, procedures, spreadsheets, decision support systems and software) can provide learning effects that affect all the capabilities of the firm (Bénézech et al., 2001).
3.  Conceivably, subcontractor size can be the driver of knowledge codification capabilities. However our analysis suggests that size is more an effect than a cause of capabilities' evolution. In other words, growth can be seen as a performance dimension of the capabilities' evolution. Since our model does not address performance effects of capabilities' evolution we do not address specifically the issue of growth in the present

chapter. However the fact that size is an effect and not a cause of the capabilities' evolution is likely to be related to the specificity of the Italian industrial context. In fact, size is seldom taken as a strategic objective by small Italian firms. Instead, subcontractors focus on different performance dimensions such as improving their products or acquiring new customers. If their strategies are successful the growth is just a consequence.

# REFERENCES

Arrow, K. (1974), *The Limits of Organization*, New York: Norton.

Bénézech D., G. Lambert, B. Lanoux, C. Lerch and J. Loss-Baroin (2001), 'Completion of knowledge codification: an illustration through the ISO 9000 standards implementation process', *Research Policy*, **30**(9), 1395–407.

Bensaou, M. and N. Venkatraman (1995), 'Configurations of interorganizational relationships: a comparison between U.S. and Japanese automakers', *Management Science*, **41**(9), 1471–92.

Berger, S. and R.M. Locke (2001), 'Il caso Italiano and globalization', *Daedalus*, **130**(3), 85–104.

Camuffo, A. (2003), 'Transforming industrial districts: large firms and small business networks in the Italian eyewear industry', *Industry and Innovation*, **10**(4), 377–401.

Camuffo, A., A. Furlan and P. Romano (2004), 'Customer–supplier integration forms. Insights from the Italian air conditioning industry', in L.N.V. Wassenhove, A. De Meyer, E. Yücesan, E.D. Günes and L. Muyldermans (eds), *Operations Management as a Change Agent*, vol. II, Conference Proceedings EUROMA, Fontainebleau: INSEAD, pp. 103–12.

Chiu, T., D. Fang, J. Chen, Y. Wang and C. Jeris (2001), 'A robust and scalable clustering algorithm for mixed type attributes in large database environment', Proceedings of the 7th ACM SIKDD International Conference on Knowledge Discovery and Data Mining, pp. 263–8.

Dosi, G., R. Nelson and S. Winter (eds) (2000), *The Nature and Dynamics of Organizational Capabilities*, New York: Oxford University Press.

Dyer, J.H. and H. Singh (1998), 'The relational view: cooperative strategy and sources of interorganizational competitive advantage', *Academy of Management Review*, **23**(4), 660–79.

Dyer, J.H., D.S. Cho and W. Chu (1998), 'Strategic supplier segmentation: the next "best practice" in supply chain management', *California Management Review*, **40**(2), 57–77.

Eisenhardt, K.M. (1989), 'Building theories from case study research', *Academy of Management Review*, **14**(4), 532–50.

Eisenhardt, K.M. and J.A. Martin (2000), 'Dynamic capabilities: what are they?', *Strategic Management Journal*, **21**(10–11), 1105–21.

Ellram, L.M. (1996), 'An application of the case study method in logistics research', *Journal of Business Logistics*, **17**(2), 93–138.

Esposito, E. and M. Raffa (1994), 'L'evoluzione del sistema della subfornitura nell'industria italiana', *Economia & Management*, **4**, 11–29.

Fine, C. (1998), *ClockSpeed. Winning Industry Control in the Age of Temporary Advantage*, Boston: Perseus Books.

Grandinetti, R. and G. Bortoluzzi (2004), *L'evoluzione delle imprese e dei sistemi di subfornitura*, Milan: Franco Angeli.

Grant, R. (1996), 'Toward a knowledge-based theory of the firm', *Strategic Management Journal*, **16**(7), 519–33.

Hakansson, H. and I. Snehota (eds) (1995), *Developing Relations in Business Networks*, London: Routledge.

Helper, S. and J. Kiehl (2004), 'Developing supplier capabilities: market and non-market approaches', *Industry & Innovation*, **11**(1/2), 89–107.

Ketchen, D. and C.L. Shook (1996), 'The application of cluster analysis in strategic management research: an analysis and critique', *Strategic Management Journal*, **17**(6), 441–58.

Kotabe, M., X. Martin and H. Domoto (2003), 'Gaining from vertical partnerships: knowledge transfer, relationship duration, and supplier performance improvement in the U.S. and Japanese automotive industries', *Strategic Management Journal*, **24**(4), 293–316.

Kraljic, P. (1983), 'Purchasing must become supply management', *Harvard Business Review*, September/October, 109–17.

Lamming, R. (1993), *Beyond Partnership*, London: Prentice-Hall.

Liu, X.R. and S. White (1997), 'The relative contribution of foreign technology and domestic inputs to innovation in Chinese manufacturing industries', *Technovation*, **17**(3), 119–25.

Lorenzoni, G. and C. Baden-Fuller (1995), 'Creating a strategic center to manage a web of partners', *California Management Review*, **37**(3), 146–63.

Lorenzoni, G. and A. Lipparini (1999), 'The leveraging of interfirm relationships as a distinctive organizational capability: a longitudinal study', *Strategic Management Journal*, **20**(4), 317–38.

Olsen, R.F. and L.M. Ellram (1997), 'Buyer–supplier relationships: alternative research approaches', *European Journal of Purchasing and Supply Management*, **3**(4), 221–32.

Petroni, A. and B. Panciroli (2002), 'Innovation as a determinant of suppliers' roles and performances: an empirical study in the food machinery industry', *European Journal of Purchasing and Supply Management*, **8**(2), 135–49.

Porter, M. (1990), *The Competitive Advantage of Nations*, New York: The Free Press.

Roper, S. and M. Crone (2003), 'Knowledge complementarity and coordination in the local supply chain: some empirical evidence', *British Journal of Management*, **14**(4), 339–55.

Sabel, C.M. and M. Piore (1984), *The Second Industrial Divide. Possibilities for Prosperity*, New York: Basic Books.

Teece, D.J., G. Pisano and A. Shuen (1997), 'Dynamic capabilities and strategic management', *Strategic Management Journal*, **8**(7), 509–33.

Un, C.A. and A. Cuervo-Cazurra (2004), 'Strategies for knowledge creation in firms', *British Journal of Management*, **15**(1), 27–41.

Voss, C., N. Tsikriktsis and M. Frohlich (2002), 'Case research in operations management', *International Journal of Operations & Production Management*, **22**(2), 195–219.

Westbrook, R. (1995), 'Action research: a new paradigm for research in production and operations management', *International Journal of Operations & Production Management*, **15**(12), 6–20.

Wynstra, F., A. van Weele and B. Axelsson (1999), 'Purchasing involvement in product development: a framework', *European Journal of Purchasing & Supply Management*, **5**(3–4), 129–41.

Yin, R. (1984), *Case Study Research*, Beverly Hills: Sage Publications.

Zanoni, A. (1992), 'La gestione strategica degli approvvigionamenti', in R. Filippini (ed.), *Progettare e gestire l'impresa innovativa*, Milan: Etas.

Zollo M. and S.J. Winter (2002), 'Deliberate learning and the evolution of dynamic capabilities', *Organization Science*, 13(3), 339–51.

# 9. The communication of corporate social responsibility (CSR) through the supply chain: an SME perspective

**Craig H. Wood and Allen Kaufman**

## INTRODUCTION

The increasing use of strategic supply chain alliances provides a potentially rich and growing communication link between suppliers and customers about how they should conduct their economic, social and environmental relations. These communications can be either intended or unintended and may be expected as part of day-to-day practical inter-actions between suppliers and customers. Intended communications include performance expectations in quality level and consistency, pricing, delivery time and demand forecasts from the customer upstream to suppliers, and technical data about component improvements and new technologies from suppliers downstream to customers. Unintended communications may include transfer of sensitive proprietary information and indications of operating problems. We postulate that many of these communications include topics about the role of business in society, which has commonly come to be known as corporate citizenship or corporate social responsibility (CSR). But, far from being accepted, the fundamental contents of these issues are constantly being debated on both the academic and the practitioner stage. And placing them in a supply chain context potentially adds several more layers of disagreement and debate (New and Westbrook, 2004, p. v). As New (2004b) points out, the subject of ethics and social responsibility in the supply chain 'remains . . . one of heated controversy, and is the subject of a vast and incoherent literature' (p. 253). We set out here to clarify the concepts and issues that define corporate social responsibility and propose an agenda for the further study of the communication of CSR principles and practices through the supply chain as a first step toward coherence.

In a market economy, corporations provide the most effective vehicle for generating new wealth and for sustaining communities. Although much attention has been given to how and why corporations voluntarily link their futures to the community and environment in which they operate, little research exists on how corporations may require or encourage one another to develop these environmental, community and social capabilities through their supply chain relations, even in the context of the partnership or relational contracting form. Because supply chains play an important, if not leading, role in global economic activity (Dyer and Chu, 2003), the influence of this communication network needs to be better understood.

CSR is an umbrella term for a wide-ranging collection of social issues of concern to the firm's stakeholders (Smith, 2003). Although CSR is generally defined as consisting of voluntary actions by businesses (European Commission, 2001, p. 5), formal legal and regulatory requirements to fulfil some obligations are mandated by governments for businesses operating within their borders and, in some cases, apply anywhere those businesses operate globally (for example, the US Foreign Corrupt Practices Act). Both voluntary and mandated CSR practices can be further classified as either internal to the firm or external to outside stakeholders (Welford, 2004; European Commission, 2001). Geographically, the importance of CSR appears to have advanced through different global regions at varying rates over the past decade (Habisch et al., 2005).

The role of different stakeholders in pressuring the firm to adopt various CSR practices provides the basis for understanding what types of topics are important at different times (Jawahar and McLaughlin, 2001). These can be categorized into two broad generic motivations for firms to communicate CSR topics: the carrot and the stick. The 'carrot' comes in the form of reward or recognition for performing 'good deeds'. Community groups, employees and both governmental agencies and nongovernmental organizations often recognize the voluntary actions of businesses. This contributes to a favourable reputation for firms that are recognized as practising good corporate citizenship (Smith, 2003; Roberts et al., 2002). Particularly for consumer products companies, this can be worth thousands of dollars in free, favourable publicity. The 'stick' can be found in the expectations of stakeholders about how their company's actions match their own image of an organization they can feel proud of, want to be associated with and want to do business with. In addition, demonstrating positive CSR can forestall or prevent the imposition of mandatory governmental requirements. A good example of this is self-regulation by the US movie industry of objectionable content in its films, which has allowed the industry to avoid direct government regulation to this day. Another valuable use of positive CSR is as 'insurance against negative events that would otherwise harm financial performance' (Peloza, 2006). In sum, there is a great deal of study required to understand how and why which CSR principles and practices may be disseminated through the supply chain.

We first describe the process that led to our interest in this research, then describe some of the national and regional differences in the meaning of CSR and give examples of how it is communicated in the supply chain context; next, we present a framework for defining CSR in a global environment, and finish with a series of questions for future research.

## HISTORICAL DEVELOPMENT OF RESEARCH

To better understand the origin of the current study and future direction we are pursuing, some background detail must be provided. As members of a group of academics at the University of New Hampshire representing a variety of specialized management fields, we started in 1991 to study how firms learn to develop and maintain competitive advantage by working with their customers and suppliers. Our first project was to study the structure of industry in the state of New Hampshire to understand how we might contribute to the Land Grant mission of the university. This study analysed 30 years of statistical data from the federal and state governments to understand trends in individual industries and identify those industries that historically were most vital to and in the future might be most promising for the state's economy. Using quantitative measures that included employment, export sales, wages and productivity, we analysed all industrial sectors in the state. The analyses produced somewhat surprising results: manufacturing, and specifically repetitive parts manufacturing, was the most important sector of the New Hampshire economy on nearly all measures. Indeed New Hampshire ranked seventh-highest in percentage of manufacturing employment of the 50 US states. From the limited information on firm size included in government data, we also found that New Hampshire had a very large percentage of small and medium-sized manufacturers – more than 90 per cent.

In order to better understand the industrial landscape of New Hampshire, we developed a survey designed around Michael Porter's contention in *The Competitive Advantage of Nations* (1990) that industrial clusters are the source of national economic superiority. The survey questions emphasized the practice and use of strategic management. On the basics of our industry studies, we mailed the survey to the company presidents of firms in the four most important manufacturing sectors in New Hampshire: fabricated metals, industrial equipment, electrical and electronic equipment, and instruments. The results (Kaufman et al., 1994) showed no industrial cluster(s) in New Hampshire, but established a solid basis for continued research in supply chain management and how small and medium-sized firms operate within their supply chains.

Manufacturing firms tend to be more capital-intensive and process-oriented than other businesses. The next enhancement to our studies was to incorporate parts of a manufacturing-based survey instrument called 'QuickView', originally designed by the Northeast Manufacturing Technology Center (1992), into our next data collection exercise to understand more fully the operations management aspects of the state's small and medium-sized manufacturer (SMM) base. We added questions to our survey on strategic and financial goals, product and process design, manufacturing technology, customer and supplier relations, and trend in gross margin, and implemented it with a telephone survey. Statistical analysis of the results proved to be quite exciting and eventually produced the Strategic Supplier Typology (Figure 9.1), a set of guidelines that help customers identify the right kind of supplier for different product architectures and capacity and knowledge needs.

This research (Kaufman, Merenda and Wood, 1996; Wood, Kaufman and Merenda, 1996; Kaufman, Wood and Theyel, 2000) results in better understanding firms' choices of partners and the nature of inter-firm contacts. It established two dimensions of customer–supplier relationships, termed *collaboration* and *technology*, that combined to form the typology of supplier strategies. These strategies connect the detailed behaviour of suppliers with the more abstract needs of customers, for example, when close collaboration (combined with specialized technology or asset specificity) is needed to deliver the right product, and when collaboration is irrelevant.

Collaboration, sometimes called *partnering*, is a term frequently used in the literature on supply chain management (Christopher, 2004; New, 2004a, 2004b; Bessant, 2004; Harland, Knight and Cousins, 2004; Dyer, 2000). With the continued disaggregation of company hierarchies producing ever more outsourcing of goods and services, and globalization offering companies the advantage of low wages and specialized expertise wherever they find it, supply chains are real-life testing grounds for the boundary-spanning governance methods required for smooth and efficient inter-firm operations. Collaboration is presented as the relational contracting alternative to arm's-length spot market transactions that suggest no requirement for joint working between buyers and suppliers (Nassimbeni, 2004; Dyer, Cho and Chu, 1998).

| COLLABORATION | |
| :---: | :---: |
| **Low** | **High** |

| | Low | |
| :---: | :--- | :--- |
| **Low** | **I Commodity supplier**<br><br>– spot market supplier<br>– low cost, low price priorities<br>– little or no differentiation<br><br><br><br><br>n = 59<br>Av. no. of employees = 28 | **II Collaboration specialist**<br><br>– detail-controlled parts supplier<br>– uses a closed network in each industry<br>– can be in many industries to maintain customer product information<br><br>n = 41<br>Av. no. of employees = 150 |

**TECHNOLOGY**

| **High** | **IV Technology specialist**<br><br>– proprietary parts supplier<br>– innovation in product technology used to produce high barriers to entry<br>– first mover advantages<br>– uses design capabilities for competitive advantage<br>n = 35<br>Av. no. of employees = 44 | **III Problem-solving supplier**<br><br>– black box supplier<br>– high differentiation<br>– cost less important<br>– small runs, high process and labour flexibility<br><br><br><br>n = 65<br>Av. no. of employees = 260 |
| :---: | :--- | :--- |

*Note:* n = 200.

*Figure 9.1  Strategic Supplier Typology*

The Strategic Supplier Typology (Figure 9.1) brings together the essential technical and social–behavioural aspects of supply chain relationships. The technology dimension consists of measured variables for both the classical competencies of manufacturing best practices (condition of tools, handling of tooling, tracking and analysis of machine downtime and idle time) and the practice of various types of advanced manufacturing technologies (CAD, CAM, MRP, QFD, SPC).

Our empirically derived collaboration dimension (Kaufman, Wood and Theyel, 2000) includes measured variables (the use of vendor certification, long-term contracts, technical assistance, concurrent engineering, strategic planning) that demonstrate transactional practices typical of long-term, trust-based relationships. The implication of scoring 'high' on the collaboration dimension is that a firm is sensitive to the value of establishing knowledge and learning networks with customers, suppliers, communities, government agencies, universities, trade associations and other stakeholders. Open and frequent communication combined with constant monitoring increases the value of social capital that can be produced by the firm's employees. This social capital can form the basis for competitive advantage. A high score on collaboration, combined with a high score on technology, results in a problem-solving supplier that is capable of successfully delivering both knowledge and capacity to the customer: innovative high-quality products employing the latest technologies available in a flexible and responsive manner.

But these practices tell very little about what causes collaboration to develop in the first place, whether it flows both upstream and downstream in the supply chain, whether it is practised with different degrees of intensity and, if so, what results are produced by different intensities. These questions led us to realize that revisions to parts of our questionnaire were necessary to better understand more of the subtleties in the relationships.

In 1994, our University of New Hampshire (UNH) research group began a joint research project on the Quebec/New England regional economy with colleagues at Université Laval. We proposed to explore the region's industrial composition through a three-stage plan: statistical analysis of government data, a survey of firms in target industries, and case studies of individual firms. Our goal was to supply useful information to state and provincial officials to guide future joint economic development initiatives.

The second stage of the joint research project was to survey firms in the leading, lagging and emerging industries identified in the statistical analysis of industries completed in the first stage of the project. We proposed using the survey instrument developed in our previous studies of the New Hampshire economy. After reviewing the instrument, our colleagues from Laval suggested the addition of a group of questions they had used in their own studies of firms in Quebec. We added the series of what the Laval group called 'networking' questions to our questionnaire and expanded all of the networking and collaboration questions to ask whether the responding firm practised these with both their customers and their suppliers in order to learn whether any directional differences existed. The 'networking' questions asked whether the firm shared equipment, personnel and new markets with their customers and suppliers, and whether they participated in joint manufacturing and product development with their customers and suppliers (see Table 9.1). The questionnaire now consisted of sections on strategic and financial goals, product and process design, manufacturing technology, customer and supplier relations, networking behaviour and trend in gross margin. The Laval and UNH groups proceeded to solicit funding to support 200 to 300 firm responses on each side of the border.

We were able to fund the UNH portion of the survey and collected 122 usable responses from firms in New Hampshire and northern Massachusetts. Statistical analysis of the data showed three distinct levels of collaboration: the collaboration dimension that we had identified in the previous survey plus two new dimensions based on the networking questions that we interpreted as operational risk-sharing and asset risk-sharing. According to the way these occurred in relation to the collaboration and technology dimensions, we viewed them as representing different levels of trust between organizations in the supply chain. The results also indicated that firms that collaborated with their customers also collaborated with their suppliers in similar ways (Table 9.1). The same was

*Table 9.1    Rotated factor loadings for collaboration and risk sharing*

| | Asset risk sharing Factor 1 | Collaboration Factor 2 | Operational risk sharing Factor 3 |
|---|---|---|---|
| Customer: partnership programmes | 0.142 | **0.604** | 0.350 |
| Supplier: partnership programmes | 0.218 | **0.645** | 0.399 |
| Customer: supplier certification | 0.116 | **0.676** | 0.128 |
| Supplier: certification | 0.101 | **0.675** | 0.202 |
| Customer: single sourcing | 0.173 | **0.579** | 0.172 |
| Supplier: single sourcing | 0.191 | **0.599** | 0.287 |
| Customer: long-term contracts | 0.045 | **0.591** | 0.234 |
| Supplier: long-term contracts | 0.149 | **0.596** | 0.241 |
| Customer: concurrent engineering | 0.193 | **0.660** | 0.365 |
| Supplier: concurrent engineering | 0.297 | **0.611** | 0.354 |
| Customer: technical assistance | 0.161 | **0.662** | 0.221 |
| Supplier: technical assistance | 0.283 | **0.616** | 0.334 |
| Share equipment with customers | **0.663** | 0.210 | 0.278 |
| Share equipment with suppliers | **0.669** | 0.173 | 0.289 |
| Share personnel with customers | **0.644** | 0.228 | 0.371 |
| Share personnel with suppliers | **0.994** | 0.197 | 0.266 |
| Share new markets with customers | 0.209 | 0.263 | **0.619** |
| Share new markets with suppliers | 0.394 | 0.279 | **0.605** |
| Joint bidding with customers | 0.213 | 0.163 | **0.705** |
| Joint bidding with suppliers | 0.194 | 0.211 | **0.504** |
| Joint manufacturing with customers | 0.400 | 0.272 | **0.635** |
| Joint manufacturing with suppliers | 0.471 | 0.419 | **0.688** |
| Joint product develop. with customers | 0.065 | 0.397 | **0.517** |
| Joint product develop. with suppliers | 0.449 | 0.451 | **0.565** |
| Percentage of variance explained | 30.36 | 12.22 | 7.59 |

*Notes:*    Extraction method: maximum likelihood; rotation method: Oblimin; loadings >0.50 are highlighted in bold face; n = 122.

*Source:*    Telephone survey.

true for operational and asset risk-sharing. As we considered how different levels of collaboration affected inter-company relations, we realized that higher levels of trust enabled more subtle messages to be communicated through the supply chain. We observed similar responses in a parallel study of software firms (Tucci et al., 2005) that was under way concurrently with the manufacturing study. These results inspired the additional areas of interest when we next expanded our questionnaire, several years later.

Having a survey instrument tested and validated by consistent results with multiple data sets, we wanted to see how partnering relationships and supply chain mechanisms would handle other possible research topics. Environmental management and corporate social responsibility were somewhat controversial areas of rapidly growing interest that have received comparatively less attention than more traditional operations and logistics topics. The results of our latest survey were collected by telephone in October 2002. The survey included firms from several industries (chemicals, rubber and plastics, and transportation equipment) in addition to our usual fabricated metals, industrial equipment, electrical and electronic equipment and instruments foursome, and split the 300 SMM respondents evenly between Northern New England (Maine, New Hampshire and Vermont) and the Mid-Atlantic states of Maryland and Virginia. The categories of questions included product and process design, technology, collaboration and risk sharing with customers and suppliers, environmental management (EM), and corporate citizenship and social issues management (CSR). The respondents were the head of operations (52 per cent), the president or CEO (20 per cent) or the plant manager (18 per cent) for firms with 20 to 500 employees.

We first statistically analysed the collaboration, technology and two risk-sharing dimensions to confirm the earlier survey results (not shown). Next we factor-analysed the responses to the corporate citizenship questions (see left-hand column in Table 9.2) to begin to understand whether they were effective in confirming our supply chain hypotheses about the way supply chain actors respond to CSR impulses that are generated through the chain. We did not include the environmental management questions in the CSR analysis, because EM is highly regulated, more readily quantified, and its effects have come to be directly related to the way it affects firm profitability.

Statistical analysis of the CSR responses produced both interesting results and a few unexpected non-results. Wood and Kaufman (2005) report three strong factors in the CSR data (Table 9.2). The first factor indicates that the respondents identify and communicate with their strategic stakeholders. This is an important finding because much of the literature on CSR suggests that the pressures on companies to demonstrate good CSR come from a wide variety of stakeholders about an equally wide variety of issues (Clarkson, 1995; Jawahar and McLaughlin, 2001). The second factor indicates that companies (think they) have and use an explicit system to measure and account for CSR activities. Given the size of the firms responding, this is somewhat surprising. Our original hypothesis was that SMMs would not have formal systems for tracking CSR activities. The third factor shows that companies are consistent in aligning their CSR activities with their corporate strategies. On the other hand, a path analysis of the CSR factors with the collaboration and risk-sharing factors shows that these CSR practices tend to be communicated effectively only to suppliers and not to customers, and then only at the higher levels of collaboration (risk sharing), not the basic level. Based on the bidirectional results of our two most recent previous surveys, this is a somewhat counterintuitive result. Some responses to questions in this CSR instrument surprisingly did not correlate to related questions as expected. For example, the measured variable 'Clear definitions for managers' community responsibilities exist' although co-located with the measurement and accountability items (Factor 2) did not load on that factor. How could a company 'Have a system to track all community activities' and not have clear definitions for their managers' responsibilities about those activities? In some cases this might be explained by the way the question was phrased, in other cases it was the content (or lack of content) in the question. In either case, as with our earlier experiences in writing and executing company surveys, modifications must be made before the next survey. What follows is a description of the work yet to be done to develop successfully an empirical data collection instrument to understand more completely the methods and motivations for the communication of CSR through the supply chain.

*Table 9.2   Rotated factor loadings for CSR practices*

| Measured variable | CSR1 Recognize strategic stakeholders Factor 1 | CSR2 Use explicit system of accountability Factor 2 | CSR3 Align CSR activities with strategy Factor 3 | Uniqueness |
|---|---|---|---|---|
| Q90 Your company identifies its strategic stakeholders | **1.037** | −0.008 | −0.060 | 0.000 |
| Q91 Your company engages in two-way communication with its strategic stakeholders | **0.895** | −0.039 | 0.064 | 0.155 |
| Q114 Business unit plans align community relationships to your firm's overall strategy | 0.069 | 0.157 | **0.535** | 0.527 |
| Q115 Your company uses financial contributions to develop its strategic relationships to community organizations with its strategic stakeholders | 0.156 | 0.045 | **0.593** | 0.475 |
| Q116 Your company uses in-kind resources to develop strategic relationships to community organizations | 0.032 | −0.028 | **0.808** | 0.343 |
| Q117 Your company engages in volunteer programmes to develop strategic relationships to community organizations | −0.020 | −0.077 | **0.902** | 0.287 |
| Q118 Your company seeks external recognition for its corporate citizenship activities | −0.056 | 0.025 | **0.815** | 0.362 |
| Q119 Your company communicates internally its corporate citizenship activities | 0.058 | 0.099 | **0.603** | 0.503 |
| Q121 A structure exists to reward managers for their corporate citizenship activities | 0.097 | **0.577** | 0.075 | 0.549 |
| Q122 A special functional area exists for corporate citizenship/ public affairs | 0.095 | **0.572** | 0.147 | 0.482 |
| Q123 The corporate citizenship office consults your company's various business units | −0.035 | **0.663** | 0.138 | 0.447 |
| Q124 Managers evaluate employees on their contributions to your company's corporate citizenship objectives | 0.006 | **0.718** | 0.041 | 0.443 |

*Table 9.2*   (continued)

| Measured variable | CSR1 Recognize strategic stakeholders Factor 1 | CSR2 Use explicit system of accountability Factor 2 | CSR3 Align CSR activities with strategy Factor 3 | Uniqueness |
|---|---|---|---|---|
| Q125 Measurements exist to evaluate the impact of community and public policy activities on the firm's strategic success | −0.053 | **0.853** | 0.005 | 0.296 |
| Q126 Measurements exist to evaluate the impact of community and public policy activities on the community and the public policy process | 0.003 | **0.884** | −0.039 | 0.258 |
| Q127 A procedure exists to review and improve these measurements regularly | −0.005 | **0.953** | −0.129 | 0.232 |
| Q128 A system exists to account for and track all of the community and public policy activities regularly | −0.040 | **0.745** | 0.086 | 0.380 |
| Weighted variance | 3.60 | 5.51 | 1.15 | |
| Alpha | 0.962 | 0.917 | 0.883 | |

*Notes:*   Extraction method: maximum likelihood; rotation method: Promax; test of 3 vs. no factors: $Chi^2(48) = 2477***$; test of 3 vs. more factors: $Chi^2(75) = 350.9***$; $***p<0.01$; $n = 300$; loadings $> 0.50$ are in bold.

## NATIONAL AND REGIONAL DIFFERENCES IN CSR

CSR is a concept that appears to have originated in the United States (Matten and Moon, 2005, pp. 325–6). Until the New Deal pushed government into active involvement in the social conditions of the country, American-style capitalism historically considered that business should be concerned only with making a profit (Friedman, 1962, 1970) and government was traditionally the protector of the rights and privileges of business. Once government mandated that businesses be responsible for some societal aspects (for example, working conditions and labour rights), employees and various external stakeholders were encouraged to press businesses for voluntary changes in other social aspects (such as community development and human rights). The consensus delineation of topics covered by CSR at a high level of abstraction is that of Carroll (Carroll, 1979; Carroll, 1991; Schwartz and Carroll, 2003) who uses a three-category classification of social responsibility: economic, legal and ethical.

Until recently the term 'CSR' did not apply to European businesses. The history of the development of their institutions was quite different from that of the US. The UK,

France and Germany for various reasons all have traditions of high social expectation and obligation for their businesses. The concept of CSR was therefore foreign (American) and did not exist for European businesses: for them it was subsumed in the standards under which they operated. But, as a result of globalization and expansion of the European Union, this has started to change: quickly, measured in bureaucratic and organizational time.

Interest in CSR has grown strongly in importance over the past decade, driven by the European Union (EU), the United Nations (UN) including the International Labor Organization (ILO), some small and medium-sized enterprises (such as Ben and Jerry's, Stonyfield Farms, Starbucks and Timberland) and a few multinational corporations (BP, GE, Levi Strauss, Nike), moderately, by fits and starts. The EU adopted CSR as a means to harmonize the many national historical traditions of the way businesses operate in society and sees CSR making a positive contribution to goals established at the Lisbon European Council in March 2000: 'to become the most competitive and dynamic knowledge-based economy in the world, capable of sustainable economic growth with more and better jobs and greater social cohesion' (European Commission, 2001). The UN's efforts are focused and spearheaded by the United Nations Global Compact (United Nations, 2005), an initiative originally proposed by Secretary-General Kofi Annan in 1999. The UN Global Compact summarizes its values in ten principles covering human rights, labour standards, the environment and anti-corruption.

The literature on comparative differences in the adoption of CSR practices is fairly small. Welford's (2004) study suggests that European companies are far ahead of Asian companies in the practice of CSR. And Tschoop (2005) finds that many more companies in Europe participate in CSR reporting, and more fully, than companies in the US, although this varies substantially by country. The recent appearance of the volume edited by Habisch et al. (2005), which details CSR practices across 21 different European countries, appears to confirm a higher level of practice in the EU than in North America or Asia. But this is one question that needs to be answered and validated empirically at the business level.

## FRAMEWORKS FOR REDESIGN

One difficulty in developing a global survey instrument is the lack of agreement and, more importantly, a standard for the topics to be included under the CSR umbrella (Krizov and Allenby, 2004). Without a standard, different groups and authors engaged in the study and reporting on the subject have advanced a wide variety of suggested standards for some or all of the categories of CSR (see Leipziger, 2003, for an extensive listing and explanations).

Welford (2004) identifies 20 elements of CSR that businesses can practise. These include having written policies on non-discrimination, equal opportunity, working hours and pay, labour standards of suppliers, responding to stakeholders, and commitment to local communities and human rights. Like the EU Green Paper (European Commission, 2001) the elements are divided into *internal* and *external* aspects (see Tables 9.3 and 9.4). This effectively divides the stakeholders into separate classes: employees and shareholders are internal and all others (customers, suppliers, communities and so on) are external. The

*Table 9.3    Internal dimension*

| Human resources | Health and safety at work | Adaptation to change | Management of environmental impacts and natural resources |
| --- | --- | --- | --- |
| Concern for employability and job security | Promote a preventive culture | Restructure in a socially responsible manner | Reduce consumption of resources |
| Employee empowerment | H&S criteria for procurement practices | Safeguard employees' rights | Reduce polluting emissions and waste |
| Better information throughout the company | Certification of management systems and subcontractors | Modernize production tools and processes | |
| Better balance of work and leisure | | Enable vocational retraining | |
| Greater workforce diversity | | Involve public authorities and employees' reps | |
| Equal pay and career prospects for women | | | |
| Profit sharing | | | |
| Non-discriminatory recruitment practices | | | |
| Lifelong learning | | | |

*Source:*    Green Paper, European Commission (2001).

UN Global Compact's ten principles (United Nations, 2005) also provide a comprehensive list of CSR topics that duplicate most of the areas covered by Welford and the EU Green Paper.

Matten and Moon (2005) lay out a conceptual framework for CSR that distinguishes between *explicit* CSR and *implicit* CSR. They argue that European companies have a long history of practising implicit CSR owing to differences in the political, social, legal and economic systems of their home countries. Implicit CSR is determined by a country's formal and informal institutions and is communicated through values and norms of the society. Further, Matten and Moon suggest that the use of the 'national business systems' approach (Whitley, 1992) is most effective in describing the rationale and workings of implicit CSR. The national business systems approach contends that the historical institutional national framework exercises a strong influence over the nature and organization of national firms. Explicit CSR describes how CSR is practised by North American corporations, which takes the form of corporate policies that define social obligations. Matten and Moon suggest a recent trend among European firms toward the use of more explicit forms of CSR.

*Table 9.4   External dimension*

| Local communities | Business partners, suppliers, and consumers | Human Rights | Global environmental concerns |
|---|---|---|---|
| Partner with communities in support of local causes | Reduce complexity and costs | Restructure in a socially responsible manner | Encourage better environmental performance through their supply chain |
| Sponsor local sports and cultural events | Increase quality | Safeguard employees' rights | Investment and activities that have a direct impact on social and economic development in third countries |
| Donate to charitable activities | Promote entrepreneurial initiatives | Adopt labour standard codes of conduct | |

*Source:*   Green Paper, European Commission (2001).

## TOWARD A CSR SUPPLY CHAIN RESEARCH AGENDA

We propose a programme of research to identify which aspects of CSR are communicated, by which members of the supply chain, to which of their stakeholders and other supply chain members. The following questions represent the most important areas of immediate practical concern:

- *What is the effect of the increasing influence of international customers on SME suppliers: do SMEs develop higher standards of CSR practice by dealing with European customers than by dealing with Asian or North American customers?*

- *How do CSR practices vary by global region, by country, by size of firm, by industry?* For instance, is the contention in Matten and Moon (2005) that European and North American companies follow different approaches to CSR valid?

- *Who are the strategic stakeholders that firms communicate with about CSR issues?* Are they always the same ones or are they situation-specific, as Clarkson (1995) and Jawahar and McLaughlin (2001) suggest?

- *What forms of communication do firms in a supply chain use to transfer CSR principles? Are they explicit (written corporate policies), implicit (based on values, norms and rules) or some combination? Are there patterns in the way firms make their CSR issues known to their suppliers and customers?*

- *How important is the level of trust established between supply chain actors in effective communication of CSR principles?*

As we have progressed in our studies of the supply chain more questions are raised than can be answered in a single thrust. The questions that we raise here represent only a small portion of the research questions that are still outstanding. Considerable work will be required of many scholars to understand and judge fully the power of communications through the supply chain.

# REFERENCES

Bessant, J. (2004), 'Supply chain learning', in S. New and R. Westbrook (eds), *Understanding Supply Chains: Concepts, Critiques, and Futures*, New York: Oxford University Press.

Carroll, A.B. (1979), 'A three-dimensional conceptual model of corporate performanc', *Academy of Management Review*, **4**(4), 497–505.

Carroll, A.B. (1991), 'The pyramid of corporate social responsibility: toward the moral management of organizational stakeholders', *Business Horizons*, **34**(4), 39–48.

Christopher, M. (2004), 'Supply chains: a marketing perspective', in S. New and R. Westbrook (eds), *Understanding Supply Chains: Concepts, Critiques, and Futures*, New York: Oxford University Press.

Clarkson, M.B.E. (1995), 'A stakeholder framework for analyzing and evaluating corporate social performance', *Academy of Management Review*, **20**(1), 92–117.

Dyer, J.H. (2000), *Collaborative Advantage*, New York: Oxford University Press.

Dyer, J.H. and W. Chu (2003), 'The role of trustworthiness in reducing transaction costs and improving performance: empirical evidence from the United States, Japan, and Korea', *Organization Science*, **14**(1), 57–69.

Dyer, J.H., D.S. Cho and W. Chu (1998), 'Strategic supplier segmentation: the next "big practice" in supply chain management', *California Management Review*, **40**(2), 57–77.

European Commission (2001), 'Promoting a European framework for corporate social responsibility', Green Paper, Luxembourg, Office for Official Publications of the European Communities.

Friedman, M. (1962), *Capitalism and Freedom*, Chicago: University of Chicago Press.

Friedman, M. (1970), 'The social responsibility of business is to increase its profits', *The New York Times Magazine*, **33**(13 Sept.), 32–3, 122–6.

Habisch, A., J. Jonker, M. Wegner and R. Schmidpeter (eds) (2005), *Corporate Social Responsibility Across Europe*, Berlin: Springer.

Harland, C., L. Knight and P. Cousins (2004), 'Supply chain relationships', in S. New and R. Westbrook (eds), *Understanding Supply Chains: Concepts, Critiques, and Futures*, New York: Oxford University Press.

Jawahar, I.M. and G.L. McLaughlin (2001), 'Toward a descriptive stakeholder theory: an organizational life cycle approach', *Academy of Management Review*, **26**(3), 397–414.

Kaufman, A., M. Merenda and C.H. Wood (1996), 'Corporate downsizing and the rise of problem-solving suppliers: the case of Hadco Corporation', *Industrial and Corporate Change*, **5**(3), 723–59.

Kaufman, A., C.H. Wood and G. Theyel (2000), 'Collaboration and technology linkages: a strategic supplier typology', *Strategic Management Journal*, **21**(6), 649–64.

Kaufman, A., R. Gittell, M. Merenda, W. Naumes and C.H. Wood (1994), 'Porter's model for geographic competitive advantage: the case of New Hampshire', *Economic Development Quarterly*, **8**(1), 43–66.

Krizov, C. and B. Allenby (2004), 'Social value added: a metric for implementing corporate social responsibility', *Environmental Quality Management*, **14**(2), 39–47.

Leipziger, D. (2003), *The Corporate Responsibility Code Book*, Sheffield, UK: Greenleaf Publishers.

Matten, D. and J. Moon (2005), 'A conceptual framework for understanding CSR', in A. Habisch, J. Jonker, M. Wegner and R. Schmidpeter (eds), *Corporate Social Responsibility Across Europe*, Berlin: Springer.

Nassimbeni, G. (2004), 'Supply chains: a network perspective', in S. New and R. Westbrook (eds), *Understanding Supply Chains: Concepts, Critiques, and Futures*, New York: Oxford University Press.

New, S. (2004a), 'Supply chains: construction and legitimation', in S. New and R. Westbrook (eds), *Understanding Supply Chains: Concepts, Critiques, and Futures*, New York: Oxford University Press.

New, S. (2004b), 'The ethical supply chain', in S. New and R. Westbrook (eds), *Understanding Supply Chains: Concepts, Critiques, and Futures*, New York: Oxford University Press.

New, S. and R. Westbrook (eds) (2004), *Understanding Supply Chains: Concepts, Critiques, and Futures*, New York: Oxford University Press.

Northeast Manufacturing Technology Center (NIST/NEMTC) and New York State Department of Economic Development (1992), 'QuickView: Manufacturing Intake Questionnaire', Troy, New York: NEMTC/RPI.

Peloza, J. (2006), 'Using corporate social responsibility as insurance for financial performance', *California Management Review*, **48**(2), 52–72.

Porter, M.E. (1990), *The Competitive Advantage of Nations*, New York: Free Press.

Roberts, S., J. Keeble and D. Brown (2002), *The Business Case for Corporate Citizenship*, Cambridge, MA: Arthur D. Little, Inc.

Schwartz, M.S. and A.B. Carroll (2003), 'Corporate social responsibility: a three-domain approach', *Business Ethics Quarterly*, **13**(4), 503–30.

Smith, N.C. (2003), 'Corporate social responsibility: whether or how?', *California Management Review*, **45**(4), 52–76.

Tschoop, D.J. (2005), 'Corporate social responsibility: a comparison between the United States and the European Union', *Corporate Social Responsibility and Environmental Management*, **12**(1), 55–9.

Tucci, C.L., A. Kaufman, C.H. Wood and G. Theyel (2005), 'Collaboration and teaming in the software supply chain', *Supply Chain Forum: An International Journal*, **6**(2), 16–28.

United Nations (2005), 'The United Nations global compact: advancing corporate citizenship', United Nations Global Compact Office, June, URL: www.unglobalcompact.org/docs/about_the_gc/2.0.2.pdf.

Welford, R. (2004), 'Corporate social responsibility in Europe and Asia: critical elements and best practice', *Journal of Corporate Citizenship*, Spring(13), 31–47.

Whitley, R. (ed.) (1992), *European Business Systems: Firms and Markets in their National Contexts*, London: Sage Publications.

Wood, C.H. and A. Kaufman (2005), 'Using the supply chain to disseminate corporate social responsibility practices: a stakeholder approach', *Innovations in Global Supply Chain Networks: Proceedings of the 10th International Symposium on Logistics*, Lisbon, Portugal, 3–5 July, Nottingham: Centre for Concurrent Enterprise, University of Nottingham Business School, pp. 638–45.

Wood, C.H., A. Kaufman and M. Merenda (1996), 'How Hadco became a problem-solving supplier', *MIT Sloan Management Review*, **37**(2), 77–88.

PART IV

Internationalization

# 10. A comparison of the pace and pattern of internationalization by US and Canadian high-growth firms

**David J. Maslach and Rod B. McNaughton**

## INTRODUCTION

Over the last decade, a shift occurred in the business rhetoric toward small firms. The orthodoxy is that small firms are only players in domestic markets. To enter international markets, firms must grow past a certain size threshold, experiment incrementally in international markets, learn gradually and build expertise before increasing their commitment. In the academic literature, this view is associated with the 'incremental' and 'stage' models of firm internationalization (for example, Johanson and Wiedersheim-Paul, 1975; Johanson and Vahlne, 1977).

The popular business press is now full of examples of small firms, often technology-based, that internationalize rapidly from inception. Portrayed as entrepreneurial in their strategy, these firms commercialize new technology or take advantage of gaps in markets left by large firms. The owners of these 'international new ventures' or 'born globals' assemble businesses in a myriad of ingenious ways, lever relationships and bring together resources often controlled by others to achieve their international success.

The phenomenon of international new ventures also attracted the attention of researchers, and there are an increasing number of articles in business journals about the rapid internationalization of smaller firms. The result is an emerging area of research at the interface of international business and entrepreneurship. A key question for researchers is why a new venture would internationalize soon after founding when it suffers the liability of newness. The emerging literature points to the importance of several broad changes in the business environment that make it more likely a small firm can successfully pursue a strategy of early entry into foreign markets. These include changes in market conditions (especially specialization, flexibility and global sourcing), changes in production, communication and transportation technologies, and the accumulation of human capital positioned to take advantage of these changes in markets and technology (Madsen and Servais, 1997).

These broad changes affect ventures in all countries. The seminal article on international new ventures by Oviatt and McDougall (1994) identified the phenomenon in the context of the United States. However researchers observing firms in smaller economies such as New Zealand, Australia, Canada, Scotland and the Scandinavian countries contribute the preponderance of literature on this topic. One explanation for this pattern is that specialization results in attempts to commercialize increasingly customized products (Madsen and Servais, 1997) and the markets for such products may be of insufficient size to meet growth (or even survival) objectives within relatively small economies. Further the markets for such products are globally dispersed nodes, connected by transnational networks at both firm and individual levels. To commercialize a product successfully, a firm must participate in this international network (Johanson and Mattsson, 1988).

A key issue is how a firm adapts its internationalization strategy to the external environment, particularly the domestic economy. Recent studies suggest an inverse relationship between international firm growth and the size and openness of the domestic market (for example, Reuber and Fischer, 1999; Bell et al., 2001; Spence, 2003). This chapter investigates the link between internationalization strategy and the domestic market by comparing the pace and pattern of internationalization of high-growth new ventures located in Canada and the US, two culturally proximate countries, but very different in terms of economic size. The Canadian market is a relatively small and open economy, while the US is a large economy that is not nearly as open (OECD, 2004). Thus this chapter addresses one of the primary themes of the 2005 Klein Symposium on Management of Technology: to what extent does existing research on international new ventures apply to a large economy like the US? To study this issue, two samples of high-growth firms, one representing Canadian firms, the other firms located in the US, were created from secondary sources. The pace and pattern of internationalization of the firms are compared between the two countries.

## DOMESTIC MARKET CONDITIONS AND INTERNATIONAL NEW VENTURES

A substantial literature is accumulating on the motives for early internationalization. For example, as preconditions like flexible manufacturing and low communication costs emerged recently, new ventures are more likely to pursue this strategy than are firms established some years ago (Oviatt and McDougall, 1997, p. 90). Another consideration is the quality of the innovation, in particular the extent to which it is proprietary. Patents and copyrights are often ineffective protections of intellectual property, especially for small firms in foreign markets. First-mover advantage offers an alternative form of protection whereby firms establish their own international presence quickly to exploit their knowledge before others appropriate it (Rao and Klein, 1994). Thus early entry into international markets is often associated with proprietary and knowledge-intensive products.

The extant literature on early internationalization also emphasizes the characteristics of the founding entrepreneur, especially international experience and personal networks (Oviatt and McDougall, 1997, pp. 93–4). The extant literature that attempts to distinguish exporting from non-exporting firms also cites the importance of individual characteristics. The key characteristic is the extent to which the founding entrepreneur sees increasing foreign sales as an important part of her or his overall business strategy, thus providing momentum for export development (Yang, Leone and Alden, 1992, p. 87). Positive attitudes toward internationalization are often associated with higher levels of education and international experience on the part of the founder.

External factors like the size and openness of the domestic market are also factors in internationalization. Openness or lack of tariffs and trade barriers in the domestic economy should increase internationalization. Trade barriers are a disincentive for firms

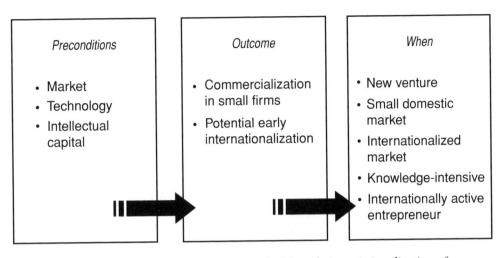

*Figure 10.1    Summary of conditions associated with early internationalization of smaller firms*

to grow internationally because profitability can be sustained in the home market (Oviatt and McDougall, 1999). The size of the domestic market is also an influence. Firms in small domestic markets have to seek international customers because they do not have a large enough customer base in their home country to sustain profitability (Bell et al., 2001). Several studies find evidence of this. For example, McNaughton (2000) found that early entry into international markets by firms in his Canadian sample is negatively correlated with the size of their domestic market. Figure 10.1 summarizes the conditions associated with early internationalization.

Both the US and Canada have a high propensity to export. Trade barriers in both countries are declining because of the GATT, WTO and NAFTA. In the US, exports account for approximately 12 per cent, and in Canada 45 per cent, of GDP (OECD, 2004). In the past ten years, Canada's propensity to export has increased, resulting in an economy that is nearly four times as open as the US as measured by exports as a percentage of GDP. In terms of domestic market size, the US, with a GDP of $US10 857.2 bn, is ten times the size of the Canadian market (GDP = $US850.5 bn) (UNDP, 2004).

It is hypothesized that the size and openness of the domestic economy influences the internationalization of high-growth firms. A domestic market that is small inhibits firm growth because it does not provide enough demand for long-term sustainability. A domestic market that is open provides opportunities for a firm to grow internationally and provides competitive forces that move a firm into the international market quickly. These two factors serve as preconditions that promote firm growth and the decision to internationalize because the firm must protect its competitive advantages. Not all high-growth firms in a small and open economy will internationalize. The decision to internationalize is highly dependent on the cognitive processes, affinity to risk and social attributes of the key decision makers. However, if the hypothesis is correct, high-growth firms located in Canada should on average internationalize more quickly and more extensively than similar firms located in the US.

Several characteristics distinguish the pace and pattern of internationalization. Kandasaami (1998) identifies three: speed of entry, pattern of entry and market coverage. Speed of entry is 'the degree of speed with which the firm enters international markets from inception'. The speed of entry is a measure of the pace of internationalization and shows the propensity of a firm to internationalize.

*H₁: Canadian high-growth firms will enter foreign countries more quickly than similar firms located in the United States.*

Pattern of entry is the 'degree to which a firm enters international markets simultaneously and proactively'. The pattern of foreign entry can reveal a proactive strategy and determinedness of a firm to enter international markets. Smaller firms in small economies will pursue international activity with much more vigour and determination because internationalization and tackling foreign markets is a key aspect of their strategy.

*H₂: Canadian firms will enter more countries than similar firms located in the United States.*

Market coverage is the 'degree to which a firm covers a large number of culturally diversified countries'. A firm with operations and sales in a large number of countries is more internationalized than a firm with less market coverage. High-growth firms from small domestic economies will likely have operations and sales in a larger number of countries in more diverse regions because they will have to participate in many more markets to overcome the demand shortcomings in their domestic market.

*H₃: Canadian firms will have more market coverage than similar firms located in the United States.*

## DATA COLLECTION

Firms that received venture capital (VC) funding are a surrogate for high-growth new ventures. Information about a closely matched sample of Canadian and US venture-funded firms was collected from secondary sources. Information about VC-funded firms in the US was collected from the *PriceWaterhouseCoopers MoneyTree* (PWC, 2003) survey website. Canadian VC-funded firms were identified from the Canadian Venture Capital and Private Equity Association (CVCA, 2004). A list of 685 VC portfolio firms was generated from the PWC website, from which a random sample of 98 firms was identified. Canadian high-growth companies were identified using a two-stage random sampling process. First, a list of 109 venture capital firms belonging to the CVCA was completed and randomized. Of the 109 venture capital firms, 36 VC firms were randomly selected and their portfolios analysed. A list of 705 high-growth portfolio firms was generated, from which 104 firms were randomly selected. The sample was identified and data collected during July and August 2004. Firms were subsequently excluded if they were not established in the US (or Canada), or had more than 500 employees.

The data were collected from each company's corporate website and from various other secondary sources, such as the Canadian Company Capabilities online database and

*Table 10.1    Profile of VC-funded firms in the Canadian and US samples*

| Characteristic | Canada | US |
|---|---|---|
| Number of publicly listed firms | 13 | 1 |
| Average firm age | 9.4 (n=94) | 6.26 (n=89) |
| Average number of employees | 64.9 (n=85) | 62.7 (n=72) |
| Average annual revenues[1] | $US11.6 mn (n=69) | $US12.1 mn (n=54) |

*Notes:*
[1] All revenues are shown in US dollars; Canadian dollars are converted to US equivalent at a rate of $CAN 1 = $US0.75, the official exchange rate at noon on 5 July 2004.

*Table 10.2    Regional location of firms in the Canadian and US samples*

| Canada | | US | |
|---|---|---|---|
| Quebec | 49 | California | 42 |
| Ontario | 33 | Massachusetts | 15 |
| British Columbia | 12 | Texas | 5 |
| Alberta | 7 | Washington | 5 |
| Other | 3 | Other | 31 |
| Total | 104 | | 98 |

*Table 10.3    Sectors of firms in the Canadian and US samples*

| SIC Code | Number of Canadian firms | Number of US firms |
|---|---|---|
| Prepackaged software | 15 | 16 |
| Commercial physical research | 7 | 5 |
| Electronic parts and equipment | 5 | 5 |
| Drugs and sundries | 7 | 1 |
| Medical laboratories | 2 | 6 |
| Data processing and preparation | 3 | 4 |
| Surgical and medical instruments | 2 | 5 |
| Business services | 0 | 6 |
| Computer programming services | 5 | 1 |
| Computer-related services | 4 | 2 |
| Other | 54 | 47 |
| Total | 104 | 98 |

*Lexus-Nexus*. The remaining information was gathered by telephone from a principal of the firm. However there remain a large number of missing values distributed throughout the variables. Table 10.1 provides a list of the key characteristics of the samples, Table 10.2 provides the location of the firms within each country, and Table 10.3 compares the industry distribution between the Canadian and US samples.

There is no statistically significant difference between the average revenue of firms in the Canadian and US samples, or between the average numbers of employees. Firms in the Canadian sample are significantly older and a larger proportion is publicly owned. Identifying the firms from the websites of venture capitalists (rather than from an annual survey) may explain the difference. There are also fewer VCs in Canada than in the US that make seed and early stage investments. Thus Canadian firms may be older when they receive their first round of VC funding.

## MEASURES OF INTERNATIONALIZATION PACE AND PATTERN

Several measures of the pace of internationalization are used. First, the overall pace of internationalization (number of countries per number of years in operation) is used as a good overall estimate (for example, Renforth, 1998; Spence, 2003). Second, growth in numbers of subsidiaries (number of countries with subsidiaries per number of years in operation) is used as an estimate of international asset growth (foreign direct investment) (for example, Sullivan, 1994). The number of countries with subsidiaries per revenue measures how quickly the assets of a firm are internationalizing per dollar earned. In addition, the number of countries a firm serves per revenue directly measures the extent to which firms pursue international markets. The number of countries a firm enters and the number of countries with subsidiaries per number of employees measure how aggressively internationalization is pursued within a firm. Finally, the ratio of foreign sales to total sales has long been a standard measure of the extent of internationalization (Renforth, 1998). Several measures of the pattern of internationalization are used. Three measures investigate the overall pattern of internationalization: (1) the number of international subsidiaries, (2) the number of countries in which a firm has subsidiaries, and (3) the number of subsidiaries in key geographic regions.

## RESULTS

Measures from the independent samples of Canadian and US-based high-growth firms are compared using the Student's $t$ statistic for independent samples – a test of the null hypothesis that the means of two populations are equal. The exact probability of the statistic provides a one-tailed test for the proposition that firms in the Canadian sample internationalize more quickly and more extensively ($H_1$–$H_3$). Tables 10.4 to 10.6 report the averages for the two samples, Student's $t$ and the associated exact one-tailed p-value.

On average, high-growth firms in Canada do not enter more countries soon after they are founded, nor do they generate sales from a more diverse set of geographic regions (Table 10.4). Further they do not establish more subsidiaries, or have subsidiaries in a greater number of countries (Table 10.5). The only statistically significant difference is that, on average, Canadian firms establish more subsidiaries in the US (than vice versa) and none of the Canadian firms had a subsidiary in India, while a few of the US firms do have a subsidiary there.

*Table 10.4    Pace of entry into foreign countries and geographic pattern of sales*

| Variable | Canadian average | US average | Student's $t$ | p-value (1-tailed test) |
|---|---|---|---|---|
| Number of countries entered in first year | 0.523 (n=17) | 0.107 (n=28) | 1.574 | 0.112 |
| Number of countries entered by third year | 1.670 (n=15) | 0.714 (n=28) | 1.080 | 0.725 |
| Total number of countries | 10.950 (n=42) | 7.780 (n=36) | 0.726 | 0.001 |
| Has sales in US (or sales in Canada for US sample) | 0.800 (n=80) | 0.306 (n=36) | 11.152/ −3.974 | 0.000/ 0.000 |
| Has sales in EU | 0.577 (n=52) | 0.500 (n=50) | 0.774 | 0.281 |
| Has sales in India | 0.125 (n=40) | 0.250 (n=40) | −1.433 | 0.126 |
| Has sales in Asia | 0.510 (n=51) | 0.435 (n=46) | 0.733 | 0.296 |
| Foreign sales/total sales | 0.356 (n=35) | 0.043 (n=35) | 4.879 | 0.001 |

*Table 10.5    Pattern of direct foreign investment in subsidiaries*

| Variable | Canadian average (n=104) | US average (n=96) | Student's $t$ | p-value (1-tailed test) |
|---|---|---|---|---|
| Number of subsidiaries | 2.130 | 2.160 | −0.074 | 0.888 |
| Number of countries with subsidiaries | 1.590 | 1.650 | −0.253 | 0.960 |
| Canadian subsidiaries in US (or US subsidiaries in Canada) | 0.269 | 0.052 | 43.288/ −16.061 | 0.000/ 0.000 |
| Subsidiaries in EU | 0.125 | 0.198 | −1.405 | 0.180 |
| Subsidiaries in India | 0 | 0.073 | −2.846 | 0.005 |
| Subsidiaries in Asia (including Australia/NZ) | 0.058 | 0.115 | −1.442 | 0.204 |

Firms in the Canadian sample derive sales from more countries, and are more reliant on foreign sales overall (Table 10.4). However, these differences are partly explained by the firms in the Canadian sample being older on average. Table 10.6 provides measures of the extent of internationalization, controlling for the number of years of operation or firm size (measured by revenues and number of employees). When years of operation are considered, firms in the US sample entered more markets and have subsidiaries in more countries. This is not the case for firm size: controlling for either revenues or number of employees shows that Canadian firms are more internationalized per dollar or employee. However both revenues and number of employees are positively correlated with years of operation ($r = 0.25$, and $r = 0.45$, $p > 0.000$), so the difference in average age of the firms between the samples also

*Table 10.6   Pace of internationalization, controlling for firm age or size*

| Variable | Canadian average | US average | Student's *t* | p-value (1-tailed test) |
|---|---|---|---|---|
| Number of countries entered / years of operation | 1.16 (n=42) | 2.03 (n=33) | −0.821 | 0.014 |
| Number of countries / $US1 mn revenue | 2.53 (n=35) | 2.25 (n=23) | 0.658 | 0.024 |
| Number of countries / number of employees | 0.216 (n=39) | 0.207 (n=31) | 0.069 | 0.006 |
| Number of countries with a subsidiary / years of operation | 0.255 (n=94) | 0.382 (n=89) | −2.283 | 0.000 |
| Number of countries with a subsidiary / $US1 mn revenue | 1.97 (n=69) | 0.493 (n=54) | 1.293 | 0.000 |
| Number of countries with subsidiaries / number of employees | 0.0581 (n=85) | 0.0567 (n=72) | 0.109 | 0.206 |

influences this result. Unfortunately there are insufficient cases to test for three-way or higher interactions.

## DISCUSSION AND CONCLUSION

The results show few differences in the pace or pattern of internationalization between Canadian and US high-growth firms. There are statistically significant differences in only a few measures, and these are partly explained by firms in the Canadian sample being older on average. The primary difference is that Canadian firms are more likely to enter the US than US-based companies are to enter Canada. A number of factors unique to the two countries may explain the results. First, Canadian businesses are generally regarded as less risk-tolerant than their US counterparts (Innovation in Canada, 2004). This may serve, on average, to restrain Canadian firms from tackling more psychologically distant markets, especially when the US is the world's largest and leading market for technology. It makes sense to enter the US before those markets overseas. The US is also diverse in terms of its regional markets. While this research treats the US as a single country, it is a collection of markets, some closer and some more distant, in terms both of geography and of business culture. US-based firms may receive more external equity than Canadian firms. The venture capital market is much smaller in Canada ($US1.5 bn in 2003) than in the US ($US18 bn in 2003), as is the average size of VC deals (MacDonald & Associates, 2003). Thus expansion of Canadian firms, especially by establishing foreign subsidiaries, may be slowed by a relative lack of capital compared to US-based high-growth firms. There may also be industry difference in the sample that influences the propensity to internationalize. While packaged software firms are most frequent in both samples, the 'other' category accounts for many firms and the mix between the two countries for other categories is varied. Finally, macroeconomic effects, especially the relative value of the Canadian and US currency, play a role. Over the past decade, the Canadian dollar was worth considerably less than the US dollar. Thus Canadian firms had more incentive to export, but less to invest in foreign subsidiaries than did US-based firms. Despite the weaker currency, relatively more firms that are Canadian established subsidiaries in the US. Further, US firms had more incentive to invest in subsidiaries in low-cost regions, and to purchase products and services created in Canada. This finding underscores the importance to Canadian high-growth firms of having a presence in the US.

The extant literature on international new ventures suggests that the pace and pattern of internationalization of high-growth firms is a function of a number of both internal and external factors. A key hypothesis in this literature is that high-growth firms founded in countries with smaller and more open economies are more likely to internationalize earlier and more extensively (for example, Reuber and Fischer, 1999; Bell and McNaughton, 2000; Spence, 2003). The logic is that these firms must internationalize to reach a market of sufficient size, to participate in international networks and to compete with international competitors. Thus the hypothesis tested in this chapter is that Canadian high-growth firms on average internationalize sooner and more extensively than do similar ventures founded in the US. The comparison provides little support for this hypothesis, especially if the age of firms in the two samples is considered.

The primary limitation of this research is that the firms included in the study are not a true random sample, and receipt of VC funding is used to define the population of high-growth firms. Further, as data were collected from a variety of secondary sources, their reliability is unknown, and there are frequent missing values where information could not be found. The firms in VC portfolios are atypical of the general population of new ventures and, while they are chosen because of the expectation of rapid growth, this does not always eventuate. The comparison of firms in Canada and the US is also difficult to generalize to other pairings of countries because of the relatively easy access to the US market that Canadian firms enjoy because of the Free Trade Agreement. Further, the US is the largest market for technology by far, and many Canadian firms do not treat the US as a 'foreign' (or international) market. Because of this unique context, the results should not be interpreted as evidence that the small domestic market–early internationalization hypothesis does not hold true in general. It does, however, show that the pace and pattern of internationalization by US high-growth firms are similar to those of firms in a country whose domestic market is approximately one-tenth the size of the US. Thus, in answer to the question raised as a symposium theme, 'to what extent does existing research on international new ventures apply to a large economy like the US?', there is support for the notion that emerging theory on international new ventures can also apply in the US context.

# REFERENCES

Bell, J., R. McNaughton and S. Young (2001), '"Born-again global" firms: an extension to the "born global" phenomenon', *Journal of International Management*, **7**(3), 1–17.
CVCA (2004), Full Members List, Canadian Venture Capital and Private Equity Association.
Innovation in Canada (2004), *London and Region Summit Report*, Government of Canada.
Johanson, J. and L.-G. Mattsson (1988), 'Internationalization in industrial systems: a network approach', in N. Hood and J.-E. Vahlne (eds), *Strategies in Global Competition*, New York: Croom Helm, pp. 214–87.

Johanson, J. and J.-E. Vahlne (1977), 'The internationalisation process of the firm: a model of knowledge, development and increasing foreign commitments', *Journal of International Business Studies*, **8**(1), 23–32.

Johanson, J. and F. Wiedersheim-Paul (1975), 'The internationalization of the firm: four Swedish cases', *Journal of Management Studies*, **12**(3), 305–22.

Kandasaami, S. (1998), 'Factors influencing the fast-track internationalisation of born-global SMEs: a conceptual model', *ANZIBA Conference Proceedings*, Melbourne: University of Melbourne.

Knight, J., J. Bell et al. (2001), ' "Born globals": old wine in new bottles', *ANZMAC Conference Proceedings, Bridging Marketing Theory and Practice*, Auckland, New Zealand.

MacDonald & Associates (2003), '2003 Key Venture Capital Observations', CVCA.

Madsen, T.K. and P. Servais (1997), 'The internationalization of born globals: an evolutionary process?', *International Business Review*, **6**(6), 561–83.

McNaughton, R.B. (2000), 'Determinants of time-span to foreign market entry: evidence from Canadian micro-exporters', *Journal of Euro-Marketing*, **9**(2), 99.

OECD (2004), 'Country Statistical Profiles 2004', available at http://stats.oecd.org, accessed 24 September 2004.

Oviatt, B.M. and P.P. McDougall (1994), 'Toward a theory of international new ventures', *Journal of International Business*, **25**(1), 45–64.

Oviatt, B.M. and P.P. McDougal (1997), 'Challenges for internationalization process theory: the case of international new ventures', *Management International Review*, **37**(2), 85–99.

Oviatt, B.M. and P.P. McDougall (1999), 'A framework for understanding accelerated international entrepreneurship', in R.W. Wright (ed.), *International Entrepreneurship: Globalization of Emerging Businesses*, no. 7, pp. 23–40, Research in Global Strategic Management series, ed. A.M. Rugman, Stamford, Connecticut: JAI Press Inc.

PWC (2003), *National Venture Capital Association MoneyTree Survey*, PricewaterhouseCoopers/ Thomson Venture Economics (http://www.pwcmoneytree.com/moneytree/nav.jsp?page=investee, 2004).

Rao, P.M. and J.A. Klein (1994), 'Growing importance of marketing strategies for the software industry', *Industrial Marketing Management*, **23**(1), 29–37.

Renforth, W. (1998), 'Assessing internationalisation: an alternative measurement technique', *ANZIBA Conference Proceedings*, Melbourne: University of Melbourne.

Reuber, A.R. and E. Fischer (1999), 'Domestic market size, competences, and the internationalization of small- and medium-sized enterprises', in R.W. Wright (ed.), *International Entrepreneurship: Globalization of Emerging Businesses*, no. 7, 85–100, Research in Global Strategic Management series, ed. A.M. Rugman, Stamford: Connecticut, JAI Press Inc.

Spence, M. (2003), 'International strategy formation in small Canadian high-technology companies – a case study approach', *Journal of International Entrepreneurship*, **1**(3), 277–96.

Sullivan, D. (1994), 'Measuring the degree of internationalization of a firm', *Journal of International Business Studies*, **25**, 19–26.

UNDP (2004), *UN Development Statistics*, UNDP.

Wroon, V. and B. Pahl (1971), 'Relationship between age and risk-taking among managers', *Journal of Applied Psychology*, **55**, 399–405.

Yang, Y.S., R.P. Leone and D.L. Alden (1992), 'A market expansion ability approach to identify potential exporters', *Journal of Marketing*, **56**(January), 84–96.

# 11. The effects of product diversification and international diversification on SMEs' innovation

## Jane Wenzhen Lu and Zhijian Wu

## INTRODUCTION

International diversification and product diversification are two important growth strategies for firms (Burgelman, 1983; Hoskisson and Hitt, 1990). Consistent with the popularity of these two strategies, there have been extensive studies on the effects of international diversification and product diversification on firm performance. Despite the growing volume of research on this topic, there are two underresearched areas.

First, most of the existing studies focused on large firms and ignored small and medium-sized firms. Second, the majority of the studies focused on the financial performance of the firms and ignored the effects of international diversification and product diversification on firm innovation. Lu and Beamish (2001) addressed the first issue by examining the relationship between internationalization and performance of SMEs. However the relationship between internationalization and firm innovation remains unknown. The study by Hitt, Hoskisson and Kim (1997) was a notable attempt at addressing the second issue. Hitt and colleagues found that there was a positive relationship between international diversification and firm innovation. This relationship was further negatively moderated by product diversification. However they used a sample of large firms and hence the question remains whether these findings can be generalized to the context of SMEs.

In this study, we attempt to address both issues. We directly test the effects of international diversification and product diversification on firm innovation in a sample of small and medium-sized enterprises. Further, we differentiate export from foreign direct investment and investigate their independent and joint effects on firm innovation.

In a sample of 164 Japanese SMEs, we found that international diversification had a positive impact on SMEs' innovation. This positive effect was mainly derived from exporting activities rather than foreign direct investments. In contrast, product diversification did not have a significant impact on SMEs' innovation. In addition, we find that international diversification positively moderates the relationship between product diversification and SMEs' innovation.

Our study contributes to the literature by addressing the above two shortcomings simultaneously. Further, our findings have important implications for SMEs' managers in designing the growth of their companies. In the following sections, we first review the literature and develop our hypotheses. We then describe our data and report the results of our hypothesis tests. Finally, we discuss the results and implications of our findings.

# BACKGROUND

International diversification and product diversification are two of the most viable directions for the growth of both small and large firms. Product diversification refers to a firm's expansion into new industries or product markets. Studies on the relationship between product diversification and firm performance have generated mixed results (for a review, see Hitt, Hoskisson and Ireland, 1994). Many studies supported a negative relationship between product diversification and firm performance (for example, Berger and Ofek, 1995; Lang and Stulz, 1994; Servaes, 1996; Lins and Servaes, 1998). At the same time, there are studies that have reported a positive relationship (Khanna and Palepu, 1996; Chang and Choi, 1988) or no relationship at all (Lloyd and Jahera, 1994).

International diversification refers to a firm's entry into new geographic markets. The findings on the effects of international diversification are likewise mixed. There are empirical studies that supported the contention that higher levels of geographic diversification lead to better firm performance (Errunza and Senbet, 1984; Doukas and Travlos, 1988; Delios and Beamish, 1999). Other studies, however, have found no relationship (Brewer, 1981; Morck and Yeung, 1991), a negative relationship (Geringer, Tallman and Olsen, 2000; Denis, Denis and Yost, 2002), an inverted U-curve relationship (Geringer et al., 1989; Hitt et al., 1997), a U-curve relationship (Lu and Beamish, 2001) or an S-curve relationship (Contractor, Kundu and Hsu, 2003; Lu and Beamish, 2004) in different samples.

The diverging results on the relationship between product/international diversification and firm performance indicate that prior studies have not fully captured the inherent complexity in this relationship. One such complexity is that performance is a multidimensional construct and prior research primarily focused on financial performance when investigating the performance implications of product/international diversification. For example, innovation is an important dimension or predictor of firm performance. Research has suggested that innovation is a critical determinant of a firm's competitive advantage and superior long-term performance (Porter, 1990). We contend that an examination of the relationship between product/international diversification and firm innovation could help unveil how these two strategies contribute to firm performance.

To the best of our knowledge, there are very few studies conducted on the relationship between the two diversification strategies and firm innovation. The study by Hitt, Hoskisson and Kim (1997) was a notable exception. However their study focused on large firms. Given the well-documented differences between larger and smaller firms, it is important to investigate the relationship between product/international diversification and firm innovation in the context of small and medium-sized firms.

# HYPOTHESES

## Product Diversification and Innovation

Product diversification has been a popular topic of research for decades (Berger and Ofek, 1995; Khanna and Palepu, 1996). The literature has documented conflicting arguments over the relationship between product diversification and innovation. Economists propose a positive impact of product diversification on firm innovation. This positive impact is mainly based on the argument that more operations in various industries lead to a spillover effect such as increases in the pool of ideas from which to develop innovations, and some cross-fertilization and stimulation across diverse areas. As this happens, there should be increased innovation (Nelson, 1959).

However the other stream of researchers found a negative relationship between product diversification and firm innovation (Baysinger and Hoskisson, 1989). Scholars contend that, as firms diversify, the firm management shifts more emphasis toward financial rather than strategic control. There are numerous reasons for the management to shift the main focus: the corporate executives are required to have a deep under-standing of each business unit if they want to have strategic control over the firm. As firms grow through international or product diversification, managers will have to deal with new products and new geographic markets about which they may have little knowl-edge or experience. Further, different types of growth add to the complexity: horizon-tal expansion creates internal competition among different business units; vertical integration intensifies the interdepartmental conflicts and profit and loss allocation; and international acquisition often results in integration difficulties. Strategic control also requires the management to coordinate and interact effectively with the managers of each business unit. Therefore, as a firm increases its product diversification level, the management is required to process and analyse increasingly diverse information and to deal with much a heavier amount of internal transaction. In reality, however, as firms diversify into more segments, corporate executives may lack the adequate information to understand the operation of each division. In addition, they may also lack the skill required to operate each business unit efficiently (Hitt et al., 1990). Prior studies have found that the governance scope (for example, strategic control capabilities) may exceed management capabilities as a firm increases its level of product diversification (Tallman and Li, 1996).

When the firm management shifts toward financial control, they tend to be more short-term and risk-averse, which prevents them from investing in innovation such as R&D (Hoskisson and Hitt, 1988). The control over financial aims reduces the firm's long-term investments such as R&D because such investments are not attractive to the managers in the incentive compensation system (Hoskisson et al., 1993). Business unit managers may face more uncertainty and risk if they decide to invest in innovation under a financial control system. To reduce the uncertainty and risk, they would commonly consider cutting the budget on R&D expenditure. Empirically, scholars found a short-term oriented strategy to exert a negative effect on firm innovation (Baysinger and Hoskisson, 1989).

Most SMEs face a problem of limited resources, be it finance, knowledge or marketing power. In this situation, the strategy to conduct product diversification competes with the strategy to develop innovation for company resources. When there is a conflict of resource allocation between product diversification and innovation, the management tends to favour the short-term profit-oriented strategy, namely product diversification. The resource competition urges the company to develop product diversification at the cost of firm innovation. Therefore, we propose the following hypothesis:

*Hypothesis 1    Product diversification has a negative impact on SMEs' innovation.*

**International Diversification and Innovation**

Firm innovation may encourage a firm to diversify internationally in order to gain higher returns on its investment in innovation (for example, R&D). Scholars argue that geographic expansion improves the 'appropriability regime' of innovation (Teece, 1986). In addition, firms may find it difficult to recover the investment in innovation only from sales in domestic markets. Empirically it is found that the investment in innovation may not be recovered before the technology becomes obsolete in industries with rapid technology change such as information or biomedicine (Kotabe, 1990).

However the resource-based view theory suggests that the cause and effect between innovation and internationalization might be the reverse, which indicates that internationalization exerts a positive impact on a firm's innovation. This is particularly true in the perspective of global competition that it is necessary for an internationalized enterprise to invest in innovation in order to maintain its competitive advantages (Bettis and Hitt, 1995).

Internationalization not only offers an incentive for a firm to expand innovation, but it also provides favourable conditions to help a firm to innovate. Internationalization helps the firm to develop strategic advantages and core capabilities that are essential to conduct innovative activities. The advantages include knowledge advantage, such as pooling of skill, information and expertise on an international basis; policy advantage, such as tax considerations and internal price transfer; financial advantage, such as cost minimization and efficient resource allocation; and market advantage, such as market segmentation and broad and instant access to customers. With the fast development in globalization of the world's economy, increased global competition has shortened the product life cycle and increased the investment required to maintain a technology advantage.

Internationalization might help the firm to generate the necessary resources to conduct the R&D that requires a considerable amount of capital and skill investment (Kobrin, 1991). Because of the access to more resources, larger markets and greater returns, the internationally diversified companies are able to recoup the investment in innovation (Kotabe, 1990). This capability functions as an incentive to further encourage the innovation in multinational corporations.

Another important motivation for innovation is knowledge. Scholars have found that new knowledge leads to more innovation (Miller, 1996). Compared to the domestic firms, multinational corporations are exposed to more diverse markets and cultures as well, and thereafter they have the opportunity to improve their organizational knowledge.

From the resource-based view, a firm's ability to innovate is important to obtaining competitive advantage (Barney, 1991). Therefore, in the long run, a firm with a more extensive investment in innovation is expected to maintain a competitive advantage compared to the firms that do not invest in innovation, keeping the other conditions unchanged. This advantage is particularly relevant for the internationally diversified firms in a highly competitive global market. As we have argued above, internationalization provides motivations for a firm to invest the necessary resources in innovation. In the meantime, the internationally diversified firms are able to generate the necessary financial and knowledge resources to produce innovation. For SMEs, international diversification provides not only the incentive but also the resources to innovate. Therefore we expect that:

*Hypothesis 2    International diversification has a positive impact on SMEs' innovation.*

**International Diversification, Product Diversification and Innovation**

As we proposed in the first hypothesis, the literature suggests a negative relationship between product diversification and firm innovation. For example, Hoskisson and Hitt (1988) find that product diversification leads to less investment in R&D. As proposed in the second hypothesis, however, we contend that international diversification has a positive impact on innovation. Thereafter the positive effect of international diversification should moderate the relationship between product diversification and innovation. For example, the incentives of internationally diversified firms may at least offset the disincentives of product-diversified firms on firm innovation (Hitt et al., 1994). This offsetting effect can be found in analogous research areas in the literature. For example, researchers find no negative relationship between product diversification and innovation in firms with concentrated ownership. It is suggested that the non-relationship could be due to an incentive of concentrated ownership to invest in innovation to offset the disincentive created by product diversification (Baysinger et al., 1991).

The analogous logic can be leveraged on the cross-relationship between international diversification and product diversification on firm innovation. For example, the international expansion of a firm lowers the risk of innovation, which could make firm innovation more attractive even from a risk-averse perspective (Bettis and Hitt, 1995). To be specific, the jeopardy of innovation, such as the inability to appropriate sufficient returns before the technology becomes obsolete, or quick imitation by competitors, could be lowered significantly by geographic diversification (Kotabe, 1990). In addition, international expansion increases the likelihood of application of serendipitous innovations (Kamien and Schwartz, 1982). Therefore we propose the following:

*Hypothesis 3     International diversification has a positive moderating impact on the relationship between product diversification and SMEs' innovation.*

# DATA

We followed the definition of the American Small Business Administration (SBA) to define a small and medium-sized enterprise (SME). According to SBA, SMEs are stand-alone enterprises with fewer than 500 employees (Beamish, 1999). We followed this definition to construct our data pool with all the Japanese firms listed on the first and second section of the Tokyo Stock Exchange from 1985 to 1995 with fewer than 500 employees. We found 164 companies in all to qualify for the sample pool.

We matched the list of Japanese SMEs to the list of parent firms in *Kaigai Shinshutsu Kigyou Souran-Kuni Betsu* (Japanese Overseas Investments – by Country) to obtain the export revenue, number of subsidiaries and number of countries that a firm invests in. In addition, we documented the sectional revenue of all the firms in our sample to calculate their product diversification measure.

The 164 Japanese firms in our sample account for 7.5 per cent of all the firms listed on the Tokyo Stock Exchange. The average number of employees in the sample is 321, with a range of 58 to 499.

**Variables**

Our model analyses the relationship between firm innovation, product diversification and international diversification. We used R&D expense as the proxy of innovation. The main independent variables are the levels of exports, the level of foreign direct investment and product diversification. We also included a number of control variables to account for the factors that might have an impact on a firm's innovation.

**Dependent variable**

We used a firm's R&D intensity, the ratio of R&D expenditure to sales, as a measure of the firm's innovation. R&D intensity is frequently used as a proxy of innovation in the literature (Hitt et al., 1991). Scholars find that R&D intensity is positively related to other popular innovation indicators such as patents (Hitt et al., 1991) and new product introductions (Hitt et al., 1996).

**Independent variables**

Basically we are measuring the international diversification and product diversification of a firm. For international diversification, it is a complex construct (Sullivan, 1994). Consistent with prior research, we used export intensity and the number of nations that a firm has invested in to measure different dimensions of international diversification.

*Export intensity*   We defined export intensity as the percentage of parent firm sales that were derived from annual export revenues. We obtained the revenue information from Nikkei NEEDS (Nikkei Economic Electronic Database Systems) tapes.

*Foreign direct investment*   We used the counts of countries in which the firm had FDIs as the proxy of foreign direct investment. This measure is frequently used in the literature to capture a firm's foreign direct investment activity (Delios and Beamish, 1999). Both FDI and exports are proxies to measure a firm's internationalization. However they differ from each other in that FDI measures the spread of internationalization while exports measure the extent of internationalization.

*Product diversification*   According to the existing literature, scholars generally use Herfindahl (Lubatkin, Merchant and Srinivasan, 1993) to measure a firm's diversification. The Herfindahl measure is based on SIC codes. Using the information on revenues by product category, we calculated the indices in the following manner: Herfindahl index for the year $t$: $Hr\_t = 1 - \Sigma(Pi)^2$; (Pi refers to the revenue percentage of the ith business sector).

**Control variables**

We included a set of control variables in our model: the size of the firm, the advertising intensity and the exchange rate. We used the logarithm of total number of employees as a measure of firm size. Advertising intensity is included to gauge the level of propriety content in market assets and we use the ratio of advertising expense to sales. Further, we also included the US–yen exchange rates for the 1985 to 1995 period to control for the impact of exchange rates on the firms' internationalization activities such as export and/or FDI. We list all the variables and their meanings in Table 11.1.

*Table 11.1  Variable descriptions*

| Variable | Definition |
|---|---|
| *Dependent variable (T)* | |
| R_D | R&D intensity by year (R&D expenditures/sales) |
| *Independent variable (T−1)* | |
| Exp | Export intensity by year (export revenues/sales) |
| Nat | Number of countries invested in: host countries in the year |
| Herf | Product diversification: Herfindhal Index for year |
| *Interaction (T−1)* | |
| Herfsub | Herf * sub |
| Herfnat | Herf * nat |
| Herfexp | Herf * exp |
| *Control variable (T−1)* | |
| Adv | Advertising intensity by year (advertising expenditures/sales) |
| Emp | Number of employees |
| Ln_emp | Logarithm of number of employees |
| Rate | Exchange rate |

**Empirical Model**

Our model can be specified as:

$$\Pi_{it} = \alpha + \beta1*EXP_{it-1} + \beta2*NAT_{it-1} + \beta3*HERF_{it-1} + \beta4*(HERF*EXP)_{it-1}$$

$$+ \beta5*(HERF*NAT)_{it-1} + \delta*X_{it-1} + \varepsilon_{it-1}.$$

In this equation, $\Pi$ refers to a firm's innovation. We contend that a firm's innovation is influenced by the extent of export, foreign direct investment, product diversification and the cross-effect of export/foreign direct investment and product diversification strategy, in addition to a set of control variables. *EXP* here means the export intensity and *NAT* means a firm's foreign direct investment level. *HERF* represents a firm's product diversification level. *HERF*EXP* is a cross-term of product diversification and export intensity. *HERF*NAT* is the cross-term of product diversification and foreign direct investment. We included control variables in the equation, which are denoted by the vector, **X**. Because our theoretical argument posited that the international diversification and product diversification of SMEs would, over time, drive changes in firm innovation, we lagged the effects of our independent variables by one year.

We used random effects Generalized Least Square (GLS) routines to estimate the equation. The main reason that we used GLS here is that the data are a time-series and pooled-panel data. GLS would enable us to avoid bias in addressing the problem of over time correlation and heterogeneity (Lawson and Hanson, 1974). In practice, we used STATA to run the GLS test. The command we used in STATA is 'XTREG', with 'RE' as the parameter to run the random effect test.

## RESULTS

We report the means and standard deviations, as well as the correlation matrix of all the variables in Table 11.2. R_D is positively correlated with EXP (p<0.01), NAT (p<0.05) and HERF. However, the correlation between R_D and HERF is not statistically significant. Except for the expected medium-level correlation between the two measures for international diversification (EXP and NAT), the magnitude of the correlations between variables is in the range of low to medium, suggesting that multicollinearity was not a serious problem in hypothesis testing.

We report the empirical results of the GLS model for the relationship between firm innovation and export, FDI and product diversification in Table 11.3. The model's associated R-square is reported at the bottom of Table 11.3. In Model 1 of Table 11.3, we tested a baseline model with only the control variables. We found a moderately negative relationship between ADV (advertising intensity) and R_D (firm innovation), which indicates that the higher investment in advertising, the lower level of firm innovation. This finding is consistent with the conventional wisdom as advertising and innovation are competing for the limited financial resources of a firm.

In Model 2, we tested the relationship between product diversification and firm innovation. We did not find any significant relationship between product diversification (HERF) and firm innovation, which is not the same as some other empirical results in the literature (Baysinger and Hoskisson, 1989). Therefore we did not obtain support for Hypothesis 1.

In Model 3 we added another independent variable that we wanted to test: EXP. We found a significantly positive relationship between EXP and R_D, suggesting that export intensity exerts a positive effect on firm innovation. Thus Hypothesis 2 is fully supported when international diversification is measured by export intensity.

In Model 4, we replaced EXP with NAT. We wanted to examine the impact of international diversification on firm innovation. We did not find any significant relationship between NAT and R_D. Thus Hypothesis 2 is not supported when international diversification is measured by the number of nations that a firm invests in.

In Model 5 we included both EXP and NAT. Similar to the previous two models, we found a significantly positive relationship between EXP and R_D, but did not find any significant relationship between NAT and R_D. This finding confirmed our conjecture that export intensity exerts a positive impact on firm innovation.

*Table 11.2   Descriptive statistics and correlations*

| Variable | MEAN | S. D. | 1 | 2 | 3 | 4 | 5 | 6 |
|---|---|---|---|---|---|---|---|---|
| 1  R_D | 0.014 | 0.022 | 1 | | | | | |
| 2  Adv | 0.024 | 0.021 | −0.094** | 1 | | | | |
| 3  Exp | 0.128 | 0.177 | 0.181** | −0.139** | 1 | | | |
| 4  Nat | 0.968 | 1.605 | 0.055* | −0.081** | 0.331** | 1 | | |
| 5  Herf | 0.577 | 0.158 | 0.036 | 0.007 | −0.103** | 0.004 | 1 | |
| 6  Emp | 321.189 | 121.317 | −0.026 | 0.093** | 0.021 | 0.114** | 0.105** | 1 |
| 7  Rate | 127.425 | 20.921 | −0.026 | −0.060* | 0.017 | −0.127** | 0.000 | 0.009 |

*Note:*   ** correlation is significant at the 0.01 level; * correlation is significant at the 0.05 level.

*Table 11.3* Regressions of R&D intensity on export, FDI and product diversification: 164 Japanese SMEs, 1986–96

| Variable | Model 1 | Model 2 | Model 3 | Model 4 | Model 5 | Model 6 | Model 7 | Model 8 |
|---|---|---|---|---|---|---|---|---|
| Intercept | — | — | — | — | — | — | — | — |
| Ln_emp | −0.0011 | −0.0011 | −0.0014 | −0.0013 | −0.0015 | −0.0017 | −0.0015 | −0.0016 |
|  | (0.0011) | (0.0011) | (0.0011) | (0.0011) | (0.0011) | (0.0011) | (0.0011) | (0.0011) |
| Rate | 0.0050 | 0.0050 | 0.0051 | 0.0052 | 0.0050 | 0.0050 | 0.0051 | 0.0051 |
|  | (0.0052) | (0.0066) | (0.0059) | (0.0061) | (0.0060) | (0.0053) | (0.0054) | (0.0055) |
| Adv | −0.0781** | −0.0781** | −0.0735** | −0.0765** | −0.0725* | −0.0759** | −0.0746** | −0.0778** |
|  | (0.0376) | (0.0376) | (0.0375) | (0.0376) | (0.0375) | (0.0374) | (0.0375) | (0.0374) |
| Herf |  | −0.0001 | 0.0013 | 0.0012 | 0.0012 | −0.0069 | −0.0026 | −0.0102 |
|  |  | (0.0098) | (0.0096) | (0.0097) | (0.0097) | (0.0101) | (0.0099) | (0.0103) |
| Exp |  |  | 0.0122*** |  | 0.0117*** | −0.0254 | 0.0116*** | −0.0239 |
|  |  |  | (0.0040) |  | (0.0040) | (0.0155) | (0.0040) | (0.0155) |
| Nat |  |  |  | 0.0046 | 0.0003 | 0.0003 | −0.0019 | −0.0018 |
|  |  |  |  | (0.0003) | (0.0003) | (0.0003) | (0.0012) | (0.0012) |
| Herfexp |  |  |  |  |  | 0.0706** |  | 0.0677** |
|  |  |  |  |  |  | (0.0285) |  | (0.0286) |
| Herfnat |  |  |  |  |  |  | 0.0041* | 0.0038* |
|  |  |  |  |  |  |  | (0.0021) | (0.0021) |
| R² | 0.3851 | 0.3851 | 0.4042 | 0.3885 | 0.4053 | 0.4176 | 0.4003 | 0.4133 |

*Notes:*
(1) Cell entries are unstandardized coefficient estimates, numbers in parentheses are standard errors.
(2) Industry dummies and year dummies are included in the model but not reported.
(3) *** p<0.01; ** p<0.05; * p<0.1.

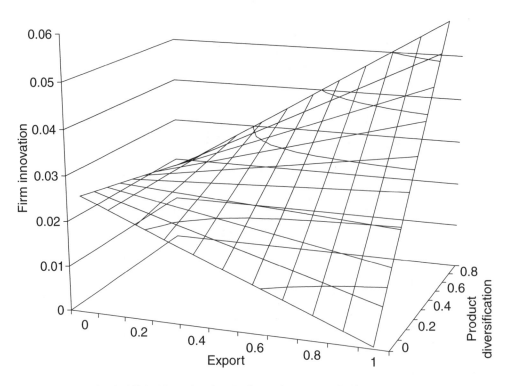

*Note:*  R_D calculated while holding values for all other various at mean levels.

*Figure 11.1   Export, product diversification and firm innovation*

In Models 6, 7 and 8, we included the cross-term to examine the impact of product diversification on the relationship between international diversification and firm innovation. In Model 6 we included the cross-term of HERF and EXP. We found a significantly positive coefficient of HERF*EXP, which suggests that international diversification exerts a positive impact on the relationship between product diversification and firm innovation. In Model 7, we replaced HERF*EXP with HERF*NAT and also found a positive, but less significant, coefficient for HERF*NAT. To verify our finding in M6 and M7, we included both in Model 8 and found both NAT and EXP to exert positive moderating impacts on the relationship between product diversification and firm innovation. Therefore Hypothesis 3 is fully supported.

We drew the findings of Model 6 in Figure 11.1. We found a conditional relationship between product diversification and firm innovation under the impact of exports. When international diversification (export) is at its low level, we found a negative relationship between product and firm innovation (R_D). As international diversification increases, however, the relationship between product diversification and firm innovation has turned positive. The figure clearly demonstrates the positive effect of international diversification on the relationship between product diversification and firm innovation.

Similarly, we drew the findings of Model 7 in Figure 11.2. We found that, when the level of foreign direct investment (NAT) is low, there is a flat or slightly negative

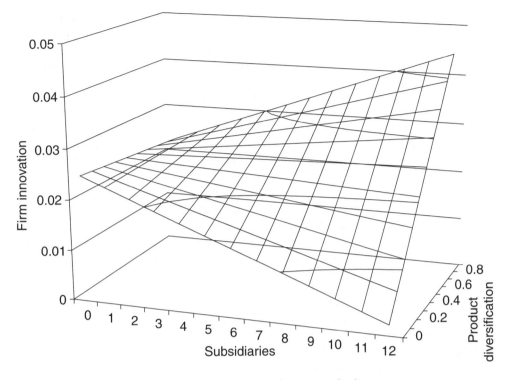

*Note:*   R_D calculated while holding values for all other various at mean levels.

*Figure 11.2    Foreign direct investment, product diversification and firm innovation*

relationship between firm product diversification and firm innovation. When the firm reaches a level of high foreign direct investment, however, the relationship between product diversification and firm innovation becomes positive. Thereafter we find a positive impact of foreign direct investment on the relationship between product diversification and firm innovation.

## DISCUSSION AND CONCLUSION

The research on firms' international diversification has received extensive attention in academic research (Hitt et al., 1997; Lu and Beamish, 2001). This topic is more relevant in the study of SMEs in the global economy as it is a vital approach for SMEs to expand. We conducted our study to address the following questions. Are SMEs with export activity motivated to innovate? Why and to what extent do exports encourage an SME to innovate?

We did not find a significant relationship between product diversification and firm innovation. This finding nullifies Hypothesis 1 and suggests that the resource competition between product diversification and firm innovation is not that significant in the 164 Japanese SMEs during 1986 to 1995. Our finding suggests that the shift toward financial control upon product diversification that has been found in large companies may not happen in SMEs. Further, as compared to large companies, SMEs are more likely to have concentrated ownership, a condition under which the negative relationship between product diversification and innovation may not exist (Baysinger et al., 1991).

However we find a positive relationship between international diversification and firm innovation, which confirms Hypothesis 2. This positive effect was mainly derived from exporting activities rather than foreign direct investment. It is worth noting that the firms in our sample represent a significant part of Japanese SMEs from the mid-1980s to the mid- 1990s. The corporations in our sample, such as Toyo and Kibun Food, all experienced high growth during that period. Exporting activity played a significant role in the growth strategy of these companies during this period. Exporting activities allowed these companies to compete at a global level and upgrade their products and services to meet the fast changing tastes of various destination countries as well as home countries. To maintain a technology advantage over international competitors in grasping market share, the firms are pressured to keep innovating and adjusting. We believe this is the reason why we find that exporting activity exerts a more positive impact on firm innovation than foreign direct investment. Our finding is consistent with previous studies in the literature (Kotabe, 1990; Bettis and Hitt, 1995) and supports the contention of the motivating effect of exports toward innovation. On the other hand, however, scholars also find innovation exerts a positive effect on exports (Bettis and Hitt, 1995; Bernard and Jensen, 1999). Our finding complements the literature in finding the other direction of effect and suggests that there may exist a virtuous circle relationship between internationalization and innovation.

The combined finding that there is no relationship between product diversification and innovation and a positive relationship between export and innovation has important policy implications. It suggests that the firms, especially small and medium-sized firms, should stay narrowly concentrated on the core business and expand geographically during its growth period. International diversification is more preferable a strategy than product diversification for small and medium-sized firms to grow.

In addition, we explored the effect of international diversification on the relationship between product diversification and innovation. We found that international diversification positively moderates the relationship between product diversification and firm innovation, which is exactly what we proposed in Hypothesis 3. The finding confirms our conjecture that the incentive from international diversification to innovate overwhelms the disincentive from product diversification. Taken together, the lack of support for Hypothesis 1 and the supporting evidence for Hypothesis 3 seems to confirm that product diversification does not lead to a significant disincentive to innovate in SMEs, which tend to have concentrated ownership and may not adopt financial controls as they diversify. In addition, our finding is consistent with the expectation that international diversification is a critical strategy for SMEs to expand, and this expansion momentum is sufficient to offset the negative impact of product diversification over firm innovation. It is consistent with the literature that there is an incentive for firms to expand geographically, through which firms are able to maximize the benefit of innovation. On the other hand, firms with international diversification are also motivated and better equipped (knowledge, culture, skill and so on) to innovate. We found that only exports and the cross-term between product diversification and export (Herf*exp) added significant explanatory power beyond the controls, which suggests that export does not conflict with product diversification. Instead our finding suggests that there is some synergy between export and product diversification which is consistent with Hypothesis 3.

Our study was conducted on SMEs in Japan, but the implication can be applied internationally. With international and product diversification as a commonly recognized approach for a firm to expand and grow, we want to raise the attention of scholars to look at the consequence of such expansion, not only over firm performance, but also over other critical firm strategies, such as innovation. In addition, this focus would be especially relevant for the SMEs to leverage the advantage of technology advance to expand internationally. We hope our study raises attention in academia to explore the expansion of SMEs in wider geographical areas (such as developing countries) and more diverse perspectives (for example, technology-oriented enterprise).

### Limitations

While the empirical results are interesting, caution should be exerted when generalizing the findings beyond the scope of this study. First, the results were derived from a sample of Japanese SMEs. Hence this raises the concern that the findings might be country-specific. Studies with comparative samples of firms from other countries should be used to test and extend the generalizability of our findings. Further, our sample consisted of publicly listed firms. Future research could investigate the performance implications of the internationalization efforts of private and smaller-sized firms to complement the picture of the relationship between diversification and innovation for the full range of firm sizes.

In addition, there are limitations to the measures employed in this study. For example, although R&D intensity is a frequently used measure of innovation in the literature, it is an indirect measure of innovation. Future studies could employ more direct measures of innovation such as new product development or patents. One of our measures of international diversification is export intensity, a widely used measure in the literature. Ideally we could also use the number of countries to which the firms export, which provides a more accurate measure of the extent of international diversification through exporting activities. However this measure was not available for our study. It would be useful for future studies to collect these data and test the robustness of our findings to alternative measures of international diversification. In future studies scholars could also use more detailed measures of product diversification such as related and unrelated diversification or relatedness among firms' resources. Finally ownership structure could have an important impact on firm strategy. It would be useful to explore the effects of ownership structure on firms' diversification strategy and innovation strategy to provide a more complete picture of the diversification–innovation relationship.

## REFERENCES

Barney, J. (1991), 'Firm resources and sustained competitive advantage', *Journal of Management*, **17**(1), 99–120.
Baysinger, B. and R.E. Hoskisson (1989), 'Diversification strategy and R&D intensity in multiproduct firms', *Academy of Management Journal*, **32**(2), 310–32.

Baysinger, B., R. Kosnik and T.A. Turk (1991), 'The effect of board and ownership structure on corporate R&D strategy', *Academy of Management Journal*, **34**(1), 205–14.

Beamish, P.W. (1999), 'The role of alliances in international entrepreneurship', *Research in Global Strategic Management*, **7**(1), 43–61.

Berger, P.G. and E. Ofek (1995), 'Diversification's effect on firm value', *Journal of Financial Economics*, **37**(1), 39–65.

Bernard, A.B. and J.B. Jensen (1999), 'Exceptional export performance: cause, effect, or both?', *Journal of International Economics*, **47**(1), 1–25.

Bettis, R.A. and M.A. Hitt (1995), 'The new competitive landscape', *Strategic Management Journal*, **16**(1), 7–19.

Brewer, H.L. (1981), 'Investor benefits from corporate international diversification', *Journal of Financial and Quantitative Analysis*, **16**(1), 113–26.

Burgelman, R.A. (1983), 'A process model of internal corporate venturing in the diversified major firm', *Administrative Science Quarterly*, **28**(2), 223–44.

Chang, S.J. and U. Choi (1988), 'Strategy, structure and performance of Korean business groups', *Journal of Industrial Economics*, **37**(2), 141–58.

Contractor, F.J., S.K. Kundu and C. Hsu (2003), 'A three-stage theory of international expansion: the link between multinationality and performance in the service sector', *Journal of International Business Studies*, **34**(1), 5–18.

Delios, A.K. and P.W. Beamish (1999), 'Geographic scope, product diversification and the corporate performance of Japanese firms', *Strategic Management Journal*, **20**(8), 711–27.

Denis, D.J., D.K. Denis and K. Yost (2002), 'Global diversification, industrial diversification, and firm value', *Journal of Finance*, **57**(5), 1951–79.

Doukas, J. and N.G. Travlos (1988), 'The effects of corporate multinationalism on shareholders' wealth: evidence from international acquisitions', *Journal of Finance*, **43**(5), 1161–75.

Errunza, V.R. and L.W. Senbet (1984), 'International corporate diversification, market valuation, and size-adjusted evidence', *Journal of Finance*, **39**(3), 727–43.

Geringer, J.M., P.W. Beamish and R.C. DaCosta (1989), 'Diversification strategy and internationalization: implications for MNE performance', *Strategic Management Journal*, **10**(2), 109–19.

Geringer, J.M., S. Tallman and D.M. Olsen (2000), 'Product and geographic diversification among Japanese multinational firms', *Strategic Management Journal*, **21**(1), 51–80.

Hitt, M.A., R.E. Hoskisson and R.D. Ireland (1990), 'Mergers and acquisitions and managerial commitment to innovation in m-form firms', *Strategic Management Journal*, **11**(1), 29–47.

Hitt, M.A., R.E. Hoskisson and R.D. Ireland (1994), 'A mid-range theory of the interactive effects of international and product diversification on innovation and performance', *Journal of Management*, **20**(2), 297–326.

Hitt, M.A., R.E. Hoskisson and H. Kim (1997), 'International diversification: effects on innovation and firm performance in product-diversified firms', *Academy of Management Journal*, **40**(4), 767–98.

Hitt, M.A., R.E. Hoskisson, R.D. Ireland and J.S. Harrison (1991), 'Effects of acquisitions on R&D inputs and outputs', *Academy of Management Journal*, **34**(3), 693–706.

Hitt, M.A., R.E. Hoskisson, R.A. Johnson and D.D. Moesel (1996), 'The market for corporate control and firm innovation', *Academy of Management Journal*, **39**(5), 1084–119.

Hoskisson, R.E. and M.A. Hitt (1988), 'Strategic control systems and relative R&D investment in large multi-product firms', *Strategic Management Journal*, **9**(6), 605–21.

Hoskisson, R.E. and M.A. Hitt (1990), 'Antecedents and performance outcomes of diversification: a review and critique of theoretical perspectives', *Journal of Management*, **16**(2), 461–509.

Hoskisson, R.E., R.A. Johnson and D.D. Moesel (1993), 'Construct validity of an objective categorical measure of diversification strategy', *Strategic Management Journal*, **14**(3), 215–35.

Kamien, M.I. and N.L. Schwartz (1982), *Market Structure and Innovation*, Cambridge, UK: Cambridge University Press.

Khanna, T. and K. Palepu (1996), 'Corporate scope and market imperfections: an empirical analysis of diversified business groups in an emerging economy', Harvard Business School.

Kobrin, S.J. (1991), 'An empirical analysis of the determinants of global integration', *Strategic Management Journal*, **12**(1), 17–37.

Kotabe, M. (1990), 'The relationship between offshore sourcing and innovativeness of U.S. multi-national firms: an empirical investigation', *Journal of International Business Studies*, **21**(4), 623–38.

Lang, L.H.P. and R.M. Stulz (1994), 'Tobin's Q, corporate diversification and firm performance', *Journal of Political Economy*, **102**(6), 1248–80.

Lawson, C.L. and R. Hanson (1974), *Solving Least Squares Problems*, Englewood Cliffs, NJ: Prentice-Hall.

Lins, K. and H. Servaes (1998), 'Is corporate diversification beneficial in emerging markets?', working paper, University of North Carolina.

Lloyd, W.P. and J.S. Jahera (1994), 'The effect of the degree of ownership control on profitability and market value', *International Journal of Finance*, **6**(4), 931–41.

Lu, J.W. and P.W. Beamish (2001), 'The internationalization and performance of SMEs', *Strategic Management Journal*, **22**(6/7), 565–86.

Lu, J.W. and P.W. Beamish (2004), 'International diversification and firm performance: the S-curve hypothesis', *Academy of Management Journal*, **47**(4), 598–609.

Lubatkin, M., H. Merchant and N. Srinivasan (1993), 'Construct validity of some unweighted product-count diversification measures', *Strategic Management Journal*, **14**(6), 433–49.

Miller, D. (1996), 'A preliminary typology of organizational learning: synthesizing the literature', *Journal of Management*, **22**(3), 485–505.

Morck, R. and B. Yeung (1991), 'Why investors value multinationality', *Journal of Business*, **64**(2), 165–87.

Nelson, R.R. (1959), 'The simple economics of basic sciences research', *Journal of Political Economy*, **67**(3), 297–306.

Porter, M.E. (1990), *The Competitive Advantage of Nations*, New York: Free Press.

Servaes, H. (1996), 'The value of diversification during the conglomerate merger wave', *Journal of Finance*, **51**(4), 1201–25.

Sullivan, D. (1994), 'Measuring the degree of internationalization of a firm', *Journal of International Business Studies*, **25**(2), 325–42.

Tallman, S. and J. Li (1996), 'Effects of international diversity and product diversity on the performance of multinational firms', *Academy of Management Journal*, **39**(1), 179–96.

Teece, D.J. (1986), 'Profiting from technological innovation', *Research Policy*, **15**(6), 285–306.

# 12. Should high-technology SMEs expect to internationalize by passing through a sequence of development stages that affect choice of export market and entry mode?

**Marian V. Jones**

## SHOULD HIGH-TECHNOLOGY SMES EXPECT TO INTERNATIONALIZE?

One of the key drivers of the globalization of the world economy is technological change. Most significant have been radical innovations in information, materials, energy, space and biotechnology that have resulted in the development of new products and markets, but also in new production systems, communication systems, transport systems and business systems (OECD, 2001). Modern technologies are complex, knowledge-intensive and require multidisciplinary inputs. They emerge from firms and organizations around the world that rely on information exchange and technology transfer to develop products and services that have international demand. An OECD report on drivers of economic growth noted that developments in ICT have made access to and diffusion of information possible at phenomenal speed (ibid., p. 11). In turn industries are being restructured internationally and, while this brings a host of international opportunities, it also brings pressures to speed up processes and find new ways of doing business. In conversation, Will Hutton stated that globalization is a powerful concept with a sense that there is no escape from the process: 'It's coming down the tracks straight at you' (Hutton and Giddens, 2000, p. 4). High-technology SMEs these days are 'born global' at least to the extent that they may have to operate from the outset in industries and markets that are international or global. High-technology SMEs should expect to internationalize because the innovation, production and marketing systems within which they operate are increasingly international, there are fewer national barriers to trade and investment behind which to shelter, and the increasing complexity of new technologies demands specialization towards niche opportunities that may extend globally.

Competition amongst the largest technology-based firms is more intense as a result of globalization. Increasingly they concentrate on core technologies while contracting out peripheral technologies to SMEs. The acquisition of patent rights from large technology firms provides start-up opportunities for spin-off and new venture SMEs that stand to benefit from international patent protection. Established international networks, and in some instances the transfer of human and social capital where the founders are previous employees of the original firm, enable the foundation of firms that are, or have the potential to become international from the outset. Gassmann et al. (2004) note that the outsourcing practices of the major pharmaceutical companies provide key opportunities for highly specialized high-technology SMEs. Reporting on a study of 12 of the world's largest pharmaceutical firms, they noted that their 193 associated R&D laboratories were located across the Triad regions. These tended to be concentrated in the northeast and midwest of the US, evenly distributed throughout western Europe and Scandinavia, and scattered along the Pacific Rim from Japan to southeast Australia.

To the extent that high-technology SMEs often provide specialist services or products for larger firms and operate within industry value chains and networks that are international, they need to internationalize because the firms they serve operate on a global basis (at least across the Triad regions). The demand for technology products is international and, on the supply side, knowledge-intensive innovation and production processes are resourced from sources of expertise located in R&D-rich countries around the world (Ernst, 2002). The latter author noted that globalization has tended to reduce the 'spatial stickiness' of innovation and the emergent global production networks of larger firms present key opportunities for SMEs (Ernst, 2002). However Stiglitz and Wallsten (1999) found strong cultural influences on national innovation systems including, for example, high rewards for individualism, which tended to cause US scientists to resist collaboration.

A greater variety of international knowledge linkages are possible now and the spread of global production networks creates opportunities for international knowledge diffusion and, in particular, opportunities for reverse knowledge outsourcing. Such opportunities emerge when large firms acquire or contract-in R&D and other specialist services from SMEs and universities. The complementary attributes of small and large firms in the innovation process have been known for some time. Early studies summarized, for example, by Acs and Audretsch (2003) suggested that larger firms have distinct advantages in economies of production and R&D scope, while smaller firms have complementary advantages of speed, flexibility and specialization in niche technologies, leading in some cases to opportunities for mutual interdependence. The same authors (1988) found that smaller firms tend to be reliant on universities to support their R&D, and are frequently found in proximity to universities or within clusters of firms involved in similar technologies or serving the same industry. Piore and Sabel (1984) found that, within these areas, local authorities are often proactive in encouraging collaboration among firms in networks that extend both locally and internationally. Furthermore some high-technology SMEs are expert at 'flexible specialization' (Garnsey and Wilkinson, 1994) meaning that they provide a specialized product or service in relation to a particular stage in the innovation or product value chain of one or several industries, and provide products or services that are unique.

Networks of firms and organizations with specialist knowledge in specific technologies, in several high-technology industries, have tended to form clusters in specific geographic locations. Examples include Silicon Valley in California, Silicon Glen in Scotland, clusters of biotechnology firms that emerged around the Cambridge area in England in the 1980s–90s, giving rise to the so-called 'Cambridge phenomenon', and more recently clusters of life sciences firms that are emerging in Finland and Scotland. A few clusters have formed across national borders within the EU; for example, the Öresund region (Denmark and Sweden) is home to a cluster of pharmaceutical and medical equipment SMEs and in Twente along the Netherlands/German border a cluster of plastics and metal-processing firms is found (Möhring, 2002). Within clusters trust is developed and knowledge shared but geographic and cultural separation between clusters may inhibit international interaction. Technological innovation is the vehicle driving the internationalization of SMEs involved in the production of *complex* technologies and 'the networks that innovate complex technologies normally operate in the context of intense international competition, faster product cycles, and shrinking time frames within which to appropriate the benefits of innovations' (Rycroft and Kash, 2002, p. 27). Firms therefore need to extend beyond the comfort of their local networks to gain access to knowledge and to technology markets. However, despite globalization, barriers to internationalization remain, for example lack of information on business opportunities, or access to it, financial barriers imposed by exchange rate, credit and political risk, the regulatory environment of different country markets and an inadequate domestic support structure (Möhring, 2002, p. 2). International networking between technology clusters is likely to be inhibited by cultural and linguistic barriers, geographic distance, the upkeep of cluster identity and the absence of a common pool of specialized labour (ibid., p. 3).

Assuming that such barriers to internationalization are surmountable, emergence of global production networks in industries such as the pharmaceutical industry should enable high-technology SMEs to exploit their advantages in the innovation process on an international or even global basis. SMEs have always played an important role in the innovation of new technology and evidence suggests that, in the US, investment in R&D by SMEs, their R&D to sales ratios and propensity to patent is increasing relative to that of larger firms (Möhring, 2002).

For high-technology SMEs and in particular those that provide products or services to larger firms such as the world's largest pharmaceutical companies, internationalization is virtually inevitable, and high-technology SMEs should expect to internationalize and to do so early. However, what is internationalization and what steps and/or stages is the firm likely to encounter in the process?

## DOES INTERNATIONALIZATION OCCUR THROUGH A SEQUENCE OF DEVELOPMENT STAGES?

Internationalization of the firm is generally understood to be a process that occurs over a period of time (Jones and Coviello, 2005). It is an extensive phenomenon that involves many aspects of the firm's activities, including its functions, processes and systems (Lehtinen and Penttinen, 1999). It is also a complex phenomenon and may be studied from a number of disciplinary perspectives, and explained by a number of different theoretical approaches, depending on the focus and perspective of the researcher. Internationalization, for example, is the process within which international technology transfer occurs, exporting is arranged and within which firms make foreign direct investments and strategic alliances. It is a process through which firms grow and develop internationally (Johanson and Vahlne, 1977), establish and manage their foreign operations (Luostarinen, 1980), increase their exposure to international business through international transactions (Beamish, 1990), establish and develop relationships and networks that extend across borders (Coviello and Munro, 1997) and which is manifest and identifiable through specific entry modes, in locations (countries) in relation to time (Jones and Coviello, 2005). The process is complex, multidimensional and difficult to define in a comprehensive or general way (Lehtinen and Penttinen, 1999).

Conventional thinking on internationalization tends to advocate a gradual move into foreign countries following an indeterminate period of development in the domestic market. The Uppsala approach (Johanson and Vahlne, 1977) describes internationalization as a process of increasing commitment to international markets, commencing with entry into psychically close markets using relatively unsophisticated market entry modes such as indirect exporting and extending over time to more distant markets and more advanced entry modes, such as the establishment of a sales subsidiary. The underlying logic of the approach is the development of knowledge and capability through experiential knowledge. Typical stages in the process start with the firm having no regular exporting activities, moving through exporting through overseas agents, establishment of a sales subsidiary and finally of overseas production. The approach is primarily concerned with the establishment of foreign markets for the firm's products.

The Finnish approach (Welch and Luostarinen, 1988) describes internationalization as the outward expansion of a firm's activities. Later, on the basis of empirical evidence, the concept was expanded to include inward, outward and cooperative activities (Luostarinen and Hellman, 1994). Based on longitudinal studies of internationalizing SMEs by Luostarinen and his team, which now extends over 30 years, the underlying logic is that firms increase their international involvement as the firm grows and develops, moving through entry modes ordered hierarchically on the basis of factors such as cost, risk, control and commitment, and distinguished by whether the investment made is indirect or direct, and whether production occurs at home or overseas (Luostarinen, 1980). Typical stages in the process are, firstly, *inward*, including the establishment of the firm's domestic operations and the importation of raw materials, components and technology, secondly, *outward*, during which the firm establishes entry modes commencing with exporting and moving through higher-order modes such as overseas production and the establishment of manufacturing subsidiaries overseas, and, thirdly, *cooperative*, during which the firm establishes alliances and partnerships with foreign firms.

Both the Uppsala and the Finnish approaches consider internationalization as a process of growth and development, and implicitly link the process of internationalization to the growth and development process of the firm itself. By extension, firms enter countries that they understand culturally, are close to geographically and therefore in which they can afford to make investments, initially through modes such as indirect export which are low-cost, low-risk and require low commitment. As resources, knowledge and capabilities grow, firms can afford to expand incrementally. The models are intuitively appealing and have been extensively supported by empirical evidence, but have also been criticized, mainly for their one-size-fits-all approach.

The so-called 'export development' or step/stage models also indicate a gradual, incremental approach to internationalization but focus almost exclusively on export sales and the development of the firm's export markets (Bilkey and Tesar, 1977; Cavusgil, 1984; Czinkota, 1982) and less, if at all, on the international growth and development process of the firm itself. Typical stages begin with the firm having no interest in exporting, fulfilling unsolicited orders, exploring the feasibility of exporting, exporting experimentally to a psychologically close country, making adjustments to optimize exporting to that country and finally exploring the feasibility of exporting to more distant countries.

Export development models are widely criticized for their assumption of reactive initiation of exports by the firms concerned, for their failure to explain adequately when and why firms might move from one stage to the next, and what exactly each stage means as regards the firm's size, resources and extent of internationalization and, generally, for lacking explanatory power (Andersen, 1993). The intuitive appeal and logic of the models, however, are difficult to refute, based as they are on a process of learning, the development of capabilities and competencies in relation to the internationalization process, and the accumulation of resources and hence firm growth as it benefits from international sales (although this last point is relatively underresearched).

Although entry modes are fundamental components of the internationalization process, Brouthers and Nakos (2004) note that SME studies tend to focus on the process itself rather than the entry modes. There is a significant literature on market entry modes that is less concerned with the process of internationalization than it is with strategic decisions about foreign market entry and servicing, and the focus of which is, not exclusively, but predominantly, on larger, already multinational firms. Questions such as which mode of business activity a firm should use to enter a particular country market, under what circumstances and when and why it should switch from one mode of activity to another are addressed in this literature in which internalization, the transaction cost approach and, more recently, the resource-based view are the favoured theoretical explanations. The emphasis in entry mode studies tends to be on rational decisions concerning competitiveness, efficiency, control and cost, on exploiting and protecting the proprietary knowledge/ownership advantage on which the firm's competitive advantage might be based, through a considered choice of entry modes, these being, chiefly, between exporting (transactional modes), direct investment (investment modes) and licensing (cooperative modes). Conventionally the entry mode literature also supports a gradual entry into foreign markets, firstly through transactional modes because, inter alia, shortages of management time, skilled management, limited managerial capacity, political naïveté and difficulties in the transition from family-controlled to management-controlled firm tend to render cooperative and investment modes more difficult for new and smaller firms (Buckley, 1989). By default, small, young firms, constrained in terms of knowledge, capabilities and other resources, would be expected to select entry modes that suited their size and capability. Typically, therefore, the first entry mode would be likely to be exporting because of its low cost and low risk. Thus, while the entry mode literature indirectly supports an incremental approach to internationalization, its logic is not explicitly based on stages of development, but rather on strategic decisions relating to the mode through which it exploits its competitive advantage internationally.

The network approach to internationalization suggests that internationalization may be triggered by a firm's contacts in its existing networks (Coviello and Munro, 1997). In the process of internationalization the firm enters new networks, creates new relationships and establishes positions in relation to foreign firms (Johanson and Mattsson, 1988). Importantly, the latter authors proposed that it is not just the firm that internationalizes, but also the actors in the network within which it operates and those network actors form the market. Markets, therefore, through their network actors, also internationalize and the firm's strategy and response to internationalization is likely to be influenced by the extent to which the market itself is internationalized. Johanson and Mattsson (1988, p. 310) present a model that attempts to explain entry mode decisions in relation to the internationalization stage of the market (low, high) and the internationalization stage of the firm (low, high). Thus an early starter, that is, a firm that enters a market that is not particularly internationalized, is predicted to follow the route of agents it has already used by investing in those relationships, or will acquire a firm with an established position in the international network to benefit from its knowledge and network links. The late starter, that is, a newly internationalizing firm in a highly internationalized market, is predicted to be highly specialized and will build bonds with customers and other network actors for the coordination of production activities. Larger, less specialized firms, they predict, may establish themselves in a highly internationalized market through acquisition or joint venture. This example aside, network approaches tend not to prescribe stages in internationalization; rather the firm in a network is seen as one variable in a sequence of causal loops over time (Weick, 1979) and foreign market entry is a process of interaction between network actors in the ever changing conditions of the network (Blankenburg, 1995). While the network approach indicates that firms internationalize through a process in which bonds and relationships are developed, and that these might culminate in formal entry mode arrangements, the network literature emphasizes an evolutionary growth pattern rather than an explicitly staged approach.

Dissatisfaction with step/stage, gradual incremental approaches to internationalization, together with emerging evidence throughout the 1980s and 1990s that increasing numbers of small firms were commencing international business activity at, or soon after inception (Turnbull, 1987; Rennie, 1993; McDougall, Shane and Oviatt, 1994; Oviatt and McDougall, 1994; Bloodgood, Sapienza and Almeida, 1996; Knight and Cavusgil, 1996; Coviello and Munro, 1997; Jones, 1999) led to the emergence of what is now commonly referred to as the international new venture approach (INV). This approach suggests that some small firms are capable of early rapid internationalization through a variety of modes other than just export, that the process involves an awareness of changes induced by internationalization, and may involve proactive behaviour, and a mindset or orientation open to the discovery and exploitation of international opportunities. Definitions have advanced accordingly; for example, Beamish (1990, p. 77) describes internationalization as 'the process by which firms both increase their awareness of direct and indirect influence of international transactions on their future, and establish and conduct transactions with other countries'. McDougall and Oviatt (2000, p. 903) accommodate the process of internationalization as central to their definition of international entrepreneurship, which, drawing on Covin and Slevin's (1991) characterization of entrepreneurial behaviour, they describe as 'a combination of innovative, proactive and risk-seeking behaviour that crosses national borders and is intended to create value in organisations'. A further refinement (Oviatt and McDougall, 2005, p. 7) incorporates a Schumpeterian perspective on innovation: 'the discovery, enactment, evaluation and exploitation of opportunities across national borders to create future goods and services'.

This evolution towards a more holistic understanding of internationalization, driven by opportunity and perhaps infinite possibilities in terms of patterns of development, emerged in some of the internationalization literature published during the 1990s. However Wolff and Pett note in their article, published in the year 2000, that two patterns of internationalization of small firms had become prevalent in the literature at the turn of this century. Studies tend to follow either the *international at foundation* pattern (following, for example, Rennie, 1993; Oviatt and McDougall, 1994) or an *international by stage* approach (following for example, Bilkey and Tesar, 1977; Johanson and Vahlne, 1977; Luostarinen, 1980; Cavusgil, 1984). In reality, patterns of internationalization are likely to be more varied, and more complex (Jones, 1999). Bell, McNaughton and Young (2001) and Bell et al. (2003) identified three patterns of small firm internationalization: the traditional 'staged' pattern, the 'born global' pattern and the 'born-again' global pattern which were distinguishable by differences in firm motivations, objectives, pace, entry modes, international strategies and financing. Rapid internationalization in particular, wherein firms are apparently able to leapfrog stages in the traditional models has been examined in relatively few studies which identify that firms may exhibit individual patterns of internationalization based on complex variations of factors internal and external to the firms, and in which response to serendipitous opportunity may be as influential as strategy (Oviatt and McDougall, 1994; Reuber and Fischer, 1997; Kutscher, Baurle and Schmidt, 1997; Jones, 1999; Wolff and Pett, 2000; Crick and Spence, 2005; Jones and Coviello, 2005).

## SHOULD HIGH-TECHNOLOGY SMES EXPECT TO INTERNATIONALIZE THROUGH A SEQUENCE OF DEVELOPMENT STAGES OTHER THAN INTERNATIONALIZATION STAGES?

To suggest that the process of internationalization is driven by a sequence of internationalization stages is somewhat tautological. However internationalization processes are embedded in multiple, overlapping processes (Araujo and Rezende, 2003). Two are considered here, the process of firm growth and development, and the process of technological innovation. Step/stage growth models were prevalent in the schools of thought pertaining to each of these processes in the 1970s and 1980s.

Frequently cited in the small firm literature, Greiner (1972) suggested that firms passed through five phases of growth characterized as five evolution stages: creativity, direction, delegation, coordination and collaboration. Each evolution stage was followed in turn by a crisis stage, that is, leadership, autonomy, control, red tape and '?' (undefined crisis). Each evolution stage in Greiner's model is marked by a specific set of attributes relating to management focus, organizational structure, top management style, control system, management reward emphasis and crisis. Each crisis stage triggers change in the attributes.

Stage models of small firm growth are widely criticized for their explicit linearity that suggests that firms follow a path through predetermined stages of growth, for failing to account for the skipping of stages or backward movements along the continuum of stages, and for their failure to accommodate path dependency: each stage is inevitable rather than influenced by the firm's history of experience. Referring explicitly to Greiner (1972), the possibility of a firm exhibiting a complex mixture of stage attributes at any one time, for example, informal organizational structure attributed to stage one in the model, with participative management style, attributed to stage five, is not accommodated (Deakins, 1999, p. 208). The combination of attributes held by the firm, in combination with various influences from the internal and external environment, at any one time, is more likely to influence internationalization than any specific stage of firm development, even if that stage could be clearly defined.

Perhaps because stage models are criticized for their limitations and tendencies towards prescription and linearity, they tended to fall out of favour and more recent stage-type approaches to firm growth have emphasized *phases in development* in a rather more fluid way than early models as typified by Greiner (1972). For example, Kazanjian (1988) discerned a staged or phased pattern of growth in two case firms that were both technology-based new ventures. The stages identified are (1) conception and development, (2) commercialization, (3) growth and (4) stability. These stages reflect the strategic and operational problems faced by management. As the dominant problems change, Kazanjian found that the firm's configuration of organizational design variables changed in response. Empirical testing of the stage model, through deductive, quantitative surveys utilizing structured questionnaires, lent some support to the notion of identifiable growth stages (Kazanjian, 1988; Kazanjian and Drazin, 1989). The sample consisted of respondents from technology-based new ventures, who were asked to select, from four stages, the one that best described their current position. It was also found, however, that 'stages are not tight, discrete packages of internal characteristics that develop in response to dominant problems, but instead are somewhat fluid, with problems overlapping in adjacent stages' (Kazanjian, 1988, p. 276). The latter also found only partial support for a predictable sequential pattern through growth stages. Further empirical testing (Kazanjian and Drazin, 1989), found modest support for progression through the four identified growth stages but cautioned that the pattern might represent a 'central tendency' only with variation around that pattern and unexplained deviance by a few firms that regressed, or skipped stages.

One of the criticisms levelled by Kazanjian (1988) on general stage models such as Greiner's is that they tend to be context-free and ignore important factors such as external influences and factors leading to the formation of the firm. Such factors may relate to the process of innovation, which is concurrent with the process of growth and development for new venture technology-based firms. In a case-based study of university high-technology spin-off firms, Vohora, Wright and Lockett (2004) identify five phases, rather than stages that their sample firms passed through. The phases are (1) research phase, (2) opportunity framing phase, (3) pre-organization phase, (4) reorientation phase, and (5) sustainable returns phase. While they found that each case firm had to pass through the previous phase to arrive at the next one, the process was noted to be iterative and nonlinear. Interestingly, progression from one phase to another was found to rely on 'critical junctures' at which firms had to have acquired specific resources and capabilities in order to move on to the next phase. In Vohora et al.'s (2004) cases, 'critical junctures' relate to resources and capabilities required to grow the firm, and simultaneously develop and commercialize the technology. The process of firm growth is apparently intertwined with the process of innovation for new venture, high-technology firms.

Stage models are also prevalent in the literature describing the process of innovation. For example, Saren (1984) in a review of the innovation literature, identifies five categories of innovation process models. These are department stage models, activity stage models, decision stage models, conversion process models and response models, the former three of which identify explicit stages in the process. Where innovation parallels the growth process of the firm itself, 'critical junctures' may emerge as the firm seeks both internally and externally to augment its resources and capabilities. For example, Forrest (1991, p. 444), in a study concerned with the firm's development of strategic partnerships throughout the innovation process, is critical of rigidly linear stage models and called for models that 'integrate(s) all the facets of the innovation process that should be recognised by those responsible for facilitating innovation in the firm'. Although stage models of innovation are as widely criticized as those relating to small firm growth and internationalization, the complexity of innovation in modern technologies often requires that some distinction between certain stages in the process of its development or transfer be identified.

For example, government support programmes normally dictate a distinction between pre-competitive and commercialization stages of innovation and tailor support packages accordingly. In most countries new drug development, for example, is subject to stringent legislative control involving several rounds of clinical trials (Figure 12.1) and the stages in the innovation process are indicated by pre- and post-trial phases. Complex technologies such as drug discovery and development require knowledge-intensive and highly specialized inputs at various points in their innovation value chain. Gassmann et al. (2004) note that the pharmaceutical industry often considers the innovation process in three phases, that is, research, pre-project and development phases, although many companies do not distinguish clearly between the phases. The new drug development value chain (Figure 12.1) therefore also suggests phases in the process that might indicate a general division of labour among contributing specialist firms and stages at which technology transfer is likely to occur.

Although production networks in high technologies such as pharmaceuticals are becoming global, Peters and Young (2006) found that life sciences firms seldom operated in global markets because of the complexity of the new drug development process. Rather they tend to take the form of several different business formats performing one or several roles in the innovation chain. Arthur D. Little (2002) defines several business models. The *vertical model* has its own complete value chain and capabilities in development, production and marketing. The *product business model* is adopted by firms that progress products towards commercialization, for example, drug development and discovery companies. Normally firms of this type would transfer the technology through licensing or alliances to larger firms with established production facilities and marketing and distribution networks. The *technology platform model* is adopted where the firm is involved in developing a platform technology; that is, one that has multiple applications across a range of technologies and/or industries and which underpins or supports a larger part of the innovation process. Finally, the *hybrid business model* may, for example, involve a firm trying to develop a sustainable business through proprietary drug discovery.

The process of technological innovation is very likely to influence the internationalization process of high-technology SMEs. Firstly, the complexity of the innovation process in some industries results in a few firms adopting fully integrated models, for example, the world's leading pharmaceutical companies, while others adopt more specialist roles. Essentially there are three value chain positions that SMEs could adopt, firstly, the *within-firm value chain* (WFVC) that is, the vertically integrated model (Little, 2002), a *within-industry value network* position (WIVN) in which specialist SMEs play distinct roles in a

| Discovery | Small-scale production | Pre-clinical testing | Phase I | Phase II | Phase III | Full-scale production | Create demand | Marketing and distribution |
|-----------|------------------------|----------------------|---------|----------|-----------|-----------------------|---------------|----------------------------|

*Figure 12.1   The new drug development value chain*

networked innovation process within a specific industry, and a *cross-industry value network* position (CIVN) in which specialist SMEs provide a product or service across several industries. Peters and Young (2006) argue that the core competencies of life sciences firms are likely to remain local. This seems to contradict their proposed model which suggests that three interrelated dimensions are important in understanding life-sciences business models. These are the location of life-science value chain functions and the significance of related local and international networks and relationships, their modes of business operation, and the internationalization of their operations, local, regional or global.

The answer to the question 'should high technology SMEs expect to internationalize through a sequence of development stages other than internationalization stages?' is probably 'yes' – where stages can be clearly defined! Firms tend to internationalize as a solution to a problem or in response to an opportunity. Where opportunities and/or solutions are found overseas or are offered by foreign partners, cross-national business activity is likely to be instigated and a process of internationalization begun. The form internationalization takes (and this might be indicated by the establishment of cross-border business modes) is likely to be influenced by the firm's resources and capabilities at that particular time rather than any particular stage in the firm's growth. Phases of development seem more pertinent and firms engaged in innovation stages such as are mentioned above are likely to seek or attract international business opportunities that supply the needs of that innovation phase. What is clear is that the role of the firm in the innovation process, and the stage of development of the technological innovation, are likely to have a significant impact on the internationalization process of high-technology SMEs and their choice of entry mode and country market, because the process of internationalization emerges from, and is dependent on, the growth process of the firm itself, and the development and commercialization of its technology.

## STAGES IN SME HIGH-TECHNOLOGY INTERNATIONALIZATION: WHAT STAGES?

Stages of development, whether of the firm, the innovation process or the internationalization process of the firm itself are not well defined and are generally criticized for being overly deterministic. In all three bodies of literature more mutable and fluid *phases* of development are now favoured over deterministic stages of growth. Development stages therefore are less likely to influence choice of entry mode than other pertinent factors, as discussed above. Internationalization is a process that occurs because the firm is seeking solutions to growth problems internationally, or responding to international opportunities. The internationalization literature, however, has tended to treat internationalization as a strategy in its own right: firms have a strategic goal to internationalize (this is actually unlikely without some other purpose or trigger for doing so) and, therefore, stages towards the goal of internationalization have been seen as having some importance.

Conventional wisdom on internationalization holds that small firms undergo a period of development in the domestic market before venturing abroad and then follow a series of incremental stages, commencing with low resource-intensive modes such as indirect exporting. It is convenient of research design, and also as a basis for policy support programmes, to categorize internationalization stages neatly according to dimensions such as the level of sophistication of entry as determined by factors such as their relative cost, risk, control and return on investment. While the intuitive and parsimonious sense of such approaches is not disputed, the results of such studies are aggregations and mask deviations from the 'central tendency' and may have been at least partially responsible for a dearth of early research on born-globals and other forms of newly internationalizing firms. For this reason, I conducted a series of investigations (published elsewhere), that looked at stages of internationalization of high-technology SMEs as unique events in the international development of individual firms, which, in a later paper, have now been labelled as 'internationalization events' (Jones and Coviello, 2005). The purpose of the research was to establish whether or not there were clear stages in the internationalization of SMEs and, if so, what the stages consisted of in terms of the types of business modes established, at what points in time they occurred during the lifespan of the firm, and how quickly they were established over a period of years.

Jones (1999, 2001) surveyed 196 small, high-technology firms in England and Scotland to determine whether in fact internationalization of small technology-based firms begins with indirect export, whether modes are established sequentially, and the extent to which internationalization patterns follow conventional development patterns or are more diverse. The key variables in the study were (1) the foundation date of the firm, (2) a comprehensive list of cross-border links (entry modes including both inward and outward modes, constructed from seminal work by Luostarinen, 1980; Young et al., 1989; Chesnais, 1988) (Figure 12.2, see Key) and (3) the date on which each cross-border link was first established. The methodology has been published elsewhere and will not be repeated here. The purpose of the study was to identify internationalization patterns of individual small technology-based firms by mapping their entry modes against the dates at which they were first established.

The findings reveal some interesting patterns (Table 12.1). In common with a number of other studies, the most frequent cross-border business link types established were exporting through an overseas-based agent/distributor and importing from overseas suppliers. Thus the most frequent modes established were trading-based modes of low resource intensity, therefore supporting similar findings by Burgel and Murray (2000). Although trading-based modes were the most frequent type of mode utilized, a wide range of cross-border links was established by the sample firms, including several forms of import and export activity, licensing in and out of technology, inward and outward contractual arrangements including R&D and overseas production under contract, and the establishment of overseas production subsidiaries. Arranged in rank order according to the number of years between firm foundation and the establishment of each cross-border link, indirect exporting was only the fourth earliest form of link to be established and not the first as predicted by conventional theory. The earliest link types formed were in fact relatively complex cooperation arrangements with overseas-based firms. The rank order of link types according to the number of years it took firms to establish them does not reflect the typical sequential pattern of low resource-intensive modes through to higher resource-intensive modes that conventional wisdom suggests. Also worth noting is that, while the frequency (popularity) of modes established tends to follow the conventional pattern of export to licensing to foreign direct investment, the time taken to establish each mode type by the firms that did so shows a different pattern suggesting that

*Table 12.1   Cross-border links by time elapsed from firm foundation*

| Years after foundation | | Type of link established* | Firms (n) |
|---|---|---|---|
| Rank | Mean years | | |
| 1 | 3.50 | Other outward links | 8 |
| 2 | 4.63 | Non-equity joint production agreements | 8 |
| 3 | 5.55 | Distribution agreements with suppliers of complementary products | 38 |
| 4 | 5.99 | Exporting through UK-based intermediary | 85 |
| 5 | 6.03 | Exporting through foreign-based agent/distributor | 117 |
| 6 | 6.42 | Imports from overseas-based supplier | 147 |
| 7 | 6.44 | Comprehensive R&D, manufacturing and marketing consortia | 9 |
| 8 | 6.93 | Technology-sharing agreements | 15 |
| 9 | 6.94 | Management/marketing service/consultancy performed overseas | 18 |
| 10 | 7.06 | Other inward involvement | 17 |
| 11 | 7.23 | Contract R&D for overseas firm | 52 |
| 12 | 7.54 | Cross-border cooperative R&D project | 68 |
| 13 | 8.20 | Technical service/consultancy performed overseas | 41 |
| 14 | 8.20 | Production in overseas subsidiary (>50% equity) | 5 |
| 15 | 8.58 | Distribution of imports in UK | 77 |
| 16 | 8.75 | Technical/service consultancy in UK for overseas firm | 52 |
| 17 | 9.21 | Contract manufacture in UK for overseas firm | 89 |
| 18 | 9.75 | Exporting through own representatives/branches overseas | 53 |
| 19 | 10.45 | Licensing out technology to overseas-based firm | 20 |
| 20 | 10.83 | Management/marketing service/consultancy in UK for overseas-based firm | 23 |
| 21 | 11.00 | Contract out manufacturing to overseas-based firm | 25 |
| 22 | 13.53 | Licensing in technology from overseas-based firm | 17 |
| 23 | 14.00 | Production in overseas subsidiary | 3 |
| 24 | 16.50 | Contract out R&D to overseas-based firm | 16 |

*Note:*   * The type of links established are also detailed in the key to Figure 12.2, which was generated from the same data set.

*Source:*   Adapted from Jones (2001, p. 200).

the aggregation of results, typical in cross-industry survey studies, tends to mask internationalization patterns that differ from convention by their relative infrequency. Most importantly, firms that follow the international new venture approach are identified here by the speed with which they commence internationalization through a variety of modes (governance structures), some of which represent the control of assets overseas (Oviatt and McDougall, 1994).

The non-sequential process of internationalization is demonstrated further if the patterns of international links formed are examined according to three key value chain activities, marketing/distribution, production and R&D, and according to whether the link was inward from an overseas-based firm, or outward towards an overseas market (Table 12.2).

*Table 12.2    Value chain composition of first steps in internationalization*

| Links established at first internationalization event* | f | % |
|---|---|---|
| All firms that established at least one cross-border link | 195 | 100 |
| All firms with a combination of links (any number and any type) | 102 | 52 |
| Firms with single inward *or* outward links only of any type | 93 | 48 |
| Firms with inward *and/or* outward marketing/distribution links | 176 | 90 |
| Firms with inward marketing/distribution combinations with production and/or R&D | 129 | 66 |
| Firms with *outward* marketing/distribution with production and/or R&D | 88 | 45 |
| Firms with production/research combinations *but with no* marketing | 19 | 10 |

*Note:*   * An internationalization event is a year in which a firm established a particular entry mode for the first time. Here entry modes are described as 'links' because they represent a business link with a firm in a foreign country. Links are described generically as related to marketing/distribution activities, R&D activities and production activities. Inward links indicate that the value adding activity occurs in the UK, outward links where it occurs overseas.

*Source:*   Adapted from Jones (2001, p. 202).

The results reveal that firms tend more often to establish combinations of cross-border links than single link types, thus again suggesting that sequential patterns of internationalization through incremental adjustments is not typical. Two main patterns were revealed; firms either commenced internationalization by establishing a single cross-border link (48 per cent), or by establishing more complex combinations of value chain links (52 per cent). A summary of the main combinations is shown in Table 12.2; for a more detailed analysis, see Jones (2001).

In an attempt to move away from linear representations of internationalization, Jones (1999) performed a temporal analysis of the entry modes established by a sample of small high technology-based firms (Figure 12.2). The analysis involved identifying the exact date on which each firm established their first link (entry mode). Links were identified according to their relationship with the firm's value chain activities, and whether the link represented an inward move from an overseas-based partner, or an outward expansion of the firm's activities towards foreign markets. Four distinct internationalization patterns emerged, illustrated in the four case examples shown in Figure 12.2. Patterns 1, 2 and 3 show some linearity in the sense that the entry modes follow relatively conventional patterns of trading arrangements followed after differing time periods by production arrangements. Within the broad label of exporting, however, the conventional pattern of low resource-intense indirect exporting through to more advanced export modes was not prevalent and there was much more variety in the order in which modes were established. Pattern 4 does not in any way support a conventional, linear sequence of entry mode establishment. The time-intense pattern of internationalization, comprising a complex combination of entry modes across all aspects of the value chain, is suggestive of the international new venture or born global (Oviatt and McDougall, 1994; Knight and Cavusgil, 1996; Rennie, 1993).

Patterns of internationalization demonstrated by high-technology SMEs are not necessarily linear or sequential. Internationalization may begin with any type of value chain activity in inward or outward directions. The diversity of link combinations suggests that these might be associated with the specific needs, competencies and goals of firms rather than to a pre-ordained and staged development process. Although export is widely supported as the means by which SMEs most frequently commence internationalization, and that for many firms the process may follow a relatively conventional, sequential process, the current prevalent view from the internationalization literature, and demonstrated here, is that a staged process is too deterministic and fails to take into account the array and complexity of factors that influence any individual firm's process of internationalization. High-technology firms should not necessarily expect to follow a standard or predetermined sequence of internationalization development stages.

## SHOULD DEVELOPMENT STAGES AFFECT CHOICE OF EXPORT MARKET AND ENTRY MODE?

In general, entry mode choice in relation to SMEs is underresearched (Burgel and Murray, 2000; Brouthers and Nakos, 2004). Interestingly the entry mode literature is virtually silent on the influence of explicit development stages on entry mode choice. There are, however, indirect influences. Burgel and Murray (2000), for example, suggest that entry mode choice is a trade-off between the resources available and the support requirements of the customer. Their results suggest that entry mode decisions represent managerial choices based on product and firm-specific considerations rather than on levels of commitment determined by past experience. However they also acknowledge an element of path dependence in that the historic channel experience of the firm in its domestic markets as well as the innovativeness of the technology are strong determinants of mode choice.

The choice of equity modes of market entry are associated with R&D intensity (Burgel and Murray, 2000), with the ability to develop differentiated complex technological products (Osborne, 1996), where there is a need to protect proprietary knowledge (Bell, McNaughton and Young, 2001) and where firms had greater international experience and had developed stronger internal control mechanisms (Delios and Beamish, 1999; Luo and Peng, 1999). While the latter example relates to experiential knowledge and the development of competence in international business, it is not linked to any specified stages of development. Brouthers and Nakos (2004) suggest that SMEs may rely on export modes because of behavioural uncertainties resulting from their inexperience and lack of systems and processes for managing internationalization. Several studies of small high-technology firms found little evidence of entry modes other than exporting modes being used by the firms in their samples (Lindqvist, 1997; Bell, 1995). However, within export modes, Burgel and Murray (2000) found the use of distributors to be favoured by the larger firms, and biotechnology and medical firms to be more reliant on intermediaries than those from other technology industries. Other influencing factors included managers who had previously lived abroad. Overall the empirical evidence that might support the influences of development stages on entry mode choice is not compelling.

Although the above argument lends little support to a structured stage approach to internationalization by small high-technology firms, the limits of their resource base, together with 'informal structures, insufficiently developed administrative procedures and techniques, and often irrational decision-making processes', may limit the possibilities of international growth and expansion (Lindell and Karagozoglu, 1997, p. 93). The argument for a gradual incremental approach allowing time for learning and adjustment is

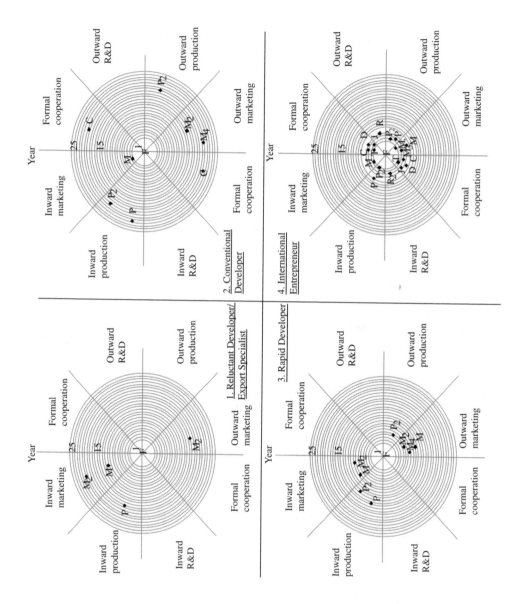

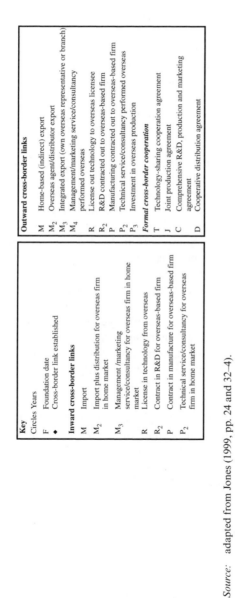

**Key**

Circles Years
F Foundation date
♦ Cross-border link established

**Inward cross-border links**
M Import
$M_2$ Import plus distribution for overseas firm in home market
$M_3$ Management/marketing service/consultancy for overseas firm in home market
R License in technology from overseas
$R_2$ Contract in R&D for overseas-based firm
P Contract in manufacture for overseas-based firm
$P_2$ Technical service/consultancy for overseas firm in home market

**Outward cross-border links**

M Home-based (indirect) export
$M_2$ Overseas agent/distributor export
$M_3$ Integrated export (own overseas representative or branch)
$M_4$ Management/marketing service/consultancy performed overseas
R License out technology to overseas licensee
$R_2$ R&D contracted out to overseas-based firm
P Manufacturing contracted out to overseas-based firm
$P_2$ Technical service/consultancy performed overseas
$P_3$ Investment in overseas production

**Formal cross-border cooperation**
T Technology-sharing cooperation agreement
J Joint production agreement
C Comprehensive R&D, production and marketing agreement
D Cooperative distribution agreement

*Source:* adapted from Jones (1999, pp. 24 and 32–4).

*Figure 12.2 Examples of firm internationalization patterns: temporal and value chain*

appealing but in the fast-moving global industries of high technology such an approach is one that few firms may be able to afford. Much more rapid market entry through relevant modes would seem more appropriate.

As already discussed, stages in the development of the firm are relevant to entry mode choice to the extent that the resource capabilities and experience of the firm will have some impact on entry mode choice as regards the cost, risk, commitment and return on investment associated with each mode. However the resource conditions and operating practices of firms at any one time may be more influential than a particular stage in the firm's growth process.

As regards the innovation process, the nature of the technology and the firm's specialist role or role with a wider innovation network is likely significantly to influence the choice of entry mode. For example, as above, different business models adopted by firms suggest particular types of link between firms in the innovation process, depending on what part of the process the firm is involved in, and the extent to which production networks are internationalized.

The nature of the technology may also influence entry mode. Buckley (2003, p. 334) suggests that the most appropriate types of international technology transfer for SMEs are small-scale technologies, labour-intensive technologies and specialized high-technology know-how. In the first type, small firms may use different production modes than large firms and satisfy demand unmet by larger MNEs. Labour-intensive technologies, especially services, Buckley argues, are likely to be transferred through relocation of the production activities to foreign locations. New technologies he suggests require external funding for commercialization, and marketing is risky. The preferred transfer modes therefore are most often equity joint ventures and non-equity licensing deals. Mode choice is explained here by the type of technology being transferred, the structure of the market *vis-à-vis* the relative positions and roles of large MNEs and SMEs, the competencies, capabilities and resources at their disposal and the nature of the production process, such as small batch, custom-made and service production processes.

The innovation process for complex technologies, then, is less likely to be staged than it is path-dependent. Early decisions regarding business modes are likely to influence later decisions, and contacts, links and relationships developed during the innovation process may influence the choice of entry mode and the sequence of development thereafter. Where high-technology firms are involved in a process of technological innovation and the technologies are complex, the process is knowledge-intensive and path-dependent (Rycroft and Kash, 2002). Typically, complex technologies by their nature cannot be fully understood by one individual expert and cannot be precisely communicated among experts across time and distance (Rycroft and Kash, 1999). Organizational learning is crucial to the development of core technological advantage but, owing to the complexity of the process, relies on the development of relationships and expert networks through which knowledge may be shared and explained. Innovation is therefore path-dependent on knowledge exchanges within the network. Rycroft and Kash (2002) suggest that time pressures reinforce local path dependence as it is quicker and easier to consult local experts than those more temporally or spatially distant, but note that firms will not necessarily follow a rigidly determined pathway.

Rycroft and Kash (2002) identified three path-dependent patterns of innovation: the *transformational pattern*, where firms are involved in the development of 'first of a kind technology', the *transitional pattern*, where major modifications are made to an existing technology, and the *normal pattern*, wherein innovation is incremental. If it is accepted that for SMEs in complex technologies innovation is likely to be the driver of internationalization, it can be hypothesized that the form and pattern of internationalization will be determined by the pattern of innovation. Table 12.3 illustrates hypothesized associations between Jones's (1999) patterns of internationalization and Rycroft and Kash's (2002) path-dependent patterns of innovation. The hypotheses are advanced tentatively here because, as Rycroft and Kash (2002, p. 22) suggest, the predictability of path-dependent systems can at times be very low, and at others very high owing to the impact of small historical events that may ultimately become important. However it is useful and interesting to make a first attempt to hypothesize interdependence between patterns of internationalization and patterns of innovation for complex technologies. The transformational pattern, because of its requirement for knowledge-intensive inputs from a considerable number of experts and expert networks, is likely to result in an instant or early internationalization process characterized by R&D collaboration, licensing agreements and buying and selling of patent rights which are more likely to be global than local. While the internationalization process commences very early, financial returns are likely to take some time to be realized but are likely to be very high when they do come in. The transitional pattern is likely to be characterized also by licensing agreements and by joint production agreements and collaborative marketing and distribution. It is likely to be rapid, but less so than for the transformational pattern, and may emerge from networks of product users who have been instrumental in the new product development process. The normal pattern is likely to be associated with local learning in local networks and less dependent on international sources of knowledge resource. However the market for incremental adjustments to existing technology is likely to be international and competitive. The associated internationalization pattern therefore is likely to be characterized by intensive exporting through overseas agents and distributors.

To the extent that internationalization is path-dependent, Wolff and Pett (2000) suggest that firms are likely to establish a base from which to commence their exporting activities. By a 'base', they mean a stock of resources and knowledge, from which exporting may become an extension of their domestic business activities. Thus the firm's modes of business in the domestic market may influence the mode choice in the internationalization process. The existing stock of knowledge accumulated in a firm is likely to shape its future trajectory and evolution (Eriksson, Majkgard and Sharma, 2000). Hence the international contacts and links encountered in the innovation process (Rycroft and Kash, 2002) are likely to influence the nature and direction of the internationalization process and, following this argument, the process is likely to be incremental and relatively gradual. However such processes may well be interrupted by the firm's ability to identify and act on new opportunities in the international market, through systematic search, and also by being open to chance and serendipitous encounters (Crick and Spence, 2005).

## CONCLUSIONS

High-technology firms should not necessarily expect to pass through a series of predetermined internationalization stages as defined by entry mode and country of entry.

*Table 12.3   Hypothesized association between internationalization patterns, and innovation patterns for complex technologies*

| Internationalization Patterns (adapted from Jones, 1999) | Innovation Patterns for Complex Technologies (adapted from Rycroft and Kash, 2002) | | |
|---|---|---|---|
| | **The transformational pattern** | **The transitional pattern** | **The normal pattern** |
| | Launches first-of-kind technologies. Organizational learning is not local, it involves accessing knowledge from outside existing networks and thus creating new knowledge. Paths of technologies and networks are launched for the first time; there is much trial and error. There are no network routines and heuristics to guide the route to success | Involves major modifications in an existing technology's design. Organizational learning as in the transformational pattern, is not local, it involves accessing knowledge from outside existing networks and thus creating new knowledge. Major design and network changes are required. Path dependence may erode or disappear | Involves incremental innovations of an established design. Local learning plays a strong role. Network strategies and structures are adjusted gradually. Local clusters of highly specialized knowledge and the existence of institutionalized arrangements that enhance trust and reciprocity may reinforce path dependence |
| | | | *The normal pattern* is likely to be associated with local learning in local networks and less dependent on international sources of knowledge resource. However the market for incremental adjustments to existing technology is likely to be international and competitive. The associated internationalization pattern therefore is likely to be characterized by intensive exporting through overseas agents and distributors |
| **2. Conventional developer** Firms tend to form simple, usually trade-related links after some years in the domestic market. Eventually they might establish more advanced links using entry modes in value chain activities other than marketing and distribution. Develop faster than the previous group with more diversity in mode type, and development pattern | | | |
| **3. Rapid developer** Firms in this group tend to establish internationalization much earlier than the previous | | *The transitional pattern* is likely to be characterized also by licensing agreements and by joint production agreements and | |

collaborative marketing and distribution. It is likely to be rapid, but less so than for the transformational pattern and may emerge from networks of product users who have been instrumental in the new product development process

group (within 3–5 years after foundation). Their first internationalization event is likely to consist of more than one type of business/value chain link, e.g. marketing, R&D and production-related links, and links are likely to be in either or both inward and outward directions

**4. International entrepreneur**
Firms in this group establish internationalization immediately or soon after firm foundation. The first internationalization event is often characterized as including several value chain-related cross-border links, including marketing, R&D and production, and often complex collaborative arrangements with overseas-based partners

*The transformational pattern,* owing to its requirement for knowledge-intensive inputs from a considerable number of experts and expert networks, is likely to result in an instant or early internationalization process characterized by R&D collaboration, licensing agreements and buying and selling of patent rights which are more likely to be global than local. While the internationalization process commences very early, financial returns are likely to take some time to be realized but are likely to be very high when they do come in

201

*Notes:*
Internationalization patterns correspond with those identified in Figure 12.2 and have been labelled accordingly.
The reluctant developer/export specialist pattern (Jones, 1999) has been omitted from the above table as it is unlikely that many high/complex technology firms in the 21st century would operate for any extended period with no international involvement.

Although exporting is the most popular mode of entry for SMEs, the choice of mode is more likely to be influenced by factors relating to the nature of the product, technology, the resource capabilities and competencies of the firm and its business model or format in relation to industry value chains. The internationalization process is only one of several interwoven and mutually dependent processes of growth and development including the start-up, growth and development process of the firm itself, and the process of technological innovation.

While each of these processes may incorporate stages, the stages relate for the most part to the internal development of the firm, and are unique to each firm. Opinion in the internationalization, small firm growth and innovation bodies of literature, respectively, has tended to shift towards the notion of fluid and mutable phases of growth rather than explicit stages. Patterns of internationalization are more diverse than literature on development stages might suggest. While patterns may be sequential and path-dependent, the path is likely to be determined by the nature of the firm's business, its role and/or position in local and/or international innovation/production value networks and its own response to opportunity. Internationalization patterns are also likely to be associated with the underlying processes that drive the growth and strategic direction of the firm. Internationalization in firms with complex technologies is likely to follow a path determined at least in part by the firm's knowledge needs in relation to the development of its technology, its dependence on local and/or global production networks and the temporal and geographical dynamics of markets for technology products.

Implications for internationalizing high-technology firms are that they should not expect to pass through a set of predetermined stages of development, whether the stages are internationalization stages, innovation stages or firm growth stages. Internationalization is a process in which firms seek solutions to problems, and seek and respond to opportunities. It may happen slowly or rapidly, and is likely to have some relationship to underlying phases of development in the firm itself. The choice of internationalization strategy at any one time encompasses choices and decisions about what aspect of the firm's business should be internationalized, through what form of cross-border business mode, with which partners and with which countries. Internationalization is essentially a platform process on the basis of which a firm may exploit opportunities relating to many factors that contribute to its growth and development, and should not be limited to a narrow focus on the development of exporting through predetermined stages of development.

Implications for policy makers are similar. While it is very convenient to aggregate firms for policy decisions such as the provision of information and support for exporters, by common stages that most firms reach, it is more important to recognize that firms might reach such stages through very different routes and over different time frames. Some innovations in policy support include the provision of one-stop shops wherein SMEs are given tailor-made advice on their start-up, growth and development and survival, and the process of internationalization is treated as part of that process, whereas historically advice on internationalization may have been available only through an export agency. Another policy innovation teams a newly internationalized firm with a mentor, another firm owner/manager who has experiential knowledge relevant to the firm and is willing to provide mentoring support through what essentially might be described as an internationalization 'buddy' scheme.

Finally, while most of the discussion in this chapter has focused on high-technology SMEs, its generalizability to firms in other sectors, or whose business is not with high technology, has not been addressed. Frustration with early step/stage models of internationalization was predominantly due to the fact that such models did not adequately consider the very diverse and often unique characteristics, circumstances and strategies within the SME sector. Recent studies on born-globals, international new ventures and rapid internationalizers have tended to take a more sector-specific approach, hence the interest in high-technology firms whose rapid internationalization tends to be driven by the speed of technological development and the globalization of technology markets. Further sector-specific research needs to be done before generalizations can be made without extreme caution.

# REFERENCES

Acs, Z.J. and D.B. Audretsch (1988), 'Innovation in large and small firms: an empirical analysis', *American Economic Review*, **78**(4), 678–90.

Acs, Z.J. and D.B. Audretsch (2003), 'Innovation and technological change', in Z.J. Acs and D.B. Audretsch (eds), *Handbook of Entrepreneurship Research*, Boston: Kluwer Academic Publishers, pp. 55–80.

Andersen, O. (1993), 'On the internationalisation process of firms: a critical analysis', *Journal of International Business Studies*, **24**(2), 33–46.

Araujo, L. and S. Rezende (2003), 'Path dependence, MNCs and the internationalisation process: a relational approach', *International Business Review*, **12**, 719–37.

Arthur D. Little (2002), *Biotechnologies: Parlons Vrai: Overview of Biotechnologies and Business Models*, London: Arthur D. Little and Associates.

Beamish, P.W. (1990), 'The internationalisation process for smaller Ontario firms: a research agenda', in A.M. Rugman (ed.), *Research in Global Strategic Management – International Business Research for the Twenty-First Century: Canada's New Research Agenda*, Greenwich: JAI Press Inc., pp. 77-92.

Bell, J.H.J. (1995), 'Internationalisation of small computer software firms', *European Journal of Marketing*, **29**(8), 16–75.

Bell, J., R. McNaughton and S. Young (2001), ' "Born-again global" firms: an extension to the "born global" phenomenon', *Journal of International Management*, **7**(3), 173–89.

Bell, J., R. McNaughton, S. Young and D. Crick (2003), 'Towards an integrative model of small firm internationalisation', *Journal of International Entrepreneurship*, **1**(2), 339–62.

Bilkey, W.J. and G. Tesar (1977), 'The export behaviour of smaller-sized Wisconsin manufacturing firms', *Journal of International Business Studies*, **8**(1), 93–8.

Blankenburg, D. (1995), 'A network approach to foreign market entry', in K. Moller and D. Wilson (eds), *Business Marketing: an Interaction and Network Perspective*, Boston: Kluwer Academic Publishers, pp. 375–405.

Bloodgood, J.M., H.J. Sapienza and J.G. Almeida (1996), 'The internationalization of new high-potential US ventures: antecedents and outcomes', *Entrepreneurship Theory and Practice*, **20**(4), 61–76.

Brouthers, K.D. and G. Nakos (2004), 'SME entry mode choice and performance: a transaction cost perspective', *Entrepreneurship Theory and Practice*, **28**(3), 229–47.

Buckley, P.J. (1989), 'Foreign direct investment by small and medium sized enterprises: the theoretical background', *Small Business Economics*, **1**(2), 89–100.

Buckley, P.J. (2003), 'International technology transfer by small and medium-sized enterprises', in D.B. Audretsch (ed.), *SMEs in the Age of Globalization*, Cheltenham, UK and Northampton, MA, USA: Edward Elgar, pp. 325–36.

Burgel, O. and G.C. Murray (2000), 'The international market entry choices of start-up companies in high technology industries', *Journal of International Marketing*, **8**(2), 33–62.

Cavusgil, S.T. (1984), 'Differences among exporting firms based on their degree of internationalization', *Journal of Business Research*, **12**(2), 195–208.

Chesnais, F. (1988), 'Technical cooperation agreements between firms', *STI Review OECD*, **4** (December), 51–119.

Coviello, N.E. and H.J. Munro (1997), 'Network relationships and the internationalization process of small software firms', *International Business Review*, **6**(4), 361–86.

Covin, J.G. and D.P. Slevin (1991), 'A conceptual model of entrepreneurship as firm behavior', *Entrepreneurship Theory and Practice*, **16**(1), 7–25.

Crick, D. and M. Spence (2005), 'The internationalisation of "high performing" U.K. High-Tech SMEs: a study of planned and unplanned strategies', *International Business Review*, **14**, 167–85.

Czincota, M. (1982), *Export Development Strategies: US Promotion Policy*, New York: Praeger.

Deakins, D. (1999), *Entrepreneurship and Small Firms*, London: McGraw-Hill.

Delios, A. and P.W. Beamish (1999), 'Ownership strategy of Japanese firms: transactional, institutional and experience influences', *Strategic Management Journal*, **20**(10), 915–33.

Eriksson, K., A. Majkgard and D.D. Sharma (2000), 'Path dependence and knowledge development in the internationalization process', *Management International Review*, **40**(4), 307–26.

Ernst, D. (2002), 'Global production networks and the changing geography of innovation systems. Implications for developing countries', *Economics of Innovation and New Technology*, **11**(6), 497–523.

Forrest, J.E. (1991), 'Models of the process of technological innovation', *Technology Analysis and Strategic Management*, **3**(4), 439–53.

Garnsey, E. and M. Wilkinson (1994), 'Flexible specialisation on a global basis and the protection of intellectual property: a problematic case', in R. Oakey (ed.), *New Technology Based Firms in the 1990s*, London: Paul Chapman Publishing Ltd., pp. 125–35.

Gassmann, O., G. Reepmeyer and M.V. Zedtwitz (2004), *Leading Pharmaceutical Innovation; Trends and Drivers for Growth in the Pharmaceutical Industry*, Heidelberg: Springer.

Greiner, L. (1972), 'Evolution and revolution as organisations grow', *Harvard Business Review* (July–Aug), 37–46.

Hutton, W. and A. Giddens (2000), 'In conversation', in W. Hutton and A. Giddens (eds), *On the Edge: Living with Global Capitalism*, London: Jonathan Cape, pp. 1–52.

Johanson, J. and L.-G. Mattsson (1988), 'Internationalisation in industrial systems: a network approach', in P.J. Buckley and P. Ghauri (eds), *The Internationalisation of the Firm: A Reader*, London: Academic Press, pp. 303–21.

Johanson, J. and J.-E. Vahlne (1977), 'The internationalization process of the firm: a model of knowledge development and increasing foreign commitment', *Journal of International Business Studies*, **8**(1), 23–32.

Jones, M.V. (1999), 'The internationalization of small high technology firms', *Journal of International Marketing*, **7**(4), 15–41.

Jones, M.V. (2001), 'First steps in internationalisation: concepts and evidence from a sample of small high technology firms', *Journal of International Management*, **7**(3), 191–210.

Jones, M.V. and N.E. Coviello (2005), 'Internationalization: conceptualizing an entrepreneurial process of behaviour in time', *Journal of International Business Studies*, **36**(3), 284–303.

Kazanjian, R.J. (1988), 'Relation of dominant problems to stages of growth in technology-based new ventures', *Academy of Management*, **31**(2), 257–79.

Kazanjian, R.J. and R. Drazin (1989), 'An empirical test of a stage of growth progression model', *Management Science*, **35**(12), 1489–503.

Knight, G. and S.T. Cavusgil (1996), 'The born global firm: a challenge to traditional internationalization theory', in C.R. Taylor (ed.), *Advances of International Marketing*, New York: JAI Press, pp. 11–26.

Kutscher, M., I. Baurle and S. Schmidt (1997), 'International evolution, international episodes, and international epochs – implications for managing internationalization', *Management International Review*, **37**(2), 101–24.

Lehtinen, U. and H. Penttinen (1999), 'Definition of the internationalization of a firm', in U. Lehtinen and H. Seristo (eds), *Perspectives on Internationalization*, Helsinki: Acta Universitatis Oeconomicae Helsingiensis, pp. 3–19.

Lindell, M. and N. Karagozoglu (1997), 'Global strategies of US and Scandinavian R&D intensive small- and medium-sized companies', *European Management Journal*, **15**(1), 92–100.

Lindqvist, M. (1997), 'Infant multinationals: internationalisation of small technology-based firms', in D. Jones-Evans and M. Klofsten (eds), *Technology, Innovation and Enterprise: the European Experience*, Basingstoke: Macmillan, pp. 303–24.

Luo, Y. and M.W. Peng (1999), 'Learning to compete in a transitional economy: experience, environment and performance', *Journal of International Business Studies*, **39**(2), 269–95.

Luostarinen, R. (1980), 'The internationalization of the firm', Helsinki School of Economics.

Luostarinen, R. and H. Hellman (1994), 'The internationalization processes and strategies of Finnish family firms', CIBR Research Papers, Helsinki School of Economics.

McDougall, P.P. and B.M. Oviatt (2000), 'International entrepreneurship: the intersection of two research paths', *Academy of Management Journal*, **43**(5), 902–6.

McDougall, P.P., S. Shane and B.M. Oviatt (1994), 'Explaining the formation of international new ventures: the limits of theories from international business research', *Journal of Business Venturing*, **9**(6), 469–87.

Möhring, J. (2002), 'Panel II: SMEs and cluster internationalisation', East West Cluster Conference, LEED, Local Economic and Employment Development Programme, 28–31 October.

OECD (2001), 'Drivers of growth: information technology, innovation and entrepreneurship', *Science, Technology and Industry Outlook*, Paris: OECD.

Osborne, K. (1996), 'The channel integration decision for small- to medium-sized manufacturing exporters', *International Small Business Journal*, **14**(3), 40–49.

Oviatt, B.M. and P.P. McDougall (1994), 'Toward a theory of international new ventures', *Journal of International Business Studies*, **25**(1), 45–64.

Oviatt, B.M. and P.P. McDougall (2005), 'Retrospective: the internationalisation of entrepreneurship', *Journal of International Business Studies*, **36**(1), 2–8.

Peters, E. and S. Young (2006), 'Emerging business models for biotechnology firms and clusters: policy responses in peripheral regions in the EU', in A.T. Tavares and A.C. Teixeira (eds), *Multinationals, Clusters & Innovation: Does Public Policy Matter?*, London: Palgrave.

Piore, M. and C. Sabel (1984), *The Second Industrial Divide: Possibilities for Prosperity*, New York: Basic Books.

Rennie, M.W. (1993), 'Global competitiveness: born global', *McKinsey Quarterly*, **4**, 45–52.

Reuber, A.R. and E. Fischer (1997), 'The influence of the management team's international experience on internationalization behavior', *Journal of International Business Studies*, **28**(4), 807–25.

Rycroft, R.W. and D.E. Kash (1999), *The Complexity Challenge: Technological Innovation for the 21st Century*, London: Pinter.

Rycroft, R.W. and D.E. Kash (2002), 'Path dependence in the innovation of complex technologies', *Technology Analysis & Strategic Management*, **14**(1), 21–35.

Saren, M.A. (1984), 'A classification and review of models of the intra-firm innovation process', *R&D Management*, **14**(1), 11–24.

Stiglitz, J.E. and S.J. Wallsten (1999), 'Public–private technology partnerships: promises and pitfalls', *American Behavioural Scientist*, **43**(1), 52–73.

Turnbull, P.W. (1987), 'A challenge to the stages theory of the internationalisation process', in P.J. Rosson and S.D. Reid (eds), *Managing Export Entry and Expansion*, New York: Praeger, pp. 296–315.

Vohora, A., M. Wright and A. Lockett (2004), 'Critical junctures in the development of university high-tech spinout companies', *Research Policy*, **33**(1), 147–75.

Weick, K.E. (1979), 'Cognitive processes in organizations', *Research in Organizational Behaviour*, **1**, 41–75.

Welch, L.S. and R. Luostarinen (1988), 'Internationalization: evolution of a concept', *Journal of General Management*, **14**(2), 34–55.

Wolff, J.A. and T.L. Pett (2000), 'Internationalization of small firms: an examination of export competitive patterns, firm size and export performance', *Journal of Small Business Management*, **38**(2), 34–47.

Young, S., J. Hammill, C. Wheeler and J.R. Davies (1989), *International Market Entry and Development: Strategies and Management*, Hemel Hempstead: Harvester Wheatsheaf.

# 13. A comparative study of Canadian and UK high-technology SMEs' internationalization processes

## Dave Crick and Martine Spence

## INTRODUCTION

A body of knowledge exists in the area of 'international entrepreneurship' which McDougall and Oviatt (2000, p. 903) consider to be 'a combination of innovative, pro-active and risk-seeking behaviour that crosses national borders and is intended to create value in organisations'. Existing studies on the internationalization of firms have found differences in the rate and mode of market entry for high-technology SMEs in comparison to those operating in low-tech markets. The former tend to internationalize more rapidly and follow market entry routes requiring higher commitment outwith exporting (McDougall and Oviatt, 1996; Knight and Cavusgil, 1996; Madsen and Servais, 1997; Andersson and Wictor, 2003).

In contributing to existing knowledge, first, it could be argued that a great deal of earlier work has been dominated by export studies (Crick and Jones, 2000); second, there is a need for more comparative research in the area of international entrepreneurship (Coviello and Jones, 2004). The broad aim of this study is to investigate selected international entrepreneurial activities in a sample of Canadian and UK high-technology SMEs. Specifically, the study focuses on internationalization decisions, taken to mean modes of entry into particular overseas markets. Two issues were investigated: first, high-technology SMEs' initial internationalization strategies and timing; and second, subsequent international expansion strategies.

The two countries are, arguably at least, significant but not dominant in terms of being perceived as bases for technological products in their respective economic groupings. Furthermore, both have relatively limited demand in their domestic market (irrespective of the geographic size) for high-tech products, suggesting that firms need to internationalize in order to exploit niche opportunities.

The chapter is structured into several sections and following this introduction a review of existing literature is provided. The conclusion from the literature review is that a 'holistic approach' should be undertaken in research investigating this topic area – in other words, an approach that considers decision making from various perspectives, for example developing competencies based on the resources employed, utilization of network relationships and being contingent on various environmental factors. A discussion of the methodology then follows, including a rationale to support the use of a qualitative approach. The results of this study are then presented, followed by a summary of the conclusions and implications arising from the investigation, before ending with avenues for further research.

# REVIEW OF THE LITERATURE

In terms of grounding this study in the context of earlier studies, two key issues seem to be relevant. First, there has been a debate about how quickly firms internationalize: in some cases, very early to take advantage of windows of opportunity, while in other cases relatively slowly, with managers learning from experience. Second, a debate exists about the extent to which managers plan for internationalization: in some cases developing strategies from experience rather than formal planning, and in other cases as a result of serendipitous events. However studies have found that internationalization decisions are a function of a number of issues, not the least of which involving resources, including experience, network opportunities and contingencies from the environment. Consequently generalizations are difficult to make from earlier studies and therefore facets of the debate are discussed as issues in their own right.

**Speed of Internationalization**

While there is no agreed definition of high-technology SMEs, they are often characterized by small and medium-sized firms with advanced knowledge and capabilities in technology, an educated workforce and the ability to adapt quickly to fast-changing environments. Consequently such characteristics assist the internationalization of high-tech SMEs by their ability to respond quickly when opportunities in overseas markets arise (Lindqvist, 1997; Baldwin and Gellatly, 1998). Unlike earlier research involving low-tech firms, in high-tech markets a key factor influencing performance appears to be speed of internationalization. Therefore high-tech SMEs do not always have a long time horizon to plan and take advantage of prior knowledge in order to formulate their international strategies as postulated in the 'stage theories' (Johanson and Vahlne, 1977, 1990; Czinkota, 1982; Cavusgil, 1984). These actions have characterized high-tech SMEs' survival in dynamic environments (Teece et al., 1997). Indeed high-tech SMEs often need to establish their respective product as the standard before their competitors, or to gain a first mover's advantage via customer loyalty, economies of scale and the like (Crick and Jones, 2000).

Consequently it could be argued that earlier studies involving the internationalization of SMEs have become somewhat dated and are not fully generalizable in today's dynamic environment: in particular, in the context of high-tech SMEs (Johanson and Wiedersheim-Paul, 1975; Pavord and Bogart, 1975; Bilkey and Tesar, 1977). There are a number of 'stage' models of internationalization, each varying by the number of stages and the labels attached to each stage. Nevertheless, in general, the models suggest that SMEs enter foreign markets in a systematic and sequential way, subsequently moving towards culturally diverse countries and through more committed modes of market entry; that is, after management learning (experience) has been acquired. In broad terms, stages range from firms being non-exporters to becoming large, experienced exporters (Andersen, 1993; Leonidou and Katsikeas, 1996; Coviello and McAuley, 1999). Criticisms of earlier work exists since, as previously mentioned, models do not fully capture the complexity of internationalizing, especially in the context of the current study involving high-technology sectors, where environmental variables are dynamic (Turnbull, 1987; Bell, 1995; Bell et al., 2004).

Recent work has therefore suggested that for reasons such as narrow product scope, fast obsolescence of their products and a limited domestic demand, particularly in smaller countries, high-tech SMEs must have an international and sometimes a global focus from inception (Litvak, 1990). This debate has characterized some firms as 'born globals' or 'international new ventures', depending on respective authors' terminology, but in overall terms these are business organizations that, from inception, seek to derive significant competitive advantage from the use of resources and the sale of outputs in multiple countries (Oviatt and McDougall, 1994). However it is still difficult to generalize across industries and markets; for example, Boter and Holmquist (1996) found that firms' strategies varied, depending on a variety of issues not least of which included the industry sector.

Industry sector considerations need to be balanced with other considerations such as the experience of the management team. For example, McDougall (1989) found that the managerial strategies of new firms that were internationally oriented differed from those with a domestic focus in respect of factors like market awareness, channel control and market penetration. Another issue affecting the rapid internationalization of firms is the absence of strong industry structure and lengthy company history. Interestingly, in dynamic environments, how quickly management teams learn to adapt is sometimes more important than previously acquired knowledge (McDougall et al., 1994; Autio et al., 2000).

Despite the speed at which firms internationalize, the criteria for measuring and predicting firms' performance is subjective and a number of studies have addressed factors associated with this issue without arriving at an agreed conclusion about how performance should be measured (Chrisman et al., 1999; Zahra et al., 2000; Shrader, 2001). For example, research has investigated a key aspect of internationalization performance in respect of firms that have de-internationalized and in some cases re-internationalized (Oesterle, 1997; Pauwels and Matthyssens, 1999; Crick, 2002). Specifically, Bell et al. (2001) found companies termed 'born-again globals' that internationalized some time previously, but then pursued a domestic strategy for a while. Critical incidents could have thrown them off their path and sent them back into the international arena: for example, a change in management or ownership, a fresh infusion of capital or a change in scope of a domestic customer. Some firms underwent rapid and structured internationalization, typically by using newly acquired networks. Consequently performance and indeed 'failure' should not necessarily be measured in terms of withdrawal from overseas markets, since this strategy may lead to superior future strategies (Crick, 2004).

**Planning of Internationalization**

Studies by Merrilees et al. (1998) and Mockaitis et al. (2006) have argued that particular aspects of internationalization strategy are not always planned in the way that some of the strategy literature suggests. Chance encounters, events and aspects of 'serendipity' have an understated role to play in explaining certain firms' internationalization. However this is a function of perceptions, since an 'opportunity' for one person may be considered as 'hopeless' by others (Crick and Spence, 2005). Indeed Shane (2000) suggests that opportunities are open to everyone, but only a small proportion of individuals will discover them. Nevertheless the issue of 'entrepreneurial alertness' is widely recognized in the literature and, as Ardichvili et al. (2003, p. 113) suggest, 'opportunities are made, not found' and require a proactive stance to develop them from an idea to a full-blown business plan. Moreover the entrepreneur needs to sense that there is a fit between market needs and resources and may find a new fit that evolves into a commercial entity.

Sarasvathy (2001) suggests that entrepreneurs have been said to formulate decisions based on a non-linear and iterative process called 'effectuation'. Entrepreneurs tend to follow their intuition rather than go through a systematic planning process to reach somewhat 'fuzzy' goals. Sometimes, given that entrepreneurs are often seen to be innovators, they identify opportunities in markets or industries which are still non-existent. Thus opportunities cannot be quantified in the way much of the planning literature suggests, as future trends cannot be predicted. However this is influenced by the level of loss or risk the entrepreneur is willing to undertake; this is a function of the resources, experience and entrepreneurial drive of individuals.

Within the field of international entrepreneurship, certain studies suggest that the process of effectuation is prevalent in expanding into foreign markets, and in some cases a firm's initial market entry abroad is chaotic, haphazard and explorative (McDougall, 1990) as opposed to following a linear and incremental process. Fletcher (2004) reports on entrepreneurs' international opportunities 'coming to them' and the risk of forgoing an opportunity was higher than that of exploiting it. Rasmussan et al. (2001) found that, for some entrepreneurs, internationalization was not part of the founding planning process but came as an afterthought thanks to the nature of the product and its limited potential in the country of origin.

Conversely McDougall et al. (1994) suggest that, for particular firms, some planning is incurred at inception, such as hiring a multilingual and multicultural workforce, using English as the language of business, and developing a world-class product, and this firmly sets the firm on an international path. Indeed Moen (2002, p. 173) suggests that 'the destiny of the firm seems to be determined at the establishment juncture', very often by managers with a global vision. Moreover Bell (1995, p. 66) found that some key decision makers 'had a clear picture, from the outset, as to which overseas markets provided the best potential for their firm's application' and used sectoral targeting (that is, targeting a trade sector) to expand into growth and/or lead markets from inception. However Bell (ibid., p. 67) also found that 'reactive and opportunistic exporting preceded any planned activities'. In short, studies have recognized that internationalization is influenced by a number of issues and consequently a contingency view has some part in explaining firms' internationalization (Reid, 1983; Yeoh and Jeong, 1995; Ibeh, 2003).

### Key Issues Affecting the Speed and Planning of Internationalization

Studies have provided some support for the 'resource-based view' of firms' internationalization. In basic terms, this approach takes an 'inside-out' firm perspective (Dicken, 1996) and resources that are valuable, rare, inimitable and non-substitutable allow the firm to develop and maintain competitive advantages (Barney, 1991). Internal resource advantages can be developed in a variety of ways, not least of which is the international orientation of the entrepreneur/management team and the resources that he/she/they are prepared to invest. A key issue, consequently, is entrepreneurial learning: that is, how this key decision maker or management team learns over time and the effect on resource allocation (Reuber and Fischer, 1997, 2002; Francis and Collins-Dodd, 1999). Slater and Narver (1995) see this as the way 'knowledge and insights' are developed by an organization or, more specifically, employees within a firm; some see this as an 'organizational memory' (Moorman and Miner, 1998). In very small firms there is a clear overlap between the resources of the entrepreneur and those of the firm, especially since, in very small firms with only one or a few employees, resource-based capabilities that accrue to the business result from the entrepreneurial learning of key individuals. Individual entrepreneurs and management teams must trade off risks in decision making and employ the appropriate resources based on experience (Shrader et al., 2000); therefore recent work has argued that internationalization should be viewed from an entrepreneurial perspective that accounts for such factors (Andersson, 2000; Spence, 2003).

Turning to the characteristics of entrepreneurs and the management team, their enthusiasm toward foreign market expansion has been found to result in higher international involvement (Cavusgil, 1984). Furthermore higher education levels, a key characteristic of high-technology entrepreneurs (Baruch, 1997), has been associated with international openness alongside the management teams' foreign origins and past international experience (Cavusgil, 1984; Bloodgood et al., 1996). Management teams of internationalizing firms develop an increasing level of intellectual capital that can be used in formulating strategies and allocating resources. Therefore elements of the 'resource-based view' of the firm can partly explain firms' internationalization (Zahra et al., 2000; Westhead et al., 2001; Knight and Cavusgil, 2004).

In respect of the management teams' international experience that could have contributed to the rapid expansion of the high-tech SMEs, prior research has shown that established international networks have been very influential, especially at the start of the internationalization process (Lindqvist, 1997). It could be argued, on the basis of the earlier discussion, that relationships offer some kind of relational capability, making network relationships part of the resource-based view of the firm. Relationships take place within personal and/or business networks that act as communication infrastructures where common interests are shared (Hallén, 1992). Various encounters with business partners and clients, representatives and ordinary citizens allow internationalizing SMEs to get a feel for the market, to gain insight into the way business is conducted, to demonstrate interest and to start the building of trust (Wilson and Mummalaneni, 1990). Moreover they potentially speed the internationalization process by providing synergistic relationships with other businesses, which complement each other's resources at various stages in the value chain (Coviello and Munro, 1997; Keeble et al., 1998; Dana et al., 1999; Jones, 1999).

Networks also include, to a certain extent, depending on an individual firm's circumstances, relationships with support organizations. Within these, various private and public initiatives exist that assist high-tech SMEs. Subsidized assistance is available in a number of countries, based on legislation and budgetary restrictions, such as those that organize various activities aimed at facilitating contacts between domestic and foreign business organizations (Welch et al., 1997; Spence, 2000). Nevertheless the usefulness of various support organizations has been criticized (Lesch et al., 1990; Seringhaus and Rosson, 1990; Kotabe and Czinkota, 1993). A particular criticism has been that much of the assistance on offer is of a generic nature and in fact export-oriented, whereas in reality many firms are engaged in multiple modes of market entry and require more specific support (Woodcock et al., 1994; Calof and Beamish, 1995; Crick and Jones, 2000). However recent UK data (Chaudhry and Crick, 2002) suggests policy makers are more effectively addressing the needs of firms with tailored rather than generic support. Therefore particular elements of the networking approach to business strategy can explain firms' internationalization.

In summary, high-tech SMEs operate in a dynamic environment and internationalization is influenced by a number of both internal and external considerations that affect the speed of, and ability to plan for, overseas operations. These considerations include managers' international orientation (and risk assessment), resources and networks, plus the way management teams react to environmental events, including 'chance' events. From an international entrepreneurial perspective, the internationalization process is not always as systematic as particular concepts, such as the 'stage' models, would suggest. A review of existing literature therefore suggests that no single agreed theory exists to explain fully firms' internationalization strategies, and a 'holistic approach' should be adopted (Bell et al., 2004; Jones and Coviello, 2005; Crick and Spence, 2005). In other words, studies should adopt an approach that investigates internationalization decision making from various perspectives; that is, development of competencies from the resources employed, use of network relationships and placement in the context of being contingent on various environmental factors.


## METHODOLOGY

Following the call for more in-depth cross-national research in the area of international entrepreneurship, identified by Coviello and Jones (2004), a qualitative, comparative methodological approach was employed in order to address the 'how and why' issues associated with Canadian and UK high-tech SMEs' internationalization strategies. A use of qualitative research is a well-documented methodological approach in identifying key points from studies in the social sciences such as this investigation (Eisenhardt, 1989).

In terms of the specific sample selection criteria, these were based on several factors. First, to help avoid a resource bias, firms employed fewer than 100 staff (Storey, 1994). Second, given that there is no single agreed definition of high-tech SMEs or sectors in which they operate (Baruch, 1997; Baldwin and Gellatly, 1998), firms were selected in sectors perceived to be 'high-technology'-oriented (electronics, software and related sectors) to reduce trade sectoral bias. Third, to avoid potential bias from parental decision making, firms were independently owned. Fourth, to avoid firms with a marginal involvement, they were committed to internationalization, and a subjective measurement of 25 per cent or more of turnover coming from international sales was used to cover this. However most firms had very high percentages of international business, in the region of 70 per cent.

Interviews involving 12 high-tech SMEs in each country were undertaken. These utilized a semi-structured approach and lasted about 60 to 90 minutes. They were undertaken with either the owner/manager or the senior member of the managerial team responsible for international activities. Potential key informant bias was recognized (Marshall and Rossman, 1995), likewise respondents' ability to recall events with the advantage of hindsight. Interviews with the main decision makers suggested that relatively little useful additional information would be gained by interviewing other members of the respective organizations since they did not have the depth of knowledge to address the questions being asked. However interview data were supplemented by using websites, collecting brochures, reports and so on where possible to triangulate the data (Yin, 1994; Denzin and Lincoln, 1998).

UK firms were drawn from a sample involving an existing database that was compiled from survey data undertaken in the past. This 'original' sampling frame had utilized the FAME database (allowing various fields of enquiry such as trade sector, number of employees and international involvement to be used). Canadian firms were drawn from the Ottawa Region database and this enabled firms to be selected on the basis of the same fields of enquiry as the UK sample. The number of interviews was constrained by time and cost considerations and, furthermore, by an ability to identify firms meeting the desired profile and employing executives that were willing to discuss potentially sensitive issues associated with their internationalization strategies.

Questions asked related to areas identified in issues drawn from a review of the literature. Within-case analysis was first undertaken and this was followed by across-case analysis. The purpose was to identify both individual and common features associated with the firms. This process was discussed among the researchers in order to obtain agreement about the way in which the data were interpreted. This process of analysis led to four main areas being identified that will be discussed in the next section: first, managers' perceptions of overseas markets (culture, distance and ways of doing business); second, influences on internationalization strategies (effects of resources, networks and contingent factors); third, strategic considerations involving the pace of internationalization and markets served; and, fourth, managerial objectives, risk assessment and the effect on internationalization.

Profiles of the firms based on selected data in both countries are detailed in Appendices 13.1 and 13.2. When comparing Appendices 13.1 and 13.2 it is apparent that the Canadian sample contained several slightly older firms whose internationalization strategies (initially at least) may have been subject to different environmental conditions *vis-à-vis* those that internationalized some time afterwards. It was not deemed to be a significant limitation to the study since interviewees were in a position to comment on internationalization strategies as they unfolded over time as they had been employed in a senior role or owned the businesses from the outset; potential bias in this respect was considered to be minimized.

## FINDINGS

Owing to the richness of the data collected, only a broad overview of the key issues are discussed in this chapter and individual cases have been omitted (albeit the profiles of the cases are shown in Appendices 13.1 and 13.2). Selected quotations are used to demonstrate key sentiments but, owing to space limitations, these are kept to a minimum. Although this chapter was initially grounded by earlier studies in the context of speed and planning of internationalization, the interviews suggested that these issues resolved themselves into four themes. The order of the points covered is not prioritized in terms of importance, rather the four themes reflect the way in which many of the interviewees discussed these areas of significance.

## Perceptions of Overseas Markets (Culture, Distance and Ways of Doing Business)

The interviews suggested there was a different attitude towards dealing with foreign markets between the two groups of entrepreneurs/management teams. Some of the Canadian managers had seemed and to some extent did still seem reluctant to cross the Atlantic or to go to markets further afield. Here the perceived expense and problems of culture, particularly in respect of language, were stated as important considerations. However other interviewees took a different perspective and claimed English was the language of business and, irrespective of the main language spoken, translation was easy in many cases. Conversely UK interviewees believed countries with potential and in particular lead markets like North America justified the time and expense in looking for opportunities in these markets.

One problem related to industry-specific considerations as regards the way in which business was undertaken. One example to demonstrate this refers to a Canadian firm in the software industry dealing with 'e' government solutions. This firm believed there were problems in the way in which different governments work across the world and particularly in Europe. A different Canadian firm had to adapt various aspects of its software between languages (French, Belgian French and so on) and this caused numerous problems in respect of time and resource constraints given the small potential of each market. As a Canadian manager noted:

> French is a very, very difficult situation because French is jealously guarded and regional variations are just too dramatic. Even the French that we have adapted has sold very, very poorly because it's usually been the wrong variations so we have decided we would not do any more unless somebody wants to pay for the adaptation.

A Canadian firm had a relationship with a German distributor that did not work out as planned, mainly because of cultural differences in business practices. It had a limited marketing budget, so a decision was made to undertake as many of the business activities as possible in Canada and leave everything else to overseas distributors. Cultural problems seemed to be far less of a problem with the UK firms, and many cited support agencies such as government advisers that could assist in addressing barriers associated with culture and business practices in foreign markets. As a UK manager commented:

> Quite frankly I don't think cultural issues as you call them are major barriers because there is always help on hand. I mean, you have just been talking about government support but there are other providers as well. Anyway, when you have been in this game as long as me there are always things to learn but things repeat themselves and it's the same problem but in another country – experience counts from the university of life!

## Influences on Internationalization Strategies (Effects of Resources, Networks and Contingent Factors)

The influences on the routes by which firms internationalized provided interesting data. A number of management teams from both countries took a somewhat cautious route towards modes of market entry, typically via agents or distributors. For the most part, the availability of financial resources played a key role in decision making generally but especially in respect of internationalization. Nevertheless, despite the higher resources and commitment involved, certain Canadian and UK firms were willing to internationalize using committed routes. For example, sales offices/subsidiaries were set up where customers required this local presence and consequently management teams were willing to commit financial resources where this was considered important.

Turning now to other factors that influenced internationalization strategies, the exploitation of technological advantages played a key role in the internationalization of many high-tech SMEs from both countries. In some cases, it was common for management teams to be able to tap into networks or utilize previous international experience they had obtained, and consequently experience as a human resource was very important. Examples were also present where overseas customers had actively approached the firms because of the reputation gained in their respective domestic markets. In particular cases unsolicited orders arrived after overseas businesses had seen the respective Canadian and UK firms' websites; therefore it was believed that technological investment in this respect had provided an important resource.

Serendipitous events also played a major part in some firms' decision making and internationalization decisions had been contingent to some extent on 'chance' rather than planned events. For example, a Canadian entrepreneur had been on the same industry committee as an executive from a US firm and this meeting led to an order being placed. In a different Canadian firm, the entrepreneur met someone from a government body and was notified of opportunities in China. In another Canadian firm, serendipity was combined with planning in that, in addition to serving the US market, the entrepreneur planned to attend trade shows, particularly in Spanish-speaking markets to increase international sales, but also received orders from a number of different markets. The entrepreneur discovered that, by targeting the US market, it was not only a lead market but also a reference point that, if successful there, firms overseas would notice and contact the supplier rather than the supplier actively needing to find customers overseas. As a Canadian manager explained in the context of targeting markets:

> International marketing activities include trade shows in the US where international buyers are being met as well as distributors for various markets. Lead markets where a distributor was proactively searched for was California. Germany is another market where potential is important but not much sales from there! Asia is where the market is moving to as a lot of manufacturers using optical devices are moving their plants there.

In the UK, 'chance' events were also observed. One entrepreneur met an overseas executive while on vacation, leading to the formation of a joint venture. In a different case the recruitment of an executive with overseas experience allowed the firm to break into foreign markets based on this executive's networks, but this had not been the purpose of recruiting him. However a number of managers in both countries believed that, to some extent, they made their own 'luck', and therefore, while certain events occurred by 'chance', decisions had been made to influence these fortuitous opportunities that arose. For example, this included managers trying to get on certain committees to extend their networks that would, in their view, increase opportunities. It could be argued that luck came to those who planned, even if not in an academic sense, as they increased their chances of identifying and exploiting opportunities. As one UK manager noted:

> We work hard trying to find good representatives but sometimes being in the right place at the right time helps. I remember when we got into the American market and this was very lucky. We had been looking to go there for some time as it is clearly the place to be for a business like mine. I was given a contact by someone I met at a business lunch that I had not planned to attend and only went at the last minute. Mind you, it was risky since, as I said, I didn't know the guy and the chap who he introduced me to might have been a fraud, but business is all about taking risks. Since then we haven't looked back in the American market.

## Strategic Considerations Involving the Pace of Internationalization and Markets Served

In nine of the UK firms and seven of the Canadian firms internationalization occurred early (within three years of start-up) and this was mainly as a planned decision. Firms from both countries that internationalized early typically served a small niche, that is, in terms of the size of the overall market and number of competitors active there. Management teams thought growth and even survival required firms to internationalize rapidly. The choice of market served was for certain firms linked to perceptions of customers' ability to pay. A Canadian firm involved with financial software for governments ensured that the contract was supported by an international agency and that this agency's payment scheme was acceptable. For a different Canadian firm, financing opportunities were linked to agencies and government contracts, involving, for example components for hydroelectric plants in Brazil. Nevertheless, as time moved on, it became evident that international organizations and contractors were not interested enough in this component or did not have the ability to pay, so the country was no longer considered as having potential; it was therefore dropped as a target market for the firm.

Examples in both groups of firms were evident where management teams had been fairly well informed from the outset about business procedures in particular markets thanks to either experience in prior employment or research via, for example, government agencies and similar organizations. It was known from prior research by particular entrepreneurs in both countries that certain markets exhibited no perceived loyalty and a lot of transactional costs; consequently there was little point in tendering in markets like these where managers knew prices would be undercut and there was little future potential to recoup investment. However, in other markets, there was a loyalty effect based to a certain extent on relationships and customers' knowledge of product quality for a fair price and these were perceived to hold better opportunities.

In certain firms in both countries there was a gradual move towards addressing some markets as technology evolved and, for example, obsolete products in developed markets could be sold in emerging ones. Many entrepreneurs were more informed about internationalization issues than certain earlier studies have suggested; specifically, those that indicated learning from experience. Entrepreneurs in both countries already had a 'general' experience from previous employment or other sources and this experience extended to dealing with new markets and situations.

A 'spill-over' effect into different markets was also observed and this has not received much attention in earlier studies. For a UK firm, the Canadian market was the target owing to perceived potential and relative ease of access in comparison to the US, and this led to US firms learning of the firm and making contact with it. The US subsequently became the firm's major overseas market. In one Canadian firm the main market was the US, but this led to opportunities in the Canadian (domestic) market that otherwise would not have been realized, because of the reputation gained in the lead market. In other words, overseas sales led to domestic market opportunities. As both a Canadian and UK manager noted, respectively:

> First, largest consumer market in the world, secondly our costs are competitive in that market and our experience has been particularly in Asia but not so much in Europe, but whenever you go in the international market outside the US, the first question they ask you is what US companies are using your software? So to a certain extent the US becomes a measure of success and it's a lot easier to leverage with other international clients if you have US clients. (Canadian firm)

> It was far easier to get into Canada first (as compared with the US) and things went well as we proved ourselves and developed a good reputation. This led to American firms coming to us since we were known over there and North America as a whole has been great for the firm. (UK firm)

**Managerial Objectives, Risk Assessment and the Effect on Internationalization**

An issue that has perhaps received limited attention in previous studies is the question of what are the objectives of entrepreneurs/the management team; that is, why was the firm created, what are the aims and did these influence internationalization? Studies tend to focus on firms looking for growth via a forward-moving internationalization route. Nevertheless, in particular Canadian and UK firms, a key objective was to maintain a lifestyle for the key entrepreneur, in others it was to develop and sell the business. Consequently risk was seen in different ways by respective entrepreneurs and management teams. Moreover interviewees in both countries suggested that some markets result in losses, whereas others compensate for these and this is a fact of business life; there is a constant balance between internationalization and de-internationalization in certain markets. Challenging the status quo to gain a competitive advantage can differentiate some firms (irrespective of their country of origin) as management teams overcome psychological barriers, although this can be affected by industry norms in some sectors in addition to risk perceptions and available resources.

The social cost of international entrepreneurship is a further underresearched topic and this was found to affect aspects of internationalization. In a Canadian firm the two owners were working long hours and consequently putting a strain on relationships with their respective spouses. This influenced the founders' strategy decisions as their wives threatened to leave them if they did not reduce their hours of work and balance this with family life. This resulted in a plan to get the firm in a position that was ready to sell; this had not previously been the goal until the ultimatum. From mainly serving the Canadian market, a move was made to enter the US market as this was seen as the lead market and success there would increase the chance of selling the business. A UK entrepreneur faced a similar ultimatum from his wife but chose to 'call his wife's bluff' – a social error since she left him! However the move was profitable in a business sense because the time that was not devoted to family life was put towards taking his firm into foreign markets, and this proved successful. As a Canadian manager noted:

> We can't spend more than we have so the next step was how do we get the company back to a breakeven point and then start building from there. In the meantime, we were looking at selling

the company because the founders were young guys, reasonably young guys who had never been through this process before. And if you have never been through this process before, it could be emotionally wrecking. I've been through three or four. It's easy to just say, 'this is not working and I'm walking away'. The guys, the founders of the company went through 'oh, we're gonna go public, we're gonna be millionaires. Oh, now we're not going public . . .' You know, that kind of stuff. It's either the company or my wife. And they chose their family.

A Canadian entrepreneur, in comparison, was risk-averse. While his firm had an international ratio (international to total sales) of 62 per cent, of this 50 per cent was in the US, not because of proximity or potential (in fact the US was not the lead market) but rather because of reduced perceived risk, as the entrepreneur was knowledgable about the characteristics of the market. The remaining 12 per cent was spread over a number of markets based on ad hoc orders from customers that had seen the firm's website. A UK entrepreneur was also risk-averse and basically, at the time of interview, was seeing his time out until retirement. Arguably this affected perceptions of costs and risks in entering and withdrawing from certain markets and therefore the firm's internationalization was constrained. In short, particular managers took a more entrepreneurial stance than others and, indeed, than some of the earlier research, such as that on 'stage' models, indicates. As one UK manager commented:

> Business is not easy and it's a case of going for opportunities when they arise. Markets come and go with orders for a firm like mine and while we concentrate on some markets others are of minor importance. We target our main markets and have to have a presence there, but others – I'm not going to put my business and jobs of my employees on the line taking on orders I think are too risky. Sure we take losses and sometimes frustration kicks in and I have to make the decision to pull the plug on a market. But that's my job and experience and gut reaction help me make these decisions.

## CONCLUSIONS AND RECOMMENDATIONS

This chapter addresses Coviello and Jones' (2004) call for more comparative research in the area of international entrepreneurship. The broad aim of this study has been to address this call and investigate selected international entrepreneurial activities in a sample of Canadian and UK high-tech SMEs. From the outset it must be emphasized that, in the broader domain of international business research, a great many (typically export-oriented) studies have been undertaken over the last few decades. Nevertheless, to reduce the scope of this chapter to manageable proportions, it was decided to investigate only UK and Canadian high-tech SMEs.

Earlier research involving the 'stage' models has suggested that firms move from the pre-export stage to more committed international involvement based to a large extent on experiential learning. In contrast, studies involving international new ventures have shown that, although firms internationalized more rapidly than the 'stage' models had suggested, this was typically still based on planned decision making, for example to exploit market niches quickly. Speed and planning were therefore seen as key dimensions in respect of grounding this study in the context of earlier research, albeit the findings highlighted that internationalization is a multifaceted issue. The first conclusion from the comparative UK and Canadian data is that the 'key' initial stimuli for pursuing and maintaining an internationalization strategy, plus the subsequent triggers for international development, could be grouped as follows: first, the management teams' utilization of existing contacts, that is, supporting the networking view (for example Coviello and Munro, 1997; Dana et al., 1999; Jones, 1999); second, the management teams' utilization of resources, considered in an overall context to include financial and managerial resources, supporting the resource-based view of the firm (Dicken, 1996; Barney, 1991; Westhead et al., 2001); third, management teams' reaction to environmental and serendipitous events, supporting the contingency view (Reid, 1983; Merrilees et al., 1998; Ibeh, 2003).

The findings in this chapter have in no way questioned the validity of existing studies and simply raised the question of their generalizability to UK and Canadian high-tech SMEs. With this in mind, the implication resulting from this first conclusion is that generalizations should not be made from the existing literature since the impact of each of these factors varied between both groups of firms, depending on the individual management teams' circumstances. Indeed these factors should not be viewed in isolation, since one theory could not on its own adequately account for high-tech SMEs' internationalization behaviour. Put another way, a combination of issues stimulated both the initial and subsequent internationalization decisions of both groups of firms.

Management teams almost exclusively gravitated towards concentrating on the 'lead' market and, given the characteristics of the firms in this study, it was arguably not surprising to find this was the US (Bell, 1995). In some sectors firms located in the lead market clearly have the benefit of being domestic players and their internationalization may be influenced by collaboration with overseas firms trying to enter the market. However, in other cases, markets are so small that firms have to internationalize to compete in a global niche; indeed this was also affected by the ability of customers to pay, as evidenced by specialized equipment being funded by agencies for projects in developing countries. The second conclusion is that international entrepreneurial decisions are made as a result of trade-offs between subjective risk assessments and the pursuit of opportunities in various markets (Crick and Jones, 2000; Shrader et al., 2000; Bell et al., 2004). Put another way, respective entrepreneurs may view the same opportunity in different ways, depending on their perception of risk at a given point in time. This could be a function of a number of factors, for example, management teams' ability to absorb losses, their experience, growth/profit objectives and so on. While the value of quantitative studies is useful for collecting generalizable data, the implication of the second conclusion is that the findings of this study cast some doubt on generalizing from quantitative studies that capture data at a given point in time. It is perhaps better to capture data at multiple points in time to build up a greater picture of firms' internationalization decisions.

Business schools tend to advocate the importance of planning based on the wide literature that is available. However, while the third conclusion is that planning was important to certain firms in this comparative study, as the strategy literature suggests, serendipity and the importance of emergent strategies should be considered alongside this (Merrilees et al., 1998; Mockaitis et al., 2005). Outside of the influence of serendipitous events, both groups of high-tech SMEs' strategies were largely influenced by the objectives of the key decision makers, that is, whether they were risk takers or risk-averse. Additionally particular firms in both groups tended to compete on reputation and address perceived lead 'niche' markets (and, as mentioned earlier, this was typically the US); however each group also contained firms that internationalized more gradually in line with earlier export-oriented research.

The implication arising from this third conclusion is that, while entrepreneurs irrespective of their country of origin can be advised on the importance of planning, consideration of serendipitous events and how management teams respond to these is more problematic. Nevertheless its importance should not be overstated either, since, in this comparative study, it was found that even if a serendipitous event was the main catalyst for internationalization, the firms still had a product ready for overseas development. Moreover management teams ensured that the financial and human resources were put in place to enable opportunities to be pursued. Hence the 'correct ingredients' were present when these serendipitous events were encountered, so that, part rationally and part intuitively, a potential synergy was recognized and opportunities were exploited by the respective management teams. In short, some of the existing studies reviewed suggest that particular theories can largely explain high-tech SMEs' internationalization behaviour. However this comparative investigation argues that no single theory could fully explain the firms' internationalization and that a 'holistic' perspective, one that incorporates features from various theories, should be taken (Bell et al., 2004; Crick and Spence, 2005; Jones and Coviello, 2005).

Nevertheless there were some differences between the two groups of firms that are worthy of mention. First, there was in some cases a different 'mindset' in terms of cultural and geographical distances and this influenced some Canadian firms to be more cautious in their mode of entry and market choice. This appears consistent with earlier research such as that involving the stage theories (Czinkota, 1982), but not recent work involving 'born global' firms (Knight and Cavusgil, 1996, 2004). Second, the advantage of price was open to the Canadian firms in certain markets, particularly the US in comparison to the UK firms, owing to the relative strength of the currencies. Third, management teams in Canadian firms often perceived themselves as technology leaders and tended to have larger margins from value-added activities than their UK counterparts. The fourth difference is that management teams from different countries may have a different mindset based on a whole host of cultural issues that affect internationalization strategy, but this is also affected by outside influences, for example perceived competitiveness based on macroeconomic constraints. The implication arising from this conclusion is that differences exist between particular high-tech SMEs and generic public policy support may not be totally useful. Trade assistance providers in various countries need to account for the various differences between their respective firms and support management teams with tailored assistance that more closely addresses their needs (Chaudhry and Crick, 2002).

## AVENUES FOR FUTURE RESEARCH

More comparative work would be useful to further understand the internationalization process of firms from particular countries (Coviello and Jones, 2004). In reality, the interaction of a number of factors makes generalizations difficult. However contributions that help formulate a model that more accurately reflects this behaviour are important. Indeed, as Jones and Coviello (2005) suggest, individual studies that address 'pieces of an emerging puzzle' help to explain firms' internationalization processes and contribute to the growing body of work in the field of research.

It is hoped that, by addressing the holistic perspective advocated in this study, researchers will help develop the emerging puzzle that Jones and Coviello (2005) advocate, but at the same time facilitate a more effective public/private sector interaction. Specifically studies will help policy makers address the need for tailored support in assisting firms with varying degrees of experience to internationalize in a manner that is appropriate to their individual circumstances, including country of origin.

## ACKNOWLEDGEMENT

At the time of writing a variation on this chapter is under review in the *International Marketing Review*. This was agreed by e-mail in advance with the Klein organizers in terms of copyright issues. Acknowledgment is made in the IMR submission to the Klein Symposium. Earlier findings from this study were reported in the 2003 McGill Conference.

## REFERENCES

Andersen, O. (1993), 'On the internationalization process of firms: a critical analysis', *Journal of International Business Studies*, **24**(2), 209–31.

Andersson, S. (2000), 'The internationalization of the firm from an entrepreneurial perspective', *International Studies of Management and Organisation*, **30**(1), 63–92.

Andersson, S. and I. Wictor (2003), 'Innovative internationalization in new firms: born globals – the Swedish case', *Journal of International Entrepreneurship*, **1**(3), 249–76.

Ardichvili, A., R. Cardozo and S. Ray (2003), 'A theory of entrepreneurial opportunity identification and development', *Journal of Business Venturing*, **18**, 105–23.

Autio, E., H. Sapienza and J. Almeida (2000), 'Effects of age at entry, knowledge intensity, and imitability on international growth', *Academy of Management Journal*, **43**(5), 909–24.

Baldwin, J. and G. Gellatly (1998), 'Are there high-tech industries or only high-tech firms? Evidence from new technology-based firms', Analytical Studies Branch, Micro-Economic Analysis Division, Statistics Canada, No. 11F0019MPE, No. 120.

Barney, J. (1991), 'Firm resources and sustained competitive advantage', *Journal of Management*, **17**, 99–120.

Baruch, Y. (1997), 'High tech organization – what it is, what it isn't', *International Journal of Technology Management*, **13**(2), 179–95.

Bell, J. (1995), 'The internationalization of small computer software firms: a further challenge to stage theory', *European Journal of Marketing*, **29**(8), 60–75.

Bell, J., D. Crick and S. Young (2004), 'Small firm internationalization and business strategy: an exploratory study of "knowledge-intensive" and "traditional" manufacturing firms in the UK', *International Small Business Journal*, **22**(1), 23–56.

Bell, J., R. McNaughton, S. Young and D. Crick (2001), 'Towards an eclectic model of small firms' internationalization', Proceedings of the 4th McGill Conference on International Entrepreneurship – Researching New Frontiers, September, Glasgow, University of Strathclyde.

Bilkey, W. and G. Tesar (1977), 'The export behaviour of smaller-sized Wisconsin manufacturing firms', *Journal of International Business Studies*, **8**, 93–8.

Bloodgood, J., H. Sapienza and J. Almeida (1996), 'The internationalization of new high-potential U.S. ventures: antecedents and outcomes', *Entrepreneurship Theory and Practice*, Summer, 61–76.

Boter, H. and C. Holmquist (1996), 'Industry characteristics and internationalization processes in small firms', *Journal of Business Venturing*, **11**, 471–87.

Calof, J.C. and P. Beamish (1995), 'Adapting to foreign markets: explaining internationalization', *International Business Review*, **4**(2), 115–31.

Cavusgil, S.T. (1984), 'Organizational characteristics associated with export activities', *Journal of Management Studies*, **21**(1), 3–22.

Chaudhry, S. and D. Crick (2002), 'A research policy note on U.K. government support and small firms' internationalization using the internet: the use of www.tradeuk.com', *Journal of Strategic Change*, **11**(2), 95–104.

Chrisman, J.J., A. Bauerschmidt and C.W. Hofer (1999), 'The determinants of new venture performance', *Entrepreneurship Theory & Practice*, **22**(1), 5–29.

Coviello, N.E. and M.V. Jones (2004), 'Methodological issues in international entrepreneurship research', *Journal of Business Venturing*, **19**, 485–508.

Coviello, N.E. and A. McAuley (1999), 'Internationalization and the smaller firm: a review of contemporary empirical research', *Management International Review*, **39**(2), 223–57.

Coviello, N.E. and H. Munro (1997), 'Network relationships and the internationalization process of small software firms', *International Business Review*, **6**(4), 361–86.

Crick, D. (2002), 'The decision to discontinue exporting: SMEs in two U.K. trade sectors', *Journal of Small Business Management*, **40**(1), 66–77.

Crick, D. (2004), 'U.K. SMEs' decision to discontinue exporting: an exploratory investigation into practices within the clothing industry', *Journal of Business Venturing*, **19**, 561–87.

Crick, D. and M.V. Jones (2000), 'Small high-technology firms and international high-technology markets', *Journal of International Marketing*, **8**(2), 63–85.

Crick, D. and M. Spence (2005), 'The internationalization of "high performing" U.K. high-tech SMEs: a study of planned and unplanned strategies', *International Business Review*, **14**, 167–85.

Czinkota, M.R. (1982), *Export Development Strategies: US Promotion Policy*, New York: Praeger.

Dana, L.-P., H. Etemad and R. Wright (1999), 'The impact of globalization on SMEs', *Global Focus*, **11**(4), 93–105.

Denzin, N.S. and Y.S. Lincoln (eds) (1998), *The Landscape of Qualitative Research: Theories and Issues*, London: Sage Publications.

Dicken, P. (1996), 'The static and dynamic mechanics of competitive theory', *Journal of Marketing*, **60**, 102–6.

Eisenhardt, K. (1989), 'Building theory from case study research', *Academy of Management Review*, **14**(4), 532–50.

Fletcher, D. (2004), 'International entrepreneurship and the small business', *Entrepreneurship & Regional Development*, **16**, July, 289–305.

Francis, J. and C. Collins-Dodd (1999), 'The impact of a proactive orientation on the export performance of high-tech firms', *Journal of International Marketing*, **8**(3), 84–103.

Hallén, L. (1992), 'Infrastructural networks in international business', in M. Forgsen and J. Johanson (eds), *Managing Networks in International Business*, Reading: Gordon and Breach Science Publishers.

Ibeh, K. (2003), 'Toward a contingency framework of export entrepreneurship: conceptualizations and empirical evidence', *Small Business Economics*, **20**(1), 49–68.

Johanson, J. and J.-E. Vahlne (1977), 'The internationalization process of the firm – a model of knowledge development and increasing foreign market commitment', *Journal of International Business Studies*, **8**(2), 23–32.

Johanson, J. and J.-E. Vahlne (1990), 'The mechanism of internationalization', *International Marketing Review*, **7**(4), 11–24.

Johanson, J. and F. Wiedersheim-Paul (1975), 'The internationalization of the firm – four Swedish cases', *Journal of Management Studies*, **12**, 305–22.

Jones, M.V. (1999), 'The internationalization of small high technology firms', *Journal of International Marketing*, **7**(4), 15–41.

Jones, M.V. and N.E. Coviello (2005), 'Internationalization: conceptualizing an entrepreneurial process of behavior in time', *Journal of International Business Studies*, **36**(3), 284–303.

Keeble, D., C. Lawson, H. Lawton Smith, B. Moore and I.F. Wilkinson (1998), 'Internationalization processes, networking and local embeddedness in technology-intensive small firms', *Small Business Economics*, **11**, 327–342.

Knight, G. and S.T. Cavusgil (1996), 'The born global firm: a challenge to international theory', *Advances in International Marketing*, **8**, 11–26.

Knight, G. and S.T. Cavusgil (2004), 'Innovation, organisational capabilities, and the born-global firm', *Journal of International Business Studies*, **35**(2), 124–41.

Kotabe M. and M.R. Czinkota (1993), 'State government promotion of manufacturing exports: a gap analysis', *Journal of International Business Studies*, **23**(4), 637–58.

Leonidou, L. and C.S. Katsikeas (1996), 'The export development process: an integrative review of empirical models', *Journal of International Business Studies*, third quarter, 517–51.

Lesch, W.C., A. Eshghi and G.S. Eshghi (1990), 'A review of export promotion programs in the ten largest industrial states', in S.T. Cavusgil and M.R. Czinkota (eds), *International Perspectives on Trade Promotion and Assistance*, New York: Quorum Books.

Lindqvist, M. (1997), 'Infant multinationals: internationalization of small technology-based firms', in D. Jones and M. Klofsten (eds), *Technology, Innovation and Enterprise: The European Experience*, London: Macmillan, pp. 303–24.

Litvak, I. (1990), 'Instant international: strategic reality for small high-technology firms in Canada', *Multinational Business*, **2**, 1–12.

Madsen, T.K. and P. Servais (1997), 'The internationalization of born globals: an evolutionary process?', *International Business Review*, **6**(6), 561–83.

Marshall, C. and G.B. Rossman (1995), *Designing Qualitative Research*, London: Sage Publications.

McDougall, G. (1990), 'Small New Zealand businesses and exporting: some observations', *New Zealand Journal of Business*, **13**, 107–16.

McDougall, P.P. (1989), 'International vs domestic entrepreneurship: new venture strategic behavior and industry structure', *Journal of Business Venturing*, **4**, 387–400.

McDougall, P.P. and B.M. Oviatt (1996), 'New venture internationalization, strategic change and performance: a follow-up study', *Journal of Business Venturing*, **11**, 23–40.

McDougall, P.P. and B.M. Oviatt (2000), 'International entrepreneurship: the intersection of two research paths', *Academy of Management Journal*, **43**, 902–6.

McDougall, P.P., S. Shane and B.M. Oviatt (1994), 'Explaining the formation of international joint ventures: the limits of theories from international business research', *Journal of Business Venturing*, **9**, 469–87.

Merrilees, B., D. Miller and J. Tiessen (1998), 'Serendipity, leverage and the process of entrepreneurial internationalization', *Small Enterprise Research*, **6**(2), 3–11.

Mockaitis, A.I., E. Vaiginiene and V. Giedraitis (2006), 'The internationalization efforts of Lithuanian manufacturing firms – strategy or luck?', *Research in International Business and Finance*, **20**(1), 111–26.

Moen, O. (2002), 'The born globals – a new generation of small European exporters', *International Marketing Review*, **19**(2/3), 156–75.

Moorman, C. and A.S. Miner (1998), 'Organizational improvisation and organizational memory', *Academy of Management Review*, **23**(Oct), 698–723.

Oesterle, M.-J. (1997), 'Time span until internationalization: foreign market entry as a built-in mechanism of innovation', *Management International Review*, **37**(2), 125–49.

Oviatt, B.M. and P.P. McDougall (1994), 'Toward a theory of international new ventures', *Journal of International Business Studies*, **25**(1), 45–64.

Pauwels, P. and P. Matthyssens (1999), 'A strategy process perspective on export withdrawal', *Journal of International Marketing*, **7**(3), 10–37.

Pavord, W.C. and R.G. Bogart (1975), 'The dynamics of the decision to export', *Akron Business and Economic Review*, Oct, 6–11.

Rasmussan, E., T. Madsen and F. Evangelista (2001), 'The founding of the born global company in Denmark and Australia: sensemaking and networking', *Asia Pacific Journal of Marketing and Logistics*, **13**(3), 75–101.

Reid, S.D. (1983), 'Firm internationalization, transaction costs and strategic choice', *International Marketing Review*, **1**(2), 45–55.

Reuber, A.R. and E. Fischer (1997), 'The influence of the management team's international experience on the internationalization behaviors of SMEs', *Journal of International Business Studies*, **28**(4), 807–26.

Reuber, A.R. and E. Fischer (2002), 'Foreign sales and small firm growth: the moderating role of the management team', *Entrepreneurship Theory & Practice*, **27**(1), 29–45.

Sarasvathy, S. (2001), 'Causation and effectuation: toward a theoretical shift from economic inevitability to entrepreneurial contingency', *Academy of Management Review*, **26**(2), 243–63.

Seringhaus, R.F.H. and P.J. Rosson (1990), *Government Export Promotion: A Global Perspective*, London: Routledge.

Shane, S. (2000), 'Prior knowledge and the discovery of entrepreneurial opportunities', *Organization Science*, **11**(4), 448–69.

Shrader, R.C. (2001), 'Collaboration and performance in foreign markets: the case of young high-technology manufacturing firms', *Academy of Management Journal*, **44**, 45–60.

Shrader, R.C., B.M. Oviatt and P.P. McDougall (2000), 'How new ventures exploit trade-offs among international risk factors: lessons for accelerated internationalization of the 21st century', *Academy of Management Journal*, **43**(6), 1227–47.

Slater, S.F. and J.C. Narver (1995), 'Market orientation and the learning organization', *Journal of Marketing*, **59**(July), 63–74.

Spence, M. (2000), 'Public–private partnerships for export: some critical considerations for their evaluation', *Journal of Public–Private Partnerships*, **2**(2), 307–22.

Spence, M. (2003), 'International strategy formation in small Canadian high-technology companies', *Journal of International Entrepreneurship*, **1**(3), 277–96.

Storey, D.J. (1994), *Understanding the Small Business Sector*, London: Routledge.

Teece, D.J., G. Pisano and A. Shuen (1997), 'Dynamic capabilities and strategic management', *Strategic Management Journal*, **18**(7), 509–33.

Turnbull, P. (1987), 'A challenge to the stages theory of the internationalization process', in P.J. Rosson and S. Reid (eds), *Managing Export Entry and Expansion*, New York: Praeger.

Welch, D., L. Welch, L. Young and I.F. Wilkinson (1997), 'The importance of networks in export promotion: policy issues', *Journal of International Marketing*, **6**(4), 66–82.

Westhead, P., M. Wright and D. Ucbasaran (2001), 'The internationalization of new and small firms: a resource-based view', *Journal of Business Venturing*, **16**, 333–58.

Wilson, D. and V. Mummalaneni (1990), 'Bonding and commitment in buyer–seller relationships: a preliminary conceptualisation', in D. Ford (ed.), *Understanding Business Markets: Interaction, Relationships, Networks*, London: Academic Press, pp. 408–20.

Woodcock, P.C., P.W. Beamish and S. Makino (1994), 'Ownership-based entry mode strategies and international performance', *Journal of International Business Studies*, **25**(2), 253–73.

Yeoh, P.-L. and I. Jeong (1995), 'Contingency relationships between entrepreneurship, export channel structure and environment', *European Journal of Marketing*, **29**(8), 95–115.

Yin, R.K. (1994), *Case Study Research – Design and Methods*, Newbury: Sage.

Zahra, S.A., R.D. Ireland and M.A. Hitt (2000), 'International expansion by new venture firms: international diversity, mode of market entry, technological learning, and performance', *Academy of Management Journal*, **43**(5), 925–50.

# APPENDICES

*Appendix 13.1    UK firms' internationalization strategies*

| Firm and start-up date | Initial Internationalization Strategies | | | | |
|---|---|---|---|---|---|
| | Timing/ years from start-up | Reasons for timing | Motives/ incentives/ stimuli | Entry strategies | First market |
| UK1 1997 | 1 year | Limited domestic market | Networks | Agents | US and several EU markets |
| UK2 1998 | 1 year | Limited domestic market | Networks | Agents | Several EU markets |
| UK3 1996 | 2 years | Limited domestic market | Gov't support | Subsidiary | US |
| UK4 1995 | 3 years | To this point the firm was not ready for overseas sales | Gov't support | Distributors | US |
| UK5 1997 | 2 years | To this point the product was not ready for overseas sales | New manager recruited | Distributors | US and several EU markets |
| UK6 1998 | 1 year | Limited domestic market | Networks | Agents | Several EU markets |
| UK7 1994 | Late 5 years | Growth and profit potential | Serendipitous encounter | Joint venture | Taiwan |
| UK8 1994 | Late 4 years | Growth and profit potential | Serendipitous encounter | Agents | Germany |
| UK9 1998 | 1 year | Limited domestic market | Networks | Agents | Several EU markets |
| UK10 1993 | Late 6 years | Growth and profit potential | Serendipitous encounter | Agents | US |
| UK11 1997 | 2 years | To this point the firm was not ready for overseas sales | Gov't support | Distributor | US |
| UK12 1996 | 3 years | Growth and profit potential | New executive team after buy-out | Distributors | Several EU markets |

| International Market Expansion Strategies | | | | |
|---|---|---|---|---|
| Subsequent markets | Motives/ incentives/ stimuli | Expansion method | Strategic orientation | Concerns |
| EU markets and Far East | Exploit niche markets | Agents | Planned | Competition undercutting prices |
| EU markets and US | Exploit niche markets | Agents and subsidiaries | Planned | Competition undercutting prices |
| EU markets | Exploit niche markets | Agents | Initially unplanned now planned | Competition undercutting prices Marketing expertise |
| EU markets | Exploit niche markets | Distributors and subsidiaries | Planned | Competition undercutting prices Managing planned growth |
| EU markets and Far East | Exploit niche markets | Distributors and joint ventures | Planned | Financial resources |
| EU markets and US | Spread sales risk over a number of markets and for growth | Agents | Planned | Financial resources Competition undercutting prices |
| EU markets and US | Growth and profit potential | Agents | Initially unplanned, now planned | Financial resources |
| EU markets and Far East | Growth and profit potential | Agents | Initially unplanned, now planned | Competition undercutting prices |
| EU markets and US plus ad hoc orders globally | Growth and profit potential | Agents | Majority planned with a few ad hoc unplanned sales | Capacity to serve demand |
| EU markets plus ad hoc orders globally | Growth and profit potential | Agents | Majority planned with a few ad hoc unplanned sales | No major concerns |
| EU | Exploit niche markets | Subsidiaries and licence agreements | Planned | Overseas gov't legislation for subsidiaries |
| EU markets plus ad hoc orders globally | Growth and profit potential | Distributors | Majority planned with a few ad hoc unplanned sales | Financial constraints |

*Appendix 13.2    Canadian firms' internationalization strategies*

| Firm | Initial Internationalization Strategies | | | | |
|---|---|---|---|---|---|
| | Timing/ years from start-up | Reason for timing | Motives/ incentives/ stimuli | Entry strategies | First market |
| C1 1981 | 15 years | Captive home market | Internet | Distributors Internet | US |
| C2 1996 | 1 year | Limited home market | Networks | Integrators Internet | US |
| C3 1984 | 6 years | Captive home market | Vertical market, similar context | 1 foreign office in Washington Internet | US |
| C4 1996 | 3 years | Growth and profit potential, US clients needed as reference | Proactive search for partners | Distributor in Denver, telemktg agency in Texas | US |
| C5 1985 | 12 years | Captive home market | Serendipitous encounter (Internet) | Distributors Integrators Internet | France |
| C6 1990 | 6 years | Captive home market | Serendipitous encounter | Distributors Internet | US |
| C7 1982 | 3 years | Growth and profit potential | Serendipitous encounter | Distributors Internet | US |
| C8 1996 | 3 years | Limited home market | Proactive search for partners | Distributors Internet | US |
| C9 2000 | 1 year | Few clients around the world, in industrialized countries | Networks | Direct sales as product is new in an emerging market Education needed | US EU Asia |
| C10 1998 | 0 years | Growth and profit potential | Serendipitous encounter (networks) | Direct sales | China |
| C11 1996 | 4 years | Limited home market, few clients around the world | Networks | Direct export | US |
| C12 1992 | 0 years | Growth and profit potential | Proactive search for partners | Distributors Internet | US |

| International Market Expansion Strategies | | | | |
|---|---|---|---|---|
| Subsequent markets | Motives/incentives/stimuli | Expansion method | Strategic orientation | Concerns |
| Mexico | Internet | Distributors Internet | Unplanned | Financial resources Marketing expertise |
| Italy Japan France | Internet | Integrators Internet | Unplanned | Marketing expertise |
| Eastern Europe EU | Vertical market, new context New product, similar context Networks | Internet Office | Planned | Knowledge of foreign markets, way of doing business |
| Negotiations with Japan but firm sold before fruition | Serendipitous encounter | NA | Planned | Assessing potential in foreign markets |
| US Japan | Vertical market, similar context | Offices Internet | Planned | Working harmoniously with foreign cultures |
| US Ukraine | Vertical market Networks | Distributors Internet Pseudo-presence | Unplanned | Financial resources |
| Australia EU | Internet | Distributors | Unplanned | Conservative owner, no need to change |
| Korea Brazil Others (only 5% sales outside US) | Internet | Distributors Strategic alliances in the US and France | Planned in the US Unplanned elsewhere | Financial resources, fear of being copied in Asia, but not in South America |
| Same but evolution in channels | Networks | Distributors in Asia, EU | Planned | None, as market is standardized and new |
| Poland Vietnam Central America | Networks | Direct sales | Unplanned | Arranging for financing Gaining a full understanding of country issues |
| Japan China EU | Networks | Office in US, distributors in Japan, China, EU | Planned | Time difference – Asia and North America |
| EU Asia | Proactive search for partners | No change in entry strategy | Planned | Customs regulations |

# 14.  SME choice of export market and entry mode: theory and research

## Gerald I. Susman and Jenna P. Stites

## INTRODUCTION

This study focuses on the exporting strategies of small and medium-sized enterprises (SMEs) and, in particular, how these firms develop or acquire assets for selling their products and services in foreign markets. Exporting is an important facet of a much broader process of internationalization, and is often one of the earliest internationalization activities that SMEs undertake. Jones (Chapter 12 in this volume) and Beamish (1990) offer different, but compatible, definitions of internationalization:

> A process through which firms grow and develop internationally, establish and manage their foreign operations, increase their exposure to international business through international transactions, establish and develop relationships and networks that extend across borders and which is manifest and identifiable through specific entry modes, in locations in relation to time. (Jones, Chapter 12 in this volume)

> The process by which firms both increase their awareness of the direct and indirect influence of international transactions on their future, and establish and conduct transactions with other countries. (Beamish, 1990, p. 77)

As these definitions suggest, internationalization is not limited to exporting. It also includes the importing and setting up of foreign-based sales and production operations either alone or in partnership with other firms. Finnish studies, for example, suggest that SMEs begin internationalizing by importing resources such as goods, services, finances and technologies (Korhonen et al., 1996). Importing allows firms to gain experience in dealing with foreign markets, and gives them the confidence that they can successfully take further steps toward internationalization, such as exporting, foreign direct investment and collaborating with foreign firms (Coviello and McAuley, 1999; Jones, Chapter 12 in this volume).

## MOTIVES FOR INTERNATIONALIZATION

Motives for internationalization are abundant and diverse. Jones (Chapter 12 in this volume) suggests it is often not a goal in itself, but simply one means for the pursuit of growth or realization of international opportunities. Similarly, since most firms do not view internationalization as a goal in and of itself, it is often pursued as a solution to a problem (Jones, Chapter 12 in this volume). For example, firms that sell high-technology products may find that domestic sales of their products are limited, or that components for their products are only available from foreign sources. Also an original equipment manufacturer (OEM) customer might ask them to export components to one of its foreign-based plants.

Firms may also internationalize because of the size and/or potential of the domestic market. SMEs often take advantage of niches, which are small market segments or gaps often ignored by large firms. Since these markets are small and specialized, niche-based firms must go abroad in order to meet growth objectives and realize their potential (Maslach and McNaughton, Chapter 10 in this volume).

Additional reasons for SME internationalization include the behaviour of competitors and pressure from larger firms (Matlay and Fletcher, 2000). Competitors who are internationalizing their own firms may provide a catalyst for others who want to remain active in the market to internationalize as well. Similarly, when larger firms internationalize, they often force small firms to do the same in order to remain competitive, for example as a supplier to the larger firm.

## THEORIES OF INTERNATIONALIZATION

We first briefly introduce the stage, network and rationalist theories of internationalization. We next examine foreign market choice, the pace of internationalization and foreign market entry mode choice from the perspective of the three different theories. The first two theories, stage and network, deal primarily with foreign market choice and the pace of internationalization, while the third theory deals primarily with entry mode choice. Each theory provides insights into the process of internationalization, but also has explanatory limitations.

Stage theory explains internationalization as a series of incremental and successive steps that firms take, dependent upon cumulative experience and learning. Firms progress through a set of lower to higher developmental stages based on choices about foreign markets, pace and entry mode. These stages generally advance through low-commitment interactions with close markets to high-commitment interactions with more distant markets.

Network theory views firms as part of a vast web of contacts and information (Bell et al., 2003). According to its proponents, formal and informal relationships within networks influence the pace of internationalization as well as choice of market and entry mode. Networks and the relationships within them can be formed through contracts and planned gatherings, or they can be formed through patterns of acquaintance and chance meetings (Meyer and Skak, 2002). Regardless of their origin, network relationships assist firms to spread from domestic to global markets by introducing them to new partners and positions within those markets (Coviello and Munro, 1995; McNaughton, 2000).

Theories that may be characterized as rationalist consider the choice of markets, entry mode and pace to be rational calculations of risk and reward. The setting for these choices may be opportunistic or planned. The essential elements of this theory include risk, uncertainty and control (Anderson and Gatignon, 1986; Erramilli and Rao, 1990; Hill et al., 1990; Root, 1987) and ownership, location and internalization (Dunning, 1980).

**Foreign Market Choice**

Stage theory suggests that the 'psychic distance' between home and host markets plays an important role in foreign market choice. Psychic distance refers to factors such as cultural and language barriers, political systems, economic development and so on that inhibit the transfer of information between the firm and its market (Johanson and Vahlne, 1977, 1990). According to stage theory, firms tend to enter foreign markets that are psychically close to their home markets before entering markets that are more psychically distant. This is because firms gain confidence as they accumulate experience in foreign markets and as a result become more willing to enter more psychically distant markets.

Psychic distance may play a stronger role in determining the location of foreign direct investment than in exporting because of what is at stake, but the evidence is mixed (Erramilli, 1991). Although studies by stage theorists Johanson, Vahlne and Wiedersheim-Paul support psychic distance, other scholars have found exceptions. For instance, a study of SMEs in the software industry found that psychic distance did not provide an adequate explanation for where firms chose to begin international activities (Bell, 1995). Bell found that demand from internationalizing clientèle, fulfilment of unsolicited orders, niche targeting and industry trends played a large role in firms' choice of markets to enter and did not necessarily take into account psychic distance.

Similarly, Korhonen et al. (1996, p. 322) suggest that firms can decrease the psychic distance between domestic and foreign markets by importing; they claim that 'a number of the actions associated with importing have the potential of diminishing perceived obstacles and generally lowering uncertainty about the later export move, through increased knowledge of and experience in the international arena'.

Network theory proposes that relationships can override psychic distance as well as any predetermined stages of international growth (that is, firms make decisions more on the basis of their network relationships than on the basis of any stage of growth). This was acknowledged by stage theorists Johanson and Vahlne (1992, 2003) who revised their original theory to encompass the effects that relationships have on market choice.

In this study, we test the proposition that psychic distance influences SMEs' choice of foreign markets to enter.

*Hypothesis I    SMEs' initial choice of foreign markets to enter is influenced by the foreign market's psychic distance from the SME's home country.*

**Pace of Internationalization**

The pace of internationalization implies how soon after inception SMEs internationalize (Bell et al., 2003; Jones, Chapter 12 in this volume; Knight and Cavusgil, 2005; McNaughton, 2000; Oviatt and McDougall, 1994).

Stage theory suggests that firms need to develop a minimal level of experience in domestic markets before pursuing foreign markets. Clearly many firms start to internationalize only after being in business for some time, but there are abundant examples of firms that are 'born global' and others that are 'born again'. McNaughton (2000) posits that, although stage theory may adequately address the process of internationalization for many large firms, there also exists a more accelerated path to internationalization that many small firms pursue (for example, 'born global' and 'born again' firms).

Born global firms refer to those that internationalize from the beginning, meaning that they are globally active upon inception (Oviatt and McDougall, 1994). Many of these firms actually ignore the domestic market until after they are globally established (Bell et al., 2003). Some firms are born global because this is imperative for their survival. Jones (Chapter 12 in this volume) claims that today's high-technology SMEs must internationalize quickly because of the increasingly global environment in which they operate. Firms are also increasingly born global because of opportunities that arise through their networks. Furthermore the management of many born global firms is entrepreneurial and globally focused from the onset.

In contrast, born again firms re-emerge as active international firms after shifting focus to the domestic market for an extended time (Bell et al., 2003). Major catalysts that are assumed to lead these firms to shift focus are top management succession, leveraged buy-out, acquisition by another firm and fulfilment of orders from domestic-based internationalized clients (Oviatt and McDougall, 1994).

Born global and born again internationalization is also described by network theory, which claims that firms need not follow a staged progression in order to internationalize; network influences are capable of providing the information and strategy necessary for a firm to internationalize (Coviello and Munro, 1997). Meyer and Skak (2002, p. 179) claim that this is a rather serendipitous occurrence: 'As events in the network are generally beyond the control of smaller firms, their strategies are subject to high degrees of serendipity, i.e. fortunate and unexpected discoveries made by chance.' Thus, although it is possible for network occurrences to be planned, such as with contracted collaboration among two firms, it is also possible that firms are extemporaneously affected by decisions and actions made on behalf of others in the network.

**Foreign Market Entry Mode Choice**

In addition to deciding whether or not to internationalize as well as what markets to enter and how soon to enter them, firms must also choose an entry mode appropriate for their market choice. The basic choice for firms is that of make-or-buy. In general, firms are able to acquire or develop sales assets (make), or they are able to contract for them (buy). Within the choice of make-or-buy there are also differing degrees of owned or contracted assets. Accordingly there are a multitude of reasons for firms choosing one mode over another. In any event, the entry mode decision of whether to make or buy sales assets is critical to a firm's success in a foreign market.

Stage theory addresses entry mode and holds that firms will make increasing commitments to foreign markets, based on experiential learning (Johanson and Vahlne, 1977). On the basis of this approach, firms begin with a low-commitment mode of entry and progress to high-commitment modes of entry through the use of acquired knowledge and experience. According to stage theory, stages of internationalization progress from no regular export activities, to exporting via independent representatives and agents, to the establishment of an overseas sales subsidiary and, finally, to overseas production (Johanson and Vahlne, 1977, 1990, 2003).

Some stage theory scholars further refine staged progression into stages of export development. For instance, the innovation-related models evaluated by Andersen (1993) generally differentiate between four to six stages of export development. These stages progress from firms that have no interest in exporting to firms that are actively increasing their exporting business. For example, the innovation-related export model proposed by Bilkey and Tesar (1977) claims that firms in stage (1) are completely uninterested in exporting and will not consider filling unsolicited orders. During stage (2), firms become willing to fulfil unsolicited orders, but are unwilling to pursue additional exporting. In stage (3), the firm begins to explore the possibility of entering the exporting business and then, during stage (4), the firm actively begins to export to a market that it feels is close in distance or is culturally similar, and so on. In stage (5), the firm becomes an experienced exporter in a single market and is able to manage its exporting business. Finally, during stage (6), the firm decides to explore the possibilities of exporting to other markets that are more distant.

There are three exceptions in which firms are expected to behave differently than is prescribed by stage theory. These exceptions include firms with large resources, firms with experience in other markets with similar environments, and firms competing in easily predictable market conditions (Johanson and Vahlne, 1990). These exceptions are made because firms with these characteristics may have less market uncertainty and thus be more inclined to make other investments that are not necessarily small and incremental, or staged.

The discussion of whether or not internationalization is staged is an interesting issue, but it requires qualification before it is applied to SMEs. Stage theory was originally developed to explain how large multinational firms (non-SMEs) make investment decisions abroad (Johanson and Vahlne, 1977, 2003). These decisions focused heavily on the impact of scale in relatively large markets, and thus it is understandable that the model describes cautious and incremental experiential learning as a basis to make further capital commitments.

From the networking perspective, another reason that firms may choose to 'make' or 'buy' sales assets is related to network connections and motivation for going abroad. For example, Erramilli and Rao (1990) make a distinction between firms that go abroad in order to follow customers that have internationalized and those that seek new markets. According to them, 'customer followers' are more likely to own (make) their own sales assets because they already have a captive sales audience waiting for them in the new foreign market (Ekeledo and Sivakumar, 1998). Conversely, 'market seekers' are more likely to contract for (buy) their sales assets because they are unfamiliar with the new territory. Thus networks can affect the choice of entry mode based on the existence of network contacts such as existing customers.

Entry mode choice can also be explained by rationalist theories on the basis of risk, uncertainty and control. Risk encompasses the issue of resource commitment and expected return. The more resources that are committed, the greater the potential return is likely to be. However it is also true that greater resource commitment offers a greater loss if the firm does not succeed. Uncertainty addresses the issue of what firms do not know externally about a foreign market or internally about the firm's future performance in the new market (Anderson and Gatignon, 1986). Many uncertainties can be alleviated through government programmes and network contacts, but there exists a level of ambiguity in entering a foreign market that affects the way that decisions are made. Control explains the level of power that a firm will have over its resources. Similar to risk, high control often gives the greatest potential return, but it also increases losses if the firm fails. For example, indirect exporting is characterized by relatively low risk (low resource commitment and low return on investment), low uncertainty and low control, while on the other hand foreign direct investment (FDI) is characterized by high risk (high resource commitment and return), high uncertainty and high control (Chung and Enderwick, 2001).

Degree of control is relative to entry mode choice; for example, exporting is considered a low-control mode of entry when compared to FDI, but exporting through a direct sales force is considered a high-control mode of entry compared to exporting through agents, representatives or distributors. Control is important because it aids the firm in developing, delivering and protecting its products and services. Thus risk, uncertainty and control are interdependent and essential factors that are considered to at least some degree in the internationalization process.

## INITIAL ENTRY MODE CHOICE

We are interested primarily in SMEs that choose exporting as their initial entry mode and focus on their choice of how to sell their products regardless of whether they start to do this early or late in their existence. Exporting involves mainly the marketing and sales functions because distribution and manufacturing in a foreign country require a substantial investment that many SMEs delay making or never make at all. The primary marketing and selling issue is whether to use the firm's own direct sales force (high control) or to contract (low control) with export agents, distributors, manufacturing representatives and so on.

A direct sales force consists of the manufacturer's employees who are paid via salary and possibly commission and who sell the product directly to the foreign buyer. The direct sales force can be either domestic or foreign-based. An export agent is an intermediary who acts on behalf of a company to open up or develop a market in a foreign country. Export agents are often paid a commission on all sales and may have exclusive rights in a particular geographic area. Independent manufacturing representatives sell products to wholesalers or other customers on a commission basis. They call on customers, demonstrate their products, point out salable features, answer questions and forward orders to the manufacturer. A distributor may make and sell its own products in its home country, but contracts to sell an exporting firm's non-competing products as part of an expanded product offering. A distributor can also be either domestic or foreign-based.

Theory that relates to entry mode choice differs from theory that relates to the decision to export or the choice of countries to enter or their sequence. This is not surprising because these respective theories are intended to explain different phenomena. Entry mode choice relies heavily on transaction cost theory and the resource-based view of the firm. When firms choose an entry mode, they consider the costs and resources required to sell and service their products effectively in foreign markets and to learn from their customers. They also consider the implications of their choice on intellectual property (IP) protection. Consequently we believe that the choice of entry mode is heavily influenced by product complexity, sales and service requirements and IP concerns.

> *Hypothesis IIa    The greater the product complexity, sales and service requirements of a firm's product, the more likely the firm will own its sales force rather than contract the marketing and sales functions to others.*

The marketing and sales functions may be limited strictly to selling products, but could include forecasting, advertising, analysis of customer profiles, trends and so on.

According to this study, product complexity is defined as modifications or customizations made to the product before it is sold. Sales requirements include the customer education, demonstrations, training and so on that are required to complete the sale, and service requirements include the provision of after-sale services such as upgrades, maintenance and spare parts.

> *Hypothesis IIb    The greater the IP concerns of a firm, the more likely the firm will own its sales force rather than contract the marketing and sales functions to others.*

According to this study, IP concerns describe the ownership and protection of processes and products that contain IP.

To support our hypotheses, we present supporting theories and empirical studies. Dunning's (1980, 1988) OLI (ownership, location, internalization) or eclectic theory is convenient for explaining our hypotheses because it is comprehensive and encompasses the resource-based view (RBV) and transaction cost (TC) theories even though the latter two theories were developed for other purposes. Eclectic theory is rational and focuses on specific advantages that influence the internationalization process. These advantages are ownership, location and internalization. Eclectic theory has been tested and is supported for its relevance as both a descriptive and a normative theory (Brouthers et al., 1999). Furthermore it has been concluded that eclectic theory is good for predicting the entry mode choice of SMEs (Nakos and Brouthers, 2002).

The ownership-specific advantages are consistent with RBV, which suggests that firms should own any assets that are core competencies and help to differentiate the firm from its competitors. Firm or ownership-specific factors include patents, trademarks, raw material possession and intellectual property referring to a product's technology or production process (Dunning, 1980).

Furthermore, Collis and Montgomery (1995) address the fact that no two companies are alike, which means that many resources are specific to a certain firm. Firm-specific resources therefore have a path-dependent component that characterizes the resources' uniqueness on account of all of the activities that have taken place in the resources' development and/or use. This path-dependent element aids in the products' inimitability and limits other companies' easily copying the firm's competitive advantage. For example, a trained and motivated direct sales force takes considerable time to develop. Similarly 'a company will be positioned to succeed if it has the best and most appropriate stocks of resources for its business and strategy' (ibid., p. 119). For example, a firm that can train and motivate its direct sales force has a strategic asset that can give it a competitive advantage.

Likewise Ekeledo and Sivakumar (2004) assert that a firm will be dissuaded from using a contracted-sales mode of entry in a foreign market when the product contains a source of sustainable competitive advantage, such as that of firm or ownership-specific inputs (for example, intellectual property pertaining to the product, its technology or manufacturing process). The TC perspective suggests that, when transaction-specific assets or asset specificity, which are similar to Dunning's determination of firm or ownership-specific advantages, become a core competency or competitive advantage, firms are better off using a direct mode of entry (Anderson and Gatignon, 1986; Hill et al., 1990). Thus, in order to sell complex products or to protect IP, a firm should own its sales assets.

The location-specific advantages concern the location or country to which the firm exports and are influenced by the attractiveness of the foreign market. Location advantages or disadvantages include natural resources, intellectual property protection, transportation costs, production costs, labour costs, tariff barriers, psychic distance and investment incentives or disincentives as well as market potential, economic or political conditions, government policies and host-country risk (Agarwal and Ramaswami, 1992; Dunning, 1988; Ekeledo and Sivakumar, 2004; Young, 1987).

Location advantages refer to the benefits enjoyed because the firm is doing business in a specific location. For example if a firm needs to transport its product to customers via freight trucks, and transporting expenses are less in the new market, that would be a location advantage for the firm. Likewise location disadvantages refer to the costs or detriments incurred because of doing business in a certain location. For example, China's lack of IP protection enforcement is a cost for firms that wish to bring their IP-intensive products into China.

Another potential location-specific advantage has to do with the location of potential partners or networks (Dunning, 1995; Zain and Ng, 2006). For instance, a market in which the entrant firm has established industrial contacts would provide a location-specific advantage for that firm, whereas a market without any contacts would not benefit or cost the entrant firm. In addition, a location that provides a niche market could also be a location-specific advantage for niche-based SMEs, and vice versa (Nakos and Brouthers, 2002).

Transaction-cost theory asserts that, when the combination of location costs and transaction-specific assets is high, it is better for the firm to use a high degree of control within its choice of entry mode (Anderson and Gatignon, 1986). For example, if the country has weak IP protection, the firm will want to own its sales assets to avoid leakage. However, if the firm's product is difficult to imitate, it might be willing to enter a foreign country with weak IP protection. Therefore firms will choose locations that best preserve or enhance existing ownership-specific advantages.

The internalization advantage is consistent with transaction cost theory, which suggests that complex transactions across firm boundaries are difficult and costly and that there are agency risks (Williamson, 1975). Transaction costs refer to the financial burdens associated with ensuring the compliance of the contracted firm (Collis, 1995), and the risks concern agents who may not act in the firm's best interest. RBV and TC theory suggest similar recommendations for complex products, high sales and service requirements, and high IP. That is, leave it in-house. The trade-off is that owning assets can be expensive and there is greater exposure to risk if the exporting venture fails. Also we recognize that choice of country to enter (L) and choice of entry mode (O, I) may interact and involve another trade-off. Therefore firms will choose the entry mode that best minimizes the cost of transactions (Coviello and McAuley, 1999).

According to eclectic theory, all three OLI factors are important to the entry mode decision. Dunning (1980, 1988) suggests that the ownership advantages of a firm will dictate the internalization advantages and that location advantages will depend on the combination of the two former advantages. Thus ownership seems to be of prime importance in the entry mode decision, followed by internalization and location factors.

However various perspectives may view each factor's importance differently. For example, the RBV perspective suggests that a firm's substantial competitive (ownership) advantages will lead it to choose to internalize its activities, viewing location advantages last (Collis, 1995; Collis and Montgomery, 1995; Ekeledo and Sivakumar, 2004). However the TC perspective suggests that internalization factors such as the agency problem will be evaluated first, leading a firm next to evaluate its ownership and location advantages (Anderson and Gatignon, 1986). Furthermore, following the OLI framework, Ekeledo and Sivakumar (1998) suggest that location advantages may be the most important factor, although this distinction is likely made on the basis of their comparison of manufacturing and service firms, as some services, such as restaurants, are non-separable from their location. Although different perspectives take differing approaches to the importance of each factor, it is clear that each factor is an important facet of entry mode choice and that the factors are interactive. Thus the overall goal is for the firm to choose the entry mode that best takes into account all of the related factors (Hill et al., 1990).

There are a number of empirical studies that provide support for the reasoning behind the OLI framework. For example, relating to product complexity, Anderson and Coughlan (1987) and Nakos and Brouthers (2002) found that products that are highly differentiated from competitors' products are likely to be sold via direct channels. Likewise a study by Anderson and Gatignon (1986) proposed that high control modes of entry are suitable for highly differentiated products as well as customized products. In the same way, Ekeledo and Sivakumar (2004) discuss 'specialized assets', which, according to their definition, include customizing the products or services being offered, such as tailoring a programme to meet a specific customer's needs. Consistent with this definition, firms that are required to customize products will likely use a direct entry mode.

Studies on the importance of sales requirements reveal that, when the sale of products requires the development of 'specialized skills and working relationships', firms tend to use direct modes of entry (Anderson and Coughlan, 1987). Accordingly, Ramaseshan and Patton (1994) found that, when before or after-sales service is necessary to make a sale, firms are more likely to use direct channels to make certain that the proper services are performed.

Moreover evidence of the significance of service requirements suggests that firms with products involving before or after-sales services tend to have a direct sales presence in the foreign market in order to guarantee that services are rendered (Chung and Enderwick, 2001; Ramaseshan and Patton, 1994). Also a study conducted on Mittelstand companies observed that Germany's SMEs prefer to use a direct sales force when dealing with services because they believe that services are too important to their reputation to risk the agency costs that accompany delegation (Simon, 1992).

Finally the importance of protecting intellectual property has been addressed in many studies and generally concludes that the best way to protect IP is to internalize it. For instance, Agarwal and Ramaswami (1992) found that the processes relating to the development of highly differentiated products are important factors in the entry mode decision and firms run the risk of losing long-term profits on such IP when it is shared with others.

Ekeledo and Sivakumar (1998) propose that protecting an IP-intensive product is sufficient merit for the adoption of a direct entry mode. Likewise Anderson and Coughlan (1987) claim that innovative or patent-worthy products should be protected, and that protection is best achieved by a direct entry mode. They suggest that patent protection is not enough and that the IP should be closely guarded to prevent leakage. This protection may be accomplished by keeping outsiders away from the development and manufacturing processes related to the product. Furthermore, when an IP-intensive product is capable of providing high returns, firms are likely to choose a high control mode of entry such as a direct sales force to ensure that the returns will be appropriated to the manufacturer (Kim and Hwang, 1992).

## SUBSEQUENT ENTRY MODE CHOICE

Researchers appear to be less interested in subsequent entry mode choice than in initial entry mode choice (Johanson and Vahlne, 1992). This is probably due to the fact that the study of subsequent entry modes requires tracking the choices of newly exporting firms over an extended period of time or reconstructing the choices of more experienced firms. However the results from such studies have the potential to be significant for entry mode literature.

There is a stage element to exporting that suggests that firms should start out with lower exposure to risk and increase commitments as they gain confidence. Thus firms will start out with agents and distributors, and move to direct sales assets. This is a testable hypothesis. A counter-hypothesis that is supported by network theory is that trust can develop between exporters and foreign-based firms, leading to initial or eventual collaboration.

*Hypothesis IIIa    As SMEs with high product complexity, sales and service requirements establish trust with foreign partners, they can move from direct sales assets to contracted relationships with their partners in subsequent mode decisions.*

*Hypothesis IIIb    As SMEs with high IP concerns establish trust with foreign partners, they can move from direct sales assets to contracted relationships with their partners in subsequent mode decisions.*

These hypotheses are consistent with the perspective of network theory in which firms increasingly externalize activities based on trust (Coviello and McAuley, 1999). However extant literature presents differing views of this activity. For example, although Coviello and Munro (1995, 1997) agree that firms that entered a foreign market alone will begin to externalize their activities on the basis of trust, they have also noted that, after a certain time of such externalization, firms once again begin to internalize so as not to risk total dependence on an external firm. A similar U-shape phenomenon has also been observed by Erramilli (1991) and Ekeledo and Sivakumar (1998, 2004). Firms that fit the U-shape pattern generally enter markets alone, then seek to collaborate with external firms, and then progress to internalizing once again. Erramilli (1991) cited ethnocentricity as a possible cause of this pattern. In the beginning, firms want to enter a foreign market alone because they believe that they are superior to firms in the foreign market. After they have been in the market for some time, they realize that they could benefit from the help of collaborators and so they externalize some of their activities. Once the firm feels that it has learned all it needs to know, it once again chooses to internalize all of its activities.

Furthermore, insofar as firm-specific resources are often path-dependent, subsequent entry modes are also path-dependent for similar reasons. For example, Bell (1995) claims that, because of path dependency (for example, the likelihood that past experience will influence future decisions), firms seldom switch modes within or between markets. The mode a firm uses in its domestic market is likely to carry over to the foreign market regardless of risk (Burgel and Murray, 2000; McNaughton and Bell, 2001).

*Hypothesis IVa   SMEs maintain the same entry mode within and between markets, that is, the mode that is used to enter a foreign market will not change.*

*Hypothesis IVb   SMEs are more likely to use their domestic sales mode in their first foreign market entry than they are to use another mode.*

Conversely another study suggests that, whatever initial mode of entry was chosen, it is likely that the mode will change and in such cases it is important for the firm to have a level of flexibility (Petersen et al., 2000). The authors claim that, although the need for changes in entry mode arises often, firms seldom plan for the future flexibility that would allow those changes to take place. They also propose that initial modes of entry are used as 'stepping stones' to other modes.

Similarly, while studying service-based SMEs, Coviello and Martin (1999, p. 51) found that subsequent internationalization 'was not, however, a controlled or planned process. Rather, it arose from the opportunities presented by various actors in each firm's network'. Their case studies also suggested that mode choice for both initial and subsequent entries was facilitated by the location of both clients and network contacts (Coviello and Martin, 1999). Their research also found that, although some firms evolved from one entry mode to another, other firms were found using multiple modes at the same time.

*Hypothesis V   SMEs are more likely to use a variety of entry modes per market and/or product than a single entry mode.*

## HYPOTHESES TESTING

We next discuss our research to test our hypotheses, which includes a review of a completed original 21-firm study, development of the current study, method of data collection and presentation of our results.

### Review of the Original Study

Our hypotheses originated from a study that was conducted in 2003–04 for the US Department of Commerce under contract from the National Institute for Standards and

Technology (NIST) (Susman et al., 2005). The objective of the study was to identify a set of SMEs that were successful exporters, understand why they became exporters, and analyse factors that contributed to their success. In all, 21 firms were identified as winners of federal or state awards for exceptional export growth. All of these firms were manufacturers, ranging in size from 5 to 600 employees. Although selected primarily because of their exporting success, these 21 firms fairly closely mirrored the NAICS codes and state locations of the population of exporting US manufacturers (ITA, 2003).

## Development of the Current Study

The data for the NIST study were collected via in-depth interviews with senior managers of the 21 firms. The interviews included 36 questions and were conducted mainly over the phone with some use of e-mail. The interviews were designed mainly to generate a descriptive profile of the firms, but they also provided anecdotal and suggestive evidence that there might be a relationship between firms with high product complexity, sales and service requirements and IP concerns, and their market and entry mode choice. In order to assess this evidence more accurately, we distributed a follow-up survey to the same 21 firms. The one-page survey asked more direct and specific questions about choice of market and entry mode than did the original interviews. The survey also included questions to test the psychic distance relationship, that is, what countries these firms initially and subsequently entered, as well as the occurrence of path dependency. The survey is reproduced as Figure 14.1.

## Method of Data Collection

We distributed the surveys via e-mail to the 21 firms that participated in the original study. The survey contained 13 questions and asked senior general managers or international sales managers to fill out and return the one-page survey. The survey was divided into two parts. Part one focused on questions related to initial and successive market and entry mode choice. Part two consisted of questions scaled from one to five that focused on product complexity, sales and service requirements, and IP concerns. Of the 21 firms, 19 participated in the follow-up study, resulting in a response rate of 90.5 per cent. Most surveys were returned via e-mail, but a few firms opted to answer the questions in a short telephone interview.

## Results

Our results are separated into two sections, part one and two, based on the hypotheses to which the survey questions and results in each part pertain. Data in part one were summarized and compared against hypotheses but were not formally tested. Data in part two were analysed with discriminant function analysis. Part one discusses hypotheses I, IIIa, IIIb, IVa, IVb and V. Hypotheses IIa and IIb are discussed separately in part two because the mode of analysis differs significantly.

### Results from part one
Hypothesis I proposed that SMEs' initial choice of foreign markets to enter is influenced by the foreign market's psychic distance from the SME's home country. Our data show

| **Part one** |
|---|
| Our questions focus primarily on how you sell your products in foreign markets. We use the term 'entry mode' to describe how you initially sold products in foreign markets as well as those in which you currently sell products. You may still be using the same mode as when you entered your first foreign market or you may now use a variety of modes based on cumulative experience or the attributes of the different markets that you serve. Types of entry modes include your own direct sales force (domestic or foreign-based), domestic-based export agents, independent manufacturing representatives and foreign-based distributors. |

| | |
|---|---|
| 1.   What country did you first enter? <br> What mode of entry did you use? | COUNTRY            _____ <br><br> MODE OF ENTRY      _____ |
| 2.   Was this entry mode the same or different than you typically use in the domestic market? | SAME ☐          DIFFERENT   ☐ |
| 3.   How many foreign countries do you currently serve? | |
| 4.   Does the choice of entry mode vary by the country served? If yes, please explain: | YES ☐              NO ☐ |
| 5.   Did the selling mode within a foreign country shift over time? If yes, why did it shift? | YES ☐              NO ☐ |
| 6.   Please distribute 100% among the selling modes that you currently use in foreign markets. If you use a selling mode other than those listed, please add it to the others and distribute percentages accordingly. If applicable, divide a single selling mode into foreign and domestic-based segments and apply appropriate percentages to each segment. | DIRECT SALES FORCE (DOMESTIC)        ____% <br><br> DIRECT SALES FORCE (FOREIGN)         ____% <br><br> DOMESTIC-BASED EXPORT AGENTS       ____% <br><br> INDEPENDENT MANUFACTURING REPS____% <br><br> FOREIGN-BASED DISTRIBUTORS           ____% <br><br> OTHER _____           ____% <br><br> TOTAL:                                               100% |
| 7.   Was the distribution the same or different five years ago? What was it five years ago? What has changed the most? Will it likely be the same or different five years from now? What do you expect to change the most? | FIVE YEARS AGO            _____ <br><br> FIVE YEARS FROM NOW  _____ |

| **Part two** |
|---|
| *Based on the statements below, please rate your company and/or your products.* <br> *Please elaborate where appropriate.* |

1 = Never true     2 = Seldom true     3 = Occasionally true     4 = Usually true     5 = Always true

| | |
|---|---|
| Selling our products requires customer education, demonstration, training, etc. | |
| Product customization or modification is essential to making a sale. | |
| After-sale service, e.g., upgrades, maintenance, spare parts, is important to making a sale. | |
| Our products or production processes contain a significant amount of intellectual property. | |
| We protect our intellectual property through patents, trademarks and trade secrets, etc. | |
| We operate in a market niche (i.e., a market so specialized that few can compete within it). | |

*Figure 14.1   Exporting practices survey questions*

that psychic distance has an impact on SMEs' initial choice of market entry. Because the firms in this study are all US-based, initial market entry was classified into three categories based on psychic distance from the US.

Category one includes markets that are psychically close to the US, that is, based on use of the English language and cultural and economic similarity. Markets included in this category are Canada, Australia, New Zealand and Mexico. Category one includes Mexico because of its proximity to US-based firms as well as the presence of Hispanic culture in the US. Eight of 19 firms (42 per cent) entered a category one market as its first international market entry. Category two includes European markets that are moderately psychically close to the US. Markets in this category include Germany, Sweden, Italy, the Netherlands, Denmark and the UK. Ten of 19 firms (53 per cent) entered a category two European market as its first international market entry. Category three includes Asian-based markets, which are the most psychically distant markets from the US-based firms involved in this study. Only one of 19 firms (5 per cent) entered a category three Asian market, namely Japan, as its first international market entry. Thus our data show that first-time exporting SMEs in our sample were most likely to enter a market that is close or moderately close in psychic distance to the US for their first international entry. A more rigorous test of hypothesis I would require that US firms rank category one ahead of category two.

Hypotheses IIIa and IIIb proposed that firms with high product complexity, sales requirements and service requirements (IIIa) and IP concerns (IIIb) would enter a foreign market with a direct sales force, establish a basis of trust with foreign partners, then shift to a contracted relationship. Considering shifts in either direction, 11 firms reported shifts in selling mode within a foreign country over time (58 per cent). Six of these shifts were between types of contracted sales force, for example agents to distributors. Clearly there are too few cases to test IIIa and IIIb. Only two firms shifted from direct sales to agents or distributors, and these shifts did not appear to be related to enhanced trust. One of the firms claims that they enter a foreign market using direct sales only until they can identify a distributor that is appropriately aligned with their product/markets. They will continue to use direct sales, however, when 'language and culture barriers can be easily overcome' and 'sales volumes and/or market opportunities are inherently limited'. Three firms shifted the other way, from agents or distributors to direct sales. Two of these three firms claimed that they enter a foreign market using distributors and then add direct sales if enough sales potential exists in the market to justify the expense. Although hypotheses IIIa and IIIb were not tested, the reported variations in entry mode shifts and rationales further our understanding of the complexities involved in entry mode choice.

Hypotheses IVa and IVb relate to path dependency and propose that SMEs do not switch entry modes within or between markets (IVa) and use the same initial entry mode in their first international market that they previously used in their domestic market (IVb). Hypothesis IVa (within markets) is not supported. Of the nineteen firms, 11 (58 per cent) claimed that their selling modes shift within a foreign country over time. Hypothesis IVa (between markets) is also unsupported; ten of 19 firms (53 per cent) claimed that their entry mode varies by country. Further, 11 of 19 firms (58 per cent) claimed that their current entry mode distribution will be different in five years.

The survey data suggest that firms make flexible use of entry modes within and between foreign countries, and expect modes to shift over time. Some qualification of this conclusion is necessary, however. There is evidence of overall stability in selling modes despite these reported shifts. For example, the selling mode used to enter the first foreign market is now the dominant selling mode in foreign markets for 16 (84 per cent) of the 19 firms. Also early shifts in mode may be infrequent. Twelve firms claim that their current distribution of selling modes is the same as it was five years ago. There is unqualified support for hypothesis IVb, however. The data show that 12 of the 19 firms (63 per cent) used the same initial entry mode in their first international market as they used in their domestic market prior to becoming exporters.

Hypothesis V proposed that SMEs are more likely to use a variety of entry modes per market and/or product than to use a single mode. Our data support this hypothesis. Although each firm uses a dominant entry mode (highest percentage of use), many also use multiple modes. Seven of the 19 (37 per cent) use a direct sales force (domestic or foreign-based) as their dominant entry mode. Three of the 19 firms (16 per cent) use independent manufacturing representatives as their dominant entry mode and nine of the 19 firms (47 per cent) use distributors as their dominant entry mode. In addition, only four of the 19 firms (21 per cent) use only one entry mode. Ten of the 19 firms (53 per cent) use two entry modes, three of the 19 firms (16 per cent) use three entry modes and two of the 19 firms (10 per cent) use more than three entry modes. Thus hypothesis V is supported. SMEs are likely to use more than one entry mode per market and/or product.

**Results from part two**

We tested hypotheses IIa and IIb with discriminant function analysis or DFA (Tabachnick and Fidell, 1996). DFA is used to predict group membership (the dependent variable) on the basis of a variety of predictor variables. Our intention in this study is to predict membership in a direct sales force or contracted sales force group on the basis of a combination of the following predictor variables: product complexity, sales requirements, service requirements, IP content and IP protection. These independent (predictor) variables were coded as MODIFY, TRAINING, SERVICE, IPCONTENT and IPPROTECT, respectively. The dependent variable (group membership) was coded as DIRECT. Hypotheses IIa and IIb were combined into a single hypothesis because of the limited sample size.

The five predictor variables were measured on five-point scales in the follow-up survey, as shown in Figure 14.1. This allowed us to use a scaled measure of analysis for the independent variables. Survey respondents were also asked to distribute 100 percent among the selling modes that they used in foreign markets; domestic-based direct sales, foreign-based direct sales, domestic-based export agents, independent manufacturing representatives, foreign-based distributors, and other (also shown in Figure 14.1). Firms were assigned to the direct sales group if the sum of their direct sales force use (domestic or foreign) was 50 per cent or higher (seven firms). Otherwise they were assigned to the contracted sales group (12 firms). A test of the equality of group means indicated that two predictor variables (TRAINING and IPCONTENT) differed significantly between groups, as shown in Table 14.1, with significance values of 0.007 and 0.008, respectively. Product customization (MODIFY) was dropped from the subsequent DFA because it showed the smallest difference between groups (see Table 14.1). Also product customization may involve engineering personnel more than sales personnel, thus limiting the relationship between direct sales and product customization. Although SERVICE and

*Table 14.1   Tests of equality of group means and group statistics*

| Group membership (dependent variable) | Independent (predictor) variables | Mean | Std deviation | F | Degrees of freedom | Significance |
|---|---|---|---|---|---|---|
| DIRECT | SERVICE | 3.42 | 1.56 | | | |
| | IPCONTENT | 4.42 | 0.69 | | | |
| 7 firms | IPPROTECT | 4.33 | 1.23 | | | |
| | TRAINING | 4.17 | 0.72 | | | |
| | MODIFY | 3.08 | 0.79 | | | |
| CONTRACT | SERVICE | 3.86 | 1.68 | | | |
| | IPCONTENT | 3.00 | 1.41 | | | |
| 12 firms | IPPROTECT | 3.43 | 1.27 | | | |
| | TRAINING | 5.00 | 0.00 | | | |
| | MODIFY | 3.29 | 1.50 | | | |
| TOTAL | SERVICE | | | 0.33 | 1, 17 | 0.571 |
| | IPCONTENT | | | 8.91 | 1, 17 | 0.008 |
| 19 firms | IPPROTECT | | | 2.33 | 1, 17 | 0.145 |
| | TRAINING | | | 9.21 | 1, 17 | 0.007 |
| | MODIFY | | | 0.15 | 1, 17 | 0.702 |

*Table 14.2   Spearman correlations between predictor variables and group membership*

| | | | DIRECT |
|---|---|---|---|
| | TRAINING | Correlation coefficient | 0.633** |
| | | Significance | 0.004 |
| | IPCONTENT | Correlation coefficient | −0.535* |
| | | Significance | 0.018 |
| Spearman's rho | SERVICE | Correlation coefficient | 0.177 |
| | | Significance | 0.467 |
| | IPPROTECT | Correlation coefficient | −0.390 |
| | | Significance | 0.099 |

*Notes:*   ** Correlation is significant at the 0.01 level (2-tailed); * correlation is significant at the 0.05 level (2-tailed).

IPPROTECT showed small differences between groups, they were retained in the subsequent DFA because they made conceptual sense and might show greater differences in a larger sample of firms.

Spearman correlations (Table 14.2) between these four predictor variables and the dependent variable, group membership, show that required customer training is significantly related in the predicted direction. However IP content is significantly related in the opposite direction of prediction. This is contrary to our hypothesis, but is likely explained by the role of IP protection enforcement in foreign countries. These results will be expanded upon later. The other two predictor variables (SERVICE and IPPROTECT) were not significantly related to group membership (see Table 14.2). The DFA shows that the four remaining variables significantly predict group membership (Wilks' Lamba = 0.492, p < 0.03). As expected, the canonical discriminant function coefficients with the highest absolute values are required TRAINING and IPCONTENT (not shown).

As mentioned earlier, required customer training, including customer education, demonstrations, training and so on, is strongly related to use of a direct sales force. Firms may prefer to invest in training a direct sales force that, in turn, will train customers in the proper use of their products because of the time, expense and risk to reputation and liability from improper use of their products. A contracted sales force may be less motivated to perform the training function as thoroughly as a direct work force, thereby raising agency risks. Firms may also want to retain the benefits of their investment in social capital because it may develop into a core competence and a strategic advantage.

Furthermore, firms that sell products with high IP content are significantly more likely to use a contracted sales force. As this outcome is the opposite of what we predicted, our explanation is more speculative. First of all, the DFA indicates that products with high IP content also have low training requirements – at least for this sample of firms. The opposite signs of the Spearman correlation coefficients support this, as do the signs of the standardized discriminant function coefficients (not shown). Firms that sell products with this combination of attributes are comfortable using a contracted sales force in the US and Europe, where IP protection is high, but not comfortable selling this way elsewhere, for example in China. We have anecdotal evidence via telephone interviews that some firms use a contracted sales force where IP protection is highly enforced, but a direct sales force where it is not.

Although these findings are provocative, some caution is in order. First, some of the firms in the sample sell multiple products to different countries. Relationships may vary by product or country (for example, intellectual property concerns). Also some relationships may vary over time, which complicates interpretation; for example, a firm may start with distributors and shift to direct sales, or vice versa. These possibilities mask the complexity that is behind these observed significant relationships.

# REFERENCES

Agarwal, S. and S.N. Ramaswami (1992), 'Choice of foreign market entry mode: impact of ownership, location and internalization factors', *Journal of International Business Studies*, **23**(4), 1–27.

Andersen, O. (1993), 'On the internationalization process of firms: a critical analysis', *Journal of International Business Studies*, **24**(2), 209–31.

Anderson, E. and A.T. Coughlan (1987), 'International market entry and expansion via independent or integrated channels of distribution', *Journal of Marketing*, **51**(1), 71–82.

Anderson, E. and H. Gatignon (1986), 'Modes of foreign entry: a transaction cost analysis and propositions', *Journal of International Business Studies*, **17**(3), 1–26.

Beamish, P.W. (1990), 'The internationalization process for smaller Ontario firms: a research agenda', in A.M. Rugman (ed.), *Research in Global Strategic Management*, vol. 1, Greenwich: JAI Press Inc., pp. 77–92.

Bell, J. (1995), 'The internationalization of small computer software firms: a further challenge to "stage" theories', *European Journal of Marketing*, **29**(8), 60–75.

Bell, J., R. McNaughton, S. Young and D. Crick (2003), 'Towards an integrative model of small firm internationalisation', *Journal of International Entrepreneurship*, **1**(4), 339–62.

Bilkey, W.J. and G. Tesar (1977), 'The export behavior of smaller-sized Wisconsin manufacturing firms', *Journal of International Business Studies*, **8**(1), 93–8.

Brouthers, L.E., K.D. Brouthers and S. Werner (1999), 'Is Dunning's eclectic framework descriptive or normative?', *Journal of International Business Studies*, **30**(4), 831–44.

Burgel, O. and G.C. Murray (2000), 'The international market entry choices of start-up companies in high-technology industries', *Journal of International Marketing*, **8**(2), 33–62.

Chung, H.F.L. and P. Enderwick (2001), 'An investigation of market entry strategy selection: exporting vs foreign direct investment modes – a home-host country scenario', *Asia Pacific Journal of Management*, **18**(4), 443–60.

Collis, D.J. (1995), *The Scope of the Corporation*, Boston, US: Harvard Business School Publishing.

Collis, D.J. and C.A. Montgomery (1995), 'Competing on resources: strategy in the 1990s', *Harvard Business Review*, **73**(4), 118–28.

Coviello, N. and K.A.-M. Martin (1999), 'Internationalization of service SMEs: an integrated perspective from the engineering consulting sector', *Journal of International Marketing*, **7**(4), 42–66.

Coviello, N. and A. McAuley (1999), 'Internationalisation and the smaller firm: a review of contemporary empirical research', *Management International Review*, **39**(3), 223–56.

Coviello, N. and H.J. Munro (1995), 'Growing the entrepreneurial firm: networking for international market development', *European Journal of Marketing*, **29**(7), 49–61.

Coviello, N. and H.J. Munro (1997), 'Network relationships and the internationalization process of small software firms', *International Business Review*, **6**(4), 361–86.

Dunning, J.H. (1980), 'Toward an eclectic theory of international production: some empirical tests', *Journal of International Business Studies*, **11**(1), 9–31.

Dunning, J.H. (1988), 'The eclectic paradigm of international production: a restatement and some possible extensions', *Journal of International Business Studies*, **19**(1), 1–31.

Dunning, J.H. (1995), 'Reappraising the eclectic paradigm in an age of alliance capitalism', *Journal of International Business Studies*, **26**(3), 461–91.

Ekeledo, I. and K. Sivakumar (1998), 'Foreign market entry mode choice of service firms: a contingency perspective', *Academy of Marketing Science Journal*, **26**(4), 274–92.

Ekeledo, I. and K. Sivakumar (2004), 'International market entry mode strategies of manufacturing firms and service firms: a resource-based perspective', *International Marketing Review*, **21**(1), 68–101.

Erramilli, M.K. (1991), 'The experience factor in foreign market entry behavior of service firms', *Journal of International Business Studies*, **22**(3), 479–501.

Erramilli, M.K. and C.P. Rao (1990), 'Choice of foreign market entry modes by service firms: role of market knowledge', *Management International Review*, **30**(2), 135–50.

Hill, C.W.L., P. Hwang and W.C. Kim (1990), 'An eclectic theory of the choice of international entry mode', *Strategic Management Journal*, **11**(2), 117–28.

International Trade Administration (ITA) (2003) 'Small and medium-sized exporting companies: statistical overview, 2003' (www.ita.doc.gov/td/industry/otea/sme_handbook/SME_index.htm).

Johanson, J. and J.-E. Vahlne (1977), 'The internationalization process of the firm – a model of knowledge development and increasing foreign market commitments', *Journal of International Business Studies*, **8**(1), 23–32.

Johanson, J. and J.-E. Vahlne (1990), 'The mechanism of internationalisation', *International Marketing Review*, **7**(4), 11–24.

Johanson, J. and J.-E. Vahlne (1992), 'Management of foreign market entry', *Scandinavian International Business*, **1**(3), 9–27.

Johanson, J. and J.-E. Vahlne (2003), 'Business relationship learning and commitment in the internationalization process', *Journal of International Entrepreneurship*, **1**(1), 83–101.

Jones, M.V. (2006), 'Should high-technology SMEs expect to internationalize by passing through a sequence of development stages that affect choice of export market and entry mode?', Chapter 12 in G.I. Susman (ed.), *Small and Medium-Sized Enterprises and the Global Economy*, Cheltenham, UK and Northampton, MA, USA: Edward Elgar, pp. 182–205.

Kim, W.C. and P. Hwang (1992), 'Global strategy and multinationals entry mode choice', *Journal of International Business Studies*, **23**(1), 29–53.

Knight G.A. and S.T. Cavusgil (2005), 'A taxonomy of born-global firms', *Management International Review*, **45** (Special Issue), 15–35.

Korhonen, H., R. Luostarinen and L. Welch (1996), 'Internationalization of SMEs: inward–outward patterns and government policy', *Management International Review*, **36**(4), 315–29.

Maslach, D.J. and R.B. McNaughton (2006), 'A comparison of the pace and pattern of internationalization by US and Canadian high-growth firms', Chapter 10 in G.I. Susman (ed.), *Small and Medium-Sized Enterprises and the Global Economy*, Cheltenham, UK and Northampton, MA, USA: Edward Elgar, pp. 157–66.

Matlay, H. and D. Fletcher (2000), 'Globalization and strategic change: some lessons from the UK small business sector', *Strategic Change*, **9**(7), 437–49.

McNaughton, R.B. (2000), 'Determinants of time-span to foreign market entry', *Journal of Euromarketing*, **9**(2), 99–112.

McNaughton, R.B. and J. Bell (2001), 'Channel switching between domestic and foreign markets', *Journal of International Marketing*, **9**(1), 24–39.

Meyer, K. and A. Skak (2002), 'Networks, serendipity and SME entry into eastern Europe', *European Management Journal*, **20**(2), 179–88.

Nakos, G. and K.D. Brouthers (2002), 'Entry mode choice of SMEs in central and eastern Europe', *Entrepreneurship Theory and Practice*, **27** (Fall), 47–63.

Oviatt, B.M. and P.P. McDougall (1994), 'Toward a theory of international new ventures', *Journal of International Business Studies*, **25**(1), 45–64.

Petersen, B., D.E. Welch and L.S. Welch (2000), 'Creating meaningful switching options in international operations', *Long Range Planning*, **33**(5), 688–705.

Ramaseshan, B. and M.A. Patton (1994), 'Factors influencing international channel choice of small business exporters', *International Marketing Review*, **11**(4), 19–34.

Root, F.R. (1987), *Entry Strategies for International Markets*, Lexington, US: D.C. Heath and Company.

Simon, H. (1992), 'Lessons from Germany's midsize giants', *Harvard Business Review*, **70**(2), 115–23.

Susman, G.I., D.T. Wilson and A.C. Warren (2005), 'Report on identification and analysis of small manufacturers that are successful global competitors', prepared for the US Department of Commerce by contract from the National Institute of Standards and Technology.

Tabachnick, B.G. and L. Fidell (1996), *Using Multivariate Statistics*, 3rd edn, New York: HarperCollins Publishers, Inc.

Williamson, O. (1975), *Markets and Hierarchies: Analysis and Antitrust Implications*, New York: Free Press.

Young, S. (1987), 'Business strategy and the internationalization of business: recent approaches', *Managerial and Decision Economics*, **8**(1), 31–40.

Zain, M. and S.I. Ng (2006), 'The impacts of network relationships on SMEs' internationalization process', *Thunderbird International Business Review*, **48**(2), 183–205.

PART V

Role of the Public Sector

# 15.  US states and the global economy: trends and policies in the mid-Atlantic and midwest

**Terrence Guay**

## INTRODUCTION

The intensification of economic activities in the global economy in recent years has had a profound effect not just on countries, but also on regions and localities within them. The effects of globalization on subnational units, e.g. US states, receive somewhat less attention than the impact on countries as a whole (Bhagwati, 2004; Friedman, 2005). Yet global economic forces do not affect a country's regions uniformly. In the US, certain states (and even smaller territories within states) have benefited from the transformative effects of the international economy, while others have been adversely affected. In part this is due to the mix of industries in each state, with some sectors better positioned to take advantage of the liberalization of global markets, but government policies also play a role in shaping a state's business environment.

In their study comparing small and medium-sized enterprises (SMEs) in Europe and the US, Karmel and Bryon (2002) conclude that the institutional environment is more heterogeneous in Europe. While this may be true when comparing the US as a country with an EU consisting of (then 15 but now) 25 member countries, it is also true that the 50 US states vary (sometimes dramatically) along a number of criteria, including size of economy, exports, population, tax rates and industrial concentration, as well as a host of other factors. Thus much can be learned by examining the international economic activity and associated policies of individual states (Eisinger, 1988; Kline, 1983; Scott, 2001).

In an attempt to better understand these variations, this chapter examines the international activities, specifically exporting and inward foreign investment, of Pennsylvania and ten neighbouring states (Connecticut, Indiana, Maryland, Massachusetts, Michigan, New Jersey, New York, North Carolina, Ohio and Virginia) with the objective of explaining patterns in the relative performance of these states in the global environment. In keeping with the theme of this book, particular attention is given to the role of SMEs. The chapter will conclude by examining efforts made by state governments to expand their state's international economic activities.

## INTERNATIONALIZATION AND EXPORTING

As the world's second-largest exporter in merchandise trade (behind Germany), the US and its 50 states have a lot at stake in their ability to compete in the international environment. Table 15.1 shows exports by state between 2001 and 2005 for all 50 states.

*Table 15.1  State merchandise export totals to the world, 2001–05 (US$mn), ranked by 2005 export value*

| Rank | State | 2001 | 2002 | 2003 | 2004 | 2005 | Dollar change, 2001–05 | Per cent change, 2001–05 |
|---|---|---|---|---|---|---|---|---|
| 1 | Texas | 94 995 | 95 396 | 98 846 | 117 245 | 128 761 | 33 766 | 35.5 |
| 2 | California | 106 777 | 92 214 | 93 995 | 109 968 | 116 819 | 10 042 | 9.4 |
| 3 | **New York** | **42 172** | **36 977** | **39 181** | **44 401** | **50 492** | **8 320** | **19.7** |
| 4 | Washington | 34 929 | 34 627 | 34 173 | 33 793 | 37 948 | 3 020 | 8.7 |
| 5 | **Michigan** | **32 366** | **33 775** | **32 941** | **35 625** | **37 584** | **5 218** | **16.1** |
| 6 | Illinois | 30 434 | 25 686 | 26 473 | 30 214 | 35 868 | 5 434 | 17.9 |
| 7 | **Ohio** | **27 095** | **27 723** | **29 764** | **31 208** | **34 801** | **7 706** | **28.4** |
| 8 | Florida | 27 185 | 24 544 | 24 953 | 28 982 | 33 377 | 6 192 | 22.8 |
| 9 | **Pennsylvania** | **17 433** | **15 768** | **16 299** | **18 488** | **22 271** | **4 838** | **27.8** |
| 10 | **Massachusetts** | **17 490** | **16 708** | **18 663** | **21 837** | **22 043** | **4 553** | **26.0** |
| 11 | **Indiana** | **14 365** | **14 923** | **16 402** | **19 109** | **21 476** | **7 111** | **49.5** |
| 12 | **New Jersey** | **18 946** | **17 002** | **16 818** | **19 192** | **21 080** | **2 135** | **11.3** |
| 13 | Georgia | 14 644 | 14 413 | 16 286 | 19 633 | 20 577 | 5 933 | 40.5 |
| 14 | **North Carolina** | **16 799** | **14 719** | **16 199** | **18 115** | **19 463** | **2 664** | **15.9** |
| 15 | Louisiana | 16 589 | 17 567 | 18 390 | 19 922 | 19 232 | 2 643 | 15.9 |
| 16 | Tennessee | 11 320 | 11 621 | 12 612 | 16 123 | 19 070 | 7 750 | 68.5 |
| 17 | Arizona | 12 514 | 11 871 | 13 323 | 13 423 | 14 950 | 2 436 | 19.5 |
| 18 | Wisconsin | 10 489 | 10 684 | 11 510 | 12 706 | 14 923 | 4 435 | 42.3 |
| 19 | Kentucky | 9 048 | 10 607 | 10 734 | 12 992 | 14 899 | 5 851 | 64.7 |
| 20 | Minnesota | 10 524 | 10 402 | 11 266 | 12 678 | 14 705 | 4 180 | 39.7 |
| 21 | South Carolina | 9 956 | 9 656 | 11 773 | 13 376 | 13 944 | 3 988 | 40.1 |
| 22 | Oregon | 8 900 | 10 086 | 10 357 | 11 172 | 12 381 | 3 480 | 39.1 |
| 23 | **Virginia** | **11 631** | **10 796** | **10 853** | **11 631** | **12 216** | **585** | **5.0** |
| 24 | Alabama | 7 570 | 8 267 | 8 340 | 9 037 | 10 796 | 3 225 | 42.6 |
| 25 | Missouri | 6 173 | 6 791 | 7 234 | 8 997 | 10 462 | 4 289 | 69.5 |
| 26 | **Connecticut** | **8 610** | **8 313** | **8 136** | **8 559** | **9 687** | **1 077** | **12.5** |
| 27 | Iowa | 4 660 | 4 755 | 5 236 | 6 394 | 7 348 | 2 688 | 57.7 |
| 28 | **Maryland** | **4 975** | **4 474** | **4 941** | **5 746** | **7 119** | **2 144** | **43.1** |

| | | | | | | | |
|---|---|---|---|---|---|---|---|
| 29 | Colorado | 6125 | 5522 | 6109 | 6651 | 6784 | 658 | 10.7 |
| 30 | Kansas | 5005 | 4988 | 4553 | 4931 | 6720 | 1716 | 34.3 |
| 31 | Utah | 3506 | 4543 | 4115 | 4718 | 6056 | 2549 | 72.7 |
| 32 | Oklahoma | 2661 | 2444 | 2660 | 3178 | 4314 | 1653 | 62.1 |
| 33 | Vermont | 2830 | 2521 | 2627 | 3283 | 4240 | 1409 | 49.8 |
| 34 | Mississippi | 3557 | 3058 | 2558 | 3179 | 4008 | 450 | 12.7 |
| 35 | Nevada | 1423 | 1177 | 2033 | 2907 | 3937 | 2513 | 176.6 |
| 36 | Arkansas | 2911 | 2804 | 2962 | 3493 | 3862 | 951 | 32.7 |
| 37 | Alaska | 2418 | 2516 | 2739 | 3157 | 3592 | 1174 | 48.5 |
| 38 | Idaho | 2122 | 1967 | 2096 | 2915 | 3260 | 1138 | 53.6 |
| 39 | West Virginia | 2241 | 2237 | 2380 | 3262 | 3147 | 906 | 40.4 |
| 40 | Nebraska | 2702 | 2528 | 2724 | 2316 | 3004 | 302 | 11.2 |
| 41 | New Hampshire | 2401 | 1863 | 1931 | 2286 | 2548 | 147 | 6.1 |
| 42 | New Mexico | 1405 | 1196 | 2326 | 2046 | 2540 | 1136 | 80.9 |
| 43 | Delaware | 1985 | 2004 | 1886 | 2053 | 2525 | 540 | 27.2 |
| 44 | Maine | 1812 | 1973 | 2188 | 2432 | 2310 | 497 | 27.4 |
| 45 | Rhode Island | 1269 | 1121 | 1177 | 1286 | 1269 | −23 | 0.0 |
| 46 | North Dakota | 806 | 859 | 854 | 1008 | 1185 | 379 | 47.1 |
| 47 | Hawaii | 370 | 514 | 368 | 405 | 1028 | 658 | 178.0 |
| 48 | South Dakota | 595 | 597 | 672 | 826 | 941 | 347 | 58.3 |
| 49 | Montana | 489 | 386 | 361 | 565 | 711 | 222 | 45.5 |
| 50 | Wyoming | 503 | 553 | 582 | 680 | 669 | 166 | 33.0 |
| | Unallocated | 41 506 | 34 468 | 35 168 | 35 080 | 36 812 | −4 693 | −11.3 |
| | United States | 731 026 | 693 257 | 723 743 | 817 936 | 904 380 | 173 354 | 23.7 |

*Note:* The 11 states compared in this chapter are highlighted in bold.

*Source:* Office of Trade and Economic Analysis, International Trade Administration, US Department of Commerce (http://www.ita.doc.gov/td/industry/otea/state/2005_year_end_dollar_value_05.pdf).

Several aspects of these data are significant. First, total US exports increased by 23.7 per cent over this period. Of the 11 states considered here, all but Virginia, Connecticut and Maryland rank among the top 14 states in terms of 2005 exports, and five (Ohio, Pennsylvania, Massachusetts, Indiana and Maryland) surpassed the 23.7 per cent increase in total US exports between 2001 and 2005. Pennsylvania's performance (a 27.8 per cent increase between 2001 and 2005) was boosted by a surge in exports in 2005 – a 20.5 per cent increase over 2004 figures. This is a considerable rebound, since the state's exports in 2002 and 2003 were below 2001 levels. Pennsylvania's ranking has climbed two spots from being the country's eleventh-largest exporting state in 2001 to ninth place in 2005, overtaking Massachusetts and New Jersey over this period. Of the 11 states reviewed in this chapter, Virginia has experienced by far the smallest increase in exports (5.0 per cent) between 2001 and 2005, and surpassed only Rhode Island among all 50 states.

Although Pennsylvania's 27.8 per cent export growth is impressive, 29 states turned in even better performances over the 2001–5 period. Southern and western states experienced the greatest increase in exports. The ten states with the largest percentage increases are Hawaii (178 per cent), Nevada, New Mexico, Utah, Missouri, Tennessee, Kentucky, Oklahoma, South Dakota and Iowa (57.5 per cent). Significantly, eight of the 15 states in the south (below the Mason-Dixon line and whose borders include Kentucky, Missouri, Arkansas and Texas) had increases of more than 40 per cent. This emphasizes the trend in the US over the past few decades whereby the economic activity in the Sunbelt[1] has generally been more impressive than in northern and midwestern states (Sawers and Tabb, 1984). The figures for Sunbelt states are also boosted because they started at a lower base. The fact that in 2005 eight of the top 12 exporting states in terms of value were states in the Northeast and Midwest reflects the longer experience in international trade by this region.

The reasons behind the variations in export growth vary by state, even among the 11 states considered here. Table 15.2 compares the 11 states in terms of export growth for the four largest product categories for each state (in terms of 2004 export value). At the present time, 2005 state export figures by product category are not available, so the figures shown in Table 15.2 are for the period 1999–2004. Despite this timing difference, several points can be made. First, large movements in exports among the top four product categories can have a major influence in a state's overall export record. Indiana, for example, experienced export growth of 40 per cent or more in each of its four major product areas between 1999 and 2004. Maryland, Massachusetts and North Carolina had export increases of 40 per cent or more in three of their top four products, with only computers and electronic products flat (in Maryland), slightly less (in Massachusetts) or slightly more (in North Carolina). Transportation equipment exports increased by 27.2 per cent in Ohio and, since this sector accounted for 36.2 per cent by value of the state's 2004 exports, it helped magnify the state's 25 per cent overall increase in exports during this period. On the other hand, export growth can appear sluggish for states with a large reliance on one or two sectors. Transportation equipment accounted for a whopping 52 per cent of Michigan's exports in 2004. However exports in this sector actually declined by 0.2 per cent between 1999 and 2004. Consequently Michigan's exports increased by only 14.6 per cent over this period, and about one-third of this increase came from oil and gas extraction. Pennsylvania would appear to have a fairly diversified economy, since no

Table 15.2  *Percentage change in exports by industrial classification (1999–2004)*

| State | Transportation equipment NAICS 336 | Machinery manufactures NAICS 333 | Computers & electronic products NAICS 334 | Chemical manufactures NAICS 325 | Miscellaneous manufactures NAICS 339 | Fabric mill products NAICS 313 | Primary metal manufactures NAICS 331 |
|---|---|---|---|---|---|---|---|
| Connecticut | 22.3[b] | 46.5 | −8.4 | 11.0 | | | |
| Indiana | 41.2[b] | 68.3 | 40.0 | 89.4 | | | |
| Maryland | 43.1 | 44.9 | 0.1 | 50.6 | | | |
| Massachusetts | | 44.1 | −7.2[b] | 262.7[c] | 108.2 | | |
| Michigan | −0.2[a] | −6.1 | 42.1 | 44.1 | | | |
| New Jersey | −10.0 | 13.3 | 14.7 | 17.6[c] | | | |
| New York | 23.0 | 20.9 | 14.3 | | 83.3 | | |
| North Carolina | | 44.1 | 4.5 | 73.3 | | 71.1 | |
| Ohio | 27.2[b] | 14.6 | 18.6 | 40.5 | | | |
| Pennsylvania | | −2.0 | −19.1 | 28.2 | | | 44.5 |
| Virginia | 6.4 | 21.1 | −29.7 | 8.5 | | | |

*Notes:*
Includes top four categories for each state by export value.
[a]: more than 50 per cent of state's total 2004 exports by value.
[b]: more than 30 per cent of state's total 2004 exports by value.
[c]: more than 20 per cent of state's total 2004 exports by value.

*Source:*  Data derived from Office of Trade and Industry Information (OTII), Manufacturing and Services, International Trade Administration, US Department of Commerce, *TradeStats Express* (http://tse.export.gov/).

sector accounts for more than 17.5 per cent of exports, but only two of its top four product groups (chemical manufactures and primary metal manufactures) showed export increases, while the other two experienced export declines. Finally Virginia experienced growth in three of its four top product categories. However beverage and tobacco products, which was Virginia's leading export category in 1999, declined in each of the next five years, for a cumulative 65.4 per cent drop by 2004. While each of the 11 states has a somewhat different story behind the export performance over this time period, for most of the 11 states export growth was weak for computers and electronic products, while chemical manufactures did rather well.

A final approach to analysing the export performance of US states is through the experience of SMEs. In its June 2005 report on SMEs engaged in exporting, the US International Trade Administration (ITA) presents considerable data on the subject (US ITA, 2005). In 2002 (the most recent statistical year), 215 754 SMEs exported from the US, accounting for 97 per cent of all US exporters and a 26.4 per cent share (by value) of merchandise exports. The known export revenue of SMEs rose from $103 billion in 1992 to $158 billion in 2002, an increase of 54 per cent. Non-manufacturing companies dominate exporting by SMEs, with wholesalers and other non-manufacturing firms (such as resource extraction, transport services, communications, and engineering and management services) comprising 68 per cent of all SME exporters and 64 per cent of total SME exports. The major foreign markets for SMEs are Canada (16 per cent of the value of merchandise exports from SMEs); Mexico (13 per cent); Japan (9 per cent); United Kingdom (5 per cent); and China, South Korea and Germany (each with 4 per cent). However the fastest-growing markets for SMEs over the period 1992–2002 were China (262 per cent increase in exports by SMEs), Malaysia (228 per cent), Brazil (138 per cent) and Mexico (132 per cent).

Table 15.3 suggests that there are considerable differences among these 11 states in terms of the importance of SMEs. New Jersey has more exporting SMEs relative to the size of its gross state product (GSP) than any of the other states, although New York is close behind. With 36.9 exporting SMEs per billion dollars of GSP, New Jersey's figure is more than twice as much as Virginia's (16.1) and Maryland's (17.8). Pennsylvania (at 25.4) ranks seventh among the 11 states. This may suggest that states like New Jersey and New York provide a particularly attractive environment for export-oriented SMEs, and/or that they host industries that are heavily export-dependent. Both explanations are supported by data in the 'SME Exports as % of all Exports' column in Table 15.3. In New York, SME exports account for 47.6 per cent of all of that state's exports (nationally, only Alaska and Florida had a higher percentage). Among the 11 states, New Jersey has the second-highest level, of 36.4 per cent. Indiana has by far the lowest percentage of SME-originated exports (12.3 per cent), while SMEs in Michigan and Ohio account for only 16.3 per cent of exports, which suggests that large companies dominate the exports of these three states. While data on SME exports in each product category by state are not available, we can propose some possible implications based on national-level data. SMEs account for 44.6 per cent of the value of all US 'miscellaneous manufactures' exports, 38.0 per cent of 'fabric mill products' exports, and 30.4 per cent of 'primary metal manufactures'. So, for example, it is very likely that SMEs in New York, where exports of 'miscellaneous manufactures' increased by 83.3 per cent between 1999 and 2004, saw many of the benefits, since this is the largest export category for that state (comprising 19.0 per cent

Table 15.3  *SMEs and exports (2002)*

| State | Gross state product, GSP ($ millions) | 2002 Population estimates (thousands) | Number of exporting SMEs | Value of SME exports ($ millions) | SME exports as % of all exports | Number of exporting SMEs per $ billion GSP | Number of exporting SMEs per thousand population |
|---|---|---|---|---|---|---|---|
| Connecticut | 167 235 | 3 458 | 4 403 | 1 727 | 23.2 | 26.3 | 1.27 |
| Indiana | 203 296 | 6 155 | 4 842 | 1 665 | 12.3 | 23.8 | 0.79 |
| Maryland | 202 840 | 5 442 | 3 614 | 885 | 24.7 | 17.8 | 0.66 |
| Massachusetts | 287 191 | 6 412 | 8 945 | 3 883 | 25.5 | 31.1 | 1.40 |
| Michigan | 347 014 | 10 039 | 10 573 | 5 065 | 16.3 | 30.5 | 1.05 |
| New Jersey | 377 824 | 8 576 | 13 943 | 5 044 | 36.4 | 36.9 | 1.63 |
| New York | 802 866 | 19 165 | 27 973 | 15 029 | 47.6 | 34.8 | 1.46 |
| North Carolina | 301 254 | 8 313 | 6 624 | 3 006 | 22.8 | 22.0 | 0.80 |
| Ohio | 385 657 | 11 405 | 10 887 | 4 039 | 16.3 | 28.2 | 0.95 |
| Pennsylvania | 424 820 | 12 324 | 10 802 | 3 988 | 29.6 | 25.4 | 0.88 |
| Virginia | 288 840 | 7 286 | 4 641 | 2 327 | 25.4 | 16.1 | 0.64 |
| US Total | 10 412 244 | 287 985 | 215 754 | 158 492 | 26.4 | 20.7 | 0.75 |

*Sources:*  Data derived from US International Trade Administration (US ITA) (2005), *Small & Medium-Sized Exporting Companies: A Statistical Handbook* (results from the Exporter Data Base), June (http://www.ita.doc.gov/td/industry/otea/docs/SMEstat-hbk2002.pdf), US Bureau of Economic Analysis (US BEA), Gross State Product Data Table (http://www.bea.gov/bea/regional/gsp/action.cfm), and US Census Bureau, Population Estimates Program (http://factfinder.census.gov).

of New York's 2004 exports). SMEs in other states with high levels of SME-dominated sectors likely benefited from export increases over this period.

A final way of comparing exporting SMEs in these 11 states is relative to state population. Here again we find that New Jersey leads, with 1.63 SMEs per thousand residents. New York and Massachusetts follow, with 1.46 and 1.40 SMEs per thousand population, respectively. At 0.64 SMEs per thousand people, Virginia lags behind the other ten states, but is not far behind the US national average of 0.75. With nine of the 11 states above the national average (and Connecticut, Massachusetts, Michigan, New York and New Jersey significantly ahead), the mid-Atlantic/midwest region appears to have a thriving segment of exporting SMEs, and a strong pool of potential entrepreneurs capable of building international-oriented SMEs.

## INTERNATIONALIZATION AND FOREIGN INVESTMENT

While exports may be the most popular measure of a state's international economic activity, levels of foreign direct investment (FDI) can present a picture of the attractiveness of a state to foreign firms and contribute to the economic health of a region. The most popular explanation for companies engaging in international production is the 'eclectic paradigm' (Dunning, 1992). This approach uses three sets of factors (organization, location and internalization) to explain why, where and how the internationalization of production occurs. Other scholars, such as O'Farrell, Wood and Zheng (1998), suggest that the reasons for companies going abroad are diverse – including being pulled abroad by customers (in the case of suppliers to larger companies) and seeking connections to networks – as is the timing, with some firms capable of 'going international' early in a product's life cycle. While it is beyond the scope of this chapter to explain why and how foreign firms have invested in the 11 states, we can sketch patterns and implications.

Between 1999 and 2003, the amount of gross property, plant and equipment (PP&E) of non-bank US affiliates (one measure of foreign direct investment) increased by 15.2 per cent in the US. However, as shown in Table 15.4, states have varied widely in their receipt of such investment. Of the 11 states, Maryland (96.2 per cent) and Massachusetts (52.2 per cent) had the largest increases. In Pennsylvania, foreign PP&E increased by 10.2 per cent – below the national average but sixth-best of the 11 states studied in this chapter. Ohio, North Carolina and Virginia actually experienced declines in foreign investment. In regional comparisons, the northeast and mid-Atlantic states generally attracted the largest percentage increases in foreign investment, with the Plains states declining, and the south mixed.

More worrying, however, is the change in employment. Non-bank US affiliates employed 52 thousand more American workers in 2004 than 1999 – an increase of 1 per cent (Anderson and Zeile, 2006). But manufacturing employment experienced steep cuts, dropping 23 per cent, from 2037 thousand jobs in 1999 to 1574 thousand in 2004. Pennsylvania, with 110 thousand manufacturing jobs attributable to foreign firms in 1999 (sixth most in the country), has witnessed a drop of 26 per cent to 81 thousand jobs (fourth most in the US) in 2004. Manufacturing job losses were also high in Indiana (21 per cent), Massachusetts (29 per cent), Michigan (26 per cent), Ohio (26 per cent), North Carolina (33 per cent) and Virginia (24 per cent). On the other hand, non-bank US

*Table 15.4  Gross property, plant and equipment of non-bank US affiliates, by state, 1999–2003 (US$mm), presented by region*

| State | 1999 | 2000 | 2001 | 2002 | 2003 | % change 1999–2003 |
|---|---|---|---|---|---|---|
| US Total | 1 075 364 | 1 175 628 | 1 181 091 | 1 192 710 | 1 239 214 | 15.2 |
| **Connecticut** | **11 297** | **13 604** | **14 468** | **13 925** | **14 094** | **24.8** |
| Maine | 4 404 | 5 087 | 5 266 | 5 820 | 6 103 | 38.6 |
| **Massachusetts** | **17 344** | **23 875** | **25 563** | **26 763** | **26 396** | **52.2** |
| New Hampshire | 2 852 | 5 124 | 5 321 | 4 536 | 4 657 | 63.3 |
| Rhode Island | 2 505 | 3 394 | 3 310 | 3 074 | (D) | 22.7 |
| Vermont | 1 296 | 2 146 | 2 614 | 1 315 | (D) | 1.5 |
| Delaware | 5 552 | 6 114 | 6 603 | (D) | 6 179 | 11.3 |
| Dist. of Columbia | 3 859 | 4 247 | 5 187 | 5 828 | 5 263 | 36.4 |
| **Maryland** | **11 277** | **13 157** | **12 866** | **11 268** | **22 120(S)** | **96.2** |
| **New Jersey** | **34 855** | **35 115** | **36 918** | **36 264** | **40 504** | **16.2** |
| **New York** | **61 900** | **68 522** | **68 860** | **76 614** | **75 439** | **21.9** |
| **Pennsylvania** | **33 742** | **34 106** | **33 528** | **34 000** | **37 200** | **10.2** |
| Illinois | 44 988 | 48 425 | 48 910 | 46 676 | 47 871 | 6.4 |
| **Indiana** | **29 378** | **30 179** | **29 744** | **30 683** | **32 336** | **10.1** |
| **Michigan** | **41 561** | **39 238** | **52 465** | **42 731** | **44 137** | **6.2** |
| **Ohio** | **38 622** | **37 530** | **35 158** | **36 635** | **37 117** | **(3.9)** |
| Wisconsin | 10 900 | 13 961 | 15 842 | 16 717 | 17 076 | 56.7 |
| Iowa | 7 432 | 7 186 | 7 169 | 7 092 | 7 276 | (2.1) |
| Kansas | 7 151 | 9 036 | 5 098 | 5 362 | 5 843 | (18.3) |
| Minnesota | 11 413 | 13 472 | 12 089 | 12 338 | 13 271 | 16.3 |
| Missouri | 15 360 | 15 773 | 14 918 | 15 170 | 15 093 | (1.7) |
| Nebraska | 2 649 | 2 737 | 2 106 | 2 063 | (D) | (22.1) |
| North Dakota | 1 819 | 1 824 | 1 753 | (D) | (D) | (3.6) |
| South Dakota | 932 | 1 011 | 1 157 | (D) | (D) | 24.1 |

Table 15.4 (continued)

| State | 1999 | 2000 | 2001 | 2002 | 2003 | % change 1999–2003 |
|---|---|---|---|---|---|---|
| Alabama | 17 758 | 16 646 | 17 037 | 17 120 | 17 582 | (1.0) |
| Arkansas | 4 540 | 4 613 | 6 103 | 6 055 | 6 005 | 32.3 |
| Florida | 36 263 | 38 755 | 35 481 | 33 731 | 34 206 | (5.7) |
| Georgia | 27 378 | 29 510 | 29 362 | 29 399 | 30 761 | 12.4 |
| Kentucky | 18 021 | 22 091 | 23 116 | 24 984 | 26 936 | 49.5 |
| Louisiana | 31 868 | 31 160 | 32 551 | 31 944 | 34 076 | 6.9 |
| Mississippi | 4 417 | 4 121 | 4 800 | 6 253 | 7 170 | 62.3 |
| **North Carolina** | **28 932** | **29 931** | **22 875** | **25 426** | **26 492** | **(8.4)** |
| South Carolina | 21 680 | 23 563 | 22 762 | 23 022 | 21 823 | 0.7 |
| Tennessee | 19 331 | 20 842 | 20 961 | 18 103 | 19 141 | (1.0) |
| **Virginia** | **21 491** | **23 570** | **20 668** | **19 273** | **19 609** | **(8.8)** |
| West Virginia | 7 288 | 7 061 | 7 115 | 7 604 | (D) | 4.3 |
| Arizona | 10 597 | 10 716 | 9 390 | 10 198 | 11 012 | 3.9 |
| New Mexico | 5 534 | 5 801 | 5 482 | (D) | 4 366 | (21.1) |
| Oklahoma | 6 834 | 7 635 | 7 743 | 8 131 | 8 885 | 30.0 |
| Texas | 96 570 | 110 032 | 103 573 | 104 247 | 101 187 | 4.8 |
| Colorado | 10 352 | 15 319 | 12 654 | 13 997 | 14 101 | 36.2 |
| Idaho | 2 253 | 2 749 | 2 598 | (D) | 2 202 | (2.3) |
| Montana | 2 488 | 3 099 | (D) | 2 362 | 2 876 | 15.6 |
| Utah | 9 336 | 14 340 | 13 552 | 12 228 | 13 395 | 43.5 |
| Wyoming | 5 396 | 8 072 | 10 215 | (D) | (D) | |
| Alaska | 28 205 | 28 964 | (D) | 30 140 | (D) | 6.9 |
| California | 111 629 | 121 040 | 118 426 | 115 961 | 115 566 | 3.5 |
| Hawaii | 11 460 | 10 369 | 9 787 | 7 816 | 7 836 | (31.6) |
| Nevada | 10 217 | 10 128 | 8 164 | 8 268 | 8 268 | (19.1) |

| | | | | | | |
|---|---|---|---|---|---|---|
| Oregon | 9 479 | 13 178 | 12 265 | 10 747 | 10 866 | 14.6 |
| Washington | 19 001 | 22 257 | 18 946 | 18 517 | 20 032 | 5.4 |
| | | | | | | |
| Puerto Rico | 2 157 | 2 169 | 2 337 | 2 344 | (D) | |
| Other US areas | 29 121 | 34 105 | 35 404 | 40 392 | 40 150 | |
| Foreign | 1 635 | 2 406 | 3 582 | 2 336 | (D) | |
| Unspecified¹ | 61 046 | 66 526 | 84 941 | (D) | (D) | |

*Note:* The 11 states compared in this chapter are highlighted in bold.
¹ Includes aircraft, railroad rolling stock, satellites, undersea cable and trucks engaged in inter-state transportation.
D: suppressed to avoid the disclosure of data of individual companies; S: more than 50 per cent of the value for the data cell is estimated, to account for data not reported by respondents.

*Source:* Data derived from US Department of Commerce, Bureau of Economic Analysis (http://www.bea.gov/bea/di/fdiop/all_gross_ppe.xls).

affiliates of foreign companies exported between $140 and 153 billion of goods each year between 1999 and 2004. This represents about 20 per cent of all US exports, thus making inward investment an important component of US trade. US affiliates also spent about $30 billion annually on research and development during this period. Thus, while FDI is increasing, generating exports and providing technological contributions to the US economy, the number of jobs associated with it has declined. It is understandable that state governments are seeking to avert this decline and add to their manufacturing industrial base by seeking out foreign firms.

## STATE-LEVEL POLICIES

Competing in foreign markets is difficult for all businesses, but 'going international' can be particularly difficult for SMEs because of limitations of capital, management expertise, experience and information (Buckley, 1989). Thus SMEs often look to government for assistance in the early stages of internationalizing. At the same time, most governments understand the impact that SMEs have on their territory, in terms of employment, exports, tax revenues and economic growth. Given the federal political structure of the US, state governments play a key role in industrial policy and in supporting the international activities of companies located within their boundaries (Vogel, 1996).

Fry (1998) presents six reasons for the increased international activities of state governments in the 1980s and 1990s. First, states are becoming increasingly aware of the effects of economic globalization and interdependence, and are seeking to bring the benefits of globalization to their constituents. An increasing number of governors and state legislatures are convinced that they must keep abreast of international activities, and try to maximize and protect state interests in a rapidly changing environment. Second, the growing dependence of the US on the global economy has forced state governments to look abroad for new marketing and investment opportunities. Third, electoral factors have convinced state leaders to become more actively involved abroad, particularly in attracting foreign investment and expanding trade opportunities and tourism, which will diversify their economic bases, expand tax revenues and generate jobs. Fourth, state governments are learning to be more entrepreneurial in generating economic growth in response to the decrease in transfer payments from Washington. Fifth, advances in communications and transportation and a growing trend towards the internationalization of production have combined to bring the world closer together and to facilitate the interaction of state governments with both governmental and non-governmental actors (including business) abroad. Sixth, a constitutional ambiguity in the limits to state actions in the foreign policy area has facilitated the growth in state activities overseas. As Shuman (1986) argues, the current foreign policy activities of state governments do not fit neatly into constitutionally defined categories. Activities such as courting foreign investment, lobbying on behalf of local business and meeting foreign government officials are not barred by the Constitution. Policies designed in response to these pressures represent an increasing awareness of the impact of the global economy. Consequently states have undertaken a variety of efforts to help their firms become more global. Policies can be divided into two broad categories: those that are firm-specific and those that more broadly support the state's business environment.

Of the firm-specific policies, the most widely utilized support consists of advice on how to begin the process of exporting. This may include introducing firms to the basic paperwork associated with exporting, market research, finding foreign distributors and/or providing contact information for other state and national government agencies or private sector organizations. For example, the Office of International Development (within the Pennsylvania Department of Community and Economic Development) provides advice on other export and overseas investment finance programmes offered by the federal government, including the US Export Import Bank, US Small Business Administration, Overseas Private Investment Corporation, and private sector banks. A Regional Export Network provides manufacturing and service firms with export development services, including market research, market entry strategy development, technical supports and export counselling, export finance programmes and promotion of Pennsylvania-led trade events. The Commonwealth also sponsors PASourceNet, which matches export opportunities with suitable SMEs. All 11 states provide advice, of varying degrees of thoroughness.

Only four states (Pennsylvania, New York, Ohio and Virginia) provide state-sponsored financing programmes. Pennsylvania's Export Finance Program provides SMEs with access to pre-export working capital and post-export accounts receivable financing through a direct loan programme (up to $350 000 for each). New York's Global Export Market Service (GEMS) helps SMEs expand through increased export activity by providing up to $25 000 in export marketing consultant services for individual companies and up to $50 000 for groups of companies or industry associations. Most states do not provide direct export financing, but work with local banks and federal programmes (such as the Small Business Administration) to guide SMEs to appropriate financing options. For example, the New Jersey Economic Development Authority (EDA) works with New Jersey banks to provide revolving lines of credit to finance confirmed foreign orders.

Other state-provided services include the ExportNY programme, provided by Empire State Development's International Division, which is an export training programme for CEOs that runs weekly for eight months. A number of states recognize the accomplishments of their best exporters through 'Governor's awards'. In Pennsylvania, for example, the Governor's Export Excellence Awards provide recognition to firms with a successful export record. While most international support comes from divisions within state economic development offices, others are situated more closely to offices associated with small business interests. For example, the Massachusetts Export Center is part of the Massachusetts Small Business Development Center Network, while the commonwealth also operates the Massachusetts Office of International Trade & Investment (MOITI).

Firm-specific policies also include state government efforts to open offices abroad and lead trade missions to other countries. The US ITA (2005) suggests that many SMEs could sharply boost exports by entering new markets, since 62 per cent of all SME exporters posted sales to only one foreign market. Many state officials are similarly concerned about this lack of export breadth, and are conducting trade missions to selected markets. Most trade missions address established markets (for example, Europe, Canada and Japan) or large emerging markets (such as China or Brazil). Between September 2005 and June 2006, the Pennsylvania Office of International Business Development sponsored trade missions to China, Brazil (and Chile), India, Germany, South Africa, Mexico, Spain, Japan (and Korea and China), Australia, Southeast Asia and Israel (and Turkey). Virginia had 25 trade missions scheduled between September 2005 and July 2006. North

Carolina's International Trade Division had 14 trade missions scheduled between September 2005 and the end of 2006. Of the 11 states, these three have the busiest trade mission schedule, while Connecticut, Indiana and Ohio appear to conduct few of these.

Foreign offices of states tend to serve two purposes. First, they are points of contact for businesses exporting from the home state to a foreign market, and thus can provide information about foreign markets. Second, they serve as gateways for foreign firms looking to invest in specific US states, and assist with eliminating barriers that foreign companies might encounter in investing, expanding and operating a business in a specific US state. Foreign firms in the US often pay higher wages than domestic firms (Coughlin, 1992). FDI also can lead to the build-up of a supplier network, disseminate technology and innovation and strengthen the tax base, and it may generate exports (Dunning, 1992). Thus government officials spend a considerable amount of time marketing their state to foreign firms. Foreign offices may be staffed by state government officials on assignment abroad, or by locals with expertise in the foreign market. Every one of the 11 states has overseas offices, with many clustered in the same countries. The European Union (EU) is the US's largest export market, accounting for over $170 billion in US exports. Firms from EU countries account for approximately 55 per cent of FDI in the US (with Switzerland accounting for an additional 20 per cent). Consequently an estimated 3.1 million US jobs were supported by EU investment in the US in 2004 (Anderson and Zeile, 2006). Thus it is not surprising that Europe is one of the most popular locations for the foreign offices of US states. The growing markets of Asia, particularly China, also are popular destinations to site foreign offices. Pennsylvania has the largest number of overseas offices of the ten countries surveyed, with 17. In addition, Pennsylvania has foreign representatives in France, Germany, Italy and the United Kingdom, serving the tourist industry.

Another firm-specific policy tool to attract foreign investment is a promise of tax waivers or reductions, reduced electrical costs and/or subsidized labour training. In 2004, New Jersey's Office of International Trade and Protocol was directly involved in securing 16 new FDI projects valued at more than $54 million. The effort resulted in 265 new jobs being created. Because of its efforts, the Office won second place honours for 'Best Foreign Direct Investment Promotional Strategy' from *Foreign Direct Investment Magazine* as part of the publication's search for the US Cities and States of the Future 2005/2006. The Massachusetts Office of International Trade & Investment and Michigan Economic Development Corporation websites provide foreign firms with a list of the range of tax and other incentives available for FDI. Such information makes it easier for firms to 'shop around' and base their location decisions, at least in part, on such incentives.

Some of the Sunbelt states have been very successful in offering attractive financial packages to foreign firms evaluating locations in the US (as well as US companies considering additional domestic investment), often at the expense of states in the northeast and midwest (Grant, 2003). Attracting foreign firms has become very expensive for state governments, as they attempt to outbid each other to be selected for investment. The Center for Automotive Research estimates that the average, per-job cost of incentives across the south has risen to $102 000, from about $60 000 in 1989. Much of this spending may be a waste of taxpayer dollars, since research suggests that few of these efforts have a significant impact on FDI flows to specific states. Head et al. (1999) argue that such incentives tend to offset each other and have a small impact on location decisions. Consequently these incentives are sometimes regarded as 'corporate welfare' for firms that were going to invest somewhere in the US whether or not subsidies would be forthcoming. Axarloglou (2005) finds that relatively higher real wages and labour costs as well as higher crime rates depress the share of inward FDI flow to a specific state, while higher labour productivity, industry agglomeration, slack in the labour market and higher per capita spending on education expands a state's share of FDI inflows. It is only when the FDI contest is narrowed down to two states that relative taxes also become an important factor. Still, the 11 states reviewed regularly use such incentives.

The second type of policies broadly strengthens the state's overall business environment, rather than assisting specific firms or industries. All companies would benefit directly or indirectly from state investments in education, worker training, infrastructure, technology clusters, and research and development. Such policies are often a problem since they are more expensive than firm-specific ones, and the pay-off is long-term. Johnson and Turner (2003) identify five types of intervention that appear to be most effective in aiding SMEs: regulatory reform, lowering the cost of loan transactions, 'light touch' technical and marketing support, facilitating demand-driven access to training and technology, and providing institutions and policies that enhance SMEs' networks and clusters. All of these policies should be aimed towards stimulating entrepreneurship. Much of the literature on the internationalization process tends to support such policies. Andersen (1993) suggests that the gradual process of internationalization is due mainly to a lack of knowledge by the firm about how to internationalize, and uncertainty about the decision to internationalize at all.

## CONCLUSION AND FURTHER RESEARCH

This chapter has provided a brief overview of the international economic activity of 11 US states, and the policies utilized by state governments to enhance the international dimension of their state. We propose four areas where further research would be helpful. First, it is not clear how effective the range of policies actually are in enhancing exports, investment or internationalization in general. Trade missions, for example, are sometimes criticized as being simply political propaganda or a photo opportunity for government officials, since contract negotiations between a local firm and a foreign customer are often fully or almost completed in advance of a trade mission. On the other hand, some research on the relationship between networks and the internationalization process of SMEs suggests that business and social contacts can play a critical role in overcoming size-related challenges of internationalization (Coviello and Munro, 1995; Holmlund and Kock, 1998). It is also possible that government-provided programmes are underutilized and, therefore, ineffective if firms are unaware of them or find the paperwork or bureaucracy involved not worth the effort. Thus it would be helpful for additional research to evaluate the efficacy of such international-oriented policies, assuming the amount of state government expenses to support international programmes is available. Perhaps more fundamentally, it would be helpful to know what kinds of policies are most useful from the perspective of business.

Second, it follows that further research on the relevance of exporting to the health of a state's economy would be helpful. For example, a state's companies, including SMEs, may do very well selling products and services to customers in other US states. Just because these transactions are regarded as domestic business activities does not necessarily mean that a state is losing out in the global economy. Additional research might focus on whether companies really are better off by seeking foreign markets, or whether competing in a domestic economy populated by 300 million people is sufficient. It is possible that the promotion of exports could be distracting companies and state governments from potentially more attractive opportunities within the US.

Third, it might be useful to compare state government policies with those of other federal political systems. Canadian provinces and especially German länder may employ policies that are more effective in promoting exports and/or attracting foreign investment. The diffusion of such policies to the US could be beneficial to the 50 states.

Finally more research should be done on the circumstances under which state governments pursue proactive or reactive policies, and the roles that SMEs play in the decision-making process. Not all SMEs are enthusiastic about trade liberalization (Alden, 2005). The membership of the National Association of Manufacturers (NAM), traditionally one of the strongest voices for freer trade in Washington, appears to be increasingly divided between larger multinationals, which find liberalization advantageous for both exporting and the relocation of production facilities overseas, and SMEs concerned about the threat of cheap imports, being dropped from the supply chain of multinationals and the country's deindustrialization (including the loss of 2.8 million manufacturing jobs since January 2001). Thus, while the US ITA can show that exports among SMEs are increasing, certainly some SMEs are experiencing difficult times owing to the intensity of international competition. Of course, US ITA figures reflect a 'survivor effect', since SMEs that have gone out of business as a result of the intensification of global competition are no longer counted. How state governments balance the interests of SMEs that are aided by globalization and those that are harmed is not well understood.

## NOTE

1.   The 'Sunbelt' refers to the southern US states, from the southeast to the southwest.

## REFERENCES

Alden, E. (2005), 'Small manufacturers drive trade protectionism up the US agenda', *Financial Times*, 1 February, p. 4.
Andersen, O. (1993), 'On the internationalization process of firms: a critical analysis', *Journal of International Business Studies*, **24**(2), 208–31.
Anderson, T.W. and W.J. Zeile (2006), 'US affiliates of foreign companies: operations in 2004', *Survey of Current Business*, **86**(8), August, 195–211 (https://bea.gov/bea/ARTICLES/2006/08August/0806_US_Affiliates_WEB.pdf).
Axarloglou, K. (2005), 'What attracts foreign direct investment inflows in the United States', *The International Trade Journal*, **XIX**(3), 285–308.
Bhagwati, J. (2004), *In Defense of Globalization*, New York: Oxford University Press.
Buckley, P.J. (1989), 'Foreign direct investment by small- and medium-sized enterprises: the theoretical background', *Small Business Economics*, **1**(2), 89–100.
Coughlin, C.C. (1992), 'Foreign-owned companies in the United States: malign or benign?', *Federal Reserve Bank of St. Louis Review*, **74**(3), 17–31.

Coviello, N.E. and H.J. Munro (1995), 'Growing the entrepreneurial firm: networking for international market development', *European Journal of Marketing*, **29**(7), 49–61.

Dunning, J. (1992), *Multinational Enterprises and the Global Economy*, Wokingham: Addison-Wesley.

Eisinger, P.K. (1988), *The Rise of the Entrepreneurial State: State and Local Economic Development Policy in the United States*, Madison, WI: University of Wisconsin Press.

Friedman, T. (2005), *The World is Flat: A Brief History of the Twenty-First Century*, New York: Farrar, Straus and Giroux.

Fry, E.H. (1998), *The Expanding Role of State and Local Governments in U.S. Foreign Affairs*, New York: Council on Foreign Relations Press.

Grant, J.G. (2003), 'Special report on southern exposure: autos', *Financial Times*, 24 September, p. 10.

Head, C.K., J.C. Ries and D.L. Swenson (1999), 'Attracting foreign manufacturing: investment promotion and agglomeration', *Regional Science and Urban Economics*, **29**, 197–218.

Holmlund, M. and S. Kock (1998), 'Relationships and the internationalization of Finnish small and medium-sized companies', *International Small Business Journal*, **16**(4), 46–63.

Johnson, D. and C. Turner (2003), *International Business: Themes and Issues in the Modern Global Economy*, London: Routledge.

Karmel, S.M. and J. Bryon (2002), *A Comparison of Small and Medium Sized Enterprises in Europe and in the USA*, New York: Routledge.

Kline, J.M. (1983), *State Government Influence in U.S. International Economic Policy*, Lexington, MA: D.C. Heath and Company.

O'Farrell, P.N., P.A. Wood and J. Zheng (1998), 'Regional influences on foreign market development by business service companies: elements of a strategic context explanation', *Regional Studies*, **32**(1), 31–48.

Sawers, L. and W.K. Tabb (1984), *Sunbelt/Snowbelt: Urban Development and Regional Restructuring*, New York: Oxford University Press.

Scott, A.J. (2001), *Global City-Regions: Trends, Theory, Policy*, Oxford: Oxford University Press.

Shuman, M.H. (1986), 'Dateline main street: local foreign policies', *Foreign Policy*, **65**(Winter), 154–74.

US International Trade Administration (US ITA) (2005), 'Small & medium-sized exporting companies: a statistical handbook (results from the exporter data base), June, URL: (http://www.ita.doc.gov/td/industry/otea/docs/SMEstathbk2002.pdf).

Vogel, D. (1996), *Kindred Strangers: The Uneasy Relationship Between Politics and Business in America*, Princeton, NJ: Princeton University Press.

# 16.  University research parks: untapped source of exports from innovation-based SMEs

## Paul M. Swamidass and Venubabu Vulasa

## INTRODUCTION

The ties between university research output and small/medium enterprises are most evident in university research parks located around university campuses. The earliest university research park was established in 1953 in the Silicon Valley in Northern California. This first park, together with Research Triangle Park, established in 1958 in North Carolina, and Waltham Industrial Center, established in 1954 along Boston's Route 128, have made their marks on US economic development. These university-dependent centres of economic development have taken high-technology products to the market at unprecedented levels through small start-up companies; many of the companies founded in university research parks are no longer small. Over the years, the small start-ups in university parks have matured into large firms with significant exports.

Studies have shown that small firms commercialize 60 per cent of all commercialized academic research-based innovations. It is also reported that firms are ten times more likely to have ties to an institution that is within a 100-mile radius than one that is farther away. The small, innovation-based firms located in university research parks have the potential to serve world markets but may not have the internal resources to do so. How could they export more? What assistance could be given them? What policies are needed? Answers to these questions would help the US tap into the export potentials of university innovation-based small firms.

## US COMPETITIVE EDGE

In the 25 years since 1977, the contribution of US manufacturing to the GDP has remained roughly the same, about 22 per cent. However, manufacturing employment as a percentage of total US employment has shrunk substantially because labour productivity in manufacturing has steadily increased. US labour productivity has reportedly a 31 per cent advantage over OECD countries, yet, with all the gain in manufacturing productivity, it is hard to keep up with Asian manufacturers on cost competitiveness.

Consequently the import of manufactured goods into the US from Asia has grown in leaps and bounds. Manufacturing employment has grown in Asia at a rapid rate, while manufacturing employment has declined in the US. In recent decades, the US's ability to create new jobs increasingly comes from the exploitation of newer ideas and technologies.

In 1980, Microsoft, Dell, Cisco and Yahoo! had no employees (except perhaps Microsoft), whereas, today, they generate combined revenues in excess of $120 billion, with 160 000+ employees in relatively higher-paying jobs (Microsoft: $40bn, 61 000 employees; Dell: $54bn, 55 200 employees; Cisco: $24bn, 38 400 employees; Yahoo!: $4.4bn, 7600 employees). Microsoft and Yahoo! have a dominant or strong position all over the world in their respective markets. *US exports are desired less for their manufacturing excellence (there are too many less expensive options for importers today) but more for the intellectual property behind them.*

US competitiveness and growing exports in the last 25 years were based, not on manufacturing, but on technological prowess. The future is not going to be any different; if anything, US export competitiveness will depend more and more on technological innovativeness. To maintain this edge, there is need for a steady source of new marketable products, entrepreneurs, investors and businesses that could bring more and more new ideas to the market in a sustainable manner.

## THE CHALLENGE

The US cannot afford to lose its edge in innovation, which is the last remaining competitive edge for maintaining and expanding US exports. In some companies, products have a life cycle that is less than one year. In Hewlett-Packard and similar technology companies, 40 per cent of their product line in any given year may not have existed four years ago; they must innovate and introduce new products rapidly each year. Recently, in the fall of 2005, Jeff Immelt, the CEO of GE, in a speech at Auburn University, said that he personally keeps track of the progress of about 100 new projects and ideas within the company. To maintain its current growth rate, the company's challenge is to create new revenue each year that equals the revenue of the entire Nike Company in the year 2005 ($14 billion). Successful large US companies such as GE, HP and many others have close to half or more than half their revenues from outside the US. Their technological leadership enables them to grow in overseas markets. See Table 16.1 for corporate expenditure on R&D for the largest US firms.

In a nutshell, while we know that efficiency, cost advantage, quality, speed and flexibility are critical to business success, 'These factors are no longer enough for long-term competitiveness. To survive and thrive, enterprises must now constantly innovate to re-invent products and services' (Lipscomb and McEwan, 2001, p. 2). How could small firms have the resources to be creative and innovative to launch new products to remain competitive at home and abroad? This is a challenge for the nation.

## PUBLIC POLICY: BAYH–DOLE ACT

Even the best US corporations, such as IBM, 3M and others, know that they cannot invent everything. In order to blunt the competitive edge of developed nations such as Japan and Germany, and to buttress large US corporations, senators Birch Bayh and Bob Dole sponsored the now famous Bayh–Dole Act (Public Law 96–517) in December 1980, called the Patent and Trademark Act Amendments of 1980. In 1980, large companies were the focus of the senators' attention.

*Table 16.1    R&D expenditures of large corporations*

| 1996 rank | 1986 rank | Company | R&D expenditures (millions) | R&D/net sales (%) |
|---|---|---|---|---|
| 1 | 1 | General Motors | 8 900.0 | 5.6 |
| 2 | 3 | Ford Motor | 6 821.0 | 4.6 |
| 3 | 2 | IBM | 3 934.0 | 5.2 |
| 4 | 9 | Hewlett-Packard | 2 718.0 | 7.1 |
| 5 | 20 | Motorola | 2 394.0 | 8.6 |
| 6 | 4 | Lucent Technologies | 2 056.0 | 13.0 |
| 7 | 66 | TRW | 1 981.0 | 20.1 |
| 8 | 18 | Johnson & Johnson | 1 905.0 | 8.8 |
| 9 | 46 | Intel | 1 808.0 | 8.7 |
| 10 | 31 | Pfizer | 1 684.0 | 14.9 |
| 11 | 12 | Chrysler | 1 600.0 | 2.7 |
| 12 | 22 | Merck | 1 487.3 | 7.5 |
| 13 | — | Microsoft | 1 432.0 | 16.5 |
| 14 | 47 | American Home Products | 1 429.1 | 10.1 |
| 15 | 5 | General Electric | 1 421.0 | 1.8 |
| 16 | 35/63 | Bristol Myers Squibb | 1 276.0 | 8.5 |
| 17 | 33 | Pharmacia & Upjohn | 1 266.0 | 17.4 |
| 18 | 23 | Procter & Gamble | 1 221.0 | 3.5 |
| 19 | 38 | Abbott Laboratories | 1 204.8 | 10.9 |
| 20 | 11 | Boeing | 1 200.0 | 5.3 |

*Source:*    National Science Board's science and engineering indicators
(http://www.nsf.gov/statistics/seind98/access/c4/c4s 2.htm).

Speaking of the said Act, Odza (2005) says,

> It reaffirmed that ownership and control of patents derived from federally-funded research belonged to the performing institution, not to the sponsoring federal agency. Bayh–Dole took the decision about commercialization out of federal hands. With later amendments, it allowed non-profits to offer exclusive licenses, which provided the incentive for the venture capital industry to invest in unproven university technology, and it required the institutions to share proceeds with the inventors. Clarification of the title helped give companies the confidence to make investments in unproven technologies.

The growth in university patents and their commercialization since the Act could be justifiably attributed to this Act.

In 1979, the Comptroller General of the US concluded that the government held 28 000 discoveries costing more than $30 billion, but only 5 per cent had been developed into commercially viable products. The government policy at that time retained title to all government-sponsored research discoveries made in university labs and in small businesses. The Bayh–Dole Act gave the rights to inventions to the universities and small business, where they were invented. The following is a compilation of patents issued to universities:

| Year | Patent applications | Licences | Royalties to universities | |
|------|---------------------|----------|---------------------------|---|
| 1991 | 1 584 | 1 229 | $218 million | |
| 2003 | approx. 7 500 | 4 516 | $1.3 billion | 374 new companies |

The biotech industry that began around 1980 is a major beneficiary of this Act.

> Consider the biotech index, which is a fair proxy for the industry. The combined market cap of its 157 companies is around $319 billion . . . The legislation also made it possible for venture capitalists to bring companies public quickly and thus see a return on their initial investment. (Leaf, 2005, p. 266)

It is understood that biomedical discoveries 'account for more than half' of university invention disclosures and 'most of their licensing revenues' (ibid., p. 267).

In the 1980s, we saw a boom in biotech firms based on university research. Overall the Bayh–Dole Act has given ownership of inventions to universities that resulted in more innovation-based small business creation and more commercialization of inventions from university labs. The critics of the Act point to the endless stream of litigations over claims and counterclaims of IP ownership (Leaf, 2005). In summary, regardless of the legal costs, which are bound to be higher during the transition since 1980, the Act has a net beneficial effect on the economy through commercialization of American ingenuity, better use of tax dollars, new business creation and, above all, use of the market economy to reward university ingenuity.

## THE EFFECT OF THE ACT

The growth in research parks is one indication of the effect of the Bayh–Dole Act. According to the Association of University Research Parks (AURP) and the Center for Urban and Regional Economic Development, University of North Carolina-Chapel Hill,

1. In 1998, there were more than 150 research parks in North America: 136 in the US; a further 140 research parks were in various stages of development in the US;
2. with half the parks responding to their survey in 2002, AURP found that
   a. a majority of the parks were established in the 1980s and 1990s,
   b. medical/biotechnology is the leading technology, with the biotech business estimated to exceed $40 billion a year (Leaf, 2005),
   c. the respondents had 2900 tenants, 235 000 employees and $9 billion in investment.

The trend continues. Among the latecomers, in 2005, Auburn University, Alabama, broke ground for a substantial, multimillion dollar research park of its own near the Auburn campus. Newer research parks such as the one coming up in Auburn, to a great degree, develop because of the stimulation provided by the Act. The parks are the symbol of the partnership between universities and innovation-based small businesses.

# MANSFIELD'S WORK

Mansfield (1991, 1998), and Mansfield and Lee (1996) studied the extent to which indus-trial innovation in the US depended on university research during the periods 1975–85 and 1986–94. Since Mansfield's studies include 1980 to 1994, the years after the Act, they provide some insight into the effect of the Act. One observation by Mansfield encourages caution while studying the impact of university research on industry/economy: 'Because the results of academic research are so widely disseminated and their effects are so fun-damental, subtle, and widespread, it is difficult to identify and measure the links between academic research and industrial innovation' (Mansfield, 1991, p. 11) His findings are as follows:

1.  one-tenth of new products and processes commercialized in seven industries depend on university research;
2.  during the period 1975–85 it took seven years to transform the innovation from the university lab to the market; and
3.  the estimate of academic research's social rate of return is 28 per cent.

During the period 1986–94, the time to take an innovation from the lab to the market decreased to six years (Mansfield, 1998). One-year earlier introduction into the market has a sizable economic effect: sales revenues begin to come in a year earlier, and employ-ees are hired a year earlier; both having a positive economic effect. To what could we attribute the speeding of the invention to market? We need focused studies to understand the phenomenon, but has the Bayh–Dole Act contributed to this? Perhaps. With more and more universities bringing inventions to the market, their commercializing skills get better with time; this may partially explain the reduction in the time-to-market. The one-year saving in time-to-market is more significant than it sounds. It could mean that more applied research and less basic research is being conducted at universities. We need further investigation to confirm this.

Mansfield (1991), citing Gellman Associates (1976), says that, 'Whereas about 20 percent of [non-academic-research-based] innovations are carried out by firms with under 100 employees, almost 60 percent [of academic-research-based] innovations were carried out by such small firms, some of which were probably established to exploit the relevant academic research' (Mansfield, 1991, p. 5). Clearly, small firms play a dominant role in commercializing university research.

Mansfield and Lee found that 'R&D supported by the firms in our sample at a partic-ular university less than 100 miles away tends to be at least ten times as great as at a more remote university' (Mansfield and Lee, 1996, p. 11). Clearly the value of research parks near a university for commercializing university research is underscored by this finding. The fact is that research parks bring small firms to a location near the campus with the explicit purpose of commercializing university research; this combination of small firms and proximity to universities is unbeatable for rapid and broader commercialization of university research. To enhance SME participation in university research-based commer-cialization, Mansfield's (and related) findings likewise indicate that university research parks are unbeatable.

# UNIVERSITIES AS A SOURCE OF INNOVATIONS

It is well known that the number of inventions, patents and licensing activities by American research universities is growing steadily (Colyvas et al., 2002). For example, according to Mowery and Share (2002), during the last 20 years, the volume of university patents has increased fourfold, and the number of universities involved in licensing has increased eightfold.

## 1996 and 1998 AUTM Reports

According to the survey-based report by the Association of University Technology Managers (AUTM, 1997), there were about 10 178 pre-patent disclosures (formal US patent office process) of inventions from research institutes, and 3800 new patent applications in 1996. The report also mentions that the cumulative total of active university licences reached 12 951 in 1996.

The sixth annual licensing survey released by AUTM (1999) confirms that the transfer of research conducted at academic research institutes to companies plays a vital role in the US economy. AUTM estimates that 'sales of products developed from inventions made in the course of academic research and licensed to industry amounted to $20.6 billion in 1996, and licensee companies, including 248 new ones, invested an estimated $4.2 billion prior to sales to bring the early-stage inventions to market' (AUTM, 1999). AUTM credits the creation of 212 500 primarily high-wage, high-skill jobs in 1996 to university research. According to AUTM, SMEs consumed 64 per cent of the licences of inventions by universities in 1997; thus SMEs are bigger consumers of academic research innovations than their larger cousins.

## 2004 AUTM Report

According to the 2004 survey summary, the AUTM's membership increased from 1015 in 1993 to more than 3600 in 2004. The survey states that there were 23 per cent more start-ups in 2004 than in 2003 and the sponsored research expenditures by 192 research institutes were $41.245 billion in 2004, which is an increase of 7 per cent over the previous year. As a result of university research, there were about 16 871 new invention disclosures, 10 517 new patent applications, and 4783 licences executed in 2004 (AUTM, 2005).

There is a long list of large companies that benefit from university association. Among the larger firms, Hewlett-Packard (HP) is an example; it has benefited from its association with universities such as Carnegie-Mellon University, Purdue University and the Georgia Institute of Technology (HP, 2006).

## SME–University Partnership Creates Innovation-based Businesses

Woolgar et al. (1998) note that the partnership between universities and SMEs in technology transfers is profitable for both sides. The growth in the volume of technology transfer activities by American universities indicates not only the creativity and innovation needs of industry, but also universities' need to turn their intellectual properties into cash. The process also builds lasting partnerships with industry, particularly with SMEs.

While larger firms sponsor university research, a sizable majority of their R&D funds is spent on corporate R&D (Acs et al., 1994). However, because of the size of their R&D budgets, even the small percentage used for sponsoring university research is sizable in dollar amounts. For example, GE's current R&D budget is almost $5 billion and most of it goes for internal R&D. SMEs, in contrast, without an internal research infrastructure, must explore how they could leverage the resources of universities through sponsored university research. University research parks seem to be the best vehicle for small businesses to exploit university research.

Sikka (1999) notes a weakness of smaller firms. Unlike larger firms, SMEs lack human, information and economic resources to plan and execute R&D. Table 16.2 shows the

*Table 16.2 Innovations and R&D expenditures of small and larger firms, by state*

| State | Total number of innovations | Number of innovations by larger firms | Number of innovations by smaller firms | Industry R&D expenditures (million $) | University research (million $) |
|---|---|---|---|---|---|
| CALF | 974 | 315 | 659 | 3 883 | 710.4 |
| NY | 456 | 180 | 276 | 1 859 | 371.0 |
| NJ | 426 | 162 | 264 | 1 361 | 70.8 |
| MASS | 360 | 148 | 212 | 954 | 245.3 |
| PA | 245 | 104 | 141 | 1 293 | 139.2 |
| ILL | 231 | 100 | 131 | 894 | 254.9 |
| OHIO | 188 | 76 | 112 | 926 | 76.2 |
| CONN | 132 | 77 | 55 | 650 | 54.7 |
| MICH | 112 | 61 | 51 | 1 815 | 103.2 |
| MINN | 110 | 64 | 46 | 399 | 55.7 |
| WISC | 86 | 33 | 53 | 224 | 65.0 |
| FLA | 66 | 21 | 45 | 375 | 70.1 |
| GA | 53 | 20 | 33 | 78 | 57.8 |
| IND | 49 | 20 | 29 | 398 | 51.3 |
| COLO | 42 | 13 | 29 | 167 | 77.2 |
| ARIZ | 41 | 23 | 18 | 201 | 37.4 |
| VA | 38 | 19 | 19 | 207 | 45.9 |
| NC | 38 | 16 | 22 | 193 | 64.6 |
| RI | 24 | 4 | 20 | 32 | 14.9 |
| OKLA | 20 | 12 | 8 | 93 | 19.9 |
| IOWA | 20 | 12 | 8 | 135 | 46.4 |
| KANS | 15 | 3 | 12 | 66 | 26.6 |
| UTAH | 11 | 2 | 9 | 72 | 32.5 |
| NEB | 9 | 1 | 8 | 9 | 20.4 |
| KY | 9 | 6 | 3 | 72 | 17.5 |
| LA | 5 | 0 | 5 | 65 | 33.4 |
| ARK | 5 | 5 | 0 | 9 | 12.0 |
| ALA | 5 | 0 | 5 | 54 | 28.3 |
| MISS | 4 | 1 | 3 | 420 | 61.4 |

*Note:* Industry R&D and University Research Expenditures are in millions of dollars.

*Source:* Jaffe (1989).

number of research innovations (inventions) by small and larger firms, and compares industry R&D and university research expenditures. From Table 16.2, we see that SMEs produce more innovations (patents) than larger firms. Please note that Table 16.2 uses the data published in 1989; more recent information is desirable. However the pattern seen in Table 16.2 is unlikely to be different today.

## ENHANCING SME–UNIVERSITY TECHNOLOGY TRANSFER

### Inexpensive Source of Innovation

Thomas (1999) points out that universities are an inexpensive source of innovation for businesses. According to Thomas, businesses could gain access to inexpensive laboratories, libraries, advanced computers and other university resources necessary for innovation. Universities are also a good source for training through short courses, when needed. Lipscomb et al. (2001) describe a model of collaborative partnerships with universities and SMEs to strengthen the competitive edge of SMEs in European countries. Their model provides necessary training for the partner SMEs, and enriches them technically through the translation of academic knowledge into real-time business solutions. The partner SME learns various aspects of innovation in product, process and service to gain and retain competitive advantage.

Chesbrough (2003) studied the governance and performance of various spin-off companies of Xerox Corporation. He found that the spin-offs by venture capitalists were more successful than Xerox's corporate entities because venture capitalists' searches for commercialization were broader than searches by Xerox insiders.

Chesbrough and Rosenbloom (2002) studied the role of a business model for the successful commercialization of innovation from the lab to the market. They observe,

> The ultimate role of the business model for an innovation is to ensure that the technological core of the innovation delivers value to the customer. Because discovery-oriented research often produces spillover technologies that lack a clear path to market, discovering a viable business model for these spillovers is a critical and neglected dimension of creating value from technologies. (Chesbrough and Rosenbloom, 2002, p. 25)

There is need for more investigation to find more ways of harnessing the spillover technologies from university research.

### SBIR Route

Small businesses could receive SBIR grants to exploit university research in partnership with universities. Wallsten (2001) found that most award-winning SBIR firms were located near university research centres and the chance of winning seems to be linked to the geographical location of the small firms. Boston (10.7 per cent), Washington, D.C. (8.5 per cent), Los Angeles (5.3 per cent), San-Jose/Santa Clara (5.2 per cent) and San Diego (4.5 per cent) are the top destinations for SBIR grants. These cities are near centres of multiple universities.

**Strategic Orientation**

The top management's strategic posture is the single most powerful driving force in technology-intensive companies that seek and use new innovations aggressively. Technology-based competitiveness and growth are no short-term fixes for short-term problems. Innovation and sustained competition are long-term issues that are imbedded in business strategies. The solution lies in training and exposing SME top management to strategic thinking, planning and implementation of an innovation-based strategy.

**Networking for Technology-based SMEs**

If a small firm is not already innovation-based, it needs to consider the following steps to increase its access to university innovation:

1. Examine company strategy and define technology/innovation needs. Define new areas for market entry using university inventions. Adopt a clear strategy of seeking worthwhile university technologies that complement corporate product strategy.
2. Sponsor university research for access to their research, and for access to world-class researchers and experts in universities.
3. Become familiar with the sources of funds that support new ventures or new investments using new technologies from universities. Become familiar with university research parks and venture capitalists operating in these parks.
4. Develop a technology evaluation capability to assess the value and usefulness of new and emerging technologies.
5. Become familiar with conferences where company-relevant technologies are described and presented by university researchers.
6. Explore federal grants including National Science Foundation grants for commercializing, exploiting and developing university inventions jointly with universities.
7. Become familiar with private entities and technology brokers who are acquiring university inventions to build an inventory of such inventions for resale to businesses. The nanotechnology area is active in this regard.
8. Create an R&D budget to sponsor university research in areas of interest. Recognize that university research could be done less expensively compared to in-house research (the fixed cost and variable cost could outweigh the risk and rewards).
9. Study successful small businesses that have close ties with universities for the sake of access to new technologies/innovations.
10. Work with the AUTM. They offer numerous courses to assist universities, businesses and investors.
11. Sponsor doctoral dissertations and master's theses in research universities: this is a proven method for SMEs actively to steer university research in the direction of their interest.
12. Consider employing new graduates who concluded a master's thesis or doctoral dissertation on research sponsored by the company.

**Why more SMEs are not Benefiting from University Research**

Several factors hinder small businesses from making more use of university research. Major reasons are as follows:

1. A lack of a strategic focus on technology-based or innovation-based competence building.
2. Unawareness of ways university research could help their business.
3. Non-familiarity with the process of licensing university inventions.
4. Unawareness of how one may steer university research for company purposes. This is an area in which large, savvy companies know how to sponsor research at universities for company gain; this is how the 'Big Boys' do it.
5. Kenney (1986) mentions the lack of start-up funds, the lack of internal capital for development, uncertainty about patentability, and the lack of qualified labour as limiting the entry of SMEs into innovation-based businesses and their eventual success.

## WHAT UNIVERSITIES COULD DO

It is not uncommon for university inventions to languish on 'the shelf' because universities do not actively commercialize all new inventions from their labs. To increase the commercialization of their inventions, universities could do three things.

First, if they have not already done so, universities must invest and staff an Office of Technology Transfer to take new inventions quickly to businesses that could develop and/or commercialize them. There are a number of universities with effective Offices of Technology Transfer (Rice University, 2006).

Second, universities may tap the faculty and student resources of their colleges of business and engineering to evaluate new inventions for commercialization purposes, and proactively seek potential licensees for the university's new inventions. Such an effort would produce students skilled in commercialization of new inventions; this is a rather rare skill, of which the US economy is in short supply, because technology commercialization is rarely taught in universities.

The Technology Commercialization Initiative of the Thomas Walter Center at Auburn University started in January 2004. Over a period of 22 months, 18 graduate students from the colleges of business and engineering evaluated 37 inventions from Auburn's Ginn College of Engineering. Two inventions have been optioned to a new start-up so far. This continuing initiative assists the Office of Technology Transfer in deciding whether a patent application is justified, who the potential licensees are in the US or abroad, and whether more development of the idea is necessary and who might be appropriate to develop the product in the US or abroad. Graduate students are appointed as Technology Transfer Interns to work part-time on commercialization projects. The skills they learn help them immensely in their job search.

Third, universities can invest in research parks near campuses. The number and size of university research parks have grown since the Bayh–Dole Act came into effect. University research parks have increased the number of academic research-based small firms. Their number is expected to grow.

It is not evident how export-minded are the small firms in university research parks. It is likely that they do not have the internal capability to test export markets. Given their size, their products are perhaps fully absorbed by the domestic market. However, since the Bayh–Dole Act came into being, the growing number of small, academic research-based firms in university research parks represents a rapidly emerging source of exports. Their products do not have to compete with Chinese products on low cost. The products of the firms in university research parks have a built-in technological advantage that comes from intellectual property rights. Such rights give the firms some pricing power in domestic as well as international markets. Export potential for small firms in university research parks is addressed in the next section.

## CONCLUSIONS AND RECOMMENDATIONS

SMEs have not fully benefited from what research universities could offer in the area of innovation for competitive advantage. In the coming years, with a shrinking manufacturing advantage, US manufacturers must turn more towards technological innovation in products, processes and services to remain competitive in the global market. Companies such as Microsoft, Yahoo!, GE, Dell and others have shown that it is possible to capture and win global markets with technological superiority. Big firms also know how to use university innovations; they are able to steer university research their way through sponsored research. These large successful firms have a clear and distinct strategy to acquire, develop and use all new technologies of relevance to their business.

The Bayh–Dole Act has caused universities to invest in university research parks, resulting in an increase in the number of small, new, academic innovation-based firms. These firms have a ready market for their products in the US. Most may not look beyond the US markets. Further, they may not have the internal skills to open international markets and succeed in them, for want of internal skills.

A conclusion of this study is that, because of the Bayh–Dole Act, university research parks that are home to a growing number of small innovation-based firms are an untapped source of exports. Given that the small firms in university research parks do not have the resources of a Coca-Cola or Citibank, we need policies to help these firms gain access to international markets and to help them develop exporting skills. The Department of Commerce and other export-promoting agencies must develop a special focus on firms located in university research parks to increase the exports from these academic innovation-based small firms. Their innovation-based products are likely to be more competitive in global markets than traditional goods manufactured in the US.

## BIBLIOGRAPHY

Acs, Z.J., D.B. Audretsch and M.P. Feldman (1994), 'R&D spillovers and recipients' firm size', *Review of Economics and Statistics*, **76**(2), 336–40.
Adams, J.D., G. Black, J. Clemmons and P. Stephan (2005), 'Scientific teams and institutional collaborations: evidence from US universities, 1981–1999', *Research Policy*, **34**(3), 259–85.
Ahern, R. (1993), 'Implications of strategic alliances for small R&D intensive firms', *Environment and Planning*, **25**, 1511–26.

Audretsch, D. and E. Lehmann (2005), 'Do university policies make a difference?', *Research Policy*, **34**(2), 343–7.

AUTM (1997), AUTM U.S. Licensing Survey, FY 1996: A Survey Summary of Technology Licensing (and Related) Performance for U.S. and Canadian Academic and Nonprofit Institutions, and Patent Management Firms, Association of University Technology Managers, URL: (http://www.autm.org/surveys/dsp.surveyDetail.cfm?pid=23).

AUTM (1999), AUTM U.S. Licensing Survey, FY 1998: A Survey Summary of Technology Licensing (and Related) Performance for U.S. and Canadian Academic and Nonprofit Institutions, and Patent Management Firms, Association of University Technology Managers, URL: (http://www.autm.org/surveys/dsp.surveyDetail.cfm?pid=21).

AUTM (2005), AUTM U.S. Licensing Survey, FY 2004: A Survey Summary of Technology Licensing (and Related) Performance for U.S. Academic and Nonprofit Institutions, and Technology Investment Firms, Association of University Technology Managers, URL: (http://www.autm.org/events/File/FY04%20Licensing%20Survey/04AUTM-USLicSrvy-public.pdf).

Brown, B. and J. Butler (1993), 'Networks and entrepreneurial development: the shadow of borders', *Entrepreneurship and Regional Development*, **5**, 101–16.

Buratti, N. and L. Penco (2001), 'Assisted technology transfer to SMEs: lessons from an exemplary case', *Technovation*, **21**(1), 35–43.

Chapple, W., A. Lockett, D. Siegel and M. Wright (2005), 'Assessing the relative performance of U.K. university technology transfer offices: parametric and non-parametric evidence', *Research Policy*, **34**(3), 369–84.

Chesbrough, H. (2003), 'The governance and performance of Xerox's technology spin-off companies', *Research Policy*, **32**(3), 403–21.

Chesbrough, H. and R. Rosenbloom (2002), 'The role of the business model in capturing value from innovation: evidence from Xerox Corporation's technology spin-off companies', *Industrial and Corporation Change*, **11**(3) 529–55.

Cohen, W., R. Nelson and J. Walsh (2002), 'Links and impacts: the influence of public research on industrial R&D', *Management Science*, **48**(1), 1–28.

Colyvas, J., M. Crow, A. Gelijns, R. Nelson, N. Rosenberg and B. Sampat (2002), 'How do university inventions get into practice?', *Management Science*, **48**(1), 61–72.

Curran, J., R. Jarvis, R. Blackburn and S. Black (1993), 'Networks and small firms: constructs, methodological strategies and some findings', *International Journal of Small Business*, **11**(2), 34–45.

Debackere, K. and R. Veugelers (2005), 'The role of academic technology transfer organizations in improving industry science links', *Research Policy*, **34**(3), 321–42.

Dietz, J. and B. Bozeman (2005), 'Academic careers, patents, and productivity: industry experience as scientific and technical human capital', *Research Policy*, **34**(3), 349–67.

Falamo, B. (1989), 'The firm's external persons: entrepreneurs or network actors?', *Entrepreneurship and Regional Development*, **1**, 167–77.

Gankema, H., H. Snuif and P. Zwart (2000), 'The internationalization process of small and medium-sized enterprises: an evaluation of stage theory', *The Journal of Small Business Management*, **38**(1), 15–27.

Gelinas, R. and Y. Bigras (2004), 'The characteristics and features of SMEs: favorable or unfavorable to logistics integration?', *The Journal of Small Business Management*, **43**(3), 263–78.

Gellman Associates (1976), 'Indicators of international trends in technological innovation', report to the National Science Foundation, Washington, D.C.

Goldfarb, B. and M. Henrekson (2003), 'Bottom-up vs. top-down policies towards the commercialization of university intellectual property', *Research Policy*, **32**(4), 639–58.

Hall, R. (1992), 'The strategic analysis of intangible resources', *Strategic Management Journal*, **13**(2), 135–44.

Hewlett Packard (HP) (2006), URL: (http://government.hp.com/hls_whyhp_uni.asp?agencyid=111).

Jaffe, B.A. (1989), 'Real effects of academic research', *American Economic Review*, **79**(5), 957–70.

Johanson, J. and L. Mattsson (1987), 'Interorganizational relations in industrial systems: a network approach compared with the transaction cost approach', *International Studies of Management and Organization*, **17**(1), 34–48.

Kenney, K. (1986), 'Schumpeterian innovation and entrepreneurs in capitalism: a case study of the U.S. biotechnology industry', *Research Policy*, **15**(1), 21–31.

Leaf, C. (2005), 'The law of unintended consequences', *Fortune*, 7 September.

Link, A. and J. Scott (2003), 'U.S. science parks: the diffusion of an innovation and its effects on the academic missions of universities', *International Journal of Industrial Organization*, **21**(9), 1323–56.

Link, A. and J. Scott (2005), 'Universities as partners in U.S. research joint ventures', *Research Policy*, **34**(3), 385–93.

Link, A. and D. Siegel (2005), 'University-based technology initiatives: quantitative and qualitative evidence', *Research Policy*, **34**(3), 253–7.

Lipscomb, M. and A. McEwan (2001), 'Technology transfer in SMEs: the TCS model at Kingston University', Proceedings of the Fourth SMESME International Conference, Manufacturing Information Systems, Aalborg University, Denmark.

Mansfield, E. (1991), 'Academic research and industrial innovation', *Research Policy*, **20**(1), 1–12.

Mansfield, E. (1998), 'Academic research and industrial innovation: an update of empirical findings', *Research Policy*, **26**(7–8), 773–6.

Mansfield, E. and J. Lee (1996), 'The modern university: contributor to industrial innovation and recipient of industrial R&D support', *Research Policy*, **25**(7) 1047–58.

Markmana, G., P. Phanb, D. Balkinc and P. Gianiodis (2005), 'Entrepreneurship and university-based technology transfer', *Journal of Business Venturing*, **20**(2), 241–63.

McAdams, R., W. Keogh, B. Galbraith and D. Laurie (2005), 'Defining and improving technology transfer business and management processes in university innovation centers', *Technovation*, **25**(12), 1418–29.

Melin, L. (1992), 'Internationalization as a strategy process', *Strategic Management Journal*, **13** (Winter Special Issue), 99–118.

Miyata, Y. (2000), 'An empirical analysis of innovative activity of universities in the United States', *Technovation*, **20**(8), 413–25.

Morrissey, M. and A. Almonacid (2005), 'Rethinking technology transfer', *Journal of Food Engineering*, **67**, 135–45.

Motohashi, K. (2005), 'University–industry collaboration in Japan: the role of new technology-based firms in transforming the National Innovation System', *Research Policy*, **34**(3), 583–94.

Mowery, D. and S. Share (2002), 'Introduction to the special issue on university entrepreneurship and technology transfer', *Management Science*, **48**(1), 61–72.

Narula, R. (2004), 'R&D collaboration by SMEs: new opportunities and limitations in the face of globalization', *Technovation*, **24**(2), 153–61.

Numprasertchai, S. and B. Igel (2005), 'Managing knowledge through collaboration: multiple case studies of managing research in university laboratories in Thailand', *Technovation*, **25**(10), 1173–82.

Odza, M. (2005), 'From the ivory tower to the marketplace', 21st C, issue 3.1, URL: (http://www.columbia.edu/cu/21stC/issue-3.1/odza.html).

O'Shea, R., T. Allen, A. Chevalier and R. Roche (2005), 'Entrepreneurial orientation, technology transfer and spinoff performance of U.S. universities', *Research Policy*, **34**(7), 994–1009.

Premaratne, S.P. (2001), 'Networks, resources and small business growth: the experience in Sri Lanka', *The Journal of Small Business Management*, **39**(4), 363–71.

Rice University, Office of Technology Transfer Home Page, URL: (http://ott.rice.edu/NewsDetail.cfm?NewsID=13, 2006).

Rothaermel, F. and M. Thursby (2005), 'University–incubator firm knowledge flows: assessing their impact on incubator firm performance', *Research Policy*, **34**(3), 305–20.

Sikka, P. (1999), 'Technological innovations by SMEs in India', *Technovation*, **19**(5), 317–21.

Tassey, G. (2005), 'The disaggregated technology production function: a new model of university and corporate research', *Research Policy*, **34**(3), 287–303.

Thomas, B.G. (1999), 'University–steel industry interaction', R&D in the Steel Industry, ILAFA 40 Congress, Buenos Aires, 12–15 Sept, Inst. Argentino de Siderurgia, 65–7.

Tseng, C., P. Tansuhaj and J. Rose (2004), 'Are strategic assets contributions or constraints for SMEs to go international? An empirical study of the US manufacturing sector', *The Journal of American Academy of Business*, **5**(1/2), 246–54.

Van Dijk, B., R. den Hertog, B. Menkveld and R. Thurk (1997), 'Some new evidence on the determinants of large- and small-firm innovation', *Small Business Economics*, **9**(4), 335–43.

Wallsten, S.J. (2001), 'An empirical test of geographic knowledge spillovers using geographic information systems and firm-level data', *Regional Science and Urban Economics*, **31**(5), 571–99.

Woolgar, S., J. Vaux, P. Gomes, J. Ezingeard and R. Grieve (1998), 'Abilities and competencies required, particularly by small firms, to identify and acquire new technology', *Technovation*, **18**(8/9), 575–84.

# 17. Issues surrounding the internationalization of SMEs: implications for policy makers and researchers

## Paul Westhead, Mike Wright and Deniz Ucbasaran

### INTRODUCTION

There is growing appreciation that entrepreneurship does not solely relate to the creation of new private firms. The entrepreneurial process can be viewed through a variety of broader lenses. For example, the entrepreneurial process can be viewed as all the functions, activities and actions associated with the perception of opportunities (Shane and Venkataraman, 2000) and the ownership of organizations to pursue them. The entrepreneurial function is a vital component in the process of economic growth (Organisation for Economic Co-operation and Development (OECD), 1998). Some small and medium-sized enterprises (SMEs) may generate earnings in international markets. To encourage this process and to secure greater international competitiveness, governments throughout the European Union are concentrating their attention on the development of policy measures aimed at both new and established private SMEs (Department of Trade and Industry (DTI), 2004). Policy towards SME internationalization (or exporting) has several strands. One strand is to encourage new private SMEs to trade internationally from the outset. A second element concerns the encouragement of 'export capable' and 'inexperienced exporter' firms to sell their goods and services outside the domestic market (Philp, 1998). The promotion of further internationalization/exporting by existing internationalizing/exporting SMEs has become an area of critical policy interest (Julien et al., 1997). The decision made by a firm (and entrepreneur) to internationalize/export is regarded as an important strategic choice (Melin, 1992) that warrants additional research and policy attention. Consequently there is a need for greater understanding of the factors associated with SMEs (and entrepreneurs) that create and/or identify opportunities in foreign markets.

A policy challenge relates to the inability and/or reluctance of many SMEs to internationalize. For some firms, their products or services may not be tradable on international markets. However many SMEs lack the resources to meet the global challenge to internationalize. It may, therefore, be more appropriate to concentrate policy support on the relatively smaller proportion of SMEs that have the resource pools to circumvent obstacles to internationalization. An important issue concerns the extent to which internationalization research can guide policy design in this area. Drawing upon insights from traditional internationalization research and the emerging international entrepreneurship literatures, a case for more balanced policy support towards the private SME internationalization process is suggested that takes into account the diversity of SMEs (and entrepreneurs) that operate, or may be capable of operating, in foreign markets.

Two broad theoretical streams have emerged in the internationalization research literature. First, traditional internationalization theories, such as stage theory (Johanson and Vahlne, 1977) have focused on the factors influencing internationalization, especially in larger firms. These traditional internationalization approaches have been the subject of considerable criticism (Anderson, 1993; Oviatt and McDougall, 1994; O'Farrell et al., 1998; Peng, 2001). Second, the inability of traditional internationalization theories to explain why some SMEs internationalize from the outset has been highlighted in the emerging international entrepreneurship theory. Entrepreneurship-related aspects of internationalization have been purported as a counterpoint to the received wisdom associated with traditional internationalization theories.

Currently there is no agreed definition of internationalization (Bell and Young, 1998) or international entrepreneurship (Young et al., 2003). Internationalization has been viewed as the process of increasing involvement in international markets (Welch and Luostarinen, 1988). A distinction can be made between inward and outward activities. Inward processes relating to internationalization (that is, importers, licensees and franchisees) have received relatively limited attention, despite the belief that many firms begin their first international activity on the inward side (Korhonen et al., 1996; Welch, 2004). Most internationalization studies focus on the outward processes associated with exporting, licensing, franchising and foreign direct investment (FDI), with exporting being the main mode of internationalization for SMEs. Consistent with the literature, this review will focus on the outward processes relating to the internationalization (mainly exporting) of smaller private SMEs.

McDougall and Oviatt (2000, p. 903) defined international entrepreneurship as 'a combination of innovative, proactive, and risk-seeking behaviour that crosses national borders and is intended to create value in organizations'. Similarly Zahra and George (2002, p. 261) defined international entrepreneurship as 'the process of creatively discovering and exploiting opportunities that lie outside a firm's domestic markets in the pursuit of competitive advantage'. International entrepreneurship is a relatively new and emerging field (Giamartino et al., 1993; Wright and Ricks, 1994) still seeking a focus. The novel contribution of international entrepreneurship theory to knowledge, as well as policy debates, is still not clearly positioned by international entrepreneurship scholars who acknowledge that a unifying and clear theoretical direction has not been presented (McDougall and Oviatt, 2000; Acs et al., 2003; Young et al., 2003). This perspective, however, provides important insights into the internationalization process that should be appreciated by policy makers.

The restrictive nature of traditional internationalization theories is being increasingly recognized. Inappropriate resource allocation decisions may be made by policy makers and practitioners who refer to the well established textbooks that relate to themes that are solely appropriate to the traditional internationalization theories. O'Farrell et al. (1998), focusing on the service sector, recommended a flexible theoretical approach to explore internationalization by SMEs. They suggested that theory should consider the strategic choices open to entrepreneurs and how the home region context may be linked to foreign market decisions. Jones and Coviello (2005) note that, while current understanding of internationalization is informed by integrating multiple theoretical perspectives, there remains a need to incorporate understanding of entrepreneurial behaviour into models of internationalization. Drawing on traditional internationalization theory and insights from entrepreneurship, they developed a time-based process model of entrepreneurial internationalization where entrepreneurship and internationalization were seen as inter-dependent. The latter discussion represents an important recognition of the need for conceptual models to be sufficiently flexible to accommodate a range of conditions that might explain a firm's internationalization decision, its actions and its dynamic processes. In turn, Jones and Coviello suggest that broader perspectives that appreciate the resources, choices and decisions made by entrepreneurs should guide policy makers seeking to help more firms to internationalize.

For theoretical insights to be converted into policy a robust evidence base is required (DTI, 2004). Whilst there is a considerable pool of knowledge relating to the internationalization of large and multi-plant companies (Coviello and McAuley, 1999; Roper and Love, 2002; Etemad, 2004), until recently there has been comparatively limited information relating to the internationalization of new and smaller private firms. Several studies have begun to explore the complex array of factors associated with the reasons 'why' and 'how' SMEs internationalize (Hollenstein, 2005). On the downside, many of these studies are fraught with methodological problems (Coviello and Jones, 2004) relating to definitions, sampling and the misspecification of empirical models.

There has been limited 'dialogue' between the alternative theoretical perspectives. This study explores the policy implications associated with recent conceptual and empirical developments relating to private SME internationalization. Other conceptual perspectives have been subject to extensive criticism in the policy context (O'Farrell et al., 1998). Because of its emerging importance, we focus our analysis on the international entrepreneurship perspective and compare it to traditional internationalization theories. Here we take a broad perspective by suggesting that policy towards internationalization needs to appreciate private firm heterogeneity. The spectrum of SMEs can range from those that do not and cannot internationalize, through to those that internationalize from their inception. Policy may need to be differentiated according to the circumstances and contexts of firms along this spectrum. Various conceptual perspectives may help shed light on the types of support appropriate for SMEs at different points on the spectrum.

This review seeks to stimulate policy discussion relating to the internationalization of private SMEs in developed economies. Our review of the internationalization (particularly, the exporting) and international entrepreneurship literatures (O'Farrell et al., 1998, esp. Figure 2; Jones and Coviello, 2005) suggests six key themes that need to be examined from a policy perspective. In the following sections, we identify and discuss the following themes with regard to the internationalization of private SMEs:

Theme 1    The propensity of private SMEs to internationalize.
Theme 2    The timing of private SME internationalization.
Theme 3    Reasons for internationalization cited by owners of private SMEs.
Theme 4    Informational obstacles to private SME internationalization.
Theme 5    The mode of private SME internationalization.
Theme 6    The effect of internationalization on SME performance.

By highlighting these six themes, we seek to create greater awareness of the implicit views that may be held by policy makers and entrepreneurs. With reference to theory and the evidence base, alternative perspectives for consideration are highlighted. Material discussed generally relates to the exporting rather than the broader internationalization literature. In the final section, implications for policy makers and researchers associated with the six themes are discussed.

# THEMES SURROUNDING THE INTERNATIONALIZATION OF SMES

## Theme 1   The Propensity of Private SMEs to Internationalize

Given the potential job generation and wealth creation benefits associated with internationalization, some policy makers may seek to encourage more SMEs to internationalize. Many firms (and entrepreneurs), however, do not want to internationalize because they are reluctant to commit their (limited) resources to enter foreign markets (Christensen, 1991; Westhead et al., 2001b). In fact, most SMEs 'stay at home' (Acs et al., 1997). Westhead et al. (2002) found with regard to their sample of 'micro' (that is, businesses that employ between one and nine employees) and 'small' (that is, businesses that employ between ten and 49 employees) independent firms in Great Britain that only 31 per cent were exporters. A significantly smaller proportion of 'micro' rather than 'small' firms were exporters (24 per cent of 'micro' firms compared with 48 per cent of 'small' firms). Further, among those firms that did export, the proportion of their sales derived from foreign markets was rather small (on average, 9 per cent for 'small' firms compared with 4 per cent for 'micro' firms).

'Small' firms, however, exported a significantly larger proportion of their sales outside the UK than 'micro' firms. A similar pattern was detected by Westhead et al. (2004) with reference to a sample of 377 independent limited liability companies located throughout the UK engaged in a variety of manufacturing, construction and service industries. They noted that only 33 per cent of firms were exporters, while the mean proportion of sales from exporting was only 8 per cent. This pattern is not confined to the UK. Empirical evidence, for example, suggests a similar pattern in the European Union, where only 18 per cent of SMEs were found to be exporters (EIM, 2005).

The attitudes, resources and behaviour of the non-exporters warrant additional attention. Further, the majority of the non-exporters may not have the inclination and/or ability to export. Evidence suggests that the vast majority of non-exporting private firms do not export because they are focusing on their domestic market (Westhead et al., 2002). Consequently, while some policy makers may hold the belief that internationalization is desirable, they need to acknowledge that attitudinal (and resource) barriers need to be addressed if the pool of internationalizing private SMEs is to be increased.

## Theme 2   The Timing of Private SMEs Internationalization

The timing of internationalization is an important distinguishing factor between traditional internationalization studies and international entrepreneurship studies. Most notably, international new venture (INV) theorists question the stage model theory, and they suggest that many new private SMEs should internationalize from the inception of business operations (Autio et al., 2000).

McDougall et al. (1994) have asserted that international entrepreneurs try to avoid domestic path-dependence by establishing ventures which have routines for managing multicultural workforces, for coordinating resources located in different nations and for addressing customers in multiple geographic locations simultaneously. INVs are viewed as organizations which, from inception, seek to derive significant competitive advantage from the use of resources and the sale of output to multiple countries. Moreover INV theorists assert that many firms no longer regard international markets as simple adjuncts to the domestic market. SMEs with specific competitive advantages linked to their technological level and product and/or service characteristics may be alert to opportunities in international markets from the outset (Oviatt and McDougall, 1994, 1997). These opportunity-driven firms, therefore, do not follow an incremental internationalization path (Bell et al., 2001). Firms that internationalize from the outset may be associated with the asset of newness. Most notably, new SMEs do not have to unlearn procedures focused on developing a domestic market presence (Autio et al., 2000).

Evidence from Finland suggests that the time from the establishment of a firm (that is, the length of time in domestic markets) to the time of the first export delivery is becoming shorter (Luostarinen and Gabrielsson, 2004). Some technology and non-technology-based firms may ground their international competitive pattern on unique resources (human capital resources such as entrepreneurial capabilities relating to entrepreneurial orientation, alertness, information search and processing, cognitive mindset and so on) (Obrecht, 2004). INVs or born globals (BGs) (Oviatt and McDougall, 1994, 1997; Preece et al., 1999) generally offer products and/or services that involve substantial value added based on a breakthrough in process or technology.

Unwittingly INVs theorists may have encouraged a growing policy belief that more new private firms should internationalize, and that they should internationalize from the outset (EIM, 2005). The development of policy based on these notions may apply only to a distinct subgroup of SMEs. If policy makers only contextualize support for knowledge and technology-based firms, this support may not be appropriate for the vast majority of SMEs that do not offer products and/or services that involve substantial value added based on a breakthrough in process or technology. Insights from other perspectives need to be considered by policy makers seeking to encourage more of the latter types of SMEs to internationalize. Findings and relationships detected with regard to INVs may not be universally applicable to other 'types' of private new SMEs, for the following reasons.

First, some SMEs may produce goods and services that are not tradable. It is necessary to understand the distinction between those cases where the goods and services are not tradable and those where they are tradable in principle, yet the firm does not engage in internationalization. This may be attributable to the attitudes, resources and behaviour of the entrepreneurs and SMEs involved. As earlier intimated, the majority of non-exporting SMEs may not have the inclination and/or ability to export.

Second, the findings from a number of empirical studies may be associated with low external validity. Some studies are restricted to small countries where high-technology firms may have to internationalize if they are to identify sufficient customers.

Third, the nature of the industrial sector selected by the SME to operate in may be important. With reference to a random sample of 377 independent companies in the UK, Westhead et al. (2004) detected that younger and manufacturing firms were more likely to be exporters, and they reported higher internationalization intensities. Further, Bell et al.'s

(2004) case study evidence relating to 15 'knowledge-intensive' and 15 'traditional' man-ufacturing firms located in three regions in the UK suggested that, whilst 'traditional' firms generally followed an incremental approach both domestically and internationally, 'knowledge-intensive' manufacturing firms were more likely to have an international ori-entation from inception, and they internationalized rapidly.

Fourth, there is a need to consider the nature of the support system which may be an important source of knowledge leveraged by the new venture to circumvent attitudinal, resource, operational and strategic obstacles to internationalization. With reference to the development of high-technology spin-off firms from universities located across Europe, Clarysse et al. (2005) concluded that an incubator model involving heavily resourced and intensive activities over a considerable period of time and based on world-class science was needed to promote firms that have the potential to internationalize. Studies have tended to ignore this potentially important influence on the timing and extent of internationalization (Autio et al., 2000).

Fifth, the notion of SMEs internationalizing from the outset ignores the potential impact of the changing international competitive landscape and the associated corporate restructuring. The reassessment of the scope of larger corporations in response to these changing market pressures is leading to the outsourcing of activities, and the divestment of often modest-sized subsidiaries and divisions to management and leveraged buy-outs that have greater discretion to select their markets and customers. These developments raise opportunities for SMEs that may have been domestic market-oriented (or heavily dependent on trading with their former parent) to become niche players with a special-ized set of customers on a global scale.

This discussion suggests there is a need to recognize that the internationalization deci-sion, as well as its timing, may vary greatly by 'type' of SME.

## Theme 3   Reasons for Internationalization Cited by Owners of Private SMEs

If SMEs (especially 'micro' firms) internationalize, it may not be because they planned or intended to do so. Proactive reasons for internationalization (that is, the desire to gain access to new and larger markets as well as know-how and technology) (EIM, 2005) are not universally cited by SME owners, particularly owners of 'micro' firms with more limited resource pools that could be leveraged to pursue strategic choices.

Evidence suggests that many private firms internationalize following unsolicited orders (Welch, 2004). Further, some SMEs reported that they were 'pulled' into exporting by cus-tomers who demanded their products/services abroad (O'Farrell et al., 1996). A report published by the European Commission (2003) also highlighted that the majority of SMEs in Europe started exporting because of an unsolicited order and/or an informal contact.

The reasons for exporting have been explored with regard to proactive–reactive behav-iour by the firm and internal–external environmental factors. Westhead et al. (2002) found that reactive–external stimuli were the main stimuli reported by exporting 'micro' and 'small' firms located in Great Britain. The reactive–external stimuli of being 'pulled' into exporting as a result of 'being contacted by foreign customers who place orders' or receiv-ing a 'one-off order' were particularly important for 'micro' rather than 'small' firms. They also noted that a larger proportion of respondents in 'small' firms rather than 'micro' firms reported proactive–internal and proactive–external stimuli (that is, 'export markets pro-actively targeted by other members of staff' and 'excess capacity "pushed" the business into exporting'). This discussion suggests that numerous SMEs become exporters (or internationalize) without much rational analysis or deliberate planning.

### Theme 4   Informational Obstacles to Private SME Internationalization

Policy makers are seeking to address attitudinal, resource, operational and strategic barriers to SME development. Information is seen as a key resource (DTI, 2004) that can enable SMEs to create and discover opportunities as well as pursue and exploit opportunities in domestic and foreign markets. Policy makers support the provision of additional information to SMEs to enable owners to make more informed strategic decisions, as well as to enable them to circumvent obstacles to business development (and internationalization).

Why some people identify opportunities and others do not may be related to the information (Kaish and Gilad, 1991; Fiet, 1996; Shane, 2000; Casson, 2003) and knowledge (that is, the human capital relating to prior information already possessed) they possess (Venkataraman, 1997). If information facilitates the identification of an opportunity, individuals may choose to increase their access to opportunities by searching for new/current information (Fiet, 1996; Shane, 2003). In some instances, opportunities can be identified when an entrepreneur combines prior information with new information. Entrepreneurs differ with regard to their stocks of prior information (Shane, 2003). Prior information can direct attention, expectations and interpretations of market stimuli as well as the generation of ideas (Gaglio, 1997). Experienced entrepreneurs with specialist knowledge may restrict their scanning and concentrate their information search within a more specific domain based on routines (and information sources) that worked well in the past (Cooper et al., 1994; Fiet, 2002). Moreover some experienced entrepreneurs with higher levels of alertness (Kirzner, 1997) may not need to gather large amounts of information to identify business opportunities. By focusing on a smaller number of diagnostic items of information, experienced entrepreneurs can avoid information overload, which can degrade their decision-making capabilities (Jacoby et al., 2001). Nevertheless, for a given level of prior information (that is, specific human capital), entrepreneurs may be able to exploit opportunities by searching for up-to-date information. Some entrepreneurs, therefore, collect and process information to make calculated judgments regarding the feasibility and risks associated with the pursuit of an identified opportunity (Casson, 2003). SME owners with limited information (and networks) may be unaware of opportunities in domestic and/or international markets.

Empirical evidence, however, suggests that the major reason for many firms not exporting is that they make the decision to focus on servicing customer needs in local domestic markets. Informational obstacles (Leonidou, 1995; Morgan and Katsikeas, 1997) do not appear to be the most frequently cited main obstacle to exporting (EIM, 2005). Westhead et al. (2002), for example, found that 61 'micro' firms (85 per cent) compared with 18 'small' firms (78 per cent) considered strategic obstacles to be the main obstacle to exporting. Conversely they detected that only three 'micro' firms (4 per cent) compared with two 'small' firms (9 per cent) considered informational obstacles to be the main obstacle to exporting.

The above discussion suggests that most SMEs, particularly more resource-constrained 'micro' firms, do not perceive that information is the key obstacle to SME internationalization. The latter SMEs may also be unaware of government programmes that provide information (or assistance) which could enable more informed strategy formulation by owners of SMEs.

## Theme 5    The Mode of Private SME Internationalization

Stage model theorists who suggest a unilinear evolutionary internationalization process, with incremental stages and a well-defined mode of internationalization at each stage, have attracted extensive criticism (Bell et al., 2004). O'Farrell et al. (1998) asserted that the internationalization/transaction cost framework of internationalization is inappropriate when exploring business services SMEs. This is because business services firms require an understanding of what is required to best support collaboration with clients. Moreover they suggested that the transaction cost framework is unable to handle complex choices among alternative modes, and it is difficult to differentiate between experienced and inexperienced business firms.

The mode of internationalization selected by a firm is an important decision (or strategic choice) that can influence the firm's position in the selected markets, and its ability to gain access to vital information and acquire resources (Holmlund and Kock, 1998). Firms can internationalize through a variety of modes (O'Farrell et al., 1998), and each mode is associated with risk, control and cost issues that need to be considered by the SME. The modes most frequently cited by private SMEs relate to direct exporting without an overseas base or establishing an overseas base through some form of foreign direct investment (FDI) associated with a greenfield site, an acquisition or a joint venture.

Studies focusing on new technology-based firms suggest that these firms are able to develop networks that raise the probability of selecting a joint venture to enter the foreign market (Dana and Wright, 2004). Growing enthusiasm for new technology-based firm internationalization has led to a general perception that all SMEs, irrespective of industrial activity, should enter foreign markets through FDI (EIM, 2005). However this mode may only be applicable to the internationalization of a small subsample of private SMEs engaged in knowledge and technology-based activities.

Westhead et al. (2002) found that the most important mode of entry cited by owners of a representative sample of SMEs was direct exporting. Owners of firms generally engaged in traditional manufacturing and service activities rarely cited joint ventures and partnerships. The reported preferences regarding mode of entry reflected their limited social and business networks, as well as their desire to have greater control over their resources (O'Farrell et al., 1996).

The modes of entry into foreign markets are likely to differ on key dimensions such as the amount of resource commitment, the extent of risk, the potential for returns and the degree of managerial control. Some modes of entry involve higher levels of commitment and higher transaction costs and costs relating to acquiring resources. Zahra et al. (2000) found important relationships between the international mode of entry and learning in new high-technology ventures. Most notably, they detected that foreign acquisitions and other higher control modes of entry facilitated greater breadth and speed of technological learning than low control modes such as international export and licensing agreements. However this approach may not be appropriate for all SMEs that internationalize.

A broader resource-based perspective would suggest that the appropriate mode of entry is dependent on the nature of foreign market resource access. Firms that internationalize may be exploiting their existing resources or may seek to enhance them. If a firm has resources that are geographically fungible, low resource access modes of entry, such as exporting, may be selected to utilize existing resource pools. Some SMEs are, therefore, able to internationalize through low resource access modes if they build links with larger companies and are drawn to internationalize on the back of these linkages. If a firm's resources are location-specific, high resource access modes (FDI, acquisition and greenfield entry) may be necessary.

### Theme 6    The Effect of Internationalization on SME Performance

There is no consensus regarding ways to measure internationalization performance (Katsikeas et al., 2000). Most studies focusing on private SMEs have failed to explore whether internationalizing firms report superior levels of firm performance. The view that internationalizing firms report superior performance is a widely received wisdom, and can be regarded as theme 6. We acknowledge that this view is assumed although not directly stated (or validated) by some academics and practitioners (EIM, 2005). A review of the evidence indicates no clear and consistent relationship between an SME's propensity to export and ability to report superior firm performance. The variety of performance indicators explored in studies makes comparison across studies difficult. Moreover results may be affected by the sectors analysed and the time frames of analysis. Indeed many studies have failed to consider inter-industry differences between non-exporters and exporters.

McDougall and Oviatt (1996) noted that firms that had increased international sales exhibited superior performance in terms of both relative market share and return on investment (ROI). Further, Bloodgood et al. (1996) found that internationalization was marginally significantly associated with ventures that reported higher profits. Burgel et al. (2001) detected that exporters reported higher levels of productivity and sales growth but not employment growth. These three studies focused on internationalizing firms engaged in new technology-based sectors.

In contrast, Lu and Beamish (2001) found with reference to a sample of smaller listed Japanese firms covering 19 industries that the proportion of sales exported had a negative relationship to return on assets. With regard to a sample of private SMEs located in the UK engaged in a variety of manufacturing, construction and service activities, Westhead et al. (2001a) detected that the propensity to export was only significantly positively associated with operating performance relative to competitors. The propensity to export was not found significantly to encourage subsequent sales and employment growth or firm survival. Similarly Westhead et al. (2004), who utilized a weighted average performance score (Naman and Slevin, 1993) to control for industry differences, found that the propensity to export variable was not significantly associated with superior weighted firm performance reported by firms located in the UK. A weak positive relationship was, however, detected in relation to the exporting intensity variable. On the downside, the latter studies relating to samples of firms generally engaged in traditional manufacturing and service activities suggest that the relationship between the propensity to export and firm performance may be context-specific.

It should be noted that studying the relationship between internationalization and firm performance could be fraught with a number of other methodological problems. For example, it may be difficult to establish a causal relationship between internationalization and performance if studies rely on cross-sectional evidence. Even when longitudinal evidence is analysed (Bloodgood et al., 1996; McDougall and Oviatt, 1996; Lu and Beamish, 2001; Westhead et al., 2001a), the results are still inconsistent. This may be partly due to the role of context and/or differences in the time lag used to explore the impact of internationalization on SME performance. Lu and Beamish (2001) highlighted the importance of time by demonstrating that FDI activity was initially associated with a decline in profitability, but later greater levels of FDI were associated with superior performance.

Another important consideration relates to the possibility that the relationship between internationalization and SME performance is moderated by other strategic variables. This may be particularly relevant to SMEs in small open economies, whereby SMEs pursuing a growth strategy may be more likely to expand by entering foreign markets. With reference to the United States context, McDougall and Oviatt (1996) detected that increased international sales in technology-based new ventures required simultaneous strategic changes in order to enhance venture performance. Further, Lu and Beamish (2001) found that exporting moderated the relationship FDI had with firm performance. They detected that pursuing a strategy of high exporting concurrent with high FDI was less profitable than one that involved lower levels of exporting when FDI levels were high.

Reviewed evidence fails to suggest that internationalization consistently enhanced the performance of SMEs with regard to several performance indicators. The studies discussed highlight the need to consider industry context, timing issues and firm-specific strategic issues within multivariate statistical frameworks, and the need to consider selection bias issues within econometric models.

## IMPLICATIONS

### Context

Policy is increasingly aimed at encouraging more new and established private SMEs to internationalize, particularly from the outset. Inevitably owners of smaller private firms concerned with uncertainty and risk will face attitudinal, resource, operational and strategic barriers to the internationalization of their ventures. Assuming an interventionist stance, a case for more balanced policy support for SMEs is suggested with reference to the internationalization process. There is a need for awareness that knowledge relating to the SME internationalization process is emerging and not well established. Further, there is a need to consider carefully the context of the evidence base, which is used to guide policy options and decisions. Failure to do so could lead to the formulation of inappropriate policies for private SMEs, entrepreneurs (or entrepreneurial teams) and networks seeking to internationalize their activities. The implications of the six themes analysed above are discussed below.

**Theme 1**

Our discussion of theme 1 emphasizes that it cannot be assumed that all private SMEs should internationalize. A differentiation of policy may be warranted. Policy makers may benefit from acknowledging that many SMEs do not want to internationalize. There is a need to consider the variable propensity to internationalize reported by SMEs. Evidence focusing upon size of firm differences confirms that a larger proportion of 'small' rather than 'micro' firms had the ability to enter export markets. If policy initiatives were aimed at encouraging all SMEs to become exporters, there would appear to be a need to better understand the target groups for assistance. Initiatives for more resource-constrained 'micro' firms may need to be tailored with care. As a first step, policy might usefully focus on aiding existing exporters to become 'export-committed' exporters and more effective exporters.

Evidence suggests that many 'micro' firms do not want to internationalize and/or do not have the resources required to internationalize. If the goal of policy is to increase the 'quantity' of internationalizing firms, policy makers may need to support initiatives that address attitudinal and resource barriers to internationalization cited by the owners of 'micro' firms. Policy makers, for example, could highlight the benefits associated with keying into new and larger markets as well as the take-up and utiliza- tion of broader know-how and innovative technologies for more owners of private SMEs. Also policy makers may seek to provide initiatives that seek to improve the 'quality' rather than solely increasing the 'quantity' of internationalizing SMEs. Policy makers may only provide resources to smaller firms that have already circumvented attitudinal barriers to internationalization. The latter firms may be seeking additional resources (information, technology, market know-how and so on) that can be lever- aged in combination with existing resources to achieve dynamic capabilities that enable them to gain competitive advantages and wealth creation in foreign (and domestic) markets.

**Theme 2**

Our discussion of theme 2 suggests that firms might reconsider their decision to interna- tionalize and exit from foreign markets. The dissemination of information relating to actual local role models could encourage entrepreneurs who have withdrawn from inter- nationalization as well as those with no internationalization experience to (re)consider the internationalization route.

A central issue for internationalizing SMEs relates to their ability to sustain repeat busi- ness, which may be especially important for business services firms. This suggests that SMEs that internationalize may particularly need to consider the sunk costs associated with entry, and the implications associated with the exit decision. SMEs that internation- alize may also need to consider the skills and resources that they need to develop in order to sustain their internationalization activity. The lack of skilled personnel and the need to develop more informal and tacit knowledge have been identified as major barriers to SME growth in general (DTI, 2004) and these issues would seem to extend to the inter- nationalization process. There appears to be a need to develop policy support that helps SMEs to consider the dynamics of the internationalization process over time rather than seeing it as a one-off activity.

## Theme 3

Our discussion of theme 3 suggests that policy makers need to appreciate that SME owners internationalize their activities for a variety of reasons, and relatively few owners cite solely proactive reasons. As intimated earlier, it may be necessary to fine-tune assistance to private SMEs. Evidence suggests that 'micro' firms were more likely to internationalize for reactive reasons, particularly if they were 'pulled' abroad by being contacted by foreign customers. The assistance required by 'micro' firms may not be the same as that required by 'small' firms. Assistance may be provided to firms (and entrepreneurs) that have a higher probability of citing reactive reasons for internationalization. The advantages (and disadvantages) associated with reactive forms of internationalization, such as unsolicited orders, need to be drawn to the attention of owners of 'micro' firms. The latter firms could be provided with assistance in order to deal with the various types of unsolicited export order opportunities.

## Theme 4

Our discussion of theme 4 suggests that policy makers should not widely assume that insufficient information is a key barrier to SME internationalization. Presented evidence suggests that many smaller private SMEs had insufficient pools of resources, not only the information resource, which led to the creation of strategic obstacles. To circumvent strategic rather than information obstacles, many firms make the rational decision to service the requirements of customers located in local domestic markets. There may be a need to encourage owners of private SMEs to create advantages for their firms by accumulating idiosyncratic firm resources. Internal sources (for example, skills relating to imagination and creativity as well as technological sophistication and an ability to create and/discover opportunities) and external sources (for example, through networks) may be leveraged by more SMEs as a source of competitive advantage in domestic and foreign markets. There may, therefore, be a need to aim policy towards enhancing the resource profiles of different types of private SMEs.

## Theme 5

Our discussion of theme 5 suggests that more SMEs should consider the benefits and costs associated with various modes of entry into foreign markets. Further, there is a need to appreciate more widely that the owners of SMEs are engaged in a dynamic and non-linear internationalization learning experience. There may be a need to provide customized support to SMEs/entrepreneurs who are at various points along the internationalization experimental learning spectrum. This suggests a need to provide support for SMEs/entrepreneurs who are experienced as well as for those with no or little internationalization experience. While not being as restrictive as the stage theory view of internationalization, this approach recognizes the importance of the time dimension in the internationalization process.

Owners of established private SMEs could be provided with assistance to address attitudinal, resource, operational and strategic barriers to internationalization. When considering assistance, policy makers should also acknowledge that, whilst exporting SMEs may cite several barriers to internationalization, the more experienced exporters may perceive themselves to be better equipped to overcome these barriers. In parallel with policies focused on new firm creation, internationalization policy may, therefore, need repeatedly to help some SMEs/entrepreneurs to develop their internationalization activities. This suggests a need to develop internationalization initiatives to include those firms that have some international experience, but which face problems in exploiting opportunities to increase further the share of sales exported. Issues related to the potential 'learning race' between large and small partners, in addition, should be brought to the attention of owners of SMEs. Mechanisms to protect the intellectual property of smaller private SMEs should be developed. The provision of further information and networking opportunities may enable more entrepreneurs to hone their opportunity creation, discovery, pursuit and exploitation skills, which can be leveraged to pursue and exploit internationalization opportunities.

**Theme 6**
Our discussion of theme 6 suggests that the link between internationalizing firms and superior firm performance appears to be related to the type of sector firms were engaged in, as well as firm-specific strategies and methodological issues. For example, technology-based firms that had internationalized generally reported superior performance, but this was not necessarily the case for firms in more mature sectors. Policy concerns for wealth and job creation and a focus on maximizing returns on investments may, therefore, require concentrating on assistance to firms with the potential to trade internationally. It should be noted, however, that, while studies may have identified a positive correlation between internationalization and technology-based firm performance, it can be very difficult to establish a statistically significant causal link. We return to this point below.

## IMPLICATIONS FOR RESEARCHERS

The above discussion suggests implications for researchers in respect of both theory building and empirical analysis. Internationalization by SMEs introduces a need for further conceptual approaches that incorporate the behaviour and characteristics of the entrepreneur (or entrepreneurial team). Jones and Coviello (2005) have attempted to present a synthesis of various approaches to the internationalization process. Their general model of the entrepreneurial internationalization process incorporates a time dimension. Additional theory building research (Bell et al., 2003) is required to develop this line of argument further to encompass the range of SMEs that internationalize.

In respect of empirical analysis, it is important to recognize that research relating to SME internationalization is associated with several methodological problems. Some studies are not keyed into debates relating to the internationalization of private smaller firms as opposed to larger multinational firms. There are also a number of concerns surrounding the size and representativeness of samples, the techniques used, and the validity and reliability of measures operationalized in SME studies. Particular problems relate to establishing whether there is a causal link between internationalization and firm performance. On the basis of cross-sectional analysis, it is unclear whether any causal link runs from internationalization to superior performance, or vice versa. Moreover some firms develop their internationalization activities over time and they adapt their modes of internationalization at different points in time as part of the process of learning and development. This suggests a need for deeper understanding of the determinants of internationalization. The design of measures to promote smaller private firm internationalization needs to consider carefully the evidence upon which these policies are based. Additional research in this area is warranted to provide an evidence base, which can guide policy with regard to resource allocation decisions and the selection of groups for assistance.

# REFERENCES

Acs, Z., L.-P. Dana and M.V. Jones (2003), 'Toward new horizons: The internationalization of entrepreneurship', *Journal of International Entrepreneurship*, **1**(1), 5–12.

Acs, Z.J., R. Morck, J.M. Shaver and B. Yeung (1997), 'The internationalization of small and medium-sized enterprises: a policy perspective', *Small Business Economics*, **9**(1), 7–20.

Anderson, O. (1993), 'On the internationalization process of firms: a critical analysis', *Journal of International Business Studies*, **24**(2), 209–31.

Autio, E., H.J. Sapienza and J.G. Almeida (2000), 'Effects of age at entry, knowledge intensity, and imitability on international growth', *Academy of Management Journal*, **43**(5), 909–24.

Bell, J. and S. Young (1998), 'Towards an integrative framework of the internationalisation of the firm', in G. Hooley, R. Loveridge and D. Wilson (eds), *Internationalisation: Process, Context and Markets*, London: Macmillan, pp. 3–28.

Bell, J., D. Crick and S. Young (2004), 'Small firm internationalization and business strategy: an exploratory study of "knowledge-intensive" and "traditional" manufacturing firms in the UK', *International Small Business Journal*, **22**(1), 23–56.

Bell, J., R. McNaughton and S. Young (2001), '"Born-again global" firms. An extension to the "born global" phenomenon', *Journal of International Management*, **7**(3), 173–89.

Bell, J., R. McNaughton, S. Young and D. Crick (2003), 'Towards an integrative model of small firm internationalisation', *Journal of International Entrepreneurship*, **1**(4), 339–62.

Bloodgood, J.M., H.J. Sapienza and J.G. Almeida (1996), 'The internationalization of new high-potential US ventures: antecedents and outcomes', *Entrepreneurship Theory and Practice*, **20**(4), 61–76.

Burgel, O., A. Fier, G. Licht and G. Murray (2001), *The Rapid Internationalisation of High-Tech Young Firms in Germany and the United Kingdom*, London: Anglo-German Foundation.

Casson, M. (2003), *The Entrepreneur: An Economic Theory*, 2nd edn, Cheltenham, UK and Northampton, MA, USA: Edward Elgar.

Christensen, P.R. (1991), 'The small and medium-sized exporters' squeeze: empirical evidence and model reflections', *Entrepreneurship and Regional Development*, **3**(1), 49–65.

Clarysse, B., M. Wright, A. Lockett, E. van de Elde and A. Vohora (2005), 'Spinning out new ventures: a typology of incubation strategies from European research institutions', *Journal of Business Venturing*, **20**(2), 183–216.

Cooper, A.C., F.J. Gimeno-Gascon and C.Y. Woo (1994), 'Initial human and financial capital predictors of new venture performance', *Journal of Business Venturing*, **9**(5), 371–95.

Coviello, N.E. and M.V. Jones (2004), 'Methodological issues in international entrepreneurship research', *Journal of Business Venturing*, **19**(4), 485–508.

Coviello, N.E. and A. McAuley (1999), 'Internationalisation and the smaller firm: a review of contemporary empirical research', *Management International Review*, **39**(3), 223–56.

Dana, L.-P. and R.W. Wright (2004), 'Emerging paradigms of international entrepreneurship', in L.-P. Dana (ed.), *Handbook of Research on International Entrepreneurship*, Cheltenham, UK and Northampton, MA, USA: Edward Elgar, pp. 3–15.

Department of Trade and Industry (DTI) (2004), *A Government Action Plan for Small Business. Making the UK the Best Place in the World to Start and Grow a Business: The Evidence Base*, London: DTI, Small Business Service.

EIM (2005), *Internationalization in the Netherlands*, Zoetemeer, Netherlands: EIM.

Etemad, H. (2004), 'A typology', in L.-P. Dana (ed.), *Handbook of Research on International Entrepreneurship*, Cheltenham, UK and Northampton, MA, USA: Edward Elgar, pp. 94–125.

European Commission (2003), *European Commission, Observatory of European SMEs, 2003/No. 5: SMEs and Cooperation*, Luxembourg: European Commission (http://europa.eu.int/comm/ enterprise/enterprise_policy/analysis/observatory.htm).

Fiet, J.O. (1996), 'The informational basis for entrepreneurial discovery', *Small Business Economics*, **8**(6), 419–30.

Fiet, J.O. (2002), *The Systematic Search for Entrepreneurial Discoveries*, Westport, Conn: Quorum Books.

Gaglio, C.M. (1997), 'Opportunity identification: review, critique and suggested research directions', in J.A. Katz (eds), *Advances in Entrepreneurship, Firm Emergence and Growth*, vol. 3, Greenwich, CA: JAI Press, pp. 119–38.

Giamartino, G.A., P.P. McDougall and B.J. Bird (1993), 'International entrepreneurship: the state of the field', *Entrepreneurship Theory and Practice*, **18**(1), 37–41.

Hollenstein, H. (2005), 'Determinants of international activities: are SMEs different?', *Small Business Economics*, **24**(5), 431–50.

Holmlund, M. and S. Kock (1998), 'Relationships and the internationalisation of Finnish small and medium-sized companies', *International Small Business Journal*, **16**(4), 46–63.

Jacoby, J., M. Morrin, G. Johar, Z. Gurhan, A. Kuss and D. Mazursky (2001), 'Training novice investors to become more expert: the role of information accessing strategy', *The Journal of Psychology and Financial Markets*, **2**(2), 69–79.

Johanson, J. and J.-E. Vahlne (1977), 'The internationalization process of the firm – a model of knowledge development and increasing foreign market commitment', *Journal of International Business Studies*, **8**(1), 23–32.

Jones, M. and N. Coviello (2005), 'Internationalisation: conceptualising an entrepreneurial process of behaviour in time', *Journal of International Business Studies*, **36**(3), 284–303.

Julien, P.A., A. Joyal, L. Deshaies and C. Ramangalahy (1997), 'A typology of strategic behaviour among small and medium-sized exporting businesses: a case study', *International Small Business Journal*, **15**(2), 33–49.

Kaish, S. and B. Gilad (1991), 'Characteristics of opportunities search of entrepreneurs versus executives: sources, interests, general alertness', *Journal of Business Venturing*, **6**(1), 45–61.

Katsikeas, C.S., L.C. Leonidou and N.A. Morgan (2000), 'Firm level export performance assessment: review, evaluation, and development', *Journal of Academy of Marketing Science*, **28**(4), 493–511.

Kirzner, I.M. (1997), 'Entrepreneurial discovery and the competitive market process: an Austrian approach', *Journal of Economic Literature*, **35**(1), 60–85.

Korhonen, H., R. Luostarinen and L.S. Welch (1996), 'Internationalisation of SMEs: inward-outward patterns and government policy', *Management International Review*, **36**(4), 315–29.

Leonidou, L.C. (1995), 'Empirical research on export barriers: review, assessment and synthesis', *Journal of International Marketing*, **3**(1), 29–43.

Lu, J. and P. Beamish (2001), 'The internationalization and performance of SMEs', *Strategic Management Journal*, **22**(6/7), 565–86.

Luostarinen, R. and M. Gabrielsson (2004), 'Finnish perspectives of international entrepreneurship', in L.-P. Dana (ed.), *Handbook of Research on International Entrepreneurship*, Cheltenham, UK and Northampton, MA, USA: Edward Elgar, pp. 383–403.

McDougall, P.P. and B.M. Oviatt (1996), 'New venture internationalization, strategic change, and performance: a follow-up study', *Journal of Business Venturing*, **11**(1), 23–41.

McDougall, P.P. and B.M. Oviatt (2000), 'International entrepreneurship: the intersection of two research paths, special research forum', *Academy of Management Journal*, **43**(5), 902–6.

McDougall, P.P., S. Shane and B.M. Oviatt (1994), 'Explaining the formation of international new ventures: the limits of theories from international business research', *Journal of Business Venturing*, **9**(6), 469–87.

Melin, L. (1992), 'Internationalisation as a strategy process', *Strategic Management Journal*, **13**(Winter), 99–118.

Morgan, R.E. and C.S. Katsikeas (1997), 'Obstacles to export initiation and expansion', *Omega*, **25**(6), 677–90.

Naman, J.L. and D.P. Slevin (1993), 'Entrepreneurship and the concept of fit: a model and empirical tests', *Strategic Management Journal*, **14**(2), 137–53.

Obrecht, J.-J. (2004), 'Entrepreneurial capabilities: a resource-based systematic approach to international entrepreneurship', in L.-P. Dana (ed.), *Handbook of Research on International Entrepreneurship*, Cheltenham, UK and Northampton, MA, USA: Edward Elgar, pp. 248–64.

O'Farrell, P.N., P.A. Wood and J. Zheng (1996), 'Internationalization of business services: an interregional analysis', *Regional Studies*, **30**(2), 101–18.

O'Farrell, P.N., P.A. Wood and J. Zheng (1998), 'Regional influences on foreign market development by business service companies: elements of a strategic context explanation', *Regional Studies*, **32**(1), 31–48.

Organisation for Economic Co-Operation and Development (OECD) (1998), *Fostering Entrepreneurship*, Paris: Organisation for Economic Co-Operation and Development.

Oviatt, B. and P. McDougall (1994), 'Toward a theory of international new ventures', *Journal of International Business Studies*, **25**(1), 45–62.

Oviatt, B.M. and P.P. McDougall (1997), 'Challenges for internationalization process theory: the case of international new ventures', *Management International Review*, **37**(2), 85–99.

Peng, M. (2001), 'The resource-based view and international business', *Journal of Management*, **27**(6), 803–29.

Philp, N.E. (1998), 'The export propensity of the very small enterprise (VSE)', *International Small Business Journal*, **16**(4), 79–93.

Preece, S.B., G. Miles and M.C. Baetz (1999), 'Explaining the international intensity and global diversity of early-stage technology-based firms', *Journal of Business Venturing*, **14**(3), 259–81.

Roper, S. and J.H. Love (2002), 'Innovation and export performance: evidence from the UK and German manufacturing plants', *Research Policy*, **31**(7), 1087–102.

Shane, S. (2000), 'Prior knowledge and the discovery of entrepreneurial opportunities', *Organization Science*, **11**(4), 448–69.

Shane, S. (2003), *A General Theory of Entrepreneurship*, Cheltenham, UK and Northampton, MA: Edward Elgar Publishing.

Shane, S. and S. Venkataraman (2000), 'The promise of entrepreneurship as a field of research', *Academy of Management Review*, **25**(1), 217–26.

Venkataraman, S. (1997), 'The distinctive domain of entrepreneurship research: an editor's perspective', in J.A. Katz (ed.), *Advances in Entrepreneurship, Firm Emergence and Growth*, vol. 3, Greenwich, CA: JAI Press, pp. 119–38.

Welch, L.S. (2004), 'International entrepreneurship and internationalization: common threads', in L.-P. Dana (ed.), *Handbook of Research on International Entrepreneurship*, Cheltenham, UK and Northampton, MA, USA: Edward Elgar, pp. 137–49.

Welch, L.S. and R. Luostarinen (1988), 'Internationalization: evolution of a concept', *Journal of General Management*, **14**(2), 36–64.

Westhead, P., M. Wright and D. Ucbasaran (2001a), 'The internationalization of new and small firms: a resource-based view', *Journal of Business Venturing*, **16**(4), 333–58.

Westhead, P., M. Wright and D. Ucbasaran (2002), 'International market selection strategies selected by "micro" and "small" firms', *Omega*, **30**(1), 51–68.

Westhead, P., M. Wright and D. Ucbasaran (2004), 'Internationalization of private firms: environmental turbulence and organizational strategies and resources', *Entrepreneurship and Regional Development*, **16**(6), 501–22.

Westhead, P., M. Wright, D. Ucbasaran and F. Martin (2001b), 'International market selection strategies by manufacturing and services firms', *Entrepreneurship and Regional Development*, **13**(1), 17–46.

Wright, R.W. and D.A. Ricks (1994), 'Trends in international business research: twenty-five years later', *Journal of International Business Studies*, **25**(4), 687–701.

Young, S., P. Dimitratos and L.-P. Dana (2003), 'International entrepreneurship research: what scope for international business theories?', *Journal of International Entrepreneurship*, **1**(1), 31–42.

Zahra, S.A. and G. George (2002), 'International entrepreneurship: research contributions and future directions', in M.A. Hitt, R.D. Ireland, S.M. Camp and D.L. Sexton (eds), *Strategic Entrepreneurship: Creating a New Mindset*, Oxford: Blackwell, pp. 255–88.

Zahra, S., D. Ireland and M. Hitt (2000), 'International expansion by new venture firms: international diversity, mode of market entry, technological learning, and firm performance', *Academy of Management Journal*, **43**(5), 925–50.

# PART VI

# Executive Summaries

# DIAMOND V MILLS

## Mark Kujawa

Diamond V Mills is not very well known to the general public. The company sells to the animal agricultural industry, a softer and greener industry than its heavy industry counterpart. Nevertheless, agriculture is competitive, dynamic, and interested in globalization, whether it wants to be or not.

Diamond V is a 62-year-old family-owned business that sells one product, and one product only: a feed additive. The additive is manufactured from yeast, the same yeast with which bread, beer and wine are made. The yeast is fed with waste grain products from wet and dry corn milling processing in Iowa and, through the process of fermentation, very specific organic compounds are formed. When fed to animals – cows, dogs, cats, fish, other bacteria and humans – these compounds stimulate good bacterial growth that improves performance and helps digestion. The company founders recognized the value of fermentation for animals and captured the manufacturing process and put it into a more standardized method, employing scientific technologies and procedures to measure the effects on humans and animals over time. Diamond V is involved in a very real way in technology transfer to farmers. As a science-based company, Diamond V has to prove to every farmer, every animal, every species, every day that the product works.

The US is 75 per cent of the company's market and, while it is a big market, it is not growing. The number of animals in production decreases every year as a result of efficiencies: more pounds of meat per animal, more gallons of milk per cow. Genetics and other technologies – including Diamond V's feed additive – help drive this productivity and, in turn, will drive down the number of animals that use the product.

It was a logical choice for Diamond V to look outside the US. Food production is a high priority everywhere. Until 1980, Diamond V was focused almost exclusively on the US. It had been selling in Italy for 45 years and in Japan for 25 years, but its effort was limited to responding to product orders and walking away. There was no strategy for pursuing other international business, or for supporting the business that was there.

In 1980, Diamond V decided to develop a strategy to support its customers and expand its markets. The company recognized that its product requires technical service; it also requires warehousing (so farmers or feed manufacturers that buy Diamond V's product can have it available every day to add to feed). Since the feed additive produced by Diamond V is used for animals producing protein for human consumption, there was a need for expensive resources to deal with the regulatory issues, tariffs and safety that come with that.

Diamond V developed and executed different strategies for different regions of the globe. For eight years it sold product to a feed manufacturer in China, with unacceptable growth. Joint venturing was not a route Diamond V wanted to take – it had heard too many negative stories from unsuccessful ventures. There were many issues of asset control and stability, so they waited, and when the Chinese government rescinded its 51 per cent Chinese ownership rule, Diamond V was one of the first American companies to be wholly owned in China. It now had total control over its product, warehousing, sales and marketing company. The future plan is some day to have a manufacturing facility there, too. Diamond V also has a wholly owned company in Mexico.

Diamond V's model for the EU, on the other hand, is to sell to distributors in each EU country. It offers its distributors exclusive rights to market its product in a country: one distributor per country. While Diamond V may give up some business opportunities with this strategy, the gains in sales focus and product loyalty are well worth it. It takes time for distributors to visit every farmer, every distribution channel and prove the science over and over again. In return for this commitment, the distributors get exclusivity.

With these two basic business models, Diamond V is in over 40 countries today. To support its expansion, the company uses the following tactics to support its strategies.

- *Control*. It is too costly for a small company to give its technology away in the hopes that a market will develop. Diamond V has only wholly owned companies, no joint ventures.
- *Exclusive markets*. In exchange for exclusivity, Diamond V requires acceptable growth.
- *A single price for the world*. This eliminates the problem of parallel imports. Products move around the globe very easily; if the price is lower in one country, distribution in the higher-priced country will quickly be eliminated. Diamond V does offer volume discounts, however.
- *Consistent codex classification*. Diamond V has fought hard to maintain a single code on its product. As an animal feed additive, and part of the human food pro-duction system, its product is sometimes incorrectly misclassified as human food, pharmaceuticals and so on. These classifications come with higher tariffs.
- *US dollars only*. Currency risk is controlled with all payments made to Diamond V in US dollars.
- *Persistence*. It takes time to develop relationships, to improve product performance and to develop distribution channels. For example, Diamond V's window to show a profit in China is ten years. The company is breaking even at the five-year mark.
- *Regulatory and compliance courage*. Diamond V has a full-time person who deals only with compliance, regulatory and tariff issues. In an industry with regulatory issues related to human safety, it is important to remain flexible, and to try not to predict what a regulatory body will do when evaluating your product for registration.
- *Trust*. Diamond V has developed a selection process for its distributors that takes from six to 12 months. The process involves personal contact, attending trade shows and building trust. E-mail does not work when trying to determine the character of the distributor who is going to take the company into the future.

All the tactics in the world, however, go for naught without focusing on people. Developing people is developing business. There are no books on developing a Chinese manager to fit into a multinational company. Diamond V engages its managers and employees – abroad and in the United States – in cultural sensitivity training and activi-ties. It hires only bilingual global managers today; the language itself is not important, but some fluency or competency must be demonstrated. Diamond V's experience is that people who come in with even a college-level second language have far greater success in dealing with the dynamics of international roles. Cultural programmes are held several times a year, with management reminders and international days to help develop cultural awareness of foreign customers.

Foreign customers are invited to America – their flag is raised on Diamond V's building when they arrive. Activities are held to introduce them to American society. We try to make the visit as comfortable as possible. A prayer room is available for Muslim guests. Although hardly ever used, it is very much appreciated by visiting Muslim customers. Diamond V takes photographs of visitors with their flag. Very often these photographs are visible in the offices of our visitors. This activity instils a sense of pride, and develops loyalty to the company.

In any business, people need to be inspired, and achieving that requires constant communication from upper management, no matter how big or small the company. Unless the message is sent regularly that the international business is absolutely important, people will return to doing what they know best. Managers must ask themselves what they have done this week to promote international business.

Diamond V's internationalization is a continuing process that is not yet 100 per cent complete. With its global market at 25–30 per cent, the next move is to develop manufacturing capacity outside the US to go to the next level.

# MARKEL CORPORATION

## James Hoban

In 1922, radio manufacturers were looking for a sleeving to fit over the electrical wires at the back of the radio. The product line that started Markel Corporation was a cotton sleeving line, made just for this. Frank Markel founded the company in 1922 and, since that time, the company has morphed its product line from cotton sleeving to fiberglass sleeving, heat-shrinkable tubing, silicon rubber tubing, and eventually to their current product line which is very specialized plastic tubing and high temperature wire. Markel is privately owned; the company was sold by the Markel family in 1983 to two people outside the company.

Administrative and manufacturing operations are located in one facility in Plymouth Meeting, Pennsylvania. Primary products are for the automotive industry: cable control liners for push–pull cable assemblies and sensor wire for harness assemblies that are pollution-control devices under the hood. A recent product development is for a component of power steering assemblies. The cable control liners are the company's main product. They were developed in response to the need for improved efficiencies at higher temperatures in automotive accelerator and transmission shift cables. Markel is a third-tier supplier, selling to original equipment manufacturers (OEMs) that in turn sell directly to automotive companies. Markel also manufactures speciality tubing and wire for other industries, including communications, electrical and industrial. But it is the automotive product line that is the focus of the exporting business.

Annual sales are currently $US23mn, down from a high of $US30mn a few years ago, before selling several product lines. These product lines were diluting time and resources – not a good thing for a small company. Their sale also lowered debt and provided cash for future development and capital investment. Over the last ten years, the company has undergone a major transformation, focusing now on what it knows best: fluoropolymer products, Markel's most profitable line, with proprietary processing and patents, and the highest potential for growth. This was the foundation to build on: highly specialized products engineered to specific requirements.

Markel's entry into exporting began modestly in the 1980s, when the company engaged a local sales rep agency with proficiency in handling export sales. Markel had no in-house expertise at the time. This agency in turn coordinated with a sales rep in the UK to identify certain potential customers in Europe. For 15 years this was Markel's strategy, with slow but steady growth as a result.

At the same time Markel was divesting itself of its other product lines (mid-1990s), it challenged its export sales strategy and administration and started to make major changes. The decision was made to bring the sales administration in-house and, although the relationship with the local sales rep agency was terminated, relationships with foreign sales reps expanded. Markel has only one office, and a sales rep organization was a major part of the company's domestic sales approach. Thus it was felt that this sales rep approach would also work well overseas.

Most of Markel's export customers were in Europe and, pre-EU, the products were repriced in local currency: pounds sterling, deutschmark, lira and peseta. Markel also assumed all logistical and import duty responsibilities, and changed its terms to delivered duty paid. This was a way to level the playing field, especially in the automotive world, and a way to secure and grow Markel's business overseas.

Other key strategies include negotiating long-term supply agreements with key customers, usually two to three years in duration; engaging a logistics company in The Netherlands; frequent personal contacts and visits overseas; and changing the company's Enterprise Resource Planning (ERP) system in 2005 to one that could process orders and invoices in foreign currency.

Long-term supply agreements have proved helpful, not only in raw material planning and price negotiations, but in developing Markel's foreign currency strategy. Pricing in the automotive arena is extremely important and costs have to be well managed. Markel tries to link its raw material commitments with its vendors to its customer agreements, thereby locking in a degree of profitability over a two or three-year period. This continues to work, even though inflation is starting to be seen for the first time in several years, particularly in those ancillary products that are dependent on the petrochemical industry.

The logistics company in The Netherlands handles warehouse inventories, manages inland transportation and handles all customs issues. This same company also handles warehousing issues in the UK. Shipping volume has increased, from one to two containers a month to weekly containers to Rotterdam and biweekly containers to the UK. Ocean containers provide a cost-effective way of transporting product, and there are but a few occasions when material has to be flown overseas.

Personal contacts and a high level of service are a source of pride for Markel. The President and CEO, and VP of Sales, make frequent visits to their customers overseas. Markel also has an in-house export sales manager whose time is devoted to export customers. Clerical support is being added. Equally important is the new ERP system that processes orders and invoices in foreign currency, thus improving efficiency.

Today, export sales represent about 50 per cent of Markel's business. The company exports to Europe, Asia, Mexico, Canada, South America and Australia. Europe is the only area where business is conducted in local currency. All other sales are in US dollars. Markel is looking to expand its export business with other products, particularly in the communications and industrial applications. One product in particular has done well domestically (some of this is defense-related): a coaxial core product that is essential in communications.

The past few years have produced foreign currency gains due to the weak dollar and the strong euro and pound. This is particularly important to a company of Markel's size, and foreign currency transactions have to be well managed to enhance the bottom line as well as cash flow.

Markel received the US Department of Commerce's E-Award in 2002, for export sales during the four-year period 1997–2001. From 1997 to 2004, Markel's export sales increased by 324 per cent. During the period 2003–04, sales really took off, thanks in part to the exchange rate. Markel's product, from a purchasing power standpoint, was less expensive because of the strong euro and pound.

It was a steep learning curve, and Markel reallocated responsibilities to climb it, making many changes for a small company with limited resources. But it has been a rewarding experience.

# X-RITE INCORPORATED

## Joan Andrews

X-Rite is a provider of colour management solutions for formulating colour, creating colour recipes, verifying colour accuracy, and communicating colour data throughout a supply chain. Market segments include custom colour matching of paint for major retailers, unique non-contact technologies for auto manufacturers, and the colour management in graphic arts – packaging, advertisements, brochures, posters – all of the printed materials that are crucial in consumer branding. Some of the largest brand companies in the world have strong programmes for qualifying their suppliers around the world because their 'colour' (think Coke Red) is very important to them. X-Rite supplies the application and technology solutions that assure its customers that the colour is going to be as expected.

Over 45 per cent of X-Rite's revenues today come from its international operations. It has been recognized twice for its export excellence. To get to this point required a profound cultural change in the company and a financial commitment that was perhaps unusual for a company of X-Rite's size, located in western Michigan.

In 1996, X-Rite was firmly entrenched in what it called its 'export period'. Culturally, the Michigan-based employees thought California was a foreign place. Grandville is a typical small town, a wonderful place where the people who are born there grow up, go to school, work and live. Travel means going to Canada or the Upper Peninsula. There was little understanding of markets even outside the state of Michigan, let alone the United States. Letters of credit from customers in China or Europe expired in the company's accounting folk's desks because they did not recognize the bank, understand the importance of the deadline, or how to process the LCs. The whole process was itself foreign. Products were designed for the US market and, while X-Rite was happy to sell overseas to any dealer who attended a trade show, there was no understanding of the markets the dealer was selling into, and very little visibility to its key customers.

X-Rite had a few people in Cologne to manage the dealer business in Germany and a few people in Manchester to manage the dealer business in the UK. The rest of Europe was handled by a very small staff of Michigan people. Unbeknownst to headquarters, the German and UK managers were constantly fighting over the business in Europe outside their territories, undercutting each other in prices, and causing tremendous confusion to X-Rite's customers. X-Rite was its own competitor in Europe.

The vastness of Asia was covered by two people, one sitting in Hong Kong and the other sitting in Michigan, both covering this immense territory with no other resources than their own ingenuity. Even in this environment, total international sales were 30 per cent of revenues. What would revenues be if X-Rite got to know its customers and figured out what was needed in local markets? What would it take to move from being an exporter that designed for the US market and appointed distributors?

Over the past nine years, X-Rite evolved into an international company. It began its cultural change by establishing sales and service operations in key markets, by localizing product and by understanding that Europe and Asia were growth drivers. Although X-Rite still designs and manufactures only in the US, its international customers now have a direct influence on its product development. This is very different from taking what X-Rite designed for the US and selling it internationally.

The biggest cultural shift for the company was to understand the importance of incorporating local language in product displays. X-Rite's products go out on a shop floor and are used in production. Production people in China, in Germany, in France, in the Czech Republic, do not speak English. They do not read English. X-Rite products with English displays and software with English prompts were limiting the ability to expand. Key disciplines held lengthy debates over how much more would be sold if products were localized. The bottom line: little would be sold if the product remained English only. The only way to see how much could be sold was at least to cover the minimum needed to be competitive in the market: local language product and support materials.

Today X-Rite has 12 international offices with 132 employees in these offices, and product that is routinely localized in ten languages but can be localized by dealers into many more. There are eight service and support centres outside the US. Executives and marketing staff travel regularly outside the US, and international experience is a prerequisite for hiring managerial positions in HR, IT or marketing. The learning curve for people with no international exposure is high and takes a long time; it can be accelerated by hiring people who already have an understanding of international cultures and the international marketplace.

X-Rite's business model works best when it has a local presence in a market. There is much pre-sale and after-sale support that is difficult for a dealer to do on its own. The tendency is to use dealers to go after smaller accounts, and for X-Rite to be there for the larger ones. At the same time, X-Rite's investments have to be self-funding. It does not enter a market unless there is high confidence that there will be a return in the first year – that is, all costs covered and something contributed to the corporation – a stiff challenge because the company lacked any funding to have a third party conduct market research.

X-Rite did some things to find out whether it should enter a market. Obvious geographies were the targets (industrial countries such as Germany and Italy) and large US accounts were queried as to their business internationally. X-Rite also used the US Commercial Service's free market studies and its relatively inexpensive Gold Key Service. The market studies would often provide enough information to understand whether X-Rite could grow in a market, and the Gold Key service would provide names of prospects to fit an X-Rite profile. Even if the prospects did not work out, much was learned about a market just by talking with them.

Markets were visited personally, on numerous occasions. Interviews were held with potential customers, dealers and service providers, such as bankers, lawyers, accountants (often very willing to give a half-day of time to talk about the business climate in the hopes that their services would be contracted later). Talks with competitors provided a feel for potential.

Once a decision was made to enter a market, X-Rite would pursue one of several options: try to buy an existing distributor if the staff and its business ties were good (France and Australia) or start from scratch by hiring a sales manager and a few support people (Shanghai and Tokyo). Fundamentally X-Rite believes in hiring local talent to manage its business, but, when starting up a new operation, having an expat from the home team on location with ties to the Michigan office can cut through red tape to get things done, and show the local workforce the X-Rite way of doing things. The expat in Brazil, for example, had a short-term assignment to get the local manager and staff up to speed so they could stand on their own.

Besides getting the local staff up and running with an expat, X-Rite demanded that marketing and engineering people get on planes and spend time in the field. E-mail is great for sending tremendous volumes of information back and forth, and websites can contain all sorts of technical information. But, at the end of the day, there may be someone in Italy who is six months behind in understanding a new software feature. Direct interaction with applications and marketing people was crucial to ensuring that all X-Rite offices, people and customers were up to the same technical level.

Aligning product development took much, much longer. It was an enormous task for X-Rite to move its product line to new software and platforms that could handle multiple languages. It had not been a focus of the company and had been ignored. It took a year and a half to re-release in languages because of old code and the need to translate every line. Only in the last five years has X-Rite been able to launch new releases of products, sales and marketing materials in ten languages simultaneously. Now it is in X-Rite's DNA, a part of what the company does. It was a five- to seven-year journey, with many false stops and starts.

This expansion, from a revenue point of view, far outstripped X-Rite's IT capabilities. The Grandville-based group had to deal with local home-grown systems out in the regions without any links. This got in the way of productivity, with time delays in reporting results and the inability to consolidate data on global customers. It has only been since October 2005 that X-Rite completed the integration of all its offices onto one platform for order fulfilment, financial reporting and customer management. X-Rite's numbers now have daily visibility; no more waiting for the close of a quarter to see what is happening.

Communication is crucial, and a hard thing to stay on top of in the crush of getting business done. Communication needs to be regular, it needs to be both formal and informal, and it needs multiple channels. It cannot just be the written word or just phone calls, or just face-to-face. Communication has to be exercised in all forms.

X-Rite holds an annual global sales meeting. Everyone comes. Budget planning is done with everyone in the room. As much as X-Rite employees travel and know what is happening, international managers miss things if they are not at the table during the planning sessions.

The company utilizes internal mailboxes for each business group. Once a question is posted, there will be a response within 24 hours. This is the number one tool for new appointments.

Overlaying the X-Rite culture on a local business culture is accomplished by words, deeds, actions and communications. Work done well is celebrated with a local event publicized throughout the company. Every year the company comes up with a unifying theme for the global group that is introduced at the annual meeting. Internal communications are built around this theme. It promotes the idea that X-Rite is all one team. Its future will be that of a global company with connected centres of excellence for marketing, product development, sourcing, administration and manufacturing. Stay tuned.

# REVERE COPPER PRODUCTS

## Thomas O'Shaughnessy

Revere Copper has been in continuous operation since 1801. At that time the American Navy had a problem: it was being outmanoeuvred by the British Navy. The British had wooden-hulled vessels that were sheathed with copper, and they were very, very fast. US Navy ships were wooden-hulled, covered with barnacles, and very, very slow. The federal government decided to sheath the hull of the *USS Constitution* below its waterline, a major undertaking. Copper was only available from Britain, too. A deal was struck: Paul Revere borrowed $10 000 from the government to build a mill to make the copper tiles and he would furnish the copper as payment for the loan. At the same time, Paul Revere also sold copper to the government of Massachusetts, for the roof of the state house on Beacon Hill. (Today, architectural copper is a big part of Revere's business.) Copper lasts virtually forever – Revere Copper has provided the plating to resheath the *USS Constitution* three times over the past 200 years.

Where does Revere Copper stand today? In the mid-1980s, the then-larger Revere Copper company was purchased by a financial institution, and split into smaller companies. The well-known Revere Ware business and brand was purchased by Corning. The main copper rolling business, Revere Copper Products Inc., was purchased privately, and became a 200-year-old 'new' company. Two decisions were immediately made: the first, to stick with what the company does and does well; the second, to provide a workplace that used people to the best of their abilities, to win, and to enjoy the process. They wanted a company that lived up to its 200-year-old tradition.

Revere is not a big company. It has two factories, each for a very different business, each operating with different strategies:

| Rome, New York | New Bedford, Massachusetts |
|---|---|
| Rolling mill | Large plating mill |
| High volume, commodity products | Low volume, specialty products |
| 500 employees | 100 employees |
| 150 million pounds per year production | 10 million pounds per year production |
| US competitors | No US competitors; Europeans are the primary foreign competition |
| US customer base | Worldwide customer base |

The New Bedford mill has heavy industry as its customers (power generation plants, refineries, petrochemical and chemical plants). The New Bedford plate is used in a medium that is doing some sort of heat or process exchange, usually in an environment that is somewhat corrosive. Revere's customers are looking for something that will provide heat transfer and last a long time.

The end of the cold war in the 1980s produced a subsequent decline in revenues from military applications. Revere had been a big supplier to the US Navy: submarines utilize copper nickel plate alloys, with tremendous amounts of copper nickel piping and heat exchangers. Further, the types of industries that required Revere's plate were no longer being built in the United States: no refineries, no power-generating plants. For Revere, the decision to export was a matter of the US market not being large enough. If a move to go international was not made, there would not be enough business to operate the New Bedford mill.

Revere examined the following strategies for going international:

- Buy a company like or similar to Revere.
- Look for brokers or resellers to buy and resell Revere's product, an easy way in the metals industry to move material but troublesome because of the loss of control over the marketplace. Reselling through a broker would divorce Revere from the marketplace. Revere would not know what was driving the behaviour of the company and/or the community that was buying its product.
- Find an agent or a manufacturer's representative. This is the path Revere chose. They looked for a small company that dealt in similar products and were calling on people who built equipment for power plants and refineries – and who were selling them other things. Revere decided to 'piggyback' on that path. This required much checking, sorting and contacting of people that supplied other products to Revere's customers in the US, and talking to associations in the metals industry to find the right people.

Revere were not totally unaware of the global marketplace; they knew where equipment was being built, where the major centres of heavy equipment were. Little was being built in Africa and Siberia, for example. Revere's first and foremost market was Europe, specifically Northern Europe (UK, Germany, Holland, France). It was easy to go there, too. Japan was a big market, without a comparable supplier, as Revere discovered. The Japanese competition was a steel mill that did not turn out satisfactory plate for its Japanese customers. Major manufacturing occurs in South Korea in many heavy industries crucial to Revere: power generation fabricators and shipyards. Mexico and India also became places to look.

Revere's strategy was very selective, structured around knowing who builds equipment and finding common representatives and agents who could handle the Revere product line along with others serving those customers. But the business did not grow overnight. Revere went to Japan for six years before its first order. It was not, and is not, an easy job. For 200 years, Revere did nothing offshore. In the early 1990s, they started to look and, by the turn of the century, 30 per cent of the business was offshore. In 2005, approximately 15–20 per cent of Revere's business is offshore. (The percentage change between 2000 and 2005 is due to Revere's US customer base [heat exchangers and heavy equipment manufacturers] also learning to compete and market internationally.)

Revere Copper Products competes internationally in the architectural copper and heat exchanger markets, among others. Revere competed against firms in Germany and the UK to provide the 300 tons of copper plate used for the Portcullis House of Parliament in London.

Heat exchangers for desalination plants might have 7000 pounds of copper material in them. Revere's customer for one of these was in Italy, but the product was shipped to Abu Dhabi, for construction ultimately in Dubai. Another desalination plant containing Revere's copper was built in Japan, and barged to Saudi Arabia.

Revere's Rome plant sells to many US-based companies that have global operations. Air conditioning companies that use Revere fin stock in the manufacturing of air conditioners have moved factories overseas and Revere has been able to maintain its position as a supplier of fin stock. Many large electrical industrial products companies, like GE, have also moved factories offshore. Revere continues to be a supplier of copper bus bar to new locations around the world. The strategy at Revere's Rome plant has been to follow its key accounts around the globe.

China is potentially a huge market, but Revere's experience there is that China seems to want to be able to build its own plants rather than import product from elsewhere. Nonetheless Revere's New Bedford plant landed a contract worth half a million in China, through a company in Hong Kong, in 2005.

# LAKE SHORE CRYOTRONICS, INC.

## Karen Lint

Lake Shore Cryotronics, Inc. is a family-owned business, founded in 1967 by two broth-ers, both ceramic engineers. Dr John M. Swartz is still the chairman today. David L. Swartz has retired. Dr Swartz was a professor of Electrical Engineering at Ohio State University, and together the two built a single temperature sensor in their basement, calibrating it on the night shift at the university. Their first customer bought 35 sensors for $24 apiece. This first product was also the company's first I-R 100 Award from *R&D Magazine*.

Lake Shore manufactures cryogenic temperature sensors and instrumentation to control and measure temperature. Lake Shore's products are purchased by research sci-entists studying materials at very low temperatures. In general, the study of materials almost always means changing the environment, whether through the application of radi-ation, a change in the magnetic field or a change in temperature, to see what happens. Lake Shore started out with a single temperature sensor and now has a full line of temperature sensors, monitors and controllers.

In the late 1980s, Lake Shore came out with a full line of magnetic measurement hand-held and bench-top Gaussmeters. In the 1990s, professors were asking graduate students to do more than just assemble equipment, and instead to analyse and understand mate-rials and results that the equipment generated. Lake Shore developed a fully computer-controlled system, complete with software. The company spends a lot on research and leverages it with SBIR (Small Business Innovation Research) contracts with the US gov-ernment. Its scientists have well over 60 peer-reviewed scientific publications, published in trade journals and presented at international symposiums and conferences; also 24 US patents and five I-R 100 awards.

The company has been exporting almost from its inception. In 1970, the Swartz broth-ers were in Europe and, while there, convinced an American who was living there to switch representation from another small scientific instrument company to Lake Shore. Lake Shore had added a few more temperature sensors to its product line, and was looking for a representative. At that time, the rep wanted all of Europe as his territory, which in retrospect was a mistake in two ways: the territory was too large and the rep became a gatekeeper.

The first two employees were hired in 1972 – both graduate students at Ohio State, both foreign nationals, one from China, the other from Egypt. Throughout the next two decades, the company expanded several times and added representation in Japan, India, North Africa, the Middle East, Canada, Malaysia, Denmark, Finland, Australia, New Zealand, Singapore and East Asia, South Korea, Taiwan and China. Lake Shore won the Ohio Governor's Exporting Award in 1989. International sales were well over 30 per cent of total sales.

Today Lake Shore has 27 reps or dealers in 40 different countries. It has seen significant growth in international sales since 2001. Some of the growth is attributed to spy satellites and the space industry in general – Lake Shore's equipment was on the Deep Impact probe, the Gravity Probe B project, and the James Webb space telescope, among others. The company has 96 employees in Ohio and 12 in Arizona. These employees hail from eight countries, 24 states and are graduates of 60 different colleges and universities. A map in the hallway of the Columbus, Ohio plant celebrates this diversity, and the international component impresses upon Lake Shore's reps and customers that it is a high-tech company. Unfortunately American schools are not producing the knowledge workers in the sciences that perhaps they should be; when Lake Shore needs a PhD semiconductor physics graduate, it does not find Americans to fill the position. It finds foreigners, exclusively. Some get their green card and stay; some return home. But all help Lake Shore understand international cultures.

Lake Shore has benefited tremendously from its collaboration with university professors and their graduate students. The company became known as the expert through its teaching at universities on material characterizations, both in the US and abroad, and former graduate students continue to use Lake Shore's tools when they take positions in industry all over the world. While Lake Shore has faced obstacles in the global marketplace, by and large its customers tend to be very educated people and, unlike Americans, speak three or four languages, one of which is always English. While Lake Shore sees the language barrier, its dealers and reps do not, and there are no issues with translating users' manuals. Lake Shore has not had to deal with foreign currency because it sells directly to its dealers: either the dealers handle the conversion, or letters of credit are used and banks handle the transaction.

Lake Shore's dealers also handle another potential problem: local electrical standards and codes. As an electronics company, there are a number of different plugs that Lake Shore might need to have on hand. Instead instruments are shipped with US connectors, and the dealers clip the end and/or put in their own connector. It would be a logistical nightmare to stock all the different connectors needed. The relationships that Lake Shore has formed over the years result in a willingness to do more, a willingness that goes both ways.

Conformance to regulatory and certification requirements is an area that has caused Lake Shore pain as an electronic manufacturer. There is a current focus on waste reduction and elimination of hazardous materials. Lead has been the primary target, but there are many other hazardous materials that will require attention. European directives mandate that, by the summer of 2006, shipments must be completely lead-free. This is a significant issue for a company the size of Lake Shore.

The US Department of Commerce Bureau of Industry and Security requires that every single export order be compared with Bureau lists as to what is being sold, to whom, and its intended use. Lake Shore learned a painful lesson in 2002, when it shipped one of its system products to the United Arab Emirates; 18 months later, the US government wanted to know why Lake Shore's system was in Iran. Lake Shore's products are high-tech and, while these products are not weapons, they could be used to study weaponry, or used in science and technology that the US government does not want to share internationally. This is an element of global trade whose future is unknown.

Lake Shore found that having reps and dealers, paid on commission, not expecting a raise or a promotion, works better for it than having direct sales employees overseas. Lake Shore has reps in most countries, born and raised there, entrenched in the culture and committed to the location. These reps know the people with whom they are dealing, and develop great relationships with their customers, a key aspect in any marketing and sales endeavour. There is regular communication and training between Lake Shore and its reps. Further, Lake Shore collaborates with technical papers and product development internationally: employees attend many, many trade shows, going hand-in-hand with the dealers and manning the booths with them. Lake Shore has traded equipment for knowledge, collaborated on patents, and licensed technology from around the world.

The lessons Lake Shore has learned include the following:

- Do not neglect dealers and reps. E-mail makes everything easier than it was 15 years ago, but regular communication is still a lot of work, and it is necessary work.
- It is not a good idea to have a dealer go off and be a manufacturer as well. Lake Shore suffered delinquent payments when this was tried.
- Do not allow a distributor to maintain exclusive rights to a too-large geographic area.
- Do understand the different cultures in every country.
- When registering an Internet URL (uniform resource locator), register it in more than one country.
- Wear the quality hat. ISO 9000 is more than a hoop to jump through. Putting processes in place, being disciplined to follow them and making employees believe in them go hand-in-hand in defining how your business is done.
- Define your mission, vision and values. Lake Shore focuses on four basic objectives: customer satisfaction, business growth, employee satisfaction and return on investment for all stakeholders.

# BROCK SOLUTIONS, INC.

## Vivienne Ojala

Brock Solutions, an engineering services company, sells its brainpower worldwide and thinks differently about international borders and exporting than do companies that sell products rather than services. In fact, Brock does not think of itself as an exporter and has no conscious export strategy. It responds to opportunities wherever they may arise, and now 80 per cent of its revenue comes from outside Canada. The company had been growing by 15 to 20 per cent a year since 1992, without devoting much thought to growth, strategy or exporting. Its focus is pursuit of larger, more challenging and complex projects to engage its growing cadre of 275 engineers who like to think about technical solutions and software development for real-time industrial controls.

Brock evolved from several small specialized companies that partnered and developed products and engineering solutions for different industrial problems. It was organized originally around functional skill sets, but, as larger and more complex projects came along, Brock realized that its customers did not care much about specialized engineering skills, the technology it used or how it was applied, but rather that the final solution solved their problem. Thus Brock discontinued or sold off the products of some of its legacy companies, and transformed itself into a purely professional services organization. It used the proceeds of the sale to pay off debt and allowed Brock to concentrate on developing the best solution to problems, using the best available products on the market, and the best marriage of technology to meet its customers' needs.

For Brock, the technology and the control hardware/software products are the same in any industry sector in which it works, whether the process is metal or paper. But customers in the copper industry, for example, want to know that Brock understands something about copper, about copper mills and about rolling out copper. Consequently Brock reorganized itself by industry sectors, acquiring a few more people along the way with industry-specific expertise and knowledge to bridge the gap between what customers in a given industry sector want and what technology they need in order to control their process.

Today Brock is organized by specialized business units, with each unit focusing on the changing technology needs of its customers in their given industry sector. These business units include baggage and material handling, automotive, pharmaceutical, process, food/beverage, cosmetics, metals and printing. These units create partnerships with their customers and with manufacturers responsible for the equipment to be placed on-site. Brock learned to work in smart teams, which include, not only Brock employees, but also its manufacturing partners and end customers.

Brock's work in the baggage handling sector gives a flavour of the way the company transformed itself. The bar code on luggage that a traveller checks at the airline ticket counter is a common bar code, an international standard in the baggage handling industry. Brock partnered with Vanderlande, a company in the Netherlands, to provide baggage handling solutions in the North American market. After 9/11, Americans, and indeed the whole world, felt a need for more security in the realm of airline baggage handling. The US government decided to fund more security screening in airports and Brock and Vanderlande were the first to supply a working explosive detection system in the US (in Boston at the end of 2002). Vanderlande makes the conveyors, and Brock supplies all the software that reads the bar codes, controls the conveyors, matches the bag tag and security screen information, and directs the bag to the right plane. In 2004, Brock and Vanderlande did $80mn worth of business in the US alone. Brock's 'Smart Sort' solution is basically the same software that is used by various courier services, postal systems and other warehousing and distribution systems.

One key element of Brock's exporting strategy revolves around its virtually-networked organization, its virtual teams and the electronic delivery of its solutions. Using baggage handling again as an example, it does not matter to Brock where the airport is located. Much of the project work for a new site can be accomplished electronically. However there usually is a site start-up requirement where, for example, a retrofit project for United Airlines at Chicago's O'Hare airport required a team of 20 people living in Chicago for a year. A second element of Brock's exporting strategy is having the right mix of people to be able to mobilize the right kind of team. Project teams ebb and flow with the requirements of each project. New employees understand that they are being hired for their knowledge, and that they will be travelling all over the world.

Brock's strong engineering-oriented solutions approach allows it to offer its customers in the automotive sector a worldwide standard for their plants. After General Motors saw the work Brock performed in one of its plants, Brock ended up working with the central press group (corporate) that puts in the press systems for General Motors around the world. If the press comes from Germany or Japan, and is installed in North America, Brock is the glue holding the total solution together. It makes sure the computer systems work, the system itself is operational, the appropriate electrical standard for the end jurisdiction is met and that GM's standards are met, thereby keeping consistency in a global world. There is as much commonality as makes sense. The last team Brock had working for GM coordinated groups in Japan, Germany, Detroit and Kitchener.

Brock's original funding came from a person who had run a large construction business. While he was not an automation engineer, he did understand what background was essential for a company that would be taking on large international contracts. A strong balance sheet and broad insurance coverage made Brock a viable, financially secure business to its earliest customers.

Brock's current strategy depends on what makes sense for the project at hand. Americans prefer to pay in US dollars and if Europeans want to pay in euros, Brock works it out. As an example, during a time of severe fluctuations between the Canadian/US dollar, Brock negotiated with a GM purchaser on a given project. It took some creativity, but the purchase was made through a German company's US subsidiary via a Canadian arm – and Brock got its Canadian dollar. The GM purchaser made it possible for Brock to get the original value of its proposal. Brock's experience is that large and influential customers who want Brock's services will help it through all the different cultures, currencies and foreign regulations. Brock has been fortunate to avoid the currency and regulatory challenges that have faced other companies that work internationally.

Ms Ojala returned to school to complete an MBA. She also hired a CFO to help the company to organize better and set up the right infrastructure. With over 200 people, this was challenging. Brock had to put in all the right Enterprise Resource Planning (ERP) and IT systems, making sure they were operations-driven and designed to meet Brock's project world, which is unique.

The people side of the organization has been particularly challenging. Young people hired out of engineering school are eager to travel anywhere at any time. This is fine for about five years. When they get married, however, they prefer to be home on weekends; when children are born, they really want to stay home. Brock hires people with technical expertise who come from all over the world. As an organization, Brock's 275 employees speak close to 40 different languages. They are selling brainpower, and borders and export rules are less of an issue in the virtual world.

# DALSA CORPORATION

## Savvas Chamberlain

DALSA was founded in Waterloo, Ontario, Canada in 1980 by imaging pioneer Dr Savvas Chamberlain, a former Professor in Electrical Engineering at the University of Waterloo. Originally the company concentrated on developing and generating technology in the area of Charge Coupled Device (CCD) image sensors. The company was capitalized in November 1984 and went public on the Toronto Stock Exchange (TSX: DSA) in May 1996. The company has grown into an industry leader in digital imaging and semiconductor technology, employing approximately 1000 people worldwide with sales revenue of more than $168mn. Sales offices across North America as well as in Germany and Japan support an international distribution network serving more than 40 countries.

DALSA Corporation is a company on a mission to build an environment of growth where dedicated people work together, creating innovative technology, quality products and superior imaging solutions. Its vision is to grow to $500mn (CAN) by 2010. In 1985, its start was predicated on the idea that academic research has inherent wealth, an inherent value that can be realized not only through the publication of ideas, but through the transfer of technology to the community at large.

When Chamberlain approached existing companies with a plan to capitalize on his technology, he was turned down – the projected revenue was less than the $50 million to $100 million that these potential partners required. With $350 000 in seed money from the University of Waterloo's technology transfer office, a couple of graduate students and a great deal of motivation, the part-time, one-man shop began to commercialize the silicon chips that previously had been designed for companies like IBM. DALSA's customers today include IBM, Boeing, Kodak, Dolby, HP, Motorola, Philips, 3M, NEC and Toshiba.

The path to becoming a successful, high-tech spin-off from a university was not very clearly marked in the early 1980s. University technology transfer offices today have far more to offer someone seeking to proliferate technology. Tech transfer offices link a professor with technology to transfer with a backer, help to raise funds and access to venture capital, and provide business management. It also helps today that the dynamics of the academic environment have changed. Technology transfer is no longer viewed as a non-academic endeavour.

What attributes does a tech start-up need? Chamberlain lists the following essential traits:

- motivation;
- a solution to a particular need;
- commitment and the basic raw material from the founders;
- a brief business plan, with a simple strategy, articulated in a quarter of a page or less;
- an understanding of the conservation of money;
- simple marketing.

DALSA did not take off until nearly ten years after its start, when the cost of computing began to fall. In 1975, the cost to provide one million instructions per second (MIP) was $1mn. When Sun Microsystems introduced its machine and IBM introduced the PC in

1981, the cost was $10 000 per MIP. DALSA's image sensor chips produced so much data that it was too costly for its potential customers to process them. Then the Pentium chip came along in 1990, and the cost per MIP was $100. In 2006, the cost is less than $1.00 per MIP. As the cost of computing plummeted, DALSA's business started growing.

DALSA's products include image sensor components, vision processing hardware components, image processing software algorithms and semiconductor wafer foundry services for use in MEMS, high-voltage semiconductors, image sensors and mixed-signal CMOS chips. Some of its Charge Coupled Device (CCD) imaging sensors are sold on the open market, but in general DALSA sells to OEMs. DALSA also makes a digital camera which may look like a typical consumer camera but operates at very high frame rates; for example, if an object is moving at 100 miles per hour, the DALSA camera is able to capture the image without losing the resolution. This technology is also used in other products, such as a cassette that fits into an x-ray machine for mammography biopsy. The doctor is able to look at the image at the same time as the biopsy needle is inserted into the patient. DALSA expects to commercialize a digital film camera that uses an 8-million-pixel chip that the company designs and manufactures.

DALSA uses technology as a competitive resource. There are three areas where companies compete in the marketplace: excellence in their (specialized) products, offering their services as a competitive advantage, or their pricing. In DALSA's case, the company paid the most attention to the excellence of its product. As the company grows, it is putting more emphasis on company service. Its products have become less expensive. This strategy means that DALSA has to keep developing new technology or acquire technology.

DALSA's move into the global arena came about basically because Canada was not producing the highly-qualified engineers that the company required. DALSA began to acquire companies, engineers and technology. In 1999, it acquired Silicon Mountain Design in Colorado Springs, Colorado. In 2002, DALSA acquired Zarlink's Wafer Fab in Bromont, Quebec and acquired Philips' CCD Business Unit in Eindhoven, Netherlands. In 2005, DALSA acquired Coreco in Montreal Quebec

# US SMALL BUSINESS ADMINISTRATION

## Manuel Rosales

International trade holds a number of challenges for small business, whether that small business is considering entering the global marketplace or not. Many small businesses do not even realize that they are already competing with companies abroad. The local dry cleaner, gas station, drug or hardware store is seldom an exporter, but probably imports raw material or supplies. Small businesses may also export indirectly, without even knowing it, by selling products or providing services to other US companies that are exporting. It is the job of the US Department of Commerce and the Small Business Administration to get the message across that globalization is unstoppable, and that there are programmes and resources in place to assist SMEs in entering this marketplace.

The key challenges for small business in international trade can be summarized as fear, complacency, technical expertise, time, contacts, and finance, or access to capital.

Fear of the unknown is a great paralyser in international trade just as it is in other aspects of life. Fear of foreign laws and regulations, and fear due to language barriers are two key factors that inhibit small business participation in trade. Complacency is an issue, too; because of the huge size of the US economy, small business does not feel the need to look outside with a domestic market as large as that of the US.

Technical expertise, or rather the lack of it, proves to be a barrier to exporting in the areas of customs regulations, logistics, foreign payment mechanisms, technical standards and packaging. What is the foreign price? Should it be different from the domestic price? Should it be in US dollars? What is a freight forwarder? If the technical standards are good enough for the US, should that suffice for overseas? Does the US not have the toughest standards in the world? Packaging presents unique problems because the messages that can be sent through colour or language are frequently quite the opposite of what was intended. For example, green hats in China mean a man's wife is cheating on him. You might have difficulty selling green hats in China. Also, in the Far East, white is the colour for funerals. It is important to know local customs and language.

With a business to run and payroll to be made, many small businesses do not have the time to invest in the exporting learning curve. Operations have to be kept rolling and production for domestic customers cannot suffer while a business owner works out how to do business in a foreign market.

Lack of overseas contacts is a significant challenge for SMEs. Unlike large companies, SMEs do not possess the off-shore business affiliates that can be used to circumvent trade barriers and gain market access. In 2002, just 17 per cent of all SMEs exporting to foreign markets had affiliates. In contrast, 41 per cent of large firms had related parties abroad. With no network in place, no affiliates, no distributors, how does an SME gain a foothold? How does an SME know whom to trust? The 'know-who' is often more important than the 'know-how'.

Finally, financial hurdles may preclude an SME from considering trading abroad. An SME will not pursue international business if it is not sure it can finance the extra work. Working capital for production is imperative. Small businesses do not know what a banker's acceptance is or what credit terms are abroad. Coupled with small community banks with little or no expertise because there is no demand for these kinds of services, financing and banking quickly become problems. Larger banks prefer to work on larger deals for a larger payoff for the same amount of work.

The SBA responds to these challenges with people and programmes, with training and time, with commitment and contacts. With respect to fear, complacency, technical expertise and time, the SBA works on several levels. The Senior Core of Retired Executives (SCORE) is a group of over 10 000 retired executives who volunteer their time to counsel small businesses. Within this group, there are experts in international trade, although not as many as SBA would like to see.

There are over 1100 Small Business Development Centers (SBDC), 35 International Trade Centers (ITC), 16 Export Assistance Centers (USEACs) with SBA staffing, and 70 offices of the SBA located throughout the US SBA's Export Trade Assistance Partnership programme (E-TAP) offer training that covers the A-to-Zs of exporting. SBA offices have international trade officers who field questions and refer inquires to US Export Assistance Centers (USEACs). SBA USEAC representatives provide counselling and conduct seminars – nearly 4000 counselling sessions and seminars for over 6000 small businesses in 2005. There is no shortage of information available for the business seeking to overcome its fears about exporting.

The US Department of Commerce is a great resource for making contacts. Small business needs to know what the overseas market climate is, what the market economies are. USDOC has commercial officers in most countries around the world stationed at US embassies. These individuals provide the 'know-who' through their involvement with American Chambers of Commerce (AmChams) and other contacts abroad. Commerce Foreign Commercial staff deal with local communities and business interests, through their work in embassies located near commercial centres. The Department of Commerce helps US small businesses, not only when they are in those countries, but from the US too by providing research and analysis.

The SBA has also created the SME Congress of the Americas, a hemispheric network of public and private small business service providers working to promote the participation of small businesses in trade, and the building of relationships throughout the hemisphere to promote trade and linkages among those small businesses. The voice of small businesses in the Western Hemisphere is strengthened through the SME Congress network and its relationship with the Summit of the Americas process.

Capital is power when it comes to dealing with the financial challenges to export. Banks are not going to lend on foreign receivables unless they have a guarantee. The SBA offers several programmes:

- Export Working Capital Programme: the SBA offers incentives to banks with a 90 per cent guarantee of payment, with a two-million dollar ceiling. These loans usually take the form of a line of credit for a business that has an order in hand but needs working capital to produce the product and sell it. Defaults in this programme are very low, lower than the regular standard SBA loans.
- SBA Export Express: this is another incentive programme for banks, but at lower guarantee and dollar ceilings (85 per cent guarantee up to $150 000 and 75 per cent guarantee up to $250 000). Through this programme, banks use their own paperwork and their own data, thereby freeing SBA's export working capital. In 2001, SBA handled 425 export loans; for FY 2005, the total was 2800.

- SBA-EXIM Bank: SBA has a participation agreement with EXIM, using EXIM's guarantees.
- USEAC: 16 SBA trade specialists provide counselling not only to the small business but to the bank that is hesitant to get involved in the international trade arena.

International trade is a great opportunity: 94 per cent of the world's population, and two-thirds of its purchasing power, live outside the United States. Small business has to be ready to export. Key components for export readiness are a commitment to the international marketplace and an ability to perform.

For there to be a commitment to export, there has to be a willingness to dedicate the time. Export intermediaries such as Export Trading Companies and Export Management Companies can provide major assistance in building the necessary relationships. The ability to perform, the physical component of delivery and follow-through are the same attributes a small business must have on the domestic side, a willingness to take those risks.

International trade agreements are setting the stage by opening new markets and providing new opportunities. Prior to the implementation of NAFTA in 1992, there were only 60 000 US exporters to the Canadian and Mexican markets. US exports to Canada and Mexico in 2005 totalled $331 billion. CAFTA-DR provides another opportunity.

SMEs dominate the export population: 97 per cent of exporters in the US are SMEs, and 70 per cent of those have 20 or fewer employees. But these companies are not small in terms of what is delivered ($300 billion a year in export trade): a billion dollars a day. Small business is not small. Small business is big business.

# KENNAMETAL INC.

## Markos I. Tambakeras

As a member of the President's Manufacturing Council, Markos Tambakeras is uniquely qualified to speak to what he terms 'the art of international commerce', focusing on free, fair and open trade – a topic of interest to a company of any size. The Manufacturing Council is composed of approximately 15 CEOs, five from small businesses with less than $50 million in sales, five from mid-sized (between $50 million and $1 billion) and five from larger corporations. It brings manufacturing 'a seat at the table' and representation on Capitol Hill. It is an important time in the history of the United States to think about manufacturing, the role manufacturing plays in the economy, and the future of the country. Tambakeras offered his thoughts on this, on two key free trade agreements, and concluded his remarks on the way small and medium-sized companies can leverage resources available to them to level the competitive playing field, not only in the US but also across the world.

Free, fair and open trade forces competition, which leads to innovation. Innovation leads to increased productivity, which leads to expanded economic growth and an improved standard of living overall. While the complexities or potential abuses of the system cannot be ignored, an ideal world with free, fair and open trade is better for most societies. Cross-border trade strengthens economic stability and fosters exchange of important innovations. A few statistics:

- manufacturing is responsible for almost two-thirds of private research and development in the US;
- manufacturing accounts for 15 per cent of GDP, down from 50 per cent, but, standing alone, would still represent the fifth largest economy in the world;
- manufactured goods account for 62 per cent of all US exports – twice the level it was ten years ago;
- manufacturing employs 15 million people directly and another eight million by association;
- US manufacturers face a 22 per cent structural disadvantage *vis-à-vis* their major trading partners that is unrelated to labour and wage costs: it is primarily due to higher taxation, costs of litigation and tort, costs of health care, and high regulation and compliance costs (of which the Sarbanes–Oxley Act of 2002 is the most recent).

Kennametal is in the materials business in the manufacturing world. It is essentially a powder metallurgy company. It takes powders, converts the powders to shapes and sells the shapes to its customers: machine tools, oil drills, mining drills; engineered materials for unique applications – all kinds of shapes, all kinds of applications. Kennametal competes successfully through its use of innovation and technology, high market share and global reach, delivering value by performance, linking its use of metallurgical science and engineering to what its customers do. From automobile and plane manufacturing, to drilling for oil and gas, to medical implants, Kennametal's focus is on technology that delivers superior value, and the global nature of the company. As recently as 2000,

30 per cent of sales came from outside the US; the figure is 50 per cent today. While Kennametal's US business is growing, and expectations are high that it will continue to do so, globalization is imperative for the company. A level playing field, and free, fair and open trade is critical to be able to compete globally. But there are obstacles. Currency manipulation, restrictive or unfair tariffs and trade laws, obscure business procedures, inequitable access to financial resources – these are but a few.

Fair access to foreign capital markets also means that a US firm should abide by the same rules and regulations when investing in a foreign country as do the nationals. Once invested in that country, the US company should be treated the same as the local national investor and have the same opportunities. All countries' trade systems and procedures ideally should be transparent and even-handed: operating obscurity can be as effective as restrictive foreign investment laws in terms of official policy.

For our part, American manufacturers have a responsibility to produce a competitive product. American manufacturers also have to recognize that common ethics and standards need to be applied when competing globally.

One lesson learned from the Manufacturing Council: there are over 100 free trade agreements in the world. The US thinks of itself as very open in terms of trade and free trade agreements, but the US has signed only three free trade agreements (FTAs). Implementation of NAFTA began on 1 January 1994. Once fully implemented, it will remove all trade barriers among the US, Canada and Mexico. Tariffs will be eliminated on a progressive basis over a period of 15 years.

In the contentious debates that preceded the adoption of NAFTA, critics maintained that this FTA would lead to the demise of the manufacturing and industrial sectors. However, between 1993 and 2001, US manufacturing output rose at an average annual rate of 3.7 per cent. That is 50 per cent higher than in the 80 years before NAFTA. CAFTA-DR was recently approved by Congress, after facing many of the same arguments and opponents. This FTA, which is meant to promote liberalization between Central America, the Dominican Republic and the US, actually levels the playing field for US exporters. Most of the trade the other way was already open and free as a result of previous agreements.

While FTAs open doors and help define and clarify how members will conduct themselves, they do not automatically provide a level playing field. The World Trade Organization does not do this either. No discussion about free trade and the WTO is complete without a discussion of China. China became a member of the WTO in 2001. Despite difficulties with China's pegged currency policy, its lax intellectual property protection and a decided lack of transparency in its trade laws, the fact is that China is too big a market and too active a trading partner to ignore. According to *The Economist*, China accounted for one-third of global economic growth during the past three years, measured as purchasing power parity: twice as much as the United States. China's *official* GDP grew by 9.7 per cent its imports surged 40 per cent and its industrial output increased by 50 per cent in the last year. China must be held accountable to WTO standards and practices they have contracted to uphold. Rather than impose punitive tariffs and trade sanctions, the US is in a much better position to influence compliance by being a savvy trading partner and not by being an aggressive opponent.

The US is the world's biggest trading partner. It exports more than $1 trillion in goods, and these exports support over 12 million jobs. An amazing 65 per cent of all US exporters are businesses with fewer than 20 employees. Further, according to the International Trade Administration, Small and Medium Enterprises (SMEs) account for more than 95 per cent of US exporters. This is a percentage that has varied only slightly since the 1990s. Therefore SMEs can wield tremendous influence on the future of US trade relations. The question is how.

Leaders of SMEs are very busy, often cannot afford lobbyists, have limited resources and, at the micro level, their export concerns can be very different from those of other SMEs. A recent survey by the National Association of Manufacturers found that 30 per cent of companies that do not export would like to do so. And of those companies that do export, two-thirds export to only one market. The survey also found that many SMEs enter the export market reactively rather than proactively; for example, they are driven to export in order to serve an existing customer who moves overseas, not because market research says it is a good idea.

Key obstacles to export activities cited by the NAM survey were a lack of information, lack of resources, fear of hurting domestic business by chasing the export business and no 'weaponry' to deal with trade inequities and other challenges. But there are several strategies SMEs can use to take the exporting plunge, one of which is called 'piggy-backing', where you work with a multinational company to sell your product or service as an extension to the MNC's offering. Kennametal is beginning to do more of this with its small and medium-sized suppliers, and is finding that it can deliver more value to its customers. Piggy-backing reduces the SME's exposure to foreign risk, with no initial investment in a supply chain or infrastructure.

Assistance is available from the federal and state governments, but it seems that many SMEs are unaware of this. If SMEs are not using a particular service because it is inconvenient, confusing or unhelpful, they need to tell their representatives that this is the case. SMEs must become more involved in setting the US free trade agenda.

Once in the export market, SMEs must subscribe to the same standards they would impose on themselves in the domestic market. In Kennametal's case, the centre of its business system is its code of ethics and business standards. There are always unknowns, challenges and temptations when competing in a foreign market. A clear and consistent understanding of your beliefs and values is critical to your ability to sustain and go forward.

# Name index

# Subject index